POWER,

MONEY,

AND

MEDIA

Communication Patterns
and Bureaucratic Control
in Cultural China

Edited by
CHIN-CHUAN LEE

NORTHWESTERN UNIVERSITY PRESS
EVANSTON, ILLINOIS

Northwestern University Press
Evanston, Illinois 60208-4210

Copyright © 2000 by Northwestern University Press. Published 2000. All rights reserved.

Printed in the United States of America

ISBN 0-8101-1786-X (cloth)
ISBN 0-8101-1787-8 (paper)

Library of Congress Cataloging-in-Publication Data

Power, money, and media : communication patterns and bureaucratic control in cultural
    China / edited by Chin-Chuan Lee.
        p. cm. — (media topographies)
    Includes bibliographical references and index.
    ISBN 0-8101-1786-X (cloth : alk. paper) — ISBN 0-8101-1787-8 (pbk. : alk. paper)
    1. Mass media—Political aspects—China. 2. Mass media—Economic aspects—China.
    3. China—Politics and government—1976- I. Li, Chin-ch'üan, 1946- II. Series.

    P95.82.C6 P68 2000
    302.23'951—dc21   00-056860

Contents

Editor's Acknowledgments   *vii*

A Note on Romanization   *ix*

1   *Chinese Communication: Prisms, Trajectories, and Modes of Understanding*   *3*
    CHIN-CHUAN LEE

2   *One Head, Many Mouths: Diversifying Press Structures in Reform China*   *45*
    GUOGUANG WU

3   *Improvising Reform Activities: The Changing Reality of Journalistic Practice in China*   *68*
    ZHONGDANG PAN

4   *Chinese Communist Party Press in a Tug-of-War: A Political-Economy Analysis of the* Shenzhen Special Zone Daily   *112*
    ZHOU HE

5   *Seeking Appropriate Behavior under a Socialist Market Economy: An Analysis of Debates and Controversies Reported in the* Beijing Youth Daily   *152*
    STANLEY ROSEN

6   *The Nature and Consequences of China's Unique Pattern of Telecommunications Development*   *179*
    DANIEL C. LYNCH

7   *The Media and the Legal Bureaucracy of the People's Republic of China*   208
      TAHIRIH V. LEE

8   *When Capitalist and Socialist Television Clash: The Impact of Hong Kong TV on Guangzhou Residents*   245
      JOSEPH MAN CHAN

9   *One Event, Three Stories: Media Narratives from Cultural China of the Handover of Hong Kong*   271
      ZHONGDANG PAN, CHIN-CHUAN LEE,
      JOSEPH MAN CHAN, AND CLEMENT Y. K. SO

10   *The Paradox of Political Economy: Media Structure, Press Freedom, and Regime Change in Hong Kong*   288
      CHIN-CHUAN LEE

11   *Mainland Chinese News in Taiwan's Press: The Interplay of Press Ideology, Organizational Strategies, and News Structure*   337
      RAN WEI

Notes on Contributors   367
Index   369

Editor's Acknowledgments

I am deeply grateful to Yu Chi-chung, whose generous funding for the China Times Center for Media and Social Studies at the University of Minnesota has made possible the publication of a trilogy on Chinese communication, of which the present volume is the third. Debts are owed to the New Asia Cultural Foundation in Hong Kong and the Minnesota Journalism Center for providing partial funding. Linda Wilson and Mary Achartz are worthy of a big, hearty thank-you for their good-humored assistance. Laboring and lounging in a mountaintop office overlooking the magnificent Tolo Harbor in the radiating warmth of many friends and graduate students at the Chinese University of Hong Kong for the three years straddling the city's regime change was a truly remarkable chapter in my academic life. James Schwoch, general editor of the Media Topographies series at Northwestern University Press, has been a source of unfailing support and constant encouragement. Appreciation goes further to Sage Publications for granting copyright permission to reprint, as chapter 9 herein, an article developed at the invitation of Cees Hamelink, the editor of *Gazette* (volume 61, no. 2 [1999]: 99–112), entitled "One Event, Three Stories: Media Narratives from Cultural China of the Handover of Hong Kong," by Zhongdang Pan, Chin-Chuan Lee, Joseph Man Chan, and Clement Y. K. So.

This volume is dedicated, it goes without saying, to those whom I love most dearly and who had to put up with my absence most generously: Chia-Chih, Chu-An, and Chu-Min.

A Note on Romanization

Throughout this volume, we use the pinyin system to romanize the names of people and places associated with the People's Republic of China. The Wade-Giles system is adopted for those tied to Taiwan, but for the sake of simplicity we drop the apostrophe.

People and places associated with Hong Kong are romanized according to their Cantonese pronunciation. Chinese surnames precede given names, but we have followed the Western style for Chinese with Western given names and for other Chinese who are professionally known by names that follow the Western style.

POWER, MONEY, AND MEDIA

1

Chinese Communication

Prisms, Trajectories, and Modes of Understanding

CHIN-CHUAN LEE

With what nation will America have its most important bilateral relationship in the emerging post–Cold War world? As Zbigniew Brzezinski notes, it will be, "for good or bad," China. Every major financial investor in the world has complex investment strategies already under way in China, and virtually every major global-scale telecommunications and information technology investment is significantly linked to China.[1] Yet despite constituting potentially the largest system in the world, China's expanding media and telecommunications remain little understood. China also remains unintegrated into global thinking about such issues as the globalization or fragmentation of culture, the transition to a global information society, the values and problems of establishing a free press, the rising importance of global electronic commerce, the nascent integration of domestic information networks into what we think of as a global Internet, and the protocommercial audience for popular-culture products. Indeed, China's actions and activities in the media and telecommunications spheres have the potential to make an incredible impact on the entire world's conception of cultural freedom and national security.

The world is moving from an industrial age, with its attendant policy structure of nation-states and bilateral negotiations, into an information age based on multilateral negotiations among a wide range of state and nonstate participants. Nation-states are said to be ceding power to international and nongovernmental organizations as well as to local entities. In view of these trends, China will be the major test case of the early twenty-first century as to whether the values of Western liberal democracy are — or are not — a world standard for social governance. Media culture is at the very heart of this consideration. China's media

3

and telecommunications address, reveal, and offer clues to such complex—and enduring—issues as journalistic freedom, individual identity and liberty, the opportunity to participate in a free-market economy, as well as the ambiguous attractions of an emergent consumer society based on media culture and the circulation of information.

This volume seeks to bring China to the attention of a wide range of scholars, specialists, and the informed public, all of whom no longer have the luxury of ignoring this major component of a globalizing world.[2] As part of an ongoing effort to grapple with the rapidly changing patterns of media communication in what Tu Weiming (1991) calls "Cultural China"—including the People's Republic of China (PRC) and beyond—this volume is organically connected to its generously received predecessors, *Voices of China: The Interplay of Politics and Journalism* and *China's Media, Media's China* (Lee 1990a, 1994a). While each volume pushes the trajectory and landscape in its own direction, the trilogy, it is hoped, will contribute productively to a much needed dialogue among the various interpretive communities. And keep this dialogue alive we must.

It is my belief that this volume has broken several important new theoretical and empirical grounds. In this chapter I aim to identify the central tenet of this volume and relate Cultural China theoretically and empirically to major concerns in the field of political communication.[3] Let me start by acknowledging that the primary theoretical orientation of this volume is a broadly defined approach to the "political economy of communication." Our outlook and epistemology, however, differ significantly from the dominant radical-critical perspective found in the Anglo-American literature, for a simple but profound reason. In Cultural China, we must contend with the ghosts of authoritarian states that dictate the terms and conditions of political economy, whereas critics of Anglo-American systems do not. (I shall return to this issue in the final section of this essay.) In what follows, I shall first articulate the intricately complex and paradoxical implications of "Cultural China" as a source and system of knowledge. I shall then illuminate how the contradiction between political control and economic reform has changed various aspects of China's political communication: media structure and function, professional culture and media content, as well as media law and telecommunications policy. Then my focus will shift to the dynamics of media interaction between mainland China and Taiwan. Finally, drawing on cases analyzed in this volume, I shall return to contrast the liberal-pluralist and radical-Marxist approaches to the political economy.

Cultural China as a System of Knowledge

"Cultural China" (Tu 1991) is made up of three symbolic universes. The first universe refers to the majority Chinese societies of the PRC, Taiwan, Hong Kong, and perhaps Singapore. The second incorporates the minority Chinese diaspora in North America and Southeast Asia, while the third universe is inclusive of people of all ethnic identities—scholars, specialists, traders, and entrepreneurs—who contribute to the understanding of Chinese culture. Three points regarding the first symbolic universe of Cultural China are at once noteworthy. First, this core universe has failed to fulfill its intellectual and cultural role. Authoritarian regimes in both the PRC and (until 1987) Taiwan had severely deprived academic, intellectual, and journalistic communities of their freedom and autonomy to produce significant knowledge. Colonial Hong Kong, with its coveted freedoms, provides an essential link between various parts of Cultural China, but its own economic might has dwarfed its cultural contributions. This tragic failure has created a big knowledge vacuum that could only be filled by other symbolic universes of Cultural China.

A second point is that the center-periphery axis in the first symbolic universe is not fixed or unchanging but varies with issues, spheres, and settings. Various genres of popular culture from politically peripheral Hong Kong and Taiwan seem to have set the agenda for mainland China, especially among the youthful urban audience (Gold 1993). Against the backdrop of the PRC's political dominance, Hong Kong and Taiwan can be seen as centers of cultural reinvigoration and economic innovation (Tu 1991). In this volume, Joseph Man Chan portrays Hong Kong as a center of television production for viewers in South China; greater exposure to Hong Kong television seems to be associated with greater changes in belief structure among the Chinese audience (chapter 8). Hong Kong's supposed economic and media influences on the PRC (particularly those of the broadcasting media, which can achieve greater geographical penetration than can newspapers) provide a basis for constructing "Trojan horse" stories. Conversely, as I examine the peripheral status of Hong Kong's media vis-à-vis China's political power, it seems clear that fear of China's threat, real or imagined, has resulted in self-censorship among Hong Kong journalists (chapter 10). Ran Wei's account suggests that Taiwan's media are motivated by commercial interest to promote a closer tie with mainland China's media, only to find their efforts deflated by Beijing's political authority (chapter 11). Within the PRC, the party press at various levels is politically central but commercially peripheral, while the evening and mass-appeal press is politically peripheral but commercially central. Moreover, media revenue gaps have been widening between coastal cities and interior provinces (Chen and Lee 1998).

Third, the media narratives of the PRC, Hong Kong, and Taiwan have created three distinctly different stories, based on their respective interests and ideologies, about the colony's handover to Chinese sovereignty (chapter 9). They collide most sharply on the issues of national and cultural identity: To wit, who are the Chinese? While the PRC tries to integrate the "nation" with the "state" as a "national family" headed by Beijing and encompassing global Chinese communities, Taiwan attempts to delink them by claiming that two equal sovereign states exist under one nation. The Hong Kong media displayed considerable ambivalence and uncertainty about their own fate of being absorbed into a big Chinese "national family." The contending and contentious nature of these interpretive communities is indicative of the complexity involved in sorting out their political, economic, and cultural relationships. In this regard, as Harry Harding (1993) states, the concept of "Greater China" may overlook the centrifugal tendencies and focus too much on the integrative forces that bind a transnational Chinese economy, a global Chinese culture, and a unified Chinese state. While "Economic China" evokes a mixture of positive and negative feelings, "Political China" has aroused a vast amount of anxiety, fear, and resentment about the implied domination by Beijing over China's hinterland and overseas Chinese societies. Besides and on top of economic interests or power politics, what is the role of the more enduring and less instrumentally oriented cultural discourse?

Looking more macroscopically at Cultural China as a whole, one sees a postmodern twist such that center is periphery and periphery center. Our understanding of Cultural China and its media communication has a distinct marking of *double marginalities*. In the first paradoxical sense, big failures by the first and second symbolic universes have made us dependent on the third symbolic universe—notably U.S. media and universities, supposedly Cultural China's most *marginal*, remote, and loosely connected element—to produce knowledge about Cultural China. In a second paradoxical sense, Cultural China further stands at a very *marginal* rim of the concentric circle of dominant academic, intellectual, and journalistic concerns in a continental-size world hegemon—that is, the United States—marked by a strong tradition of cultural isolation. In this country, conduct of all inquiries categorized as lying within "area studies" has been woven peripherally into different branches of the knowledge industry, according to the demands of the Cold War (Said 1979).

Ezra Vogel (1994) therefore characterizes American scholars of contemporary China as "marginals in a superpower" who were "lukewarm cold warriors, peripheral social scientists, and assertive moralists."

Knowledge is not value-free or neutral. Knowledge producers are conditioned by what phenomenologists call "relevance structures" that entail personal biography, interest, schooling, paradigmatic commitment, the larger politico-economic history, and the epochal worldview surrounding them. Edward Said (1979, 1982, 1993) coined the term "Orientalism" to describe the historical processes by which Western scholars have constructed the mosaic of "the other world," or the Orient, in light of the imperialist needs of their countries, a mosaic complete with preconceived notions, fantasies, and biases. This process is eminently applicable to the construction of Cultural China. The Cold War framework constituted the single most powerful "grammar" in the deep structure of the American mind to inform generations of China scholars and journalists (Farmer 1990, 1994; Chang 1990). This does not, of course, imply that all understanding and misunderstanding about China served U.S. imperialistic interests. But it should by now be painfully clear (Lee 1990a, 1994a) that U.S. coverage of China has oscillated between romanticism and cynicism and that this radical mood swing has often had more to do with what was happening in the United States than it did with what was happening in China. The study of contemporary China, including its media, was admittedly littered with fantasized accounts of naive revolutionary romanticism during the Cultural Revolution, thus to some extent reinforcing its low academic status. This naïveté was reminiscent of pilgrimages made by America's rebellious intellectuals to Stalin's Soviet Union, Ho Chi Minh's North Vietnam, and Castro's Cuba — all against the larger social backdrop of McCarthyism, the Vietnam War, and anti-Communism (Hollander 1981).

The study of Chinese media has begun to mature, however. Many perspectives and approaches have appeared in tandem with theoretical and methodological advances in various branches of the humanities and social sciences. This is also a direct response to a relative opening-up of research opportunities in China, coinciding with the coming of age of scholars of Chinese descent. Making their voices heard in this volume are many younger Chinese scholars who, having been educated in Western universities and having picked up the requisite vocabulary and logic for social research, now aspire to communicate with their Western colleagues in a dialogue of equals. Meanwhile, their present-day Western colleagues seem also more proficient in the Chinese language and culture than were members of the preceding generations. Together, various interpretive communities may—to use phenomenological terms—intersubjectively construct multiple and pluralistic realities about media dynamics in Cultural China. The interpenetration of the insider's perspectives, based on firsthand experience and personal participation, with the outsider's perspectives, derived from analysis and reflection, should enrich each other. But, as Robert Merton (1972) cautions us, all individuals should carry not only a single status but also a "cross-cutting status set." We are "plural persons," trying to manage the tension between the roles of "insider of the outsider" and "outsider of the insider" (Berger and Kellner 1981:34).

In this volume, the tension between differing roles is revealingly described by Zhongdang Pan (chapter 3) and Zhou He (chapter 4), who do ethnographic studies in Beijing's journalistic circles and in one of Shenzhen's leading newspaper organizations. Like good journalists, media anthropologists aspire to get into the picture without being engulfed in it; they seek to strike a balance between being committed participants and detached observers. They mine rich anecdotes of theoretical import that are broadly suggestive of the patterns of media change and the structural conflict involved. Daniel Lynch conducts in-depth interviews with scholars and policy makers with regard to China's changing telecommunications policy (chapter 6), and Joseph Man Chan completes a sample survey in Guangzhou to probe the effect of television spillover from Hong Kong (chapter 8). With notable exceptions (Polumbaum 1990; Lull 1991; Chu and Ju 1993), these projects would have been very difficult if not impossible to conduct in more restrictive periods. Other case studies by Stanley Rosen (chapter 5) and Tahirih Lee (chapter 7) use deep "textual reading" to delineate the boundaries and processes of change, while holistic interpretation of the published archives and statistics (such as that by Wu in chapter 2) is also highly illuminating.

In line with the tradition of its predecessors (Lee 1990a, 1994a), this volume exhibits a diversity of theoretical and methodological interests from a number of disciplines: media studies, political science, and legal history. The chapters included herein cut across different units of analysis, but many of them converge on media structures, bureaucracies, and organizations. This volume is unusually strong in examining institutional factors that shape the production of media content, although several chapters (such as Stanley Rosen's case study and Joseph Man Chan's survey) cover media content and audience reception of it. Moreover, we focus primarily on the information side of the media rather than on the symbols and rituals of popular culture and entertainment (such as songs and games) that circulate and knit together the social fabric. Meanwhile, we should caution ourselves against taking the term "Cultural China" too literally, for it may belie the huge developmental gaps that exist between coastal China and interior China. A large part of China is admittedly not covered in our account or in anybody else's.

Candor requires we admit to the paramount liberal underpinnings of our work. We are filled with strong and genuine hopes that the PRC's media will become ever freer from state stricture, that Hong Kong's media will withstand possible onslaughts following the regime change, and that China and Taiwan will improve their diplomatic and media communication. This list could go on, but the point is that we abhor subjugation of the media to the status of party-state organ. In analyzing the process of China's marketization and its implication for expanding media freedom in nonpolitical areas, we are also mindful of the market potential in distorting and restricting media diversity—not only in liberal democracies but also in illiberal China. Pan and He allude to the corrosive influence of money on media ethics in China. The increasingly conglomerated media in Hong Kong have also been taking the path of least resistance to political constraints by pursuing depoliticization, apoliticization, vulgarization, and sensationalism. We hope to capture the dialectical and paradoxical implications of market forces for media operation and content.

Western-trained, we have inevitably turned and returned to Anglo-American literature—on the sociology of media professionalism and organization, media effects, and the role of the media in political change—to shape our problem or sharpen our analyses. In contextualizing the literature in Chinese practices, we have had to contend with contrasting theoretical models that posit the media variously as a site of social, institutional, and ideological struggle; as a mirror or shaper of reality; or as an agent of social change or social control. This state of affairs inevitably begets a host of vexing questions. Where should theoretical perspectives meet empirical observations? How broadly relevant are the established Western perspectives to non-Western (particularly, Chinese) settings? To what extent does our culturally grounded research represent a perspective that challenges theoretical orthodoxy, or is a simply typical or deviant case to be incorporated into the general pattern? The guild of mainstream U.S. communication research has a long history of celebrating its own tedious parochialism by paying little heed to, and thus consigning to marginality, any media topologies whose visions or concerns go beyond the water's edge. Studies on Chinese communication—despite the magnitude of China's social experiments, likely to affect huge masses of geography and population, and despite the increasingly high standard of this scholarship—have yet to be "made visible," have yet to get noticed and be counted as part of the mainstream landscape.[4] Notwithstanding the epistemological and cultural gulfs, we believe, with C. Wright Mills (1959:157), that only by comparative studies can we "become aware of the *absence* of certain historical phases from a society, which is often quite essential to understanding its contemporary shape."

Media Reform of the 1990s in the PRC

One of the most central problems facing political communication in the PRC in the 1990s involves what I (Lee 1994b) call "ambiguities and contradictions" arising from the relationship between continued state control and economic reform. In this volume, Zhou He characterizes this tension as a "tug-of-war" while Stanley Rosen refers to it as a "duality." This inherent disunity speaks to the dialectic of political economy—the state versus the market—a dilemma that China's authoritarian state capitalist-market system can only hope to manage rather than resolve. The media under the old Communist commandist mode of control were first and foremost the transmission belt of the party line, but two decades of economic reform have served to weaken their still strong mouthpiece role (Lee 1990b). What Peter Berger (1985) calls "marketization of political management" in China has progressively depoliticized the state, economics, and culture, thus creating considerable room for media liberalization. Local and regional media have risen to chip away at the centralized dominance (White 1990; Yu 1990). Formal censorship has been regularized and made more predictable through efforts of bureaucratic control (Polumbaum 1994), and the media have undergone a process of increasing secularization (Dittmer 1994). In China, the state is still highly authoritarian, arbitrary, and intrusive; but it has had to reckon with innumerable manifest or latent functions unleashed by market forces. As a result, China's media have been characterized as having "commercialization without independence" and enjoying "bird-caged press freedom" (Chan 1994; Chen and Chan 1998).

MEDIA STRUCTURE[5]

Guoguang Wu (chapter 2) portrays a notable change in China's media structure: that "many mouths" have echoed the thought of "one head." Wu takes a middle course and, in my opinion, a more accurate position between the pessimistic view that the authoritarian regime would never change and the optimistic view that transformation in China has been so profound as to produce a momentum for "peaceful evolution." Instead, he argues that marketization has brought about fragmentation and diversification to China's party-state monopoly of media structure in three ways. First, various ministries and bureaus of the central government, along with local governments, have rushed to set up their media voices. Second, even though private media ownership is out of the question, many quasi-social groups—including the party-affiliated mass organizations (labor unions, women's federation, and the Communist Youth League), the nine satellite "democratic parties," and various professional associations and academic societies—have all tried to establish their own media voices. Third, marketization has reduced press dependence on the state. In sum, structural liberalization takes place primarily in the *social* rather than *political* sector, and societal liberalization is a necessary but insufficient condition for democracy. An abundance of media outlets does not, of course, ensure ideological pluralism. (The rise of local power, however, has added a new dimension to the old dynamic of media control; thus, for example, the unorthodox *Southern Weekend* has been protected by Guangdong authorities from punishment by the central Department of Propaganda.)

Marketization has produced an "uneven development" in China's press commercialization. As a consequence, press fortune has been reversed: The previously dominant central and regional papers have been losing ground in market competition to mass-appeal newspapers that used to enjoy a low status in the state hierarchy. The *People's Daily* is a most astonishing index. While still heading the list of top ten newspaper advertising revenue earners in 1990, the paper slumped to number ten three years later and to number fourteen in 1996; this raises a serious question about the future of the party press. While Mikhail Gorbachev reformed the former Soviet Union's polity without concomitant economic transformation, Deng Xiaoping steered China onto the road of economic growth as a way to forestall significant political change. With the progress of economic reform in China, the state has found it imperative to shed part of its mammoth financial obligations, thus urging all media to achieve financial self-reliance and even taking measures to curtail media subsidies. By 1997, however, only an estimated one-third of China's newspapers reached financial self-sufficiency; many of those in the impoverished and interior provinces would not have survived without state subsidies. On the rise in the bid to take the party organ's market role have been mass-appeal papers in Shanghai, Guangzhou, Shenzhen, and Beijing. The nationally broadcast Chinese Central Television (CCTV) is so lucrative (with an advertising revenue of U.S. $600 million in 1998) as to need no state subsidies, but the state, eager to retain its patron role, insists that CCTV accept its meager allowance anyway.

Market competition has significantly altered the salary structure of Chinese journalists. In the 1980s, they were paid according to professional grade (senior editor/reporter, head editor/reporter, editor/reporter, assistant editor/reporter) regardless of the size or status of their media units. At present, however, the organization's ability to garner advertising revenues is a more important determinant of the reporter's income than either the media unit's administrative status (central, provincial, municipal, or county) or the reporter's professional grade. The jealousy aroused by the extraordinary wealth of *Xinmin Evening Daily* (where a reporter was paid as much as the editor in chief of the *People's Daily*) must have contributed to its being forced to merge with the unprofitable *Wenhui Daily* in 1998. Besides, many financially lucrative papers have tried to lobby the central government for approval to expand the number of pages they publish in order to carry more advertisements. Some of them now operate their own delivery system to expand their range of circulation rather than continue to rely on the poor and yet increasingly more expensive postal service. Within the media unit, the once auxiliary managerial departments have been elevated to equal the editorial departments in status.

One of the most intriguing and perplexing developments has been a trend toward press conglomeration in the PRC. Unable to secure new publication licenses from the state, in the mid-1980s many official newspapers went ahead to publish editorially soft companion supplements disguised under a variety of names, such as "weekend editions," as income-generating devices. Hard-line propaganda officials repeatedly censured many large papers (*dabao*), which had been losing readers, for trying to support themselves by publishing tabloids (*xiaobao*) that were filled with reports of accidents, gossip, and trivia. Following the Tiananmen crackdown in 1989, the state closed down all companion publications except the few controlled by major party organs. The Communist Party had long been fiercely hostile to press conglomeration in the Western countries, denouncing it as a manifestation of how the oppressive capitalist class seeks to control public opinion. Therefore, it seemed to signal a peculiar reversal of policy when the Press and Publication Administration approved the *Guangzhou Daily* as China's first press group in 1996. The *Guangming Daily* and the *Economic Daily* followed suit. The *Nanfang Daily,* the *Yangcheng Evening Daily,* the *Shenzhen Daily,* and several others are awaiting approval.

Press conglomeration in China is strictly engineered by the state, revolving around a group of "core" party organs, which act as umbrellas incorporating a multitude of auxiliary newspapers and magazines that cater to various areas of specialized interest.[6] Official rhetoric vaguely justifies conglomeration as a measure to upgrade the quality of the Chinese press and its economy of scale. The real reasons are, of course, much more complex. The state seeks to reincorporate the core and newly affluent outlets into the state system and, in the process, to shift part of its own financial responsibility by requesting that these prosperous outlets subsidize those considered socially important but financially unprofitable. These core outlets may help the authorities cure their headache by crowding out or taking over a chaotic array of "small papers" that have repeatedly defied state orders. In turn, these core publications benefit from takeovers and mergers; some even bargain with the authorities for preferential tax treatment as a condition of conglomeration.

So far, the Chinese authorities seem to find in press conglomeration a panacea for resolving many difficult problems that must be faced sooner or later. Communist state planners may conveniently forget their harsh criticisms of Western capitalists, but they are satisfied that the Communist Party, not the capitalists, gains control of China's press conglomerates. Press conglomeration, however, does exact social prices that the Chinese authorities do not seem to have thought through. The state altered the policy by fiat, without transparency, and probably masking a series of behind-the-scenes bargains with the emergent financial forces. For press conglomeration to work, China must confront many vexing legacies of the Leninist system. To cite a few: How will the omnipresent state interfere in the process and operation of press conglomeration? In the course of controlling the pace, size, and process of press conglomeration, will the state be able to keep intact the traditional Communist mode of organizing the press? What will the relationship be between the core and its subsidiary publications? Will the core take away all or most of the profits from its affiliates? These issues warrant close scrutiny.

THE "PARTY PUBLICITY INC."

Zhou He, in a pioneering work, studies the political economy of the media in reform China using a more politics-centered and more state-oriented approach (chapter 4). As he points out, in China the party-state owns a vital part of the national economy, sets development priorities and projects, controls key resources and even the entire financial system, and regulates all crucial economic activities. On the other hand, the party-state once again lighted the flame of market reform in part to save itself at the brink of a legitimacy crisis following the Tiananmen crackdown. The real question becomes one of assessing the extent to which market factors have served to weaken, modify, or subvert various ideological dimensions of journalistic practice.

Focusing on the *Shenzhen Special Zone Daily,* one of the avant-garde and lucrative publications in a southern border city geographically and administratively remote from central control, Zhou He surmises that introducing advertising revenues into newspaper operation has affected various aspects of the newspaper in an uneven manner. Advertising and circulation management unashamedly follows the market mode; the organizational structure of the newspaper remains politically dominated but is becoming more accommodating of market needs. The party-state does not give up its authority to appoint top leaders but nonetheless lets the paper hire and fire more junior staff, thus helping to establish a reward structure based on performance rather than age or rank. Editorially, the paper exhibits what Zhou He calls "a capitalistic body" (to serve the market) that wears "a socialist face" (to pacify the party); its content is still conventionally framed, but its genre of discourse is being expanded.

Most important, Zhou He argues that China's party press is being transformed from a strict mouthpiece into what he calls the "Party Publicity Inc." Its present chief mission is to promote the party's images and legitimacy by means of softened messages rather than to achieve full-scale ideological indoctrination and brainwashing of the people. The outer ideological limits remain to be set by the party, but within them the press has gained greater room for maneuvering. As a profit center, the press has tried to commodify the politics in contrast to the old custom of politicizing commodities—in other words, instead of endowing most mundane issues with political significance, it is making serious political topics lively and interesting enough to attract the consumer's attention. The state expects the media to toe the party line in exchange for the opportunity to profit from the market. In the 1990s, the media have largely been devoting themselves to pursuing maximum market gains away from the state's interference, and so the media fervor for political reform in the late 1980s has been cooling off.

THE SOCIOLOGY OF NEWS WORK

In another piece of pioneering work, Zhongdang Pan brilliantly links the big picture of the political-economy perspective to the day-to-day practice of journalism (chapter 3). Drawing on the literature of what is generally called the "sociology of news work," especially the phenomenological writing of Gaye Tuchman (1978), Pan conducted a painstaking participant-observation study with journalists from six papers in Beijing. He tells many field tales that are most revealing of the "ambiguities and contradictions" in the current storm of news reforms. How do Chinese media and journalists manage the tension between economic reform and political control? How do they "improvise" certain strategies that may come to be routinized as part of new practices? How do such practices collide or coexist with the commandist approaches to weaken conventionality? These are the questions he asks.

The new political economy in China seems to have produced the latent consequence of creating a wider institutional space within which news organizations and journalists can improvise news practices beyond the official confines. But in view of the structural and ideological ambiguities involved, news improvisation is bound to be shortsighted, opportunistic, and subject to possible interruption by political decrees. This much-talked-about "news reform" is not guided by a coherent ideological framework but based on ad hoc tactics that grow out of the need to cope with practical problems. The media seem to have lost their zest for the usually abstract and "impractical" ideological discourse typical of the 1980s. Replacing their political energy is the goal of making money by groping for a more innovative product in format or content. To this end, the media form a new web of relationships with advertisers, run multilayered business enterprises (including such unrelated operations as hotel management), and swim around the shifting official boundary. However situational and informal, these improvisational practices may subvert official rigidity in the long haul. In Beijing, Pan seldom encounters journalists making references to orthodox party rhetoric, nor does Zhou He meet many journalists in Shenzhen defining themselves strictly as "party propagandists." Social change seems to have altered Chinese journalists' "practical ideology" if not their "pure ideology" (Schurmann 1966). But, admittedly, we still have only primitive knowledge about how this change has affected different status and interest groups (cadres, editors, and reporters) within the newsroom.

Accounts by Pan, He, and Stanley Rosen (chapter 5) have shown that news workers seem to attach much less importance to the fight for official passage of media laws in the 1990s than they did in the 1980s. Journalists have become more pragmatic and, perhaps, less idealistic. They realize that the authoritarian regime is only interested in the "rule *by* law," not the "rule *of* law," and that any explicit body of statutes does not necessarily protect their job rights or enhance their professional autonomy. Media organizations and workers have one by one jumped into the ocean of business pursuit, and in many ways business enterprises have risen to rival the party as a major influence on media operations. According to Pan's account, the ability to cultivate advertising sponsorships enhances the status of an individual editor or journalist within the organization and strengthens a news organization's power in relation to its news sources. Many news units evince enthusiasm for adopting trendy West-ern-style polls and surveys as new marketing schemes; some are prepared to fa-cilitate the efforts of their staff in revenue-producing news work by providing better resources or incentives (automobiles, cellular phones, and cash awards).

Journalists' business acumen is largely embedded in the widespread and rather informal network of personal connections (*guanxi*) built around good faith and tacit reciprocity. The editor on duty, with scarce organizational re-sources at his or her disposal, stands to profit. "Paid journalism" takes the forms of trading news for favors, leasing space and time to commercial sponsors, ex-ploiting media connections to make business deals, and disguising advertise-ments as news (Zhao 1998). It is a new and prevalent (mis)norm, partly because "everybody does it"; whoever spoils the game runs the risk of being ostracized as a troublemaker. Since corruption is so rampant and structurally embedded in government and business, official warnings have done little to curb it among journalists (Zhao 1998). It is difficult to know how far this process of improvi-sation can go without significantly changing journalistic practice or provoking an official clampdown.

MEDIA CONTENT AND IDEOLOGY

In the late 1980s, the politically boldest news outlet was Shanghai's semiofficial *World Economic Herald*. It stood at the forefront of advocating various compre-hensive programs of political and economic reform (including the rule of law, press freedom, and democracy) and was closed down by the authorities during the Tiananmen crackdown in 1989 (Hsiao and Yang 1990; Goldman 1994). Tighter press control briefly returned before the waves of economic enthusiasm began to sweep across China in 1992, bringing about increasing relaxation of restrictions in *nonpolitical* areas. But innovations by today's *Beijing Youth Daily* and the *Shenzhen Special Zone Daily* in no way match the *political* courage of the *World Economic Herald*. In retrospect, the *World Economic Herald* both benefited tremendously from the general atmosphere of political reform initiated by Zhao Ziyang and was used by his top assistants (many of whom are now in exile over-seas) as a forum to advocate their reform agendas (Goldman 1994; Zhao 1998).

Instead of directly defying state ideology in the post-1989 decade, the media have learned to invent a set of more innovative and devious approaches for coping with the terms of political requirements and economic interests. Faced with the dilemma of having to please "two masters" (the party and the public), they have had to improvise a variety of seemingly paradoxical strategies to stimulate audience interest without stepping out of official bounds. Journalistic culture has changed considerably since the 1980s (Polumbaum 1990); now newspaper editors confess in private that their front pages endorse planned economy, their second to eighth pages support mixed economy, and their ninth to sixteenth pages advocate market economy. Many popular radio phone-in shows and television exposé pieces appear juxtaposed with otherwise rigid and dogmatic programs. Many programs offer a mix of popular topics and emotional debates that attract high ratings. With the aging party leaders already in bed, the eleven o'clock national news on CCTV is said to be more daring and informative than its seven o'clock news. (CCTV is allowed greater latitude in programs such as "Focus Interviews" than the *People's Daily* is to expose such sensitive issues as corruption among the lower- or middle-ranking cadres.[7] Television is quickly becoming the most potent shaper of popular images and values, but the party press retains its status as the foremost ideological instrument.) This evolving symptom of media schizophrenia is a stone aimed to kill two birds, party needs and public wants, at the same time. The media have little reason or incentive to offend the state, since they can profit from the market as long as they ritualistically chant the chorus of official dogma. The state is trading economic benefits for media loyalty.

Stanley Rosen (chapter 5) provides a fascinating account of how the daring *Beijing Youth Daily* uses investigative reporting and debates on controversial issues as popular marketing devices. As a local paper that stands out as an example in the 1990s of experimentation in news style and layout, it picks controversial social issues, conducts independent investigations, interviews the different sides involved, and invites a lively debate from its readers. The story series is likely to be introduced and concluded by a note from the editor that deliberately casts the issue in terms of "nationalism," "patriotism," or some other conventional value. These seemingly disarming press debates can be used to reconcile conflicts experienced by the public. More subtly, the readers expand their own horizon of vision and must rethink many core values through exposure to public struggles over redefining what is right or wrong. What is a "good citizen" or "public spirit"? Should nationalism suppress individualism? Must party loyalty sacrifice personal interest? Ideas germinate.[8]

The newspaper routinizes new modes of reporting to cover "newsworthy" topics in highly improvisatory ways, to which the authorities can put a stop at any time. Therefore, the *Beijing Youth Daily* has a very pragmatic motive in striking a tolerable fit between party trust and market success. To do this, it must constantly gauge the situation, test the limits of investigative reporting and consumer advocacy, and take its potential opponents into account in playing a game that often resembles hide-and-seek. The examples of the *Beijing Youth Daily,* the *Shenzhen Special Zone Daily,* and the *Southern Weekend* show that ideological innovation always originates from the periphery rather than from the center. These politically marginal papers have greater room and take greater risk to experiment with new ideas. As a price to pay, however, the *Beijing Youth Daily* has been repeatedly pressured by the disgruntled propaganda police to re-place its chief editors. To conclude more broadly: In China, television and newspapers are more stringently controlled than are radio, magazines, books, and new media (see below); the party press is more controlled than is the non-party press; television news is more controlled than is entertainment, and prime-time news is more controlled than is non-prime-time news; political is-sues are more controlled than are social issues (such as environmentalism, gen-der, or consumer advocacy).

Telecommunications

Digitized telecommunications mark a new page in the history of communica-tion revolution: They are asynchronous in timing, instantaneous, interactive, and transmitted through multiple carriers. The user is not simply a passive con-sumer, but also an active producer of messages. The mode of communication is not linear and static but associative and interconnected. Through the new me-dia, one can talk to one individually or many can talk to many simultaneously, unlike traditional mass media that only allow a few to talk to many. Ithiel de Sola Pool (1983), a self-proclaimed *soft* technological determinant, calls the new media "technologies of freedom." He predicts that in the age of new media, more personalized and individualized modes of communication will replace the dominance of homogeneous and unidirectional mass (read: massive) media. Pool (1990) adds that the new media will overcome technological bottlenecks to produce information so abundant and diverse as to suit consumer needs and equalize the distribution of information across class or national boundaries. Many critical political economists, notably Herbert Schiller (1989), claim, on the contrary, that transnational corporations, allied with the First World states, will control the new media as added resources of global domination and hege-mony.

Will the new media displace or complement traditional mass media? In China, how will the state ultimately react to telecommunications development as an instrument of economic growth amidst political control? Daniel Lynch (chap-ter 6) provides a useful account based on painstaking examination of documents and thorough interviews with media professionals and officials. He maintains that China, for historical and organizational reasons, lacks a centralized bureaucratic locus of control for making unified telecommunications policies. While mass media are viewed as ideologically oriented propaganda tools, the state seems to regard telecommunications as common carriers, and hence it subjects them to less ideological scrutiny. Neither is the party-state as monolithic as is commonly assumed. Various units within the state—for example, the Department of Propaganda versus the Ministry of Posts and Telecommunications, central versus local—seem to have their own practical interests and agendas.

Lynch is guardedly sanguine about the potential of telecommunications to loosen "thought work" and even to mobilize actions for popular opposition or resistance in time of crisis. Elsewhere, Edward Friedman (1994) speculates on the ways in which the Chinese public might decode and subvert official messages. We are at an initial stage of coming to grips with the potential development and implications of the new media. Assessing ideological impact, especially in a closed system, is inherently difficult, for it requires a painstaking examination of the process through which the *public* (such as professionals, urban workers, or peasants) interprets the *content* (such as political information, human-interest stories, or personal e-mails). To ask but several questions that beg for better understanding: How is thought control exercised, strengthened, or weakened? What propaganda messages are produced and consumed? How do different social strata use media or telecommunications messages? How do new technologies reinforce social thought, undermine some norms, produce a new mix, mobilize bias, or depoliticize the public life?

The more relaxed censorship on telecommunications is not the result of a suddenly enlightened official policy. Despite the immense potential for development and investment in China, I suspect that the new technology is too underdeveloped to make officials anxious. Two decades of economic reform have transformed China's totalitarian regime into an authoritarian regime; the erosion of the commandist system has made the regime more tolerant of media autonomy and diversity in the *nonpolitical* areas. While the Maoist regime maintained a totalistic control over the minutest details, the Dengist regime is mainly concerned with power preservation. What is perceived to pose a threat to state power would be summarily put down, but technological genres (whose ideological import is hidden and indirect) may be tolerated. Authoritarian regimes of all stripes tend to mystify technological sophistication as a direct measure of, if not as the main source of, ideological power and social impact. Cable television is thus the least regulated and most commercial, thanks partly to its current technological crudeness and, hence, its political marginality, and partly to the difficulty of censoring 4,000 networks (fewer than 1,200 of them officially approved). Offering what is described as "Coca-Cola programming" in contrast to CCTV's "distilled water," these numerous low-budget and primitive cable systems have become a driving force behind the tabloidization of Chinese television (Gordon 1999). Here we see an intriguing parallel between today's China and yesterday's Taiwan, where the martial-law censors maintained an iron-fisted control on major media but underestimated the potential power of the "marginal" media (guerrilla-like political magazines and primitive cable outlets). Who would have expected that these "marginal" media would spearhead Taiwan's oppositional culture and political movement (Lee 1993, 1994b, 1998a)?

Telecommunications is a loose bag that contains a wide range of products, including mobile phones, fax machines, satellites, computers, and the Internet. In China, some technologies (such as the telephone) had historically been used, as Lynch points out, to coordinate communication between different units and levels of the state system, and, therefore, their public use has been too slight to cause official alarm. The more sophisticated technologies are highly underdeveloped for reasons of high cost, poor infrastructure, low funding, and market immaturity. They are more likely to be managed by the technical side rather than by the ideological side of the party-state, and the technical departments tend to regard technologies as ideologically neutral.

The Internet, despite its primitive development, has become something of a new fad in China. As of July 1999, of the close to three hundred on-line media (including 273 newspapers, or 13 percent of the total number of newspapers), the main state ideological apparatuses (such as the *People's Daily*, Xinhua News Agency, CCTV) figured prominently, but the lion's share was taken by urban mass-appeal newspapers (25 percent), economic newspapers (15 percent), and other party organs at various levels (Chui 1999a). Meanwhile, about 1,500 official Web pages have been created by a variety of central, provincial, and local government units that appear to be primarily interested in publicizing information for attracting foreign investment and enhancing business opportunities. (It is noteworthy that such sensitive agencies as foreign relations, national defense, public security, and military establishments have so far eschewed Web pages.) Most of the official Web pages, however, have a dearth of useful information for the public, process information at an excruciatingly slow speed, and are not open to two-way communication (Chui 1999b).

At the turn of this millennium, this nation of 1.4 billion people is dotted with only six million Internet users; all of them are required to be registered with the government, and most of them are urban intellectuals, businesspeople, professionals, and college students. Despite the huge potential and the amazingly rapid pace with which telecommunications industries have grown in China, only 5 percent of the nation's households have a telephone and only 2 percent of them own a personal computer. High illiteracy and cost make Internet access irrelevant to most people. In order to "catch up" with the West's technological prowess, China vowed to invest U.S. $29 billion in upgrading telecommunications infrastructures from 1995 to 2000, only one-tenth of the U.S. investment. A Gallup poll conducted in China shows that consumers' appetite for purchasing personal computers is low, lagging far behind their desires for washing machines and refrigerators. The Internet in China remains, in this sense, part of what Wilbur Schramm (1997) calls the "little media"—marked by low technological sophistication, low organizational complexity, and a low degree of capital and labor intensity. On the contrary, traditional newspapers and television are still regarded as "big media" and therefore scrutinized more scrupulously by state censors.

Schooled in the old propaganda modes of words and sounds, state censors are only slowly awaking to the policy significance and ideological implications of the new media. Apart from the peculiar historical legacy of telecommunications development in China, I believe that this lack of expertise and awareness accounts, at least in part, for why the state bureaucracy has been slow to come to grips with complex policy control issues in this field (see chapter 6). Concerned with the influx of pornographic and "subversive" messages, the government issued a directive in 1996 ordering that all Internet communication from overseas be routed to the Ministry of Posts and Telecommunications (now renamed the Ministry of Information Industries) for official screening. In many ways, China makes no secret of emulating the city-state of Singapore, whose economic prosperity and effective authoritarian control have won Beijing's admiration. Given its geographical size, China is, in essence, creating the world's most gigantic *Intra*net system so as to confine within its national borders the traffic of this increasingly important technological communication domain, thus immunizing its population from the alleged corrupting influences of Western "spiritual pollution." Outside pressures are closing in on China, however, as it joins the neoliberal World Trade Organization (WTO) to participate as a full member in the globalization of capitalism, a process that will thrust an authoritarian state into sharper conflict (and partial accommodation) with the dynamics of world economy. As part of the conditions for admission to the

WTO, China has conceded to the demands of opening up its potentially vast telecommunications industries and the Internet market to foreign ownership, especially by Western-based transnational corporations. What implications this policy shift holds for censorship, the flow of information, and the larger policy contour are far from revealed.

Media Law

Tahirih Lee (chapter 7) characterizes China's media as (1) legal educators, (2) legitimizers and enforcers of the law, and (3) sources of the law. In almost every country, the media have the educative function of promoting laws and legal policy. But China's media do more, as part of the overall ideological structure tied to the complex webs of education and propaganda efforts and to relentless campaigns (Su 1994). In transmitting centrally controlled information and interpretation, the media have inherited the Chinese Communists' guerrilla-war and mass-campaign traditions requiring the creation of words, slogans, rituals, and symbols simple and vivid enough for the masses to grasp. Because the legal system is poorly codified, the Chinese media may have a special aura of authority as transmitters of "correct" state policy and ideology. They filled a legal vacuum during the antilegal and antiprofessional era of the Cultural Revolution, and today they still continue to perform some functions of legal professionals.

Law cannot be divorced from politics; formulation and enforcement of the law is inherently a political process. The media reveal and cultivate the public images of the PRC government as being "protective" and "caring" but "harsh." Many analysts (Lukes 1974; Galbraith 1983; Boulding 1990) have aptly argued that power can be exercised not only through enactment of reward and punishment but fundamentally through a hegemonic process in which submission to authority-cum-law is assumed and recognized. Tahirih Lee notes that the Chinese media serve as sources of law in publishing statutes, policies, and official interpretations as well as in notifying local governments about their authority to enact regulations for specific statutes and policies. Nonphysical violence has been used, and the media may also amplify instances of punitive actions to achieve a wider social effect. Televised criminal convictions, for example, appeal to the viewer's sense of shame and fear; thus, undermining the viewer's sense of privacy strengthens the suggestion of surveillance of the viewer. She seems to conceive the Chinese media's legal role in more *hegemonic* than *coercive* terms.

Ideological hegemony, in Gramscian terms, means that the liberal-capitalist state maintains its rule by conditioning the people to a broad set of social-consent norms that the media and other cultural institutions manufacture instead of by invoking coercive apparatuses or resorting to rigid propaganda (Hall 1977; Williams 1977; Gitlin 1980). How hegemonic—in the sense of being persuasive rather than coercive—the Chinese media are can only be determined comparatively. Those who take exception to Tahirih Lee's implicit thesis may fault her for blunting the differences between authoritarian and democratic media. They would argue that in China formal statutes and codes remain more authoritative than the media as "sources of law" and that both China's media and its legal system are far more coercive than persuasive. Chinese media obviously lack public credibility or moral authority to persuade a people who, based on experience, generally believe that whoever follows the laws will lose out. China's legal reform seeks to achieve the rule *by* law (making the laws subservient to political goals) rather than the rule *of* law (striving for legal independence from political dictates). Dissemination of legal and other information in China is still rigidly stratified according to party membership and administrative rank (Dittmer 1994). Inasmuch as the state monopolizes "correct" legal interpretations, the media could only uphold state policy and ideology. Enforcing ideological conformity and muting the dissent are among the key roles of the Chinese media. As Tahirih Lee ably demonstrates, China used media transmissions as a policy instrument to articulate legal ramifications of the Sino-British Joint Declaration and the Basic Law before the PRC's resumption of sovereignty over Hong Kong. This legal instrument role does not seem to have been weakened by the surging waves of media commercialization.

In this sense, the "public" role of the PRC's state-owned media moves closer to the definition of "public" in the German (equivalent to *gongkai* in Chinese terms) rather than in the Anglo-American sense (*gonggong*). In the German sense, Elisabeth Noelle-Neumann's (1995) "spiral of silence" hypothesis states that the prevailing opinion creates strong public (*gongkai*) pressure on people to act in conformity; thus seemingly popular views gather further momentum, while the unpopular ones weaken and even disappear. Media persuasion in China appears to be backed by coercive state power. Its media rarely tolerate deviation from official policy and obviously do not play the "public" role in the classical (and idealized) Anglo-American sense in which people are engaged in rational discourses about issues of major consequence to them. In fact, the very concept of a "public sphere" may be dubious in China, where the primarily top-down media are conduits, interpreters, and enforcers of legal and policy pronouncements.

Esoteric Communication[9]

Media interaction between the PRC and Taiwan, as a key component of communication patterns in Cultural China, has oscillated widely as both sides try to
gain advantages from it. Cultural exchange is a form of low politics even though
media flow ranks among the most sensitive items of cultural politics. Before the
1980s, cultural flow was strictly forbidden, and in the 1980s, the PRC chastised
Taiwan for its reluctance to increase mutual contacts in direct trade, mail, and
air transport. In the early 1990s, however, Beijing became defensive, as the rapidly democratizing Taiwan started to turn to press freedom as a diplomatic front
to defuse Beijing's political pressure. The PRC ignored Taiwan's suggestion that
newspapers be allowed to establish bureaus and circulate freely on both sides of
the Taiwan Strait. Beijing has restricted Taiwanese television production sites to
seven mainland cities; it has prohibited mainland journalists from visiting Taiwan (Taiwan's journalists make four hundred visits to the mainland per year);
and China's media coverage of Taiwan has been scant and highly negative. In
addition to beaming nine shortwave radio stations at Taiwan, China's television
signals find their way through satellite linkup into the island's living rooms — but
both to little effect. By and large, barriers of access have limited Taiwan's mainland news coverage to a narrow focus on Beijing-based politics.

Prior to 1987, Taiwan's triple alliance of the party, the state, and the military controlled a half of the island's thirty-one newspapers and monopolized all
three television networks. Indigenous Taiwanese owned a small group of mar-
ginally important papers, whereas two private oligopolies claimed two-thirds of
Taiwan's newspaper advertising and circulation. Since political liberalization in
1987, as Ran Wei (chapter 11) describes, these three types of newspapers, given
their market niche and ideological interests, have shaped distinct policies toward mainland reporting. The party-state press is wavering in its attitude, but
the indigenous press — favoring Taiwan's secession from China — is downright
hostile to it. Only the Big Two have been enthusiastic about the enterprise,
even making failed and controversial attempts to establish bridgeheads in the
mainland market.

Of special interest is the role of the media in what scholars of political culture (Pool 1973; Griffith 1973; Pye 1979) call "esoteric communication" — that
is, the process by which each side tries to gauge and react to the significance of
the other side's policy cues through the window of media coverage. In Communist politics, the policy-making process is shrouded in mystery and secrecy,
with rival factions manipulating a variety of symbols — metaphors, analogies,

code words, and historical allegories—to denounce their opponents. Marlowe Hood (1994) traces the use by Chinese leaders of both public media and internal media (circulated within the party elite circle) to win factional wars, showing them going so far as to try to manage general foreign news and particular news items about China. Instead of wanting to confront their opponents face-to-face, Communist leaders prefer to conduct their struggles through mass media smoke screens that are presumably *im*personal enough to provide insulation from immediate emotional pressure. They assume that their rivals and the "people" should be able to decode motives from the ambiguous media expressions. Failure by the intended audience to draw the intended implications may lead to the heightening of the conflict.

Esoteric communication, with the media acting as a "looking-glass mirror" (Lang and Lang 1982), has filled part of the diplomatic void between the PRC and Taiwan. The media provide a thin context devoid of the rich texture necessary for the art of diplomacy and direct negotiation. But, playing the game of political gestures, leaders can use the media to score propaganda victories and to maintain legitimacy at home. The media give rise to a semblance of dialogue by amplifying what each side says and how one side reacts to the other side's reactions. In between stands "a bystander public" (Lang and Lang 1982): third-party spectators to the unfolding drama who gaze at the media stage, witnesses to the opposing regimes' hurled threats, bluffs, and insults, yet who themselves have little role to play in the actual resolution of conflict. Media sociologists maintain that media agendas are, by necessity, bureaucratically structured, that news rhythm is closely linked to government cycles of operation, and that the media, therefore, tend to follow the concentric circle of power (Tuchman 1978; Fishman 1980; Gans 1979; Chang 1990). While this is true, Taiwan's media have also often given full play to China's official positions, sometimes creating public pressure on Taiwan's decision-making body. This is not true of the PRC's controlled media. In fact, evidence suggests that some PRC media seem to have deliberately heightened the cross-strait tension and animosity to attract market attention.[10]

The media play both routine and nonroutine roles. In the China-Taiwan equation, even though deep suspicion lingers, media portrayal on both sides has moved from total demonization of the other to a point where the public can glean certain useful information from news reports. In their routine mode of operation, the media ritualistically rehash much of the official rhetoric, which is boring yet predictable enough to suggest that no major policy change has occurred to upset fragile ties. The media's routine reporting has replaced the role of secret "shuttle diplomacy" played by a few overseas Chinese scholars and politicians who had been asked to relay messages between the two sides. Moreover, a ritualistic media framework constitutes a bridge that can be put to use to start an initiative at a turning point, as shown by the Sino–U.S. talks in Warsaw prior to final rapprochement.

The media have not only reflected the contentious relationship between the PRC and Taiwan but have, in a nonroutine way, contributed to its construction and maintenance. Since 1987, Beijing has tried to endorse pro-unification candidates in Taiwan's elections, but these efforts, once publicized by the media, have backfired. The PRC's missile threat in 1996 set off a rancorous ideological warfare over Taiwan's mainland policy among the four presidential contestants. Lee Teng-hui (Li Denghui), the first local-born president, capitalized on the media's role to sharpen the us–against–them sentiment by lashing out at Beijing's hegemony, thus winning accolades from the domestic bystander-public for his courage in standing up to the Communist bully. Since then, formal official channels have been shut down, leaving the media to construct much of the bilateral understanding and misunderstanding. The media also chronicle, and thus magnify, a growing discord in Taiwan between leading capitalist interests, who eye the huge China market, and President Lee, who opposes their investment ventures. In this sense, the media play a major part in the increasingly intertwined "external" and "domestic" politics. The peace-making role of the media, as exemplified by coverage of Egyptian President Sadat's overtures to Israel (Dayan and Katz 1992), has yet to prevail in Cultural China.

Paradoxes of the Political Economy of Media

As previously noted, the perspective informing many chapters in this volume is that of a broadly defined political economy of communication. This perspective must, by definition, cope with the larger "political" and "economic" conditions of the media as well as with the interactive impact of politics and economics on the media's structure, operation, content, and ideology. If political economy is indeed "the study of the social relations, particularly the power relations" and "the study of control and survival in social life" (Mosco 1996:25–26), then the repository of power that regulates control and survival has been conceptualized very differently. Accentuating one side of political economy over the other side has led to the development of two different approaches: "economism" versus "politicism" (Staniland 1985). To summarize, the radical-

Marxist political economists of communication are more "economistic" (focusing on critiques of the capital), whereas the liberal–pluralist political economists of communication are more "politicalistic" (focusing on critiques of the state).[11] I have posited their differences in table 1.1, as a preliminary framework for analysis.

Table 1.1. Two Approaches to the Political Economy of the Media

	Liberal–Pluralist	**Radical–Marxist**
Political program	Realistic, practical, and pragmatic politics; supports responsible capitalism	Idealistic and critical politics; criticizes capitalism and supports versions of socialism
Type of political economy	Politicism	Economism; material base as "determining"
Locus of explanation	"Late developing" and Third World countries, mostly authoritarian	Advanced capitalist countries. Liberal or social democracies
Type of corporatism	State corporatism	Societal corporatism
The role of the state	Primary. Dominant shaper of economic and media policies. Repressive state power threatens media freedom	Secondary and derived: a. An instrument of capitalists, the capitalist class, or transnational corporations; b. Relative autonomy in exercising public intervention in media resources; c. Creates media symbols to further hegemony
The role of the market	Promotes diversity and countervails arbitrary state power	Capital accumulation and concentration restrict media diversity and produce communication inequalities
Media professionalism	Promotes media pluralism and freedom. "Creed of credibility"	a. "Strategic rituals" used to reinforce the established order; b. Tyranny of media professionals at the expense of public voices

Michael Schudson (1991) faults the dominant radical-Marxist approach in the communication literature, which emanates from Britain and the United States, for being "oddly insensitive to (authoritarian) political and legal determinants of news production." It is thus "more 'economic' than 'political.'"[12] John

Downing (1996) claims that assumptions about the mainstream media literature often lose their applicability beyond the "heartland nations" of the United States and Britain, for they fail to adequately address the role of the media in the process of regime change and consolidation. In turn, radical political economists (Golding and Murdock 1979; Garnham 1990:30) complain that pluralists have paid too much attention to the state-media relationship and not enough to the impact of privatized capitalism on the means of communication. James Curran (1991) has called for giving liberal conceptions "a decent funeral," because the legacy of old saws "bear[s] little relationship to contemporary reality." It is my opinion that liberal conceptions will remain as viable in media studies as authoritarian control in many Third World states will remain obstinate against popular resistance.

Neither of these two approaches should be regarded as *universal*. Privileging them on a priori grounds would not only overlook the crucial contextual differences but also commit the fallacy of misplaced concreteness. I therefore treat them as two varied yet related *historical conditions* of modern social life, with at least two major implications. First, in line with Staniland (1985), the liberal-pluralist approach may apply to authoritarian media systems, whereas the radical-Marxist approach is most powerful in criticizing liberal-capitalist media systems. In Cultural China, the radical-Marxist approach throws little light on the liberal media struggle against authoritarian states of the PRC and Taiwan under martial law (Lee 1990a, 1993, 1994a). I would add a second implication: In *transitional systems*—from authoritarian to democratic rule, or vice versa—both approaches may coexist side by side, uneasily and paradoxically, under some circumstances. As post–martial-law Taiwan renegotiates its fluid and intermeshed state-capital relationship, for example, the radical approach is increasingly central to examining how capital concentration strains media diversity, but *not* to the exclusion of the pluralist approach (Lee 2000). Hong Kong's liberal media order presents an opposite case: Fear of China's authoritarian state has heightened the relevance of the pluralist approach, but the radical approach remains all the more pertinent to the critique of media conglomeration (chapter 10). The contradictions posed between China's political control and economic reform (chapters 2 to 5) have further raised many intriguing questions.

RADICAL MARXISTS: ECONOMISM

Nicholas Garnham (1990:23) has outlined a highly cogent theory of the political economy of mass communication which is situated in historical materialism and which attempts to avoid the "twin traps of economic reductionism and of the idealist autonomization of the ideological level." What is important is that he seems to start and end his analysis with the *economic* sphere. Peter Golding and Graham Murdock (1991) call their perspective "critical political economy." *Who* are critical of *whom*, on *what?* In a rough outline, "who" characterizes radical Western Marxists; "whom" points to the capitalist order and its media dynamics; and "what" is the distorted public communication and social inequality said to be products of the capitalist order which renders full democratic expression impossible.

What constitutes the main problematic of this "critical political economy" in the media-culture realm? Political economy is, for Vincent Mosco (1996:25), "the study of social relations, particularly the power relations, that mutually constitute the *production, distribution, and consumption of resources*" (emphasis added). Although resources can also be politically based, Mosco refers primarily to the economically based resources. For Golding and Murdock (1991:198), the task is to trace "the impact of *economic dynamics* on the range of diversity of public cultural expression, and its availability to different social groups" (emphasis added). Prefacing the most comprehensive anthology on the topic (two volumes, running to nearly 1,400 pages), they note that critical political economy of communications addresses (a) "the distributional consequences of capitalism for communications processes and institutions, and of the availability of differing forms and structures of meaning," (b) "the distribution between public and private, not least in the realm of regulation," and (c) "the relative role of the state, the private corporation and the individuals in communications" (1997:xvi).

Two decades earlier, Murdock and Golding (1977) contended that development of a separate body of communication theories was not needed; rather, what was needed was the development of a coherent and comprehensive theory of society—presumably synonymous with the political-economy perspective—from which media theories could be deduced. They refused to be seen as "economistic," but their political economy was largely "economic." In the same article, they took to task Stuart Hall and Raymond Williams, two leading British cultural scholars, for "a top-heavy analysis in which an elaborate anatomy of cultural forms balances insecurely on a schematic account of economic forces shaping their production."[13] Their subsequent formulation (Golding and Murdock 1991) has softened this antagonism by adopting Williams's redefinition of "determination" and Hall's orientation toward treating economic forces as determining "in the *first* instance" rather than "in the *final* instance," as Marx originally envisaged. Williams (1977) proposes that we examine how economic infrastructure passively "sets limits" and actively "exerts pressure" on the superstructure in actual and active *processes* of social struggle. Economic infrastructure and ideological superstructure (which includes anything ranging from the media and culture to the state and law) are not to be treated as two separate *domains*. Hall's position (1983) implies that economic factors may explain general direction but not the detailed content of the ideological field, and that there may be room for intellectual autonomy and innovation within the general limits of the capitalist structure.

There are as many versions of economistic political economy as there are versions of Marxist interpretation. They are all informed by the radical humanism of the Hegelian Marx and committed to various socialist visions opposed to capitalist alienation and exploitation. Facing widespread public acceptance of the status quo, radical Marxists in the "heartland nations" ask, "Why do people not rebel more often than they do?" (Downing 1996:230). They stand at the margin of liberal or social democracies in Western Europe and North America, where their own freedom of speech is protected to a substantial degree, to launch intellectually potent but perhaps politically feeble attacks on the established capitalist order. They pursue an idealistic "third way" that rebels against the exploitative capitalist way or the repressive Leninist way (Gouldner 1980). One of the most influential and appealing "third ways" is undoubtedly Jürgen Habermas's (1989) concept of the "bourgeois public sphere." Based on this concept, James Curran (1991) has prescribed a democratic media system that incorporates the civic sector, the professional sector, the social market sector, and the private enterprise sector. Schudson (1995) doubts that such a "public sphere" ever existed historically, but the concept is charming enough to serve as a normative anchor for Curran's program. James Carey (1995), an idealistic pragmatist, also advocates the "recovery of public life"—admittedly, without vouching for its historical truth—to stimulate "imagination of a possible politics."

Many radical media political economists have taken the role of the *political* or the *state* for granted. One reason is that political censorship of the media in the liberal state is more invisible (Keane 1991). Another is that, theoretically, state power is assumed to be part of the superstructure often subservient to corporate interest. In directing their moral outrage against the capitalistic logic, radical Marxists tend to treat the state as a dependent—"secondary and derived" (Giddens 1973:32–33)—variable of economics, albeit with some variations in the perspectives of instrumentalists, structuralists, and culturalists.

Instrumentalists (Schiller 1992; Herman and Chomsky 1988) regard the state apparatuses, as embodied by the U.S. "military-industrial complex," as the principal instruments of transnational media corporate interests, whose expansion and penetration have infringed on the "national sovereignty" of Third World countries. Instrumentalists tend to consider the relationship between the state and big business as linear and unproblematic. To correct this focus, Murdock (1982) recommends examining how the general dynamics of media industries and capitalist economics structurally limit the exercise of corporate power. Even this welcomed emphasis does not begin to address the *state's* "relative autonomy" vis-à-vis the dominant classes or the globally imposed constraints (Poulantzas 1978; Skocpol 1979).

Radical political economists have a contentious relationship with structuralists and culturalists within the Marxist tradition (Hall 1986). Structuralists, notably Louis Althusser (1972) and Nicos Poulantzas (1978), pay considerable attention to the role of the state. For Althusser, the repressive state apparatuses function in the public domain, but the ideological state apparatuses function as part of the private domain. He argues that no dominant class can hold state power over a long period without at the same time exercising its hegemony over and in the state ideological apparatuses.[14] The Althusserian conception has many of its own critics among Marxists, especially from those who emphasize practice rather than formal structure. Garnham (1990:30), Althusser's critic, attempts to "shift attention away from the conception of the mass media as ideological apparatuses of the State, and sees them first as economic entities." He argues particularly for the importance of analyzing how the development of monopoly capitalism has industrialized the superstructure of culture and media. Finally, culturalists claim that the state produces and reproduces symbols in the media to consolidate "hegemony" in the Gramscian sense, thus marginalizing the dissent and closing off alternative discourses.

Radical political economists are penetrating in criticizing the impact of corporate reach on commodifying public communication but much less persuasive in analyzing political and cultural dynamics. To relate this point to Cultural China: Capital concentration mixed with political uncertainty has driven Hong Kong's media toward conglomerate ownership, under which the economic logic is pursued at the price of cultural values and media diversity (chapter 10). Besides, Taiwan's media oligopoly during martial law was formed by a client-patron relationship in relation to the state, not through "free" market competition; but the market forces unleashed since 1987 have muffled new voices in a different way (Lee 1993, 2000). The current trend toward media conglomeration in China is engineered by the state for the sake of control rather than as a consequence of capital accumulation in the market.

What role do radical Marxists assign to the *political?* Mosco (1996:200) recognizes that political economy would "benefit from a greater emphasis on the *political.*" Specifically, he outlines four areas for study: (1) how market standards, rather than public interest, establish market regulation; (2) how state intervention expands the number of participants in the market; (3) privatization; and (4) internationalization of the capital and product of the communications industry (Mosco 1996:202–3). Golding and Murdock (1991) single out "the changing role of the state and government intervention"—along with the growth of the media, the extension of corporate reach, and commodification—as the historical processes "particularly central to a critical political economy of culture." But their analysis focuses partially and narrowly on how the state intervenes on behalf of the public interest to rectify the "distortions and inequalities of market systems."[15] While Schiller (1992) and Herman and Chomsky (1988) see the state as serving transnational media corporate interests, Golding and Murdock (1991) and Mosco (1996) seem to uphold the state as a guardian of public interest in warding off corporate assault. It is noteworthy, however, that none of them are writing about authoritarian states in particular.

Phillip Schmitter (1974) uses the terms "societal corporatism" and "state corporatism" to depict the modes of intersection between public and private sectors in advanced capitalism and authoritarian countries, respectively. "Societal corporatism" takes a negotiated form that involves partial and reciprocal intersection between public and private sectors. This results in centralized economic power—including cultural and media capital—in large transnational corporations. Given its regulatory role in the management and stabilization of the national economy, however, the liberal state becomes one of the central loci for democratic struggles. By acknowledging the positive role of state intervention, Golding and Murdock (1991) and Mosco (1996) suggest a possibility for significant change in capitalist democracies. Political determinants and social movements do, under some circumstances, "overdetermine" the media industry.

Radical-critical scholars have paid scant attention to the harsh conditions produced by authoritarian or Leninist regimes. As Alvin Gouldner (1976:165) puts it, "[I]f socialism is to mean a new human emancipation, one thing is certain: it *cannot* mean the nationalization of the means of production." Many of the "socialist alternatives"—in the images of Cuba, the PRC, North Vietnam, and the former Soviet Union—once espoused by Schiller (1976), Dallas Smythe (1994), and others were nothing but repugnant. It is one thing to condemn exploitation of the world periphery by core imperialists, quite another to promote authoritarianism as an alternative to global capitalism. "Grand narratives" fail miserably when it comes to fine-grain politics. These radical writers indiscriminately displace one grand ideology with its mirror opposite, showing little tolerance for gradations. Their *totalizing* discourse should come in for a fair share of postmodern deconstruction, for which John Tomlinson (1991) shows much promise.

Finally, as media professionalism is firmly rooted in capitalistic logic,[16] radical Marxists seek to debunk it as an ideologically constructed myth that serves the interest of the status quo. Peter Schlesinger (1979) rightly argues that media professionalism is predicated on an unarticulated commitment to the established liberal democratic order. The linkage between media professionalism and national interest is most notoriously displayed in foreign policy issues (Said 1982; Herman and Chomsky 1988).[17] Gaye Tuchman (1978) shows that media professionalism relies on "strategic rituals" that enable the media to uphold the facade of objectivity when, in fact, their news net tends to be woven around centrally legitimated institutions. She argues that this dominant perspective permeates mainstream media accounts to the neglect of other alternative or deviant views. Todd Gitlin (1980) also shows that media construction of a student movement tends to support the reformist group and reject the radical group. The long-term ideological effect of the media is "hegemony" (Hall 1977; Williams 1977) and the manufacture of consent (Herman and Chomsky 1988). To others (see Manoff and Schudson 1986), even the narrative form of a news story achieves this ideological effect. Objective reporting has been, as Schudson (1978:160) summarizes, accused of "reproduc[ing] a vision of social reality which refuses to examine the basic structures of power and privilege" and "represent[ing] collusion within institutions whose legitimacy was in dispute." Moreover, from a pragmatist perspective, Carey (1995) blames media professionalism for downgrading the public from political "participants" to mere "spectators." This formulation seems to combine a nostalgic Jeffersonian vision of the past and a romantic Habermasian utopia of the future. These radical critiques are intellectually powerful but seem to have exerted only marginal influence on journalistic practice.

LIBERAL PLURALISTS: POLITICISM

The radical-Marxist premises, developed in the West, do not apply to the media controlled by authoritarian states in "late-developing countries" or in most Third World countries of Asia, Latin America, Africa, and the former Eastern

Europe. Writing about the PRC, for example, many authors in this volume assume "the determining imposition of the political order (the state) upon the economic order," with the state taking "a dominant, autonomous role in shaping both the distribution of power within society and the direction of economic development" (Staniland 1985:75-76). How does the *state* wield its dominant control on media expression? In China, for example, the authoritarian state monopolizes the national economic resources on which the media depend, while controlling the decision-making processes in the material and editorial senses (chapter 4).

Liberal politics is a politics of what is practically possible, not what is potentially ideal or ideally potential. It acknowledges human imperfection, distrusts any grand design, and advocates incremental reform rather than large-scale overhaul of the existing order. It endorses "responsible capitalism" rather than rejects capitalism in a more fundamental sense. Current theories of democracy have moved far away from the maximum conditions (the Jeffersonian images of informed, participatory citizenry in small pastoral communities) to the minimum conditions requiring procedural consensus, the rule of law, and effective communication in an urbanized and industrialized America. To the extent that liberal rhetoric is characteristically unromantic, it has nonetheless instilled a profound sense of hope and legitimacy in a wide variety of popular struggle, resistance, and liberation movements, including those in the Third World (Jansen 1991:137). Progressive student movements in modern China—from May 4, 1919, to June 4, 1989—have had a tradition of appealing to such liberal ideals as democracy, liberty, science, and human rights.[18]

John Keane (1991:95-109) notes that Western liberal states may exercise five interlocking types of political censorship: emergency powers, armed secrecy, lying, state advertising, and corporatism. Such censorious power of the state is, however, structural and, moreover, invisible. The opposite of liberal democracy is the totalitarian state: During China's Cultural Revolution era, the state maintained an omnipresent and omnipotent control over every facet of civil life. Occupying the ground between liberal democracy and totalitarianism are the "bureaucratic-authoritarian regimes" found in Latin America and Asia (O'Donnell 1973, 1978). There, a policy of capital accumulation and economic growth was single-mindedly pursued, while the army and police were mobilized to crush ruthlessly any popular movement favoring greater political participation. Instead of harnessing economic growth to political democracy, bureaucratic-authoritarian regimes justify state suppression of press freedom and civil liberties on the grounds that political stability is a precondition for economic growth. To that end, the bureaucratic-authoritarian state creates a close-knit "patron-client relationship" (Eisenstadt and Roniger 1981) to dispense political and economic favors in exchange for their allies' support. As this relationship is necessarily asymmetrical but reciprocal, the authoritarian regime demands from the media extensive but not total subservience to the state. The media procure scarce resources and seek protection from the state, but in turn they display an overall commitment to it. This interaction is frequently tacit, informal, and backed by close personal ties. The media are strictly forbidden to foster horizontal alliances with other social groups or labor unions.

The state is seen as an enemy rather than a guardian angel of public interest and media freedom. The authoritarian state organizes political expression without "determin[ing] its content in any detailed and persuasive way" (Staniland 1985:75). Jansen (1991:134) observes disapprovingly that liberal histories "portray democracy as the theory and capitalism (cum 'free enterprise') as the practice," but industrial capitalism "routinely abridges free enterprise as well as freedom of the press." While liberal writers tend to view capitalism as largely if also conditionally compatible with democracy, radical-Marxist writers tend to see them as fundamentally contradictory. The market may betray the ideals of democracy and Habermas's "public sphere," but from the pluralist perspective it is also a necessary yet insufficient condition for checking on authoritarian state power. Market competition has provided more opportunities for freedom of expression in Taiwan (Lee 1993), South Korea (Yoon 1989), Mexico (Hallin 2000), and South Africa (Hachten and Giffard 1984); even the PRC is beginning to exhibit this pattern. To wit, market competition makes the mainstream media more sensitive to public wants: They deviate from state rhetoric in moments of ambiguity and ally themselves with reformist social causes (such as environmentalism and consumer rights).

Rather than denouncing media professionalism, liberal pluralists view it as a meaningful ideal that promotes a diversity of opinion and empowers the media to "check and balance" the established power. Like democracy, media professionalism promises no political utopia. As an occupational myth, it may not be totally attainable, but as a journalistic practice it has established a realistic and reasonable record of success. In the United States, since media professionalism is deeply embedded in the "enduring values" traceable to the Progressive Movement, the media have displayed high vigilance against government corruption and corporate wrongdoing (Gans 1979).[19] It is no accident that various renditions of media professionalism and the torch of press freedom have manifestly or inadvertently energized generations of people and journalists worldwide to fight against authoritarian regimes (Lee 1993; Yoon 1989). Even though media professionalism has been given a hard time in the PRC, "objective reporting," often crudely conceptualized, remains a high calling for journalists at every juncture of political struggle (Li 1994). It is eminently evident in this volume that PRC journalists have exploited the imperatives of market competition in many ways to dilute or dodge political control. Even if their efforts may not be heroic, wholesome, or even successful, the conditioned tendency of some radical Western scholars to reject media professionalism or its correlates out of hand seems patently foolish. There is too little, not too much, media professionalism in an authoritarian country. After all, a man cannot dispose of something he does not own, just as an undernourished boy does not refuse to eat meat simply to "keep his body fit."

In sum, the radical-Marxist perspective is a "top-down" approach in the sense that its proponents critique the status quo of the liberal-capitalist media — the "incomplete emancipation," resource inequity, and cultural distortion posed by *economic* dynamics in advanced capitalism — from the high plateaus of various radical-Marxist humanist formulations. Radical writers tend to take the state for granted precisely because state control of the media is more benign in advanced capitalism. The liberal political-economy perspective seems to fit late-developing countries, including most Third World and former Communist countries, where the state takes a dominant role in shaping the distribution of power within society and the direction of economic policy (Staniland 1985:75; O'Donnell 1978). Hence, the proponents of this "bottom-up" approach struggle against the low and rough ground of naked state media repression and are encouraged by the liberal images of "checks and balances" in "the marketplace of ideas." After all, a freer market order, not abused by the state, offers an emancipatory alternative to aristocratic, oligarchical, or authoritarian dictatorship. I am reopening the issue in the belief that these two approaches represent a complex dialectic whose interactions and contradictions must be further investigated. Finally, how media technology impinges on or is impinged on by the state-capital relationship in the globalization process should receive fuller articulation.

Notes

1. The fiber-optic cables being constructed in the Pacific Ocean will directly link China with the west coast of North America for the first time. These cables will have eight times the bandwidth, or signal capacity, of the current Asia-to-North America

fiber-optic links. A similar fiber-optic link is under construction between Shanghai and Frankfurt, for the most part following the route of the old Silk Road; this means that China and the European Union will provide the gateway to one of the major information links with the new Central Asian republics. Whether the major satellite launches planned in the next five years—launches that will increase the number of communication satellites by four to five times the present capacity—can be accomplished without access to Chinese launch facilities is very uncertain.

2. This volume grew out of a working conference held under the auspices of the China Times Center for Media and Social Studies at the University of Minnesota. The conference was repeated, with most of the same papers and one new contribution, at the Chinese University of Hong Kong. At both conferences, I asked two participants, besides myself, to provide detailed feedback on each paper, so many chapters included here have profited from comments from at least five colleagues.

3. I am grateful to Yu Huang, Zhou He, Eric Ma, and especially Jim Schwoch for providing helpful comments. Thanks go also to Hugo de Burgh and John Tomlinson, who graciously invited me to present this paper as a keynote speech to a symposium at Nottingham Trent University in the United Kingdom on February 12, 1999.

4. Not by accident, however, are only a few scholars of Chinese descent on the long roster of the *China Quarterly* editorial board—a phenomenon similar to what Said (1979) describes in the field of Oriental studies. Very few "comparativists," let alone China specialists, have been so honored by communication journals. In a situation that resembles baseball's World Series, it is always a sore point to ask just how "international" the various professional communications associations and their journals, including some which include the term in their titles, are in the field of communication.

5. This section is largely adapted from Chen and Lee (1998).

6. To illustrate, the *People's Daily* publishes five newspapers (including its domestic and overseas editions, the *Market, Global Digest,* and *Caricature and Humor*) and six magazines (*News Front, Earth, Chinese Economic Express, Chinese Product Quality Bulletin, People's Forum,* and *Current Thought*). In addition, the *Liberation Daily* owns four newspapers and two magazines; the *Nanfang Daily* has six newspapers and one magazine; and the *Economic Daily* publishes four newspapers and five magazines. Other potential conglomerates include the *Zhejiang Daily* (five newspapers and two magazines), the *Yunnan Daily* (four newspapers and one magazine), the *Dazhong Daily* (four newspapers and two magazines), the *Fujian Daily* (five newspapers and one magazine), and the *Shaanxi Daily* (five newspapers and three magazines). The names of these auxiliary publications are largely revealing of social need and market demand. The subjects they cover range from art and novels to farming, fashion, and birds and flowers to English learning and public relations.

7. In China's state administrative rank system, the party press is placed somewhat higher than the television station, whereby the *People's Daily* director assumes a minister rank and the CCTV director has a deputy minister rank. A provincial party newspaper is also one rank above the provincial television station. The CCTV example is perhaps an exception to the rule for three reasons. First, adhering to this strict hierarchical order,

the media are forbidden to criticize officials of the same administrative rank; CCTV as a central-level unit can expose the corruption of provincial-level officials, whereas provincial television stations cannot. Second, CCTV's investigative exposés are known to have been encouraged by Premier Zhu Rongji. Third, counterexamples can be found: In Guangdong, what the *Nanfang Daily* is allowed to do may be off limits to Guangdong TV.

8. Parallel to this is a growing market in popular books that offer accessible analysis, reexamination of recent social history and social mores (such as sex, marriage, divorce, and extramarital relations), as well as discussion of the personal (Gordon 1999).

9. This section is adapted from Lee (1998b).

10. In July 1999, when President Lee declared, in a German television interview, that Taiwan has a "special state-to-state relationship" with the PRC, Beijing reacted strongly. The *Global Times* took an even more hawkish line toward Taiwan than its parent *People's Daily*. In what seemed to be a commercially rather than politically motivated decision, the former exaggerated the "tension in the Taiwan Strait" in the front-page headline, which was accompanied by sensational pictures of alleged landing operations by the People's Liberation Army (PLA). The *Science Times,* a weekly published by the Chinese Academy of Science, even printed a headline that read "PLA's New Guided Missile Able to Attack Lee Teng-hui at His Desk Directly."

11. Perspectives on political economy can be categorized in various ways (see, for example, Caporaso and Levine 1992), but my use of the "liberal-pluralist" and "radical-Marxist" labels partly follows Curran et al.'s "pluralist" and "Marxist" distinctions (1982), and corresponds to Murdock's treatment of "theory of industry" versus "theory of capitalism" (1982). Within the liberal-pluralist framework, some may contrast the neoclassical approach to the Keynesian approach, the neoinstitutional approach, and so on, but this internal distinction is less relevant here.

12. Michael Schudson further charges that British and American studies of Britain and the United States have "taken a liberal democratic political framework for granted." Only in the absence of comparative studies, he continues, can they "paint the news media in liberal societies in the tones of news media in authoritarian regimes."

13. Garnham (1990) is also critical of Stuart Hall and other French structuralists.

14. The repressive state apparatuses include the government, the administration, the army, the police, the courts, the prisons, and so on. The ideological state apparatuses include churches, schools, family, political parties, communication, arts, literature, and sports. This view contrasts sharply with that of Golding and Murdock (1991), who look to the state as a repository of distributive justice.

15. In the two-volume anthology they edited (totaling nearly 1,400 pages), the first volume is devoted to the "economic" side and the second volume to the "political" side of political economy. The first volume covers (1) defining political economy; (2) communication and capitalist enterprise; (3) communication, ideology, and capitalism; and (4) communication and the global order. The second volume covers (1) private interests in common goods; (2) public broadcasting and public interest; (3) policing the public interest; and (4) institutionalizing diversity.

16. Media professionalism is a vague concept that often incorporates such conventions and values as objective reporting, press freedom, media ethics, and occupational autonomy. Objective reporting as a practice separates facts from opinion. It was a historical response to the rise of capitalism and market economy as a way to embrace middle-class pluralism in a liberal democracy (Schudson 1978). The emerging capitalist life produced a "utilitarian culture" which transformed media accounts from a more normative order to a more descriptive dimension; institutionalization of objective reporting was inspired by such political and economic needs (Gouldner 1976). Media professionalism has been transferred to the Third World through institutional, historical, and ideological contexts (Golding 1977).

17. While domestically the U.S. media may reflect—and sometimes intervene in—the two-party political system and the institutional conflict between different branches of the power structure (Hallin 1986), they do not even necessarily apply the same level of fairness or balance to international reporting. They tend to "domesticate" other countries as variations on American themes (Gans 1979). They reduce complex reality to a simple and crude us-against-them dimension in light of their own prejudices, mental conceptions, and hegemonic motives (Said 1982). They also downplay human rights abuse of friendly states while exaggerating that of its enemy states in order to prove the "superiority" of the Western system (Herman and Chomsky 1988). Overall, media reports are in broad agreement with U.S. foreign policy agendas.

18. In this regard, exception must be taken to Rampal (1994) for crediting Taiwan's increasing openness mainly to the legacy of Confucian humanism. Confucian ethos may have constrained the authoritarian rulers in a general way, but Taiwan's liberal struggle for democracy and press freedom had come primarily from the U.S. influence.

19. Peter Dreier (1979) interprets this somewhat disapprovingly as symptomatic of "corporate liberalism" or an attempt by the media to forestall significant change in the interest of preserving the long-term health of the capitalist system.

Bibliography

Althusser, Louis. 1972. *Lenin and Philosophy, and Other Essays*. New York: Monthly Review Press.

Berger, Peter. 1985. *The Capitalist Revolution*. New York: Basic Books.

Berger, Peter, and Hansfried Kellner. 1981. *Sociology Reinterpreted*. New York: Doubleday.

Boulding, Kenneth. 1990. *Three Faces of Power*. Newbury Park, Calif.: Sage.

Caporaso, James, and David P. Levine. 1992. *Theories of Political Economy*. New York: Cambridge University Press.

Carey, James. 1995. "The Press, Public Opinion, and Public Discourse." In Theodore L. Glasser and Charles T. Salmon, eds., *Public Opinion and the Communication of Consent*. New York: Guilford.

Chan, Joseph Man. 1994. "Commercialization without Independence: Media Development in China." In Joseph Cheng and Maurice Brosseau, eds., *China Review 1993.* Hong Kong: Chinese University Press.

Chang, Tsan-kuo. 1990. "Reporting U.S.–China Policy, 1950–1984: Presumptions of Legitimacy and Hierarchy." In Chin-Chuan Lee, ed., *Voices of China: The Interplay of Politics and Journalism.* New York: Guilford.

Chen, Huailin, and Joseph Man Chan. 1998. "Bird-Caged Press Freedom in China." In Joseph Cheng, ed., *China in the Post-Deng Era.* Hong Kong: Chinese University Press.

Chen, Huailin, and Chin-Chuan Lee. 1998. "Press Finance and Economic Reform in China." In Joseph Cheng, ed., *China Review 1997.* Hong Kong: Chinese University Press.

Chu, Godwin, and Yanan Ju. 1993. *The Great Wall in Ruins: Communication and Cultural Change in China.* Albany: State University of New York Press.

Chui, Shaoming. 1999a. "The Mainland's News Webs Take Cities and Seize Territory." *Open Monthly (Kaifang)* (August):70–71 (in Chinese).

———. 1999b. "The Mainland's Webpages Better than Nothing." *Open Monthly (Kaifang)* (September):62–63 (in Chinese).

Curran, James. 1991. "Mass Media and Democracy: A Reappraisal." In James Curran and Michael Gurevitch, eds., *Mass Media and Society.* New York: Arnold.

Curran, James, Michael Gurevitch, and Janet Woollacott. 1982. "The Study of the Media: Theoretical Approaches." In Michael Gurevitch, Tony Bennett, James Curran, and Janet Woollacott, eds., *Culture, Society, and the Media.* New York: Methuen.

Dittmer, Lowell. 1994. "The Politics of Publicity in Reform China." In Chin-Chuan Lee, ed., *China's Media, Media's China.* Boulder, Colo.: Westview.

Downing, John. 1996. *Internationalizing Media Theory.* London: Sage.

Dyan, Daniel, and Elihu Katz. 1992. *Media Events.* Cambridge, Mass.: Harvard University Press.

Eisenstadt, S. N., and Luis Roniger. 1981. "The Study of Patron-Client Relations and Recent Developments in Sociological Theory." In S. N. Eisenstadt and Rene Lernarchand, eds., *Political Clientelism, Patronage and Development.* Beverly Hills, Calif.: Sage.

Farmer, Edward. 1990. "Sifting Truth from Facts: The Reporter as Interpreter of China." In Chin-Chuan Lee, ed., *Voices of China: The Interplay of Politics and Journalism.* New York: Guilford.

———. 1994. "Frost on the Mirror: An American Understanding of China in the Cold War Era." In Chin-Chuan Lee, ed., *China's Media, Media's China.* Boulder, Colo.: Westview.

Fishman, Mark. 1980. *Manufacturing the News.* Austin: University of Texas Press.

Friedman, Edward. 1994. "The Oppositional Decoding of China's Leninist Media." In Chin-Chuan Lee, ed., *China's Media, Media's China.* Boulder, Colo.: Westview.

Galbraith, Kenneth. 1983. *The Anatomy of Power.* Boston: Houghton Mifflin.

Gans, Herbert. 1979. *Deciding What's News.* New York: Pantheon.

Garnham, Nicholas. 1990. *Capitalism and Communication.* London: Sage.

Giddens, Anthony. 1973. *The Class Structure of the Advanced Societies.* London: Hutchinson.

Gitlin, Todd. 1980. *The Whole World Is Watching.* Berkeley: University of California Press.

Gold, Thomas. 1993. "Go with Your Feelings: Hong Kong and Taiwan Popular Culture in Greater China." *China Quarterly* 136:907–25.

Golding, Peter. 1977. "Media Professionalism in the Third World: The Transfer of an Ideology." In James Curran, Michael Gurevitch, and Janet Woollacott, eds., *Mass Communication and Society.* London: Arnold.

Golding, Peter, and Graham Murdock. 1991. "Culture, Communications, and Political Economy." In James Curran and Michael Gurevitch, eds., *Mass Media and Society.* London: Arnold.

————, eds. 1997. *The Political Economy of the Media.* 2 vols. Brookfield, Vt.: Elgar.

Goldman, Merle. 1994. "The Role of the Press in Post-Mao Political Struggles." In Chin-Chuan Lee, ed., *China's Media, Media's China.* Boulder, Colo.: Westview.

Gordon, Kim. 1999. "Special Report: China Speaks Out." *Prospect* (March):48–52.

Gouldner, Alvin. 1976. *The Dialectic of Technology and Ideology.* New York: Oxford University Press.

————. 1980. *The Two Marxisms.* New York: Oxford University Press.

Griffith, William E. 1973. "Communist Esoteric Communications: Explication de Texte." In Ithiel de Sola Pool and Wilbur Schramm, eds., *Handbook of Communication.* Chicago: Rand McNally.

Habermas, Jürgen. 1989. *The Structural Transformation of the Public Sphere.* Cambridge: Polity Press.

Hachten, William, and Anthony Giffard. 1984. *The Press and Apartheid: Repression and Propaganda in South Africa.* Madison: University of Wisconsin Press.

Hall, Stuart. 1977. "Culture, the Media and the 'Ideological Effect.'" In James Curran, Michael Gurevitch, and Janet Woollacott, eds., *Mass Communication and Society.* London: Arnold.

————. 1983. "The Problem of Ideology: Marxism without Guarantees." In B. Matthews, ed., *Marx: A Hundred Years On.* London: Lawrence and Wishart.

————. 1986. "Cultural Studies: Two Paradigms." In Richard Collins et al., eds., *Media, Culture and Society.* London: Sage.

Hallin, Daniel. 1986. *The "Uncensored" War.* New York: Oxford University Press.

————. 2000. "Media, Political Power, and Democratization in Mexico." In James Curran and Myung-Jin Park, eds., *De-westernizing Media Studies.* London: Routledge.

Harding, Harry. 1993. "The Concept of Greater China: Themes, Variations, and Reservations." *China Quarterly* 136:660–86.

Herman, Edward, and Noam Chomsky. 1988. *Manufacturing Consent.* New York: Pantheon.

Hollander, Paul. 1981. *Political Pilgrims: Travels of Western Intellectuals to the Soviet Union, China, and Cuba, 1928–1978.* New York: Oxford University Press.

Hood, Marlowe. 1994. "The Use and Abuse of Mass Media by Chinese Leaders during the 1980s." In Chin-Chuan Lee, ed., *China's Media, Media's China*. Boulder, Colo.: Westview.

Hsiao, Ching-chang, and Mei-rong Yang. 1990. "'Don't Force Us to Lie': The Case of the *World Economic Herald*." In Chin-Chuan Lee, ed., *Voices of China: The Interplay of Politics and Journalism*. New York: Guilford.

Jansen, Sue Curry. 1991. *Censorship*. New York: Oxford University Press.

Keane, John. 1991. *The Media and Democracy*. Cambridge: Polity Press.

Lang, Gladys E., and Kurt Lang. 1982. *The Battle for Public Opinion*. New York: Columbia University Press.

Lee, Chin-Chuan, ed. 1990a. *Voices of China: The Interplay of Politics and Journalism*. New York: Guilford.

———. 1990b. "Mass Media: Of China, about China." In Chin-Chuan Lee, ed., *Voices of China: The Interplay of Politics and Journalism*. New York: Guilford.

———. 1993. "Sparking a Fire: The Press and the Ferment of Democratic Change in Taiwan." *Journalism Monographs*, No. 128. Also in Lee 1994a.

———, ed. 1994a. *China's Media, Media's China*. Boulder, Colo.: Westview.

———. 1994b. "Ambiguities and Contradictions: Issues in China's Changing Political Communication." In Chin-Chuan Lee, ed., *China's Media, Media's China*. Boulder, Colo.: Westview.

———. 1998a. "State Control, Media Technology, and Cultural Concerns: The Politics of Cable Television in Taiwan." *Studies of Broadcasting* 34:127–51.

———. 1998b. "Media Market and Political Conflict: A Decade of Media Interaction between Mainland China and Taiwan." *East Asia Quarterly* (*Dongya Jikan*) 29(2):43–57 (in Chinese).

———. 2000. "State, Capital, and Media: The Case of Taiwan." In James Curran and Myung-Jin Park, eds., *De-westernizing Media Studies*. London: Routledge.

Li, Liangrong. 1994. "The Historical Fate of 'Objective Reporting' in China." In Chin-Chuan Lee, ed., *Media's China, China's Media*. Boulder, Colo.: Westview.

Lukes, Steven. 1974. *Power: A Radical View*. London: Macmillan.

Lull, James. 1991. *China Turned On: Television, Reform, and Resistance*. London: Routledge.

Manoff, Robert, and Michael Schudson, eds. 1986. *Reading the News*. New York: Pantheon.

Merton, Robert K. 1972. "Insiders and Outsiders: A Chapter in the Sociology of Knowledge." *American Journal of Sociology* 77:9–47.

Mills, C. Wright. 1959. *The Sociological Imagination*. New York: Oxford University Press.

Mosco, Vincent. 1996. *The Political Economy of Communication*. London: Sage.

Murdock, Graham. 1982. "Large Corporations and the Control of the Communication Industries." In Michael Gurevitch, Tony Bennett, James Curran, and Janet Woollacott, eds., *Culture, Society, and the Media*. New York: Methuen.

Murdock, Graham, and Peter Golding. 1977. "Culture, Communications, and Political Economy." In James Curran, Michael Gurevitch, and Janet Woollacott, eds., *Mass Communication and Society*. London: Arnold.

Noelle-Neumann, Elisabeth. 1995. "Public Opinion and Rationality." In Theodore L. Glasser and Charles T. Salmon, eds., *Public Opinion and the Communication of Consent*. New York: Guilford.

O'Donnell, Guillermo A. 1973. *Modernization and Bureaucratic-Authoritarianism*. Berkeley: Institute of International Studies, University of California.

————. 1978. "Reflections on the Pattern of Change in the Bureaucratic-Authoritarian State." *Latin American Studies* 8:3–38.

Polumbaum, Judy. 1990. "The Tribulations of China's Journalists after a Decade of Reform." In Chin-Chuan Lee, ed., *Voices of China: The Interplay of Politics and Journalism*. New York: Guilford.

————. 1994. "Striving for Predictability: The Bureaucratization of Media Management in China." In Chin-Chuan Lee, ed., *China's Media, Media's China*. Boulder, Colo.: Westview.

Pool, Ithiel de Sola. 1973. "Communication in Totalitarian Societies." In Ithiel de Sola Pool and Wilbur Schramm, eds., *Handbook of Communication*. Chicago: Rand McNally.

————. 1983. *Technologies of Freedom*. Cambridge, Mass.: Harvard University Press.

————. 1990. *Technologies without Boundaries*. Cambridge, Mass.: Harvard University Press.

Poulantzas, Nicos. 1978. *State, Power, Socialism*. London: NLB.

Pye, Lucian. 1979. "Communication and Chinese Political Culture." In Godwin Chu and Francis Hsu, eds., *Moving a Mountain*. Honolulu: University Press of Hawaii.

Rampal, J. C. 1994. "Post-Martial Law Media Boom in Taiwan," *Gazette* 53:73–92.

Said, Edward W. 1979. *Orientalism*. New York: Vintage.

————. 1982. *Covering Islam*. New York: Pantheon.

————. 1993. *Culture and Imperialism*. New York: Knopf.

Schiller, Herbert I. 1976. *Communication and Cultural Domination*. White Plains, N.Y.: Sharpe.

————. 1989. *Culture Inc*. New York: Oxford University Press.

————. 1992. *Mass Media and American Empire*. 2nd ed. Boulder, Colo.: Westview.

Schlesinger, Peter. 1979. *Putting "The Reality" Together*. Beverly Hills, Calif.: Sage.

Schmitter, Phillip. 1974. "Still the Century of Corporatism?" *Review of Politics* 36(1):85–131.

Schramm, Wilbur. 1977. *Big Media, Little Media*. Beverly Hills, Calif.: Sage.

Schudson, Michael. 1978. *Discovering the News*. New York: Basic Books.

————. 1991. "The Sociology of News Production Revisited." In James Curran and Michael Gurevitch, eds., *Mass Media and Society*. London: Arnold.

————. 1995. *The Power of News*. Cambridge, Mass.: Harvard University Press.

Schurmann, Franz. 1966. *Ideology and Organization in Communist China.* Berkeley: University of California Press.

Skocpol, Theda. 1979. *States and Social Revolutions.* New York: Cambridge University Press.

Smythe, Dallas. 1994. *Clockwise: Perspectives on Communication,* ed. Thomas Guback. Boulder, Colo.: Westview.

Staniland, Martin. 1985. *What Is Political Economy?* New Haven, Conn.: Yale University Press.

Su, Shaozhi. 1994. "Chinese Communist Ideology and Media Control." In Chin-Chuan Lee, ed., *China's Media, Media's China.* Boulder, Colo.: Westview.

Tomlinson, John. 1991. *Cultural Imperialism: A Critical Introduction.* Baltimore: Johns Hopkins University Press.

Tu, Weiming. 1991. "Cultural China: The Periphery as the Center." *Daedalus* 120(2):1–32.

Tuchman, Gaye. 1978. *Making News.* New York: Free Press.

Vogel, Ezra F. 1994. "Contemporary China Studies in North America: Marginals in a Superpower." In *The Development of Contemporary China Studies.* Tokyo: Toyo Bunko.

White, Lynn T. 1990. "All the News: Structure and Politics in Shanghai's Reform Media." In Chin-Chuan Lee, ed., *Voices of China: The Interplay of Politics and Journalism.* New York: Guilford.

Williams, Raymond. 1977. *Marxism and the Literature.* New York: Oxford University Press.

Wu, Guoguang. 1997. *Zhao Ziyang and Political Reform.* Hong Kong: Pacific (in Chinese).

Yoon, Youngchul. 1989. "Political Transition and Press Ideology in South Korea." Ph.D. diss., University of Minnesota.

Yu, Jinglu. 1990. "The Structure and Function of Chinese Television, 1979-1989." In Chin-Chuan Lee, ed., *Voices of China: The Interplay of Politics and Journalism.* New York: Guilford.

Zhao, Yuezhi. 1998. *Media, Market and Democracy in China: Between the Party Line and the Bottom Line.* Urbana: University of Illinois Press.

2

One Head, Many Mouths

Diversifying Press Structures in Reform China

GUOGUANG WU

The metaphor in the title of this chapter describes the evolving structures of the Chinese press, particularly in relation to the reforming yet still Communist state. As is widely known, in the classic Communist political system, the state (or, equally in this context, the party-state) has a "near-complete monopoly of control" of all means of effective mass communication (Friedrich and Brzezinski 1956:22), and the press serves as the "mouth" of the ruling Communist Party—for "command communication" (Wu 1994) rather than for providing social information for the people. Regime change so far has not happened in China as it did in former Communist countries (such as the Soviet Union and Eastern Europe),[1] and the relationship between the Chinese Communist state and the press has also been reorganized differently than shown in this classic model. Throughout the profound reforms in the economy, society, and (to some extent) the political system, the Chinese press, as discussed in this chapter, has featured a diverse structure. Basically, this means that many party and nonparty newspapers are being published in today's China, but the Communist party-state still exercises tight control over them.

Is this monsterlike picture of "one head, many mouths" true of the Chinese press? How can the relationship between the state and the press be reorganized when the state still exercises tight press control? Or, particularly, how can the press structures be diversified amidst authoritarian repression? Further, empirically, what does this picture mean for the transition of the Chinese media in particular and for the role of the media in politico-economic transitions from Communism in general? And, conceptually, how do socioeconomic changes alone, without accompanying political changes, alter the state-press relationship? These are the questions I am concerned with in this chapter.

In interpreting changes in China's media, some observers emphasize that state control and political repression over the mass media have continued as before (Su 1994; Lu 1994). They typically argue that political control in China is still tight, and sometimes even tighter, despite socioeconomic reforms; therefore, socioeconomic changes alone do not expand the space for press freedom if no fundamental political reform takes place. In contrast to this "continuist" perspective, another group of scholars represents a "reformist" perspective, focusing on the desirable yet gradual change either sponsored by the state from above or gained from below by journalists in their struggle against governmental policies (Goldman 1994; Hsiao and Yang 1990).

Both the "continuist" and "reformist" perspectives have certainly contained partial truth and have contributed to the understanding of the transitional Chinese media. But we still have difficulties understanding the media in relation to economic change and authoritarian politics. In particular, both approaches have neglected the structural continuity and change of the Chinese media. Evidence for changes in the Chinese media is not to be sought from the journalistic performance of reform-minded individuals, groups, and news agencies but is reflected primarily in the diversification of media structures. Instead of examining the impact of political control on the everyday activities of journalism, I shall analyze the consequence of marketization on the media structure. This political-economy approach to mass media assumes that marketization has produced a significant political impact on media structures in the Communist party-state system.

In the past twenty years, China has undertaken profound reforms to marketize its state-planned economy while maintaining its authoritarian regime, which has survived despite the global collapse of Communism in the late 1980s. Unlike the sweeping political and socioeconomic changes in the former Soviet Union and Eastern European countries, China's transformation has been gradual, instrumental, uneven, and marked by continued political repression and powerful resistance to the democratizing pressure of marketization. I am neither so pessimistic as to conclude that nothing or little has changed in China's media nor so sanguine as to declare that a sweeping change has been achieved. Basically, I argue that socioeconomic liberalization has produced substantive changes in media structures, changes significant enough to offer an increasingly larger space for journalistic reports in the *social* realm, albeit not yet in the *political* realm.

In the process of economic marketization, the Chinese press is moving from being politics-centered to being economics-centered; from being a privileged branch of the authoritarian party-state system to being an industry with "private interests within the economic system" (Bottomore 1993:12); and from being a state-monopolized structure to being a fragmented and diversified structure. This change has been effected through three critical influences: decentralization, socialization, and marketization.

Decentralization

The first aspect of structural diversification in the Chinese media is decentralization. By this I mean that the media have changed from being concentrated in the national capital to being dispersed to localities; from the provincial capitals to the city and county seats; and, within the central state system, from the power center to different branches, departments, and bureaus of the government.

Decentralization in the Chinese economic reform successfully fosters economic growth even without political reform (Montinola, Qian, and Weingast 1995). At the same time, it also stimulates the transition from state socialism to market economy, and it has significantly reshaped power distribution and political relations within the Communist party-state system. In contrast to past central dominance, local governments have a greater opportunity to speak out in their own voices, to the extent that political homogeneity seems to have broken at the seam of the policy-making process (Goodman 1992; Jia and Lin 1994; Naughton 1995). Regional diversity has developed into both economic and political localism or regionalism, such that provincial and lower-level governments are able to defend and expand their local interests (Segel 1994).

In the past twenty years, as economic, social, and even political life grows ever more regionalized and as the regional authorities seek to express their own views, at least in their localities, the media distribution system has been substantially decentralized. As table 2.1 indicates, in 1979, when the reform started, there were sixty-nine newspapers published in China, seventeen of them (24.6 percent) published in Beijing. All other newspapers were published in provincial capitals, while the few newspapers scattered at the subprovincial levels were ignored in the statistics. The percentage of newspapers located in the national center declined in the first half of the 1980s, from 19.1 percent in 1980 to 17.4 percent in 1981 and to 15.2 percent in 1982. Starting in 1983, the statistics began to cover the newspapers at subprovincial levels, which had substantially increased in number and significance. As a result, there was a sudden boom in the number of local newspapers. The percentage of centrally located newspapers drastically decreased to 6 percent in 1983 and reached bottom, at 5.2

percent, in 1984. In the 1990s, centrally located newspapers increased again, to around 9 percent, an increase often considered in the context of the coincident recentralization in economic reform (as in the years 1988 to 1991 and 1994); their decrease, likewise, coincided with the rise of localism (as in 1992).[2] Table 2.1 clearly indicates the rise of local power in the distribution of the press.

Table 2.1. Central versus Local Newspapers, 1979–1997

Year	Total	Central (% of total)	Provincial	Local
1979	69*	17 (24.6)	52	—
1980	188*	36 (19.1)	152	—
1981	242*	42 (17.4)	200	—
1982	277*	42 (15.2)	235	—
1983	773	46 (6.0)	294	727
1984	1,041	54 (5.2)	404	987
1985	1,445	79 (5.5)	619	1,366
1986	1,574	95 (6.0)	696	1,479
1987	1,611	99 (6.1)	751	1,512
1988	1,537	130 (8.5)	699	1,407
1989	1,576	138 (8.8)	714	1,438
1990	1,442	129 (8.9)	645	1,313
1991	1,524	137 (9.0)	675	1,387
1992	1,657	139 (8.4)	736	1,518
1993	1,788	153 (8.6)	790	1,635
1994	1,953	193 (9.9)	822	1,760
1995	2,089	205 (9.9)	844	1,884
1996	2,163	206 (9.5)	877	1,957
1997	2,149	206 (9.6)	871	1,943

*The total does not include newspapers published at subprovincial levels.

Sources: *Zhongguo chuban nianjian; Quanguo tushu zazhi baozhi chuban tongji ziliao;* and *Zhongguo xinwen chuban tongji ziliao huibian,* various years.

If we look at a province, we may get a more concrete impression of the growth pattern of local newspapers. For example, in 1978 five newspapers were published in Heilongjiang Province in northeastern China; this number rose to sixty-eight in 1993, including both the newspapers directly run by the party committees at the provincial and lower levels and the so-called professional newspapers (Chun 1993). In 1997, after a wave of "rectification" of the media, this province still published thirty-seven newspapers. In the rich east coast provinces, where localism is much stronger due to higher levels of economic development and to local interests (Wu and Zheng 1995; Li 1998), the number of newspapers could be much higher. In 1997, for example, Guangdong Province had sixty-two newspapers, Jiangsu had fifty-eight, and Shandong had fifty-three, a sharp comparison with the smaller numbers of local media in inner and poor provinces such as Shaanxi (twenty-four), Guizhou (twenty-seven), Qinghai (seven), and Ningxia (seven) (*Zhongguo xinwen chuban tongji ziliao huibian* 1998).

In the reform years, the media at subprovincial levels experienced an even more remarkable increase both in number and in circulation. In this context, "subprovincial" covers three different administrative levels: the city (*shi*), the district (*zhuanqu*), and the county (*xian*). In the late 1970s, only some major cities had surviving newspapers, and almost all of the newspapers sponsored by the county-level party committees (*xian bao*) were abolished during the Cultural Revolution. In the 1980s, however, every city established its own newspapers, and in rural areas some county governments entered into media enterprises by first running a newspaper. As one Chinese journalist (Feng 1994) observed, while party-organ newspapers at the national and provincial levels have suffered steep decreases in circulation since 1980, party-organ newspapers at the district, city, and county levels have increased circulation at an average of 20 percent per year (except in 1981).

Table 2.2 lists the number of county newspapers from 1983 to 1997 (statistics from 1978 to 1982 being unavailable). It shows that the development of such newspapers also basically reflected the rise, and sometimes the flux, of localism.

Such structural decentralization also occurred in the electronic media. In the 1980s, cities in the east coast area first established their own local television stations, in addition to the local newspapers; then the rural areas tried to catch up by running many local television channels, which were usually sponsored by "district" party committees. In the late 1970s, all television stations belonged to the central, provincial, and some metropolitan governments; in the early 1990s, they accounted for only one-third of national television stations. The other two-thirds are now sponsored by lower-level local governments.

Vertical decentralization of media power from the national center to localities is only one dimension of this kind of change. Another dimension is the increasing number of newspapers run by various ministries and bureaus of the

Table 2.2. Development of County Newspapers, 1983–1997

Year	No. of Newspapers
1983	79
1984	95
1985	100
1986	113
1987	114
1988	95
1989	100
1990	91
1991	96
1992	100
1993	115
1994	131
1995	150
1996	150
1997	140

Sources: *Zhongguo chuban nianjian; Quanguo tushu zazhi baozhi chuban tongji ziliao;* and *Zhongguo xinwen chuban tongji ziliao huibian,* various years.

central government. Traditionally, vertical control of local functions by ministries was regarded as a symbol of the powerful central control in the Chinese Communist system (Schurmann 1968:188–94). In the past twenty years, there has been substantial political fragmentation among different departments within the central state structure (Lieberthal and Lampton 1992; Lieberthal and Oksenberg 1988), and power was informally redistributed from the highest decision-making bodies to the administrative departments as power was decentralized from the national government to the regional localities. This seemed to be a result of rationalization of power and bureaucratic routinization (Polumbaum 1994), which were required by economic development. Considering how concentrated power was within Beijing's central governing system, the current dispersion of power among different departments and bureaus within the national government should be regarded as an important indicator of decentralization and political diversification.

For this chapter, it is analytically and practically meaningful to distinguish two different types of governmental organizations. One is the political center of national power in the party–state system, which includes decision-making bodies such as the Politburo and the Central Secretariat of the Chinese Communist Party (CCP), the State Council, and their specialized functioning departments for media management, including the Propaganda Department of the CCP Central Committee and the State Press and Publication Administration. Another type of governmental organization are those administrative ministries and functioning branches within the national governmental system (such as the Ministry of Civil Affairs, the Ministry of Labor, and so on), which are peripheral vis-à-vis the political center named above. Dispersion of power to run the press also happened along the path flowing from the political centers to those administrative departments, a process we also call "decentralization."

Before the reform era, the political centers of the party–state system monopolized the ownership and operation of all the nationwide circulated media; for example, the *People's Daily* (*Renmin ribao*) was directly managed by the Politburo of the CCP, the Xinhua News Agency was controlled by the State Council, and other newspapers were supervised by the Propaganda Department of the CCP Central Committee. Now, as listed in *The Chinese Journalism Yearbook* (*Zhongguo xinwen nianjian,* hereafter referred to as *ZXN*), each ministry or ministerial- and semiministerial-level bureau of the national government has at least one newspaper of its own. These newspapers are also organ newspapers, but usually they cover only the particular profession under the jurisdiction of the sponsoring ministry. They are thus called "professional newspapers" (*zhuanye baozhi*), in comparison with the "comprehensive newspapers" (*zonghe baozhi*), usually run by a political center.

Table 2.3 shows the development of "professional" newspapers in the 1980s and 1990s in contrast to the decreasing trend of comprehensive newspapers. The pattern is similar to that observed in table 2.1. In 1980, the comprehensive newspapers occupied 88.3 percent of the total, a number that fell drastically—to 32.2 percent—in 1981. This trend continued in stable fashion, falling to 29.2 percent in 1982, 10.6 percent in 1983, 9 percent in 1984, and reaching its low point, 8.1 percent, in 1985.

It must be noted that some newspapers sponsored by those functioning departments or semigovernmental organizations on the periphery were traditionally categorized as "comprehensive newspapers." Therefore, table 2.3 underestimates the number of "professional newspapers" that benefited from decentralization. This table is also relevant to the discussion of socialization in the next section, as some newspapers sponsored by semigovernmental and societal

Table 2.3. Comprehensive versus Professional Newspapers, 1980–1997

Year	No. of Newspapers		
	Total	Comprehensive	Professional
1980	188	166	22
1981	242	78	164
1982	277	81	196
1983	773	82	691
1984	1,041	94	947
1985	1,445	117	1,328
1986	1,574	166	1,408
1987	1,611	641	970
1988	1,537	N.A.	—
1989	1,576	N.A.	—
1990	1,442	N.A.	—
1991	1,524	N.A.	—
1992	1,657	N.A.	—
1993	1,788	803	985
1994	1,953	880	1,073
1995	2,089	929	1,160
1996	2,163	974	1,189
1997	2,149	971	1,178

*N.A. indicates that the relevant statistics are unavailable.

Sources: *Zhongguo chuban nianjian; Quanguo tushu zazhi baozhi chuban tongji ziliao;* and *Zhongguo xinwen chuban tongji ziliao huibian,* various years.

organizations as well as by some large-scale enterprises are also categorized as "professional newspapers."

The fragmentation among different branches of power, not only within the administrative departments of the executive, is politically more important, although statistically less impressive. As nonexecutive institutions, including the National People's Congress (NPC), gained greater power in the reform years (O'Brien 1990; Wu 1998a), they sought more voices of their own. It was reported that the rubber-stamp NPC, seeking greater power, has been preparing to publish its own newspaper.[3] So far their efforts have been in vain, perhaps because of the disapproval of the Politburo and the State Council. In contrast, another semiparliamentary organization, the National People's Political Consultative Council (NPPCC), has owned a daily newspaper since 1980. In 1992, the circulation of this newspaper stood at 163,000 (*ZXN* 1993), declining to 120,100 in 1997 (*Zhongguo xinwen chuban tongji ziliao huibian* 1998). Moreover, China had forty-odd newspapers run by the provincial and metropolitan PPCCs in 1997 (*ZXN* 1998:59), a significant increase from zero in 1979. No vertical supervising relationship exists between the national and local institutions of NPCs and NPPCCs. Those local institutions could use their own media to reflect regional interests (Li 1998). In this sense, decentralization of the media structure was also brought forth by the division of power in the political system.

Socialization

The second way in which media have become structurally diversified is through socialization, defined as a breakup of the state-monopolized media structure and replacement by a new structure in which various nonstate actors play an increasingly significant role. As decentralization refers to dispersion of power from the national center to peripheries within the state framework, socialization of media structures means political reallocation of media resources from the state to some social sectors.[4]

The traditional Chinese Communist regime has often been defined as a structure in which the state exerted monolithic, totalitarian control over society (Friedrich and Brzezinski 1956). It has been said that, under this regime, there existed "a technologically conditioned, near-complete monopoly of control, in the hands of the party and of the government, of all means of effective mass communication, such as the press, radio, and motion pictures" (Friedrich and Brzezinski 1956:22). Meanwhile, society was subservient to, or at least passive with regard to, the state. But economic reform has activated the society and widened its scope (White, Howell, and Shang 1996; Brook and Frolic 1997). This trend is also reflected in the media structure. Even though individual citizens are prohibited from owning a media outlet, ownership of the media by nonstate sectors is becoming more and more prevalent. The newspapers published by social organizations such as mass associations and professional societies are becoming the major competitors of the Communist party-state press. Of these nonstate sectors, I would like to discuss three major groups: the traditionally semigovernmental (semisocietal) organizations sponsored by the Communist party-state, the satellite political parties, and professional societies.

The first kind of social organization includes those sponsored and directly led by the party-state itself, including the Communist Youth League (CYL), women's associations, and official trade unions. Fully aware that it could be controversial to put them into the category "society" in the Western sense, I invoke the "one head" metaphor as a framework and am using the concept of "society" in a restricted way. I draw a distinction between peripheral semigovernmental departments as part of the "society" and the core party-state organizations.

At the national level, these semigovernmental organizations have owned newspapers or magazines since 1949, but two things changed during the reform years. First, their national headquarters established more agencies for public communications. The national headquarters of the Women's Federation of All China (Zhonghua quanguo funu lianhehui; WFAC), for example, used to have only a monthly as its mouthpiece, but it now owns a newspaper, *Chinese Women's Daily* (*Zhongguo funu bao*). Second, their local organizations have also been very active in establishing their own media enterprises. Each headquarters of the CYL at the provincial level, for example, and some at the city level now own at least one magazine or even a daily newspaper (*ZXN* 1998:52–53); for the WFAC the situation is similar (*ZXN* 1998:53–54). Some branches of such organizations even become media centers, as in the case of the Shanghai Committee of the CYL, which owns two newspapers and three periodicals (*ZXN* 1998:52).

Such nonstate media have gained greater autonomy despite their formal organizational affiliation with the party-state system in terms of finance, personnel, and journalistic endeavor. They can be more courageous than the party-state media in voicing opinions different from those of the party and the government; sometimes they try to criticize the government and its leaders. In October 1986, for example, *Shenzhen Youth Daily* (*Shenzhen qingnian bao*), a newspaper sponsored by the Shenzhen City Committee of the CYL, published an essay urging Deng Xiaoping, China's paramount leader at that time, to retire from official positions. When Deng said that the people would not allow him to retire, the paper argued that Deng misinterpreted the people's will.[5] In the 1990s, it was *Beijing Youth Daily* (*Beijing qingnian bao*), run by the Beijing City Committee of the CYL, that played a pioneering role in journalism reform.

Nine "satellite parties" make up the second group of social organizations that widen the space of media ownership and operation. As political and even financial affiliates of the CCP (Seymour 1987), they have increased their autonomy; one of the manifestations of this was their eagerness to publish their own media, jointly or separately. Now some major parties among them are publishing newspapers, others own magazines, while still others (usually small organizations) are lobbying to own periodicals.

The most substantial change in media structure in this category comes from the third group of social organizations: various professional associations and academic societies. As sociologists (Wang, Zhe, and Sun 1993; Brook and Frolic 1997; White, Howell, and Shang 1996) observed, China's reform has brought about waves of effort to organize such associations and societies in various fields, which are too numerous to count. Some of the periodicals were established under their institutional umbrellas in the so-called *gua kao* (hitch-up and lean-on, or affiliation) relationship. Before the Tiananmen movement in 1989, the well-known newspaper *World Economic Herald* (*Shijie jingji daobao*), for example, was protected under the umbrella of a research institute in Shanghai (Hsiao and Yang 1990). Another popular newspaper during that period, *Modern People Tribune* (*Xiandai ren bao*), was sponsored by the Foreign Trade Association in Guangzhou. Even individuals can establish media enterprises by encapsulating them as publications of an association or a society. On the eve of the Tiananmen event, examples of influential magazines of this kind included *Studies of National Conditions* (*Guoqing yanjiu*), edited in Beijing by some journalists from the *People's Daily* and the *Guangming Daily* but published in Changsha in the name of Hunan University Press; *Oriental Chronicle* (*Dongfang jishi*), also edited in Beijing but published in Nanjing; and *New Enlightenment* (*Xin Qimeng*), edited by several individual scholars and published in Changsha. The 1990s saw another wave of such enthusiasm, which led to the publication of such popular periodicals as *Orient* (*Dongfang*) and *Life* (*Shenghuo*) as well as some semi-independent semiacademic journals such as *Strategy and Management* (*Zhanlue yu guanli*) and *Chinese Culture Studies* (*Zhongguo wenhua yanjiu*).

Overseas capital has also been channeled to China's media industry. The open-door policy permitted foreign investment in the media in the late 1980s, though the permission was granted on a very limited basis and was contingent on political situations. Such investments came mainly from overseas Chinese capitals in Hong Kong, Singapore, and Thailand; the establishment of the *Starlight Monthly* (*Xingguang*), a failed joint venture between the Hong Kong–based Sing Tao group and the *People's Daily,* was an example in this category. Like domestic media, overseas investment in the media must seek the sponsorship from—and encapsulate in—a Chinese association or society.

Table 2.4 shows a general comparison of the numbers of organ papers of the CCP committees at various levels and of the other kinds of newspapers from 1976, the eve of the reform, to 1994, the last year for which these statistics are available. The government changed its way of compiling statistics after 1994 by deleting categories such as party newspapers (*dangbao*) and nonparty newspapers (*fei dangbao*), which made such numbers unavailable; table 2.4, therefore, does not cover the years after 1994.

Table 2.4. Party Organs versus Other Newspapers, 1976–1994

Year	No. of Newspapers	
	Party Organs	**Others**
1976	236	5
1977	238	6
1978	252	7
1979	270	10
1980	260	120
1981	250	451
1982	280	380
1983	300	490
1984	350	700
1985	384	1,326
1986	361	1,790
1987	374	1,685
1988	407	1,915
1989	410	1,496
1990	406	1,036
1991	422	1,092
1992	436	1,230
1993	440	1,350
1994	460	1,411

*The numbers here are not logically consistent with those in table 2.1 because of differences in the way statistics were reported.

Source: *Zhongguo xinwen nianjian*, various years.

It is obvious from table 2.4 that while the number of publications by the party press doubled during this period, other kinds of newspapers grew in leaps and bounds, especially during the late 1980s. The latter outnumbered the party press papers by almost five times in 1988; despite the official clampdown in the wake of the Tiananmen event in 1989, this ratio returned to about 3.5:1 in 1993 and 1994.

Marketization

Marketization aptly describes the general trend of China's socioeconomic change, including media structure, in the past twenty years. Even though China's transition away from the state-planned economy has not brought about privatization of the ownership system, market mechanism is a potent factor in allocating the material resources of mass communication. This change has substantive political implications. As Pei (1994:150) observes, "[I]n a politically repressive environment, market forces became the principal means for societal actors gradually and subtly to influence the political process and alter the balance between the state and society."

Marketization has reduced institutional dependency of the media on the state, mainly through the commercialization of the media's interests, behaviors, and, finally, their structural change. As Lynn White (1990) points out, an important institutional link between the press and the state in China is the former's financial dependence on the latter. When the media entered the sea of the market, they had to try to make money by themselves rather than "eating from the big pot" (chi daguo fan) offered by the state. Now scholars have found that mass media in China have included profit making as a plausible aim in their activities (Chan 1993). It has been argued that "mass media have had to reorient themselves to the needs of the market and to increase their financial assets by all legitimate means" (Chan 1993:6). Here I argue, further, that the activities to make money are making the media more independent from the state, structurally if not politically. Commercialization makes most media (the exception being a few "top" organizations within the party-state hierarchical system, such as the People's Daily) rely essentially on market competition for their survival and prosperity, rather than, as formerly, on their hierarchical locations within that system and their connections with the state (Wu 1994). In addition, many new media enterprises have appeared to take advantage of market opportunities.

Commercialization of China's media started with the recovery and flourishing of the advertising industry beginning in the late 1970s (Chan 1993). As table 2.5 indicates, the volume of advertising revenues has risen to renminbi (RMB) $9,700 million in 1997, or nearly 133 times that in 1983, when economic reform was introduced into urban areas.

Table 2.5. Advertising Revenues of Newspapers, 1983–1997

Year	Revenue (in million renminbi yuan)	Increase (%)
1983	73	
1984	119	38.66
1985	220	45.91
1986	256	14.07
1987	355	27.89
1988	501	29.15
1989	629	20.35
1990	677	7.29
1991	962	29.63
1992	1,618	40.55
1993	3,771	57.10
1994	5,050	25.33
1995	6,460	21.83
1996	7,760	16.76
1997	9,700	20.00

Sources: *Zhongguo xinwen nianjian* and *Zhongguo baike nianjian*, various years.

Table 2.5 raises three interesting points about the increase in newspaper advertising revenues. First, the revenues had a sharp jump in the early stage of urban economic reform, namely, during the years from 1983 to 1985. The increase from 1982 to 1984 was 38.66 percent, and from 1984 to 1985 it was 45.91 percent. Second, the lowest increase occurred from 1989 to 1990 (an increase of only 7.29 percent), when economic liberalization was hindered after the Tiananmen crackdown. Third, the years 1992 and 1993 saw further jumps, from 962 million in 1991 to 1,618 million in 1992 (an increase of 40.55 percent) to 3,771 million in 1993 (an increase of 57.1 percent), when the paramount leader, Deng Xiaoping, toured southern China to push for another wave of economic marketization. According to the official statistics, in 1997, thirty-three newspapers each surpassed RMB $100 million in advertising revenue; among them, three even exceeded RMB $600 million (*ZXN* 1998:29).

Relative statistics have shown that in 1997 television (25 percent) and newspapers (21 percent) controlled the second and third largest shares of China's advertising revenues; the largest share was taken by advertising firms (42 percent).

Radio stations (2 percent) and magazines and other channels (10 percent) were relatively insignificant (*Zhongguo jingji nianjian* 1998). Advertising revenues now account for more than 50 percent of the total revenues of some newspapers. These newspapers are often run by CCP committees in the metropolitan and wealthy areas. The most prominent example is *Haerbin Daily* (*Haerbin ribao*) in Heilongjiang Province, the organ newspaper of the Haerbin City Committee of the CCP, whose total revenues, including advertising, made it the number one profit-making unit in that city (*ZXN* 1998:29).

Newspaper distribution has also undergone a significant change. Most worthy of note is the corresponding relationship between the tides of economic reform (1987 and 1992) and the increasing circulation of nonparty newspapers, as shown in table 2.6. The table is fairly short because statistics are not available before 1985 or after 1992, as the government frequently changed the categories used in collecting the statistics.

Table 2.6. Circulation of Party-Organ Papers, 1985–1992

Year	Total	Party-Organ Papers
1985	151,870,000	29,530,000
1986	159,900,000	28,240,000
1987	176,900,000	29,420,000
1988	167,300,000	28,520,000
1989	152,480,000	25,286,000
1990	139,860,000	25,780,000
1991	153,180,000	27,030,000
1992	190,660,000	30,430,000

Source: *Zhongguo xinwen nianjian*, various years.

In this development, leading party newspapers were the hardest hit victims. The *People's Daily*, the CCP's foremost mouthpiece, declined from a high circulation of 5.2 million in 1982 to 2.13 million in 1997 (*Zhongguo xinwen chuban tongji ziliao huibian* 1998). Among the eight comprehensive newspapers whose circulations each surpassed one million in 1997, only the *People's Daily* was a party newspaper. The other seven included three evening papers (*Xinmin Evening News,* published in Shanghai; *Yangzi Evening News,* published in Nanjing; and *Yangcheng Evening News,* published in Guangzhou); one weekend paper (*Southern Weekend,* published in Guangzhou); two papers in digest form (*Baokan wenzhai,* published in Shanghai, and *Reference News* [*Cankao xiaoxi*], the digest of the overseas press, published in Beijing); and the *Paper for Pupils* (*Xiaoxuesheng bao*) (*Zhongguo xinwen chuban tongji ziliao huibian* 1998).

As a partial response to the reduced market share, the party press has established a series of umbrella newspapers and magazines under its own auspices. A party newspaper is thus partially transformed into an enterprise group in which the party newspaper remains as a core with other periodicals acting as the branch companies. This provides structural management appropriate to the political and economic environments: On the one hand, the party newspaper continues to be a tool of party propaganda, which protects its official legitimacy but is also a major cause for its decline in circulation; on the other hand, the party newspaper can make money through its satellite publications, which are usually market oriented or at least well adapted to the market mechanism. The *People's Daily,* for example, manages two smaller newspapers, the *Market (Shichang bao)* and *Satire and Humor (Fengci yu youmo)*, as well as a couple of magazines. This has been a common phenomenon in China throughout the 1980s and 1990s. It is somewhat problematic to define those satellite newspapers and magazines as "party newspapers," even if they are owned by party newspapers.

With those subordinate periodicals, therefore, the party-organ system itself is now more diversified. Even the party organs have to contend with official political control and the market drive. Market drive may not necessarily produce press freedom, but media marketization creates a situation in which games now are being played under dual rules: The entrepreneurial spirit prevails in mass media, while the party discipline is being maintained.

From Structure to Action? Discussion and Conclusion

This chapter takes a structuralist approach to the development and change of the Chinese press in the reform era, arguing that various types of diversification in media structures have occurred and have been stimulated by economic reforms and that the introduction of the market to the media industry—no matter how rudimentary, disjointed, and imperfect—is creating a new media system in China. We have discussed three major ways through which socioeconomic changes have contributed to the diversification of media structures. First, Chinese media are structurally diversified within the party-state system through decentralization, which happens along with dispersion of economic and political power among different levels and branches of the state organization. As localism rises and political fragmentation increases in the Chinese political economy, the distribution of the press is also, on the one hand, localized, while provinces, cities, districts, and counties take a larger and larger share in the media enterprise, and, on the other, fragmented, as the administrative branches intrude into the business of media management that had been monopolized by the political centers. Besides, new centers of political power such as the NP-PCC, if not yet the NPC in this field, are emerging as competitors of the old centers running the press.

Second, when the nonstate sectors arise to break the state monopoly, the media have undergone a process of what we call "socialization," referring to the changes in favor of society in state-society relations. As totally independent social organizations are not easy to find in China, some semigovernmental and semisocietal organizations occupy the place in which "civil society" functions to expand the space for media autonomy. Third, marketization has helped to diversify the financial and distribution structures of the media in general and those of the management of party organs in particular. In sum, the Chinese press is undergoing change from a nationally concentrated structure to a locally and ministerially fragmented structure; from a monolithic structure in which the party-state enjoyed the monopoly to a more pluralist structure involving both the state and social organizations; and from a structure in which the party organs dominated to one in which they must struggle to compete with the non–party-state media for survival.

With such changes, China's mass media are entering into a situation I describe as "one head, many mouths," borrowing a metaphor that characterizes the media as the "mouths and tongues" of the party-state in the Communist political system. We clearly realize the existence and periodic tightening of political repression under the Communist authoritarian regime in China. But at the same time we find that socioeconomic structural pluralization coexists with political repression, so that many "mouths" may open up even though they are within the structure of a single head and are often restricted in operation by that head. Do these different mouths necessarily express different voices? This is a question about the political implications of structural diversification for press freedom, which deserves a brief discussion, though basically it is beyond the scope of our study.

The primitive but most fundamental effect of the structural diversification of the press is the increasing difficulty of exercising state control. Decentralization, for example, places many of the decentralized newspapers beyond the scope of direct control by the central propaganda department; more than before, the department must rely on local authorities to implement its political disciplines. The local authorities, in comparison with the central regime, are mainly concerned with economic development, not ideological correctness (Wu and Zheng 1995). Similarly, in terms of the socialization of the press structures, the linkages between those social organizations and the newspapers and periodicals under their sponsorship are usually loose, which means even organizational sponsors find it difficult to control their own "mouths"; the party-state's political control over these publications, therefore, becomes ineffective.

Further, marketization becomes a strong driving force behind the press to keep testing the line drawn by the state for judging what is politically correct. The reason is simple: The press needs to struggle for expanding circulations in order to make money, and political taboos are often eye-catching topics for news stories. Basically, the state exerts control over sensitive political topics. The space for freedom of the press is therefore larger in the social realm than in the political one.[6] In reality, however, no impenetrable fence stands between the social and the political, and a "spillover" effect could be at work here, particularly as the profit-making mentality becomes more and more prevalent in press management.

The authoritarian regime has been taking action against this trend. Even so, the nature and degree of political repression of the media have changed due to changes in the media. While the authoritarian regime is as intent as before on maintaining tight political control (Chan 1995), it has to respond to a rapidly changing economy by adjusting its means of repression. As media liberalization and limited press freedom are mainly reflected in the overall structural diversification of the media rather than in the professional performance of everyday journalistic activities, the Chinese authoritarian regime seems to recognize the difficulty posed by having so many "mouths" expressing the thoughts of one "head." In 1996 and 1997, the regime tried hard to "reorganize" and "rectify" the media structures, and the targets of the close-down wave were mainly newspapers and magazines published by local governments, governmental departments, and bureaus and by social organizations.[7] One-third of the periodicals at and below the provincial levels would be closed down, according to the rectifying plan made by the central propaganda department.[8] The system of the Chinese Peoples' Bank, for example, had 152 newspapers and magazines, but 119 of them at local levels were closed down in 1996.[9]

From table 2.1 we know that none of the central newspapers was closed down during these two years, but fourteen local newspapers were. According to an official report, 227 newspapers were cut in 1997, or 10.4 percent of the total number of newspapers in China (ZXN 1998:28). Among them, seventy-nine had been run by administrative departments of local governments and professional societies (*ZXN* 1998:29). The state did not deny that one purpose of such "rectification" was to strengthen party newspapers and that it had "held in check the competition of various kinds of newspapers with party newspapers for circulations and for market" (*ZXN* 1998:29).

Actually, such "reorganization" has taken place several times since 1989, but the trend of media diversification has not stopped. Even if the authoritarian government can deprive a certain newspaper or magazine of its freedom, it proves much more difficult to "reorganize" the entire media field. When an authoritarian regime feels the pressure to detest many voices to the extent that it must seek to deal with them, we know that China's media are now more pluralistic, if not democratic.

In concluding, freedom of the press is expanded in China with the diversification of media structures. As liberty is conceptually concerned with diversity (Jones 1995), structural diversification is a prerequisite for liberalizing the Chinese press. If we define "liberalization" as either the occurrence of competition (Dahl 1971) or the expansion of individual rights (O'Donnell and Schmitter 1986), we may further conclude that partial liberalization of the press is happening in China. In general, what makes the case of China striking in the worldwide transition from nondemocracy to democracy is its uneven and paradoxical relationship between political repression and economic reform. When regime change is delayed, economic and social changes are significant in both the developmental and the structural sense. In China, given the coexistence of the intransigence of the old regime and internal structural changes, as well as the coexistence of the party-state command and fresh market drive, gradual liberalization is more likely to occur than sweeping democratization. This gradual liberalization is economic in nature, but its effect may eventually spill over into the political arena. As it is economic in nature, and as it happens structurally, it could occur in the frictions under political repression, and it will not be reversed, even though the authoritarian regime struggles against it.

Notes

Special thanks go to Dr. Xiaoying Liao for her substantial contribution in collecting data and exchanging ideas with the author and to Professor Chin-Chuan Lee for his help of various kinds, including careful editing of earlier drafts of this chapter. The author also thanks Professors Joseph M. Chan, Huailin Chen, Leonard L. Chu, Yu Huang, Anxiang Ming, Zhongdang Pan, Xupei Sun, and Xu Yu for their comments but nevertheless takes full responsibility for contents of this chapter.

1. For regime change in the former Soviet Union and Eastern European countries, see, for example, Bermeo (1992); Fish (1995); Offe (1996); and Maravall (1997). For comparative studies of the Soviet Union and China, see Pei (1994).

2. For the rise and flux of localism in the reform years, see, for example, Wu (1998b).

3. *Ming Pao,* May 12, 1996.

4. For state-society relations as an analytical framework, see, for example, Stepan (1978); Badie and Birnbaum (1983); Migdal (1988); Migdal, Kohli, and Shue (1994); and Evans (1997).

5. See the essay "Wo zancheng Xiaoping tongzhi tuixiu" ["I Prefer that Comrade Xiaoping Retire"], written by Qian Chaoying in *Shenzhen qingnian bao,* October 21, 1986. For Deng's statement in his conversation with an American reporter, see Deng (1993:167–75). This event led to a thorough reshuffling of the leading editors of that newspaper.

6. For the distinction between the social and political dimensions, see Bottomore (1993).

7. *Mirror Monthly (Jingbao yuekan)* 232 (November 1996): 37.

8. *Sing Tao Daily* (November 14, 1996): A6.

9. *Ming Pao* (January 8, 1997): A10.

Bibliography

Badie, Bertrand, and Pierre Birnbaum. 1983. *The Sociology of the State.* Chicago: University of Chicago Press.

Bermeo, Nancy, ed. 1992. *Liberalization and Democratization: Change in the Soviet Union and Eastern Europe.* Baltimore: Johns Hopkins University Press.

Bottomore, Tom. 1993. *Political Sociology.* Minneapolis: University of Minnesota Press.

Brook, Timothy, and B. Michael Frolic, eds. 1997. *Civil Society in China.* Armonk, N.Y.: M. E. Sharpe.

Chan, Joseph Man. 1993. "Commercialization without Independence: Trends and Tensions of Media Development in China." In Joseph Cheng Yu-shek and Maurice Brosseau, eds., *China Review 1993.* Hong Kong: Chinese University Press.

———. 1995. "Calling the Tune without Paying the Piper: The Reassertion of Media Control in China." In Lo Chi Kin, Suzanne Pepper, and Tsui Kai Yuen, eds., *China Review 1995.* Hong Kong: Chinese University Press.

Chun, Chun. 1993. "A Quiet Revolution: Comments on the Journalistic Reform in the Mainland" ("Yi chang jing qiaoqiao de geming: ping dalu xinwen gaige"). *Democratic China (Minzhu zhongguo)* 16 (July):69–74.

Dahl, Robert A. 1971. *Polyarchy: Participation and Opposition.* New Haven, Conn.: Yale University Press.

Deng Xiaoping. 1993. *Selected Works of Deng Xiaoping (Deng Xiaoping wenxuan),* vol. 3. Beijing: People's Press.

Evans, Peter, ed. 1997. *State-Society Synergy: Government and Social Capital in Development*. Berkeley: University of California Press.

Feng, Yuan. 1994. "Changes in China's Newspapers since the 1980s" ("Bashi niandai yilai zhongguo dalu baoye de bianqian"). *Modern China Studies (Dangdai zhongguo yanjiu)* 42 (June):21–30.

Fish, M. Steven. 1995. *Democracy from Scratch: Opposition and Regime in the New Russian Revolution*. Princeton: Princeton University Press.

Friedrich, Carl J., and Zbigniew K. Brzezinski. 1956. *Totalitarian Dictatorship and Autocracy*. Cambridge, Mass.: Harvard University Press.

Goldman, Merle. 1994. *Sowing the Seeds of Democracy in China: Political Reform in the Deng Xiaoping Era*. Cambridge, Mass.: Harvard University Press.

Goodman, David S. G. 1992. "Provinces Confronting the State?" In Kuan Hsin-chi and Maurice Brosseau, eds., *China Review 1992*. Hong Kong: Chinese University Press.

Hsiao, Ching-chang, and Yang Mei-rong. 1990. "Don't Force Us to Lie: The Case of the *World Economic Herald*." In Chin-Chuan Lee, ed., *Voice of China: The Interplay of Politics and Journalism*. New York: Guilford.

Huntington, Samuel P. 1991. *The Third Wave: Democratization in the Late Twentieth Century*. Norman: University of Oklahoma Press.

Jia, Hao, and Lin Zhimin, eds. 1994. *Changing Central-Local Relations: Reform and State Capacity*. Boulder, Colo.: Westview.

Jones, Peter. 1995. "Two Concepts of Liberalism, Two Concepts of Justice." *British Journal of Political Science* 25:515–50.

Li, Jiehui. 1998. "Politicians, Legislature, and Localism in Guangdong: Toward an Institutionalized Autonomy." M.Phil. thesis, Chinese University of Hong Kong.

Lieberthal, Kenneth G., and David M. Lampton, eds. 1992. *Bureaucracy, Politics, and Decision-Making in Post-Mao China*. Berkeley: University of California Press.

Lieberthal, Kenneth, and Michel Oksenberg. 1988. *Policy Making in China: Leaders, Structures, and Processes*. Princeton: Princeton University Press.

Lu, Keng. 1994. "Press Control in 'New China' and 'Old China.'" In Chin-Chuan Lee, ed., *China's Media, Media's China*. Boulder, Colo.: Westview.

Maravall, José M. 1997. *Regimes, Politics, and Markets: Democratization and Economic Change in Southern and Eastern Europe*. Oxford: Oxford University Press.

Migdal, Joel S. 1988. *Strong Societies and Weak States: State-Society Relations and State Capacities in the Third World*. Princeton: Princeton University Press.

Migdal, Joel S., Atul Kohli, and Vivienne Shue, eds. 1994. *State Power and Social Forces: Domination and Transformation in the Third World*. New York: Cambridge University Press.

Montinola, Gabriella, Yingyi Qian, and Barry R. Weingast. 1995. "Federalism, the Chinese Style: The Political Basis for Economic Success in China." *World Politics* 48 (October):50–81.

Naughton, Barry. 1995. *Growing Out of the Plan: Chinese Economic Reform, 1978-1993*. New York: Cambridge University Press.

O'Brien, Kevin J. 1990. *Reform without Liberalization: China's National People's Congress and the Politics of Institutional Change.* New York: Cambridge University Press.

O'Donnell, Guillermo, and Philippe C. Schmitter. 1986. *Transitions from Authoritarian Rule: Tentative Conclusions about Uncertain Democracies.* Baltimore: Johns Hopkins University Press.

Offe, Claus. 1996. *The Varieties of Transition: The East Europe and East German Experience.* London: Polity.

Pei, Minxin. 1994. *From Reform to Revolution: The Demise of Communism in China and the Soviet Union.* Cambridge, Mass.: Harvard University Press.

Polumbaum, Judy. 1994. "Striving for Predictability: The Bureaucratization of Media Management in China." In Chin-Chuan Lee, ed., *China's Media, Media's China.* Boulder, Colo.: Westview.

Quanguo tushu zazhi baozhi chuban tongji ziliao (National Statistics of the Publication of Books, Magazines, and Newspapers). Various years. Beijing: China Statistics Press.

Schurmann, Franz. 1968. *Ideology and Organization in Communist China,* enlarged ed. Berkeley: University of California Press.

Segal, Gerald. 1994. *China Changes Shape: Regionalism and Foreign Policy.* Adelphi Paper, No. 287. London: International Institute for Strategic Studies.

Seymour, James D. 1987. *China's Satellite Parties.* Armonk, N.Y.: M. E. Sharpe.

Stepan, Alfred. 1978. *The State and Society: Peru in Comparative Perspective.* Princeton: Princeton University Press.

Su, Shaozhi. 1994. "Chinese Communist Ideology and Media Control." In Chin-Chuan Lee, ed., *China's Media, Media's China.* Boulder, Colo.: Westview.

Wang, Ying, Zhe Xiaoye, and Sun Bingyao. 1993. *Shehui zhongjian ceng: gaige yu Zhongguo de shetuan zuzhi (The Middle Level of Society: Reforms and Social Organizations in China).* Beijing: Chinese Development Press.

White, Gordon, Jude Howell, and Shang Xiaoyuan. 1996. *In Search of Civil Society: Market Reform and Social Change in Contemporary China.* Oxford: Clarendon Press.

White, Lynn T., III. 1990. "All the News: Structure and Politics in Shanghai's Reform Media." In Chin-Chuan Lee, ed., *Voices of China: The Interplay of Politics and Journalism.* New York: Guilford.

Wu, Guoguang. 1994. "Command Communication: The Politics of Editorial Formulation in the *People's Daily.*" *China Quarterly* 137 (Summer):194–211.

———. 1998a. "From Factional Conflict to Institutional Competition: The Dynamics of Congressional Role Change in Reform China." Paper presented at conference "Party-State Transformation and Democratization on Both Sides of the Strait," Fairbank Center for East Asian Research, Harvard University, Cambridge, Mass., February 17–18.

———. 1998b. "Political Control, Institutional Decay, and Flux of Localism." Paper presented at conference "Structural Changes in Reform China," Kobe, Japan, November 15–16.

Wu, Guoguang, and Zheng Yongnian. 1995. *On Central-Local Relations (Lun zhongyang difang guanxi)*. Hong Kong: Oxford University Press.

Zhongguo baike nianjian (Chinese Encyclopedia Yearbook). Various years. Beijing: Chinese Encyclopedia Yearbook Press.

Zhongguo chuban nianjian (Chinese Publications Yearbook). Various years. Beijing: Chinese Publications Yearbook Press.

Zhongguo jingji nianjian (Almanac of China's Economy). 1998. Beijing: Chinese Economic Yearbook Press.

Zhongguo xinwen chuban tongji ziliao huibian (Collections of Statistics of Journalism and Publishing in China). Various years. Beijing: Chinese Statistics Press.

Zhongguo xinwen nianjian (ZXN; Chinese Journalism Yearbook). Various years. Beijing: Chinese Journalism Yearbook Press.

3

Improvising Reform Activities

*The Changing Reality of Journalistic
Practice in China*

ZHONGDANG PAN

hina's "journalism reforms" have attracted scholarly attention for some
time (for example, Polumbaum 1990; Chan 1993; Chu 1994). The reforms in the 1990s have been characterized as a wave of commercialization and marketization (Chan 1993; Li 1995; Chen and Huang 1997). Some
scholars have noted that these reforms are taking place within a context of continuing political and ideological control of the media by the Chinese Communist Party (Chan 1993, 1995). These writings depict China's "journalism
reforms" as a process involving two contradictory forces—state control by the
Communist Party and commercialization (Lee 1994). This mode of change in
China's media institution presents us with a theoretical riddle: How do such reforms, many of which do not seem to be compatible with the ruling Communist ideology, take place, and where are the chaotic, incoherent, and sometimes
even erratic reforms heading? One view is that the reforms represent a "peaceful evolution" toward establishment of a market system (Huang 1994). Others
with a more cautious view argue that the fundamentals of the party press system
remain unchanged during the reforms (X. Zhang 1993; Yuan 1996). It is questionable whether the concept of "peaceful evolution" can be appropriately applied to interpret China's journalism reforms (Pan 1997b).

To address this theoretical challenge, in this chapter I argue that changing
journalistic practices constitute the essence of China's journalism reforms. Journalistic practices are here defined as the activities of news gathering and reporting as well as the activities that directly influence the ways and contexts in
which news gathering and reporting are carried out.[1] Informed by Giddens's
structuration theory (1984) and the "routine theory" in the sociology of news

production (Schudson 1991), this chapter examines these practices in terms of journalists' and media organizations' interactions with China's "commandist" journalism institution (Lee 1990). By "journalism institution," I mean the rules and principles revealed in routine journalistic practices. Based on these premises, I interpret China's "journalism reforms" as a process in which certain routine practices are questioned, challenged, and modified and certain nonroutine practices are designed, implemented, and justified. In a broader theoretical framework, such unroutinization and change of practices constitute what observers see as social change (see Giddens 1984:227–62). As a particular mode of social change, China's journalism reforms are unique in that they are taking place within the general framework of the "commandist system" (Lee 1990; Yuan 1996; Pan 1997a). Consequently, China's "journalism reforms" reveal a rather murky trajectory, that is, the patterns and direction of institutional change (Giddens 1984:246). Most often, the reform practices may be "improvised" activities (Anagnost 1985; Berkowitz 1992) that are strongly microsituational, opportunistic, shortsighted, and ideologically localized or particularized.

To elaborate this thesis, I interpret evidence from an ongoing field study. Much of my description falls on the activities and justifications for the activities that influence the media organizations' internal and external configurations as well as journalists' networks vital to their news making. After visiting the newsrooms (better called editorial offices) of the six newspapers examined in my study, I observed that the real story of the reforms lies in how routine news making is carried out and in what institutional settings. I am not referring to journalists working on the phone, writing stories, going over articles with contributing authors, interviewing sources to check factual details, and arguing with their department heads and sometimes even with the editor in chief over the treatment of an article or even the choice of a word. These things occur on a daily basis, but the social and economic settings and the social and cultural texture of these production routines are changing. At all of the six newspapers that I examined, the completion of these routines required only around ten hours per week of the journalists' time. As a matter of fact, at all of these papers, reporters and editors would only show up in their offices one or two days each week. Most of their activities took place outside their offices and served to sustain or improve the conditions for their production routines. The significant differences among the newspapers I examined are related to the hospitality of the activity locale for an organization and for the individual journalist. Most improvised activities were undertaken to construct such a locale. These improvised activities are thus the focus of this study.

My account is also highly person-specific. As in any ethnographic study, I function as both the data gatherer and the interpreter. My account represents only one version of China's journalism reforms. In addition, in this chapter, my aim is not to seek for causal explanations of China's journalism reforms or of journalists' activities. Rather, I set out to understand their activities as the journalists themselves understood them, interpreted via sociological concepts. My account is only my story of China's journalism reforms, albeit a story told in sociological terms (compare Geertz 1973). My story should be contested via different theoretical approaches, but it does not answer well to the challenge of its "ontological validity" (compare D'Andrade 1986; Gergen 1986). My account conforms to the methodological principle articulated in Giddens (1984:284): "Sociological descriptions have the task of mediating the frames of meaning within which actors orient their conduct. But such descriptions are interpretive categories which also demand an effort of translation in and out of the frames of meaning involved in sociological theories."

Journalism Reforms under Communist Hegemony

China's "commandist media system" is built upon one cardinal principle: The media are not first and foremost commercial entities; rather, they are instruments through which the party can propagate the party line and party policies of its revolutionary struggle. The theoretical argument for this principle is that, in the struggle against bourgeois control, the proletariat should use the media as a tool to "denaturalize" the bourgeois ideology, to "enlighten" the proletariat and the mass public, and to achieve the proletariat's "intellectual, moral, and philosophical leadership" (compare Bocock 1986:63). In other words, the mass media are the key instrument with which the proletariat can seek to replace the bourgeois hegemony with its own hegemony and subsequently maintain it (Gramsci 1971). In China, these ideas provide powerful and necessary symbolic resources (Berger and Luckmann 1966) to legitimize the "commandist system" in the Communist Party's struggle for social change, as well as in its defense against subsequent challenges to it (compare Ransome 1992; Yuan 1996). Writings in Marx, Lenin, and Mao explicating such ideas are repeatedly referred to and further elaborated by the Communist leaders in the post-Mao era (see Hu 1985; Jiang 1993, 1996). Elaborating these basic ideas remains a central task of many contemporary journalism texts and scholarly writings (for example, J. Liu 1991; Yuan 1996).

Such ideas, until recently, have legitimized a series of taken-for-granted practices at various levels of the party press system (compare Cheek 1989). At the structural level, the state subsidizes the media, and the committees at various levels of the Communist Party hierarchy appoint key personnel, decide major topics for news coverage, and censor journalists' work. The Propaganda Ministry of the party oversees the content control at all levels through official publication and editorial guidelines as well as through prepublication censorship. Further, journalists are trained first and foremost as "party propagandists." At the organizational level, all work units (for example, schools, government agencies, and factories) subscribe to party newspapers, and all media outlets reprint or rebroadcast the editorials and other important materials of the official organs of the *People's Daily* and Xinhua News Agency (G. Wu 1994). Before the reforms, journalists carried out their news-gathering and reporting activities within these parameters.

The "journalism reforms" that started in the late 1980s consist of a set of far-reaching changes in media operations (see Li 1995). In spite of uncertainties and ambiguities at all levels of the media industry and occasional course reversals (for example, the party's return to a tighter grip on the media immediately after 1989 student uprising), the macroenvironment of media operations is seen to be moving toward loosening political controls and relaxing ideological orthodoxy (X. Zhang 1993). Three major measures brought significant changes to the politico-economic environment of media operations in China: the reduction and gradual termination of state subsidies to almost all media organizations except a handful of party organs, starting in the late 1980s (Song 1994; Chan 1993); the reestablishment of the State Press and Publication Administration in 1987 (Polumbaum 1994);[2] and the resurgence of the advertising industry.

These steps turned out to be interlocking measures. Together, they fostered a trend toward increased media commercialization (Chan 1993; Song 1994; Li 1995). Typical of China's reforms, they were not measures formulated as part of an overall design. Rather, they were developed more or less in an ad hoc fashion. When the state took the step of reducing its media subsidies, the primary motive was to reduce the government's skyrocketing budget deficit and to unload a heavy financial burden from the state rather than to marketize the media industry (Chen and Huang 1997). Showing this ad hoc approach, the official framework for such measures was to turn media outlets into public units under business management (*shiye danwei qiye guanli*). In other words, those units that traditionally drew their revenue from the state budget would now get only a limited amount of state support for infrastructural investment, and they themselves would be responsible for additional financial resources needed for their normal operations. In this official stipulation, a line not to be crossed is clearly drawn. That is, media organizations should not become profit-making entities. The official discourse laboriously distinguishes media as a means of symbolic production as opposed to a means of material production (J. Liu 1991; Song 1994). Even today, while the media industry is polarized on the issue of the distribution of advertising billings (Chen and Huang 1997), the official discourse remains ambiguous as to whether media organizations should seek profit in market situations.

Nevertheless, reducing the state subsidies did force media organizations to plunge into the market. As media professionals like to say, after the "milk supply is terminated" (*duannai*), the media have to look for food on their own initiative. They soon found that many other entities traditionally operating under the command system also had had their "milk supply" terminated. Some newly formed private or semiprivate enterprises never had the opportunity to get on the "milk-supply lines." These commercial entities found advertising indispensable, and so did the media. Between 1985 and 1995, the advertising industry grew from 234 million yuan (U.S. $30 million) to 13.4 billion yuan (U.S. $1.65 billion). In 1993 in particular, annual advertising revenue nearly doubled that of 1992. By then, China had more than thirty thousand commercial advertising entities. Almost all of the top international advertising agencies had branch offices in China. By 1993, it was estimated that more than one-third of the 2,039 officially registered newspapers were self-sufficient, and many of those were making handsome profits.[3] Only around this time, between 1992 and 1993, did "marketization of media industry" start to appear in the official vocabulary of journalism reforms (see, for example, Liang 1992; W. Liu 1993). Today, the ways in which newspapers and broadcast media compete in a market environment have become the central topic of discussions among policy makers, media professionals, and scholars (Tong 1993; Li 1995).

During this process, the reestablishment of the State Press and Publication Administration (SPPA) was a major event, and its significance has been severely underrated and, by some, misinterpreted (Cheek 1989; Polumbaum 1994). One of the major consequences of the deepening economic reforms moving toward marketization is the increasing tension between the party and the state. The latter nominally owns all major means of production, including those for symbolic production. The tension reached such a level that a call for a separation between party and state powers (*dangzheng fenkai*) entered the official discourse. Re-creating the SPPA to take over the regulatory and administrative activities concerning the print media industry makes it possible for the party to continue its ideological domination in that its ideological principles have now been translated into administrative regulations enforced by the state apparatus (Song 1994). This change in government structure was, therefore, a major step undertaken by the Communist Party to respond to the changing environment.

By 1994, a new wave of journalism reforms moving toward commercialization reached a new height with encouragement from a speech by Deng during his visit to the Shenzhen special economic zone in early 1992. During these few years, the newspaper industry had seen dramatic changes. The total number of newspapers reached 2,108 by the end of 1994, a 31 percent increase above the 1991 level; among the newly published papers, a majority of them were market-oriented "readers digest" publications, newspapers on service (for example, *Shopping Guide* and *Stock Exchange Herald*), and entertainment (for example, various weekend and sports specials). Advertising revenues for the industry reached 3.77 billion yuan (U.S. $4,700 million) by the end of 1993, four times the 1991 figure. A market-driven distribution structure was beginning to emerge. *Yangcheng Evening News* from Guangzhou, for example, marched into the Beijing market; *Shopping Guide* became a nationwide chain newspaper; *People's Daily* started its East China edition; and *Beijing Youth Daily*, a small paper traditionally targeted at youths in Beijing, became the third most influential Beijing local paper for the general audience and started nationwide distribution. At the same time, journalists were getting rich, famous, and ever more intricately tied to commercial activities by virtue of the need to cover the economic reform activities and of the opportunities for shuttling their tasks among news, public relations, and advertising (Pan 1997b). These changes form the background of this study.

Journalistic Routines and Ideological Hegemony

Situated against this background, this chapter does not aim at understanding how journalistic practices *constitute* the macroscopic changes that can be characterized as media commercialization (Chan 1993; Chen and Huang 1997). At this level, the concept of "improvisation" may best help us to understand the sociocultural meanings of journalism reforms. Here, "improvising" refers to the way in which journalists design, implement, and justify their nonroutine journalistic practices that function to *weaken, circumvent, and erode the hegemony of the commandist system associated with the Communist ideology.*

Routine practices constitute the "social ontology" of hegemony (Williams 1973). When such routine practices are found to be incapable of handling erupted crises or dramatic changes, the logic behind them ceases to be transparent. It is called into question, and what used to be an accepted reality becomes an area of contention (see Gitlin 1980:273–75; Hallin 1986). When that happens, the original state of hegemony is threatened and sometimes weakened or circumvented. In China, given the Communist Party's continuing tight grip on the "ideological state apparatuses" (Althusser 1971), such a period of uncertainties requires that some "extraordinary measures" be taken to "repair" the process usually governed by routines (see Gitlin 1980; Bennett, Gressett, and Halton 1985). China's reforms called for incorporating the principles of market economy that had long been delegitimized. Therefore, some "extraordinary" or "nonroutine" measures must be invented, implemented, and justified *collaboratively* by journalists and the agents of the commandist system, who are often driven by different concerns, in order to "repair" the exiting system. While the agents of the system may wish to salvage the commandist system by "domesticating" (Gitlin 1980) some nonroutine measures associated with the market economy, journalists may find system maintenance the only legitimate and practical framework within which they can try something new. Through such "collaborative efforts," the overall framework of the "commandist system" is maintained and reproduced, and along the way some forms of "nonroutine measures" are incorporated.

The process of forming nonroutine practices in such a context, therefore, takes away any explicit appearance of an ideological opposition. Rather, this is a process of reinforcing the supremacy of the ruling ideology by employing new symbolic resources and improvising new practices to expand the boundary of the dominant ideology (Pan 1997a).[4] By symbolic resources, I mean those concepts and interpretive schemes that journalists as strategic actors use to reason, invent, explicate, and justify what they do (Berger and Luckmann 1966; Zelizer 1993). The symbolic resources come from both endogenous and exogenous sources, that is, from Maoist ideology, traditional elite and folk cultures, and imported contemporary Western ideas (Whyte 1989). Those who uncover and utilize such resources tend to be young, well educated, and entrepreneurial. They are familiar with orthodox ways of doing things, but they no longer treat them as "natural." In other words, they are much less likely to confine themselves within the framework of "routines" and "conventions." They are more likely to *innovate* and *improvise* when interacting with the changing environment. Meanwhile, due to the lack of a well-developed professional community and a community culture and the lack of a sufficient degree of predictability in the macro politico-economic environment, these actors appear to be opportunistic and shortsighted, despite being strategic within limited settings. Such widening of the pool of symbolic resources and of the range of social actions takes place for two reasons: to maintain the ideological supremacy of the Communist Party and to advance the reforms. It is well understood among Chinese journalists that no reform needs to be or can be carried out in "oppositional" terms. Rather, as a senior reporter told me, "We are essentially consistent with the party and the government, and that's how we get things done." As a result, a significant feature of their reform activities is the definition of those activities in microsituational terms. In other words, these journalists apply the overarching ideological principles in terms of "local particulars" (Hall 1980).

This description of the journalism reform process is driven by my theoretical concern with changes in China's media system in relation to the broader social change occurring in China, and I am guided by Giddens's principle on where to focus sociological attention. Giddens (1984:25) points out that understanding the conditions and processes of social systems involves "studying the modes in which such systems, grounded in the knowledgeable activities of situated actors who draw upon rules and resources in the diversity of action contexts, are produced and reproduced in interaction." The concept of improvising is well suited to this style of analysis. More formally, the concept denotes the process by which journalists as knowledgeable actors design, implement, and justify their activities, with the understanding of the "unnaturalness" of the dominant ideology and the simultaneous recognition of the real-world supremacy of the same ideology because this ideology lives on powerful coercive apparatuses as well as on the deeply rooted social practices that remain prevalent. Through these activities, journalists interact with the commandist institution and "negotiate" the boundary of the official ideology by broadening the sources of symbolic resources and by diversifying social practices within the official ideology. The remaining sections of this chapter describe and interpret the evidence from my fieldwork in light of this conception.

Background and Procedures

I arrived in City A in mid-January 1995 at the height of the media commercialization wave.[5] I started my fieldwork with the overall objective of understanding how journalists were carrying out their work in a market environment. My journalist friends in City A had already informed me that most Chinese journalists no longer *acted* as if they were party propagandists and that they were much less oriented toward the Maoist doctrine of journalism than they were officially portrayed as being. I was aware of journalists' frustrations over having

to please "two masters," the tensions in their day-to-day work, and their desire
to change, at least toward the direction of more job autonomy and professionalism and toward having a legal framework in which to operate (see Polumbaum 1990). I understood that although most of them were making efforts to
adapt to—and some of them were even excelling in—the changes brought
about by the reforms, they had no clear idea what the overall practical goal of
the journalism reforms could be or what the resulting media system would look
like. Many of them also had some limited knowledge of media operations and
journalistic work in Western countries. These ideas were based on my past observations in China and my readings about China's journalism reforms. With all
these points in mind, I started observing and experiencing Chinese journalists'
daily activities and media operations, in the light of some of the questions raised
in classic American studies on the subject (see Tuchman 1978; Gans 1980; Fishman 1980).

I chose to start with the newspaper industry because it had more fully developed practices in the revolutionary tradition and a clearer designation of the
party organs through the "organ paper" (jiguan bao) system, as compared with
other media. I distinguished six categories of newspapers based on degrees of
control (party organs; nonparty organs, that is, organ newspapers of official or
semiofficial agencies; and nonorgan newspapers, that is, newspapers nominally
affiliated with an organization) and on scope of circulation (national versus local). I then planned to choose one or two newspapers from each of the categories. The selection of the newspapers for this study, however, could not be
probabilistic due to extreme difficulties in gaining access.[6] Rather, which papers
were chosen depended largely on how far my contacts in the industry could
take me. This chapter reports my interpretive account of the observations and
interviews I have conducted in City A since that time. The journalists whom I
interviewed came from a variety of officially registered daily newspapers.

The core of my evidence comes from the observations in six newspapers in
City A. Table 3.1 summarizes the basic characteristics of these newspapers. Because I am still in the process of analyzing the field notes from my observations
and interviews at four of the newspapers, evidence from Paper X and Paper Y
will be discussed in greater detail than will that from the other newspapers.

These newspapers differ in a number of ways. First, as Chen and Huang
(1997) show, measured by annual advertising revenue, metropolitan papers are
much better off than are nonmetropolitan papers, whether they are distributed
nationally or provincially; among the metropolitan papers, nonorgan papers are
much better off than organ papers and party organs. In this group of six papers,

Table 3.1. Key Features of the Six Newspapers Studied

Newspaper	Category	Administrative Level	Circulation Area	Circulation (1,000)
Paper U	Party Organ	Bureau	City A metropolitan area	465.4
Paper V	Nonorgan	Bureau	Nationwide	200.0
Paper W	Nonparty organ	Bureau	Nationwide	1,190.0
Paper X	Nonparty organ	Branch	City A metropolitan area	151.8
Paper Y	Nonparty organ	Bureau	Nationwide	263.9
Paper Z	Nonorgan	Bureau	Nationwide	100.0

The circulation figures are reported in *Chinese Journalism Yearbook 1995*, reflecting the condition of the newspapers at the end of 1995.

for example, the smallest, Paper X, has the highest advertising revenue. By the end of 1994, it had already reached 30 million yuan (nearly U.S. $4 million). In comparison, Paper Y has a nationwide circulation, but its 1994 advertising revenue was only 8 million yuan (about U.S. $1 million). Paper U is a typical city party-organ paper; its advertising revenue reached 7.89 million yuan (about U.S. $0.99 million) in 1994.[7] Two variables strongly influence a newspaper's advertising revenue: the density of its circulation in a major metropolitan area and the degree of the party's political control, measured roughly by the three categories in terms of levels of control. The latter factor plays such an important role that the more distant a newspaper is from the political and ideological center, the more active and appealing it is to readers (see Pan 1997b).

Another important difference among the six newspapers is their respective location on the administrative ladder. The hierarchy comprises four categories in descending order of power: ministry (*bu*), bureau (*ju*), branch (*chu*), and section (*ke*). Paper X, for example, is an organ paper of City A's official youth league, and it had only branch-level status until 1995 when it was elevated to the subbureau (*fu ju*) level. All the other newspapers have a bureau-level status. The four major administrative levels are generally associated with different degrees of access to news sources in the system, different levels of control of resources, and, at the same time, different degrees of proximity to the political center.[8] This issue came up repeatedly in my fieldwork. My interviewees repeatedly referred to being a "*bureau*-level paper" or "*branch*-level paper" to explain resource constraints and their (in)ability to cover certain stories. In general, the higher the level of a news organization, the closer the surveillance to which it is subjected by party officials and the wider its access to news sources.

These organizational characteristics form the immediate context of the journalistic practices that I observed. My purpose is not to compare these papers. Rather, I want to point out these variations among them because they allow me to connect my situational observations to the newspaper industry in general. With only six papers from one city, I am far from having a "representative sample" of newspapers in China, nor do I have what Przeworski and Teune (1970) call the "maximum variance design." The variations among these newspapers, however, together with my formal and informal interviews with journalists from other papers in the city and my observations of newspapers sold on newsstands across the city, do enhance my confidence about interpreting my data in more general terms.[9]

Routine, Nonroutine, and Improvisation

Research in the West shows that journalists use nonroutine or "extraordinary measures" when they encounter events that are not easily classifiable within the existing typification schemes (see Gitlin 1980; Tuchman 1978). Clearly, "non-classifiable" events occur more frequently during periods of social change. In China's reform era, nonroutine practices take place daily, to the extent that some of them even take on the appearance of being routinized.

To understand how nonroutine journalistic practices are invented in China, we must have a clear idea of the unique macroenvironment in which such practices take place. Three characteristics of this macroenvironment stand out. First, no coherent conceptual framework of reform or set of clearly formulated and articulated depictions of the system to which the reforms are directed has been developed. The most famous line is the alleged statement by Deng Xiaoping, the so-called chief architect of the reforms: "Crossing a river by groping after rocks," meaning improvising and experimenting. A popular statement that carries the equivalent meaning is "follow your instinct" (*genzhe gan-jue zou*).

Second, a great degree of uncertainty prevails among journalists concerning the "true" meaning of the party line and policies. In practice, this also means that bureaucratic and ideological hurdles are placed before anyone who wishes to take an innovative step.

Third, journalists and media organizations all face the immediate concern of financial survival: A media organization must pay its employees, house them, and provide them with medical care and other benefits. After the state subsidies were reduced or terminated, most media organizations barely had enough funds to cover employees' salaries and benefits, not to mention investing in the infrastructure. In their memoirs commemorating their newspapers' anniversaries, the founding editors and publishers of Paper W and Paper X all talked about the resource shortage and their efforts to gain more. Resource shortages at the organizational level are closely related to resource shortages at the individual level. The salary and benefits provided by the organization are far from enough to match the rising expectations for material life and the increasing market availability of consumer goods. For some, journalists' income could hardly meet their basic needs. As a result, a journalist must extend his or her practice beyond organizational boundaries. This is widely referred to as "the second career."

In this macroenvironment, journalists must design and/or engage in activities that arise from specific occasions. These activities are doable and may help accomplish some immediate goals in a narrowly specified situation, although sometimes they are tactical moves within a vaguely stated vision for an organization's future. Further, they are not easily characterizable ethically within a specific interpretive framework. In brief, they often reflect the actors' short-sighted, opportunistic, and entrepreneurial efforts to improve their chances of "success," usually defined in terms of financial well-being and/or of acquiring professional prestige, in a situation that is full of constraints, contradictions, and uncertainty.

One example will illustrate the key elements of improvised nonroutine practices. A veteran editor from the East China edition of *People's Daily* presented a case in one of our conversations: A new law regulating the advertising industry had become effective not long before. The law prohibits cigarette advertising in mass media. One tobacco company in Anhui Province, however, where the scenic Yellow Mountains are located, was willing to pay 170,000 yuan (U.S. $21,250) for a full-page ad promoting a packaged tour to the area. The ad featured a scene from the Yellow Mountains and a caption that read, "Stop smoking, come to tour the Yellow Mountains," along with the key features of a tourist package, and the name and address of the tobacco company that had paid for the ad. The question from the editor was, "If someone from the Commerce Bureau questions the legality of printing this ad, do I have any justifiable defense?" Clearly, whether printing the ad had *actually* violated the law was not in question. The offer from this advertiser was much higher than the standard rate for a full-page ad. Apparently, this was an offer that the editor could not refuse. He decided to print the ad. In his words, "It [170,000 yuan] is too good an opportunity to pass up."

Opportunistic leaning is strategic for actors in a macroenvironment filled with diverse symbolic resources, fluidity, uncertainty, and constraints (Pan 1997a). This does not mean that actors do not have any long-term orientation or planning. They do: Sometimes, such long-term orientations are revealed through reconfigurations of an organization or through programmatic activities. In 1993, the newspaper industry, short of capital, found an increasingly hospitable environment for diversification; it developed business ventures in other areas, especially in advertising, packaging, real estate, theme-park tourism, and restaurants. Some newspapers even launched joint ventures with overseas capitals (for example, Chan 1993). Paper X, a metro nonparty organ, owned twelve different enterprises by the end of 1993, including an advertising firm, a public-relations agency, a packaging and decoration business, and a joint venture called, after the island province in the South China Sea, Hainan Island Tourist Company. By 1994, five of these had turned out to be modestly profitable. In addition, Paper X was also publishing three additional periodicals. Many of these business ventures reflect the newspaper's intention of making good use of its human resources in art design, information gathering, and networking. Others simply reflect efforts by the newspaper's management to chase the hottest investment areas of the day, such as, in the early 1990s, real estate and the tonic medicine businesses. Still others reflect the decision by the newspaper management to expand the newspaper's target market by publishing, for example, a biweekly magazine tailored to the growing number of yuppies.

Newspapers vary in their organizational strategies as they diversify. Aiming for business expansion, Paper X formally registered itself as a corporation in 1993, with the publisher named as the president of this corporation. Due, however, to the lack of any "spirit from the top" (the Chinese way of describing official guidelines for action from the government), this infant corporation could not seek capital investment from other investors — domestic or foreign, state owned or private enterprise — to develop its main business: publishing Paper X. Further, the head of the corporation was still held accountable to the paper's supervising agency and to the party. (Indeed, he was removed from his post in 1996. The removal was triggered by the paper's controversial coverage of a company's product quality.) In comparison, Paper W adopted a different model. It formed a corporation headed by its deputy publisher as a venue for launching other business ventures. The corporation's businesses included a toy manufacturing company, an interior design company, and a technological development company, among others.[10]

There are still other models. In Paper Y, the leadership wished to become the largest corporation offering sports information and entertainment in China. In the last few years, it had expanded into other businesses, including, not surprisingly, advertising. All these are separate small businesses owned by the paper and supervised by the paper's managing director. The paper also had four other spin-off publications managed in a similar fashion. Only one of these publications was truly profitable, however; two barely broke even, and one was even losing money. Because an official regulation prohibited any financial investment in a newspaper, Paper Y management subcontracted one of its spin-off periodicals to another organization. The editorial personnel of this periodical was from Paper Y. The contractor brought in advertisement and other sponsors, and the periodical became financially "independent," in that it generates its own revenue and sets journalists' monthly and end-of-year bonuses.

Some of these activities may be construed as being strategic for a newspaper's long-term developmental goals. These strategic activities remained tentative and often short-lived, however. Paper X has already folded one of its periodicals. Paper Y was forced to reconsider its contract for its spin-off periodical because the head of the contractor encountered serious "economic problems," the Chinese euphemism for corruption. The leadership of these papers frequently sighed when talking about their "reform" activities: "We don't know how to proceed. Nothing is on the normal track. We can only explore."

The need to explore unknown territories is felt at all levels of an organization. Individual journalists would be financially rewarded if they brought financially gainful opportunities to their organizations. As a result, some journalists with keen business senses became known as "point men" (*xue tou*). They often engage in activities outside of their organizational and professional boundaries, doing what is called "exploring caves" (*zou xue*), that is, pressing enterprises for financial deals. These activities are usually situational and even spontaneous rather than being charted in or predicted by any routine framework. Because no framework exists to guide routine practices in this area, the only guide is one's "instinct."

Following one's instinct is also a means to sort through the confusing and multilayered instructions from above, whether from the editor in chief, the leaders of the supervising agency, or the Party Propaganda Ministry. Very often, such instructions are relayed to individual journalists verbally. Many journalists seem to have concluded that the best strategy for dealing with such confusion is not to take anything seriously. At Paper W, I encountered an illustrative scene at a regular weekly meeting of the Weekend Special Department. The head of the department announced that he needed to inform everyone of new instructions from the Editorial Committee, the body that frames the editorial policies of the newspaper, consisting of the chief editor, his deputies, and some department heads. Immediately after he made that announcement, journalists at the meeting started to complain: "Again!" "Now what?" "What is it this time?" The speaker continued by saying that the Editorial Committee wanted the department to organize a special issue on a widely praised government official who had died on duty. Further, this special issue ought to report the memorial activities that had been planned in City A for this "model party official." At this point, the meeting turned into total chaos: "They want us to do this today, to do that tomorrow, and to do some other things the day after. They change their focus every day. What do they really expect us to do?" "Who is going to read that kind of stuff?" "Well, it doesn't matter whether anyone reads it. What does readability have to do with anything?" More than once, my journalist subjects told me they "just don't pay attention. Do what you have to do."

By no means can journalists do whatever they wish. As a matter of fact, all my journalist subjects emphasize the importance of "minding the degree" (*ba wo du*), that is, being sensitive to what can be done, what can be reported, how it can be done, and how it might be reported. One department head at a paper told me: "After the June fourth incident in 1989, my work became easier because reporters were no longer interested in 'poking holes,' they were more aware of the 'degree'; as a result, reviewing news became rather easy."[11] In Paper X, one veteran editor said, "Politics comes first, communication comes second; propaganda comes first, news comes second; this is the reality in our country. Every young journalist must learn this." Many veteran journalists claimed that they had internalized the "degree," but when I asked them to articulate such a parameter, they had difficulties: "It's something we are all aware of, we sense it, but we can't really express it. You will know it after being around for a while." Clearly, such an internalized parameter becomes part of the journalists' professional instinct.

Following one's instinct, of course, cannot be problem free. Problems may arise from some unexpected areas. Sometimes, even a seasoned journalist might encounter problems. One incident at Paper U illustrates the point. Not long before my fieldwork, this paper published a story about a renowned university professor who had evaded the income tax. The story went through the organizational venues per a well-understood routine procedure: One department head initiated the story. The idea was then pitched to the deputy chief editor in charge of this department and won his approval. The department head then gave the assignment to a veteran reporter. The resulting story also went through the normal three-layer review process: first by the department head, then by the deputy chief editor in charge of the section where the article was designated to appear, and finally by the editor in chief. They all signed the authorization slip for its publication. After the story appeared, however, the propaganda chief of the city's party committee was concerned that such reports might agitate the intellectuals who already harbored acute discontent. The editor in chief received a call one day from the official's office: The journalists involved in producing this story were not sensitive enough to the broader context of intellectual discontent. They must submit a self-criticism in writing. Of course, they all did.

Clearly, the changes in the conditions of media operation called for innovative activities that would not be considered "journalistic" in the tradition of the party press. They constitute what I call "nonroutine" activities in this chapter. The lack of predictability in the political environment and the pressure of making financial gains both at the individual and the organizational levels give these activities opportunistic and shortsighted features. Further, under the present macrocondition, there is only room for nonroutine activities at the micro level, and these activities must not contradict the broad parameters of the party press at either the organizational or the institutional level. Improvisation thus displays the unique feature of the relationship between the microagents, that is, individual journalists and media organizations, and the macroconditions.

Weaving the "Web of Subsidies"

Most journalistic routines pattern and reproduce social relationships for news production (Tuchman 1978). Journalists are network builders on both the professional and the personal levels. Such networks inform them of various occurrences; provide them with the access to and verification of information they need for their reportage; and help them to achieve "factuality" based on the existing social order, that is, "facts" uncovered and verified by sources with recognized authority or expertise. Based on this interpretation of source–journalist relationships, Tuchman (1978) coined the phrase "web of facticity" to characterize such a network. Tuchman's conception gets further support from the observation that a journalist's professional prestige often is indicated by the number and composition of the exclusive sources that he or she has amassed (Fishman 1980). "Web of facticity" is thus a very useful concept with which to examine how the existing social order functions in journalistic work to determine facts and factuality.

Chinese journalists are also excellent network builders. The journalists that I met and conversed with in City A are all well connected. Their contacts spread to almost all walks of the city's life, as well as to other cities. Many of such contacts constitute important sources. Paper Y, for example, specializes in sports coverage. The editor in chief and a senior editor both told me that their newspaper was facing tough competition from some newly emerging small papers that specialize in the same area. Their reporters, however, have developed much closer relationships with the key individuals in the area, such as star athletes, coaches, and officials in the National Sports Commission. As a result, whenever a major news event in national sports occurs, their reporters are among the first to know. Their reporters even know of many behind-the-scenes dealings and nuances involving various sports teams. The most effective means for those smaller newspapers to compete with Paper Y in covering news about national sports would be to attract Paper Y's reporters to write for them.

Through their nonroutine activities, however, Chinese journalists also work hard to exploit their network of potential sources for financial gains. From a political-economic perspective, cultivating this particular function of "news net" (Tuchman 1978) reduces the cost of news production, a cost reduction accomplished through the "subsidy" of the news media by potential sources (Gandy 1982). To parallel Tuchman's term, I call this aspect of the "news net" a "web of subsidies." This concept refers to the type of source-journalist relationship that has a significant agent-client aspect.

This aspect of source-journalist relationship is not something unique in China (see, for example, Gandy 1982). In the United States, a source organization "subsidizes" news production by supplying packaged information to the media free of charge (see Maltese 1994 for an example). In this case, a source organization claims certain information-gathering and -packaging tasks from media organizations, and through this claim it contributes to covering part of the cost incurred in news production. In China, this "public relation" or "public information" practice of information subsidy is still at an early stage of development. The more prevalent practice is for journalists and media organizations to seek financial sponsorships from the news sources for editing a page or writing an in-depth story. Often, such sponsorships take the form of an advertisement or a direct cash contribution to a newspaper through individual journalists. This particular aspect of source-journalist relationships reflects a unique way in which news production is financed in contemporary China. Cultivating this aspect of source-journalist relationships requires many nonroutine activities and also makes many of these activities possible. These practices of weaving the "web of subsidies" help to develop a new symbiotic relationship between news media and other social organizations, one built upon a Chinese style of the "commodification" of news information (Murdock and Golding 1977; McManus 1994).

In City A, the journalists' "web of subsidies" is a vital means for media organizations to sustain and house nonroutine news production activities. Two processes are operating here. First, China's advertising industry is far from large enough to support all the media organizations. As a result, media must rely on various enterprises to sustain their operations. Given the explicit rules against any direct investment by a corporation in a media organization, media must attract "contributions" through informal networks in noninvestment forms. Second, the advertising market in China is far from mature. Competition for advertising billing is far from being a fair game. Advertising billing is often distributed among media organizations through personal networks. Therefore, weaving the "web of subsidies" has a significant impact on a newspaper's organizational dynamics and journalistic practices. Often, one important measure of a journalist's contribution to his or her media organization is the amount of "sponsorship" and advertising billing he or she has brought in. At Paper V, for example, a reporter who had brought in a million yuan (U.S. $125,000) was awarded a large apartment, even though many of his more senior and needy colleagues were ahead of him on the waiting list. The practice of mixing news with various forms of monetary transactions has been branded "gold-based journalism" or "paid journalism" (H. Wu 1995).

Enterprise sponsorship in journalism takes various forms. An enterprise could sponsor the publication of a story, a section or page, or a column; it could also sponsor some reporters' news-gathering trips by covering their travel expenses and providing free meals and accommodations or by offering some cash compensation, called "red packets."[12] Although these practices have been condemned by the authorities and by the semiofficial journalist association (see H. Wu 1995), they remain common. As one senior editor from Paper U said: "It [paid journalism] is quite common. The editors-in-chief do it; the bureau chiefs do it. Everybody does it."

Soliciting and accepting sponsorship from enterprises for some columns or sections actually started at the *People's Daily* (H. Wu 1995). The paper's former director of the Economic News Bureau initiated an "economic information" section back in 1979, with each issue being paid for by the enterprise featured in that day's paper. This veteran journalist, now retired, has expressed his regret publicly. He claimed that he had wanted to "serve the economic reforms" by facilitating the diffusion of economic information, but his initial idea has been misapplied, resulting in corruption of the journalism profession.

All the papers examined in my fieldwork continue with this practice. Paper Y, for example, often prints one-by-two- or two-by-three-inch boxes together with its headline news stories on the front page. These boxes contain advertisers' or sponsors' logos and telephone numbers. Sometimes, a particular page of the paper declares "This page is sponsored by [name and telephone number of the sponsoring organization]."

The management of a newspaper usually implicitly or explicitly assigns the task of soliciting such sponsorships to individual journalists. No newspaper publisher or editor would admit in public that his or her paper requires its journalists to engage in such solicitation. Such task assignment often results from specific management strategies designed for other purposes. I discussed one such means earlier: Journalists' contributions to their papers are assessed not only on their quality of news making but also on their level of revenue generation. Another means is the system of "duty editorship." In this system, editors rotate responsibility for a page or section, editing it for a period of time (for example, one month). When a journalist is the "editor on duty" for a page, he or she must organize the articles to fill the page, edit the articles, submit the articles for review to the editor in chief or a deputy chief editor, and work with the layout-design editor. This person is also provided with financial incentives to attract ads and sponsors for this page: a 10 to 20 percent commission.

One day, I met with a journalist working for the official organ of the State Press and Publication Administration in a Pizza Hut restaurant for an informal interview. She said to me: "It's on me today. I got paid extra." What happened was that she had closed a deal with a state-owned enterprise. The general manager of the enterprise happened to be a good friend of hers. When she became the editor on duty for the "social news" page that month, the enterprise would "donate" 100,000 yuan (U.S. $12,500) to the newspaper, in exchange for an acknowledgment statement for a week. My informant received 20 percent of that amount as a commission.

Another incident also shows the nature of the relationships in the "web of subsidies." At Paper Y, the general manager and the editor in chief asked me and a friend of mine, who specializes in marketing research and advertising, to conduct marketing research for them. They wished to find out where their paper stood against the mushrooming numbers of small newspapers specializing in the same area of coverage. I was willing to work on the project free of charge as a way to gain access. But my friend was operating a marketing research agency and wanted to be paid for this project. The general manager sighed after receiving an invoice from my friend: "We usually ask for money. Now, we have to pay. It takes some effort to get used to this idea."

Other practices are undertaken in a similar spirit. An increasingly prevalent one is for a newspaper to contract another party, usually an enterprise, to edit an insert or a special section. Paper X, for example, publishes "Automobile Special" and "Computer Special" every Wednesday. Each section is edited by an enterprise contractor. In this practice, the contracted party pays a fixed amount to the paper for printing its own materials. One supervising editor from the paper is assigned to look over the content of the contracted pages to make sure that they do not contain things that might embarrass the paper, for example, reference to sensitive political issues or use of politically inappropriate terms.

Clearly, one can find the newspaper's desire for more revenue behind this measure. This is not how journalists interpret this practice, however. They justify it by claiming that it makes use of reporting and writing talents not easily channeled into a newspaper under the current personnel management system. Indeed, the personnel management system in the Chinese media industry remains highly restrictive. Although many papers have gained autonomy in hiring reporters and editors on a contractual basis, the Personnel Ministry or Bureau at a higher level sets quotas for more permanent employees. Because many fringe benefits, such as health insurance and housing, are only covered under the personnel management system, contractual terms are not sufficient to attract more talented or senior journalists. Many newspapers design such "contracting-out-space" schemes to circumvent the strict personnel management system.

This contracting-out-space practice bears close resemblance to selling newspaper space to advertisers. The difference here, however, is that the paper keeps the right to specify in the contract that such pages will print news or entertainment-oriented information and that advertising will not exceed a fixed portion of a page. Practices of this sort cannot be judged in legal or even ethical terms because in neither sphere can one find a coherent framework. The vocabulary in the reform discourse, which urges newspapers to "walk toward the market" (*zouxiang shichang*) and to "face the society at large" (*mianxiang shehui*), seems to have provided the legitimacy for practices of this kind. The caveat here is that such legitimacy is fragile because the same vocabulary could be used to delegitimize such practices when the authorities invent a new interpretation of these concepts.

Obviously, these practices lead to the concern over mixing the "web of facticity" with the "web of subsidies." Would this mixture further undermine journalists' or a media organization's editorial autonomy?[13] I raised this issue a number of times during my fieldwork. The people of whom I asked this question never gave me a straight "yes" or "no" answer. Usually, the answer went like this: "Well, I don't think reporters like me are affected by how the advertisers or sponsors might react. But, when you encounter some stories that are potentially damaging to a really significant advertiser, you hesitate a little. You have to decide what to do and how to do it on a case-by-case basis." One reporter was more forthcoming: "When your paper is doing well financially, you can occasionally do a piece offensive to one of them [big advertisers or sponsors]."

One editor from Paper X responded to my inquiry by telling me a story of how he "whipped" the city's largest McDonald's restaurant. Two years ago, this restaurant had a management-labor dispute. The management laid off an employee who allegedly posted petitions in the employee locker room calling on the employees to get together to demand a benefit package. This reporter first interviewed some employees and gathered evidence of the alleged mistreatment of the employees by the management. Then, on a Friday afternoon, he went to see the restaurant's general manager. The general manager, according to this reporter, was quite arrogant, demanding that nothing be printed about this incident and even threatening to call on the city government to intervene if the reporter insisted on doing the story. The reporter went back to his paper and filed a story on Saturday that appeared on Sunday. By Monday morning, when the city government was scheduled to respond to the call from the restaurant's general manager, calls from citizens started to flood in, demanding that the government take actions to protect Chinese workers from "being exploited" by foreign capitalists. Although the city government was irritated by Paper X's story for "spoiling City A's investment atmosphere," under the pressure of public sentiment, it intervened in the management-labor dispute instead. Two weeks later, the reporter went back to the restaurant to see the general manager. By then, the restaurant had offered to hire back the fired employee and to make some concessions to improve working conditions. The general manager talked to the reporter at length about the management's efforts to improve employees' working conditions and promised a 20,000 yuan (U.S. $2,500) sponsorship payment to the paper. A story on the restaurant's improved working condition was duly published. The lesson from this story, according to the reporter, is that it is possible to write a critical report without jeopardizing financial relationships with the subjects of the report.

In the unique macroenvironment of China's journalism reforms, the concept of "web of subsidies" captures the essence of various venues associated with nonroutine activities circumventing the restrictions of the commandist system. Observations from Paper Y help illustrate my point. Reporters at Paper Y complained loudly that the paper's supervising agency would not let them print many stories that were judged highly newsworthy, for example, incidents in which Chinese athletes were disciplined by international sports organizations for using illegal drugs. Some of the reporters had to leak such stories to their colleagues on competing newspapers or file the stories themselves in those newspapers using pen names. As a result, the only national sports paper did not have "real" sports news, as the journalists in this paper told me; the tragedy accelerated the decline of its circulation, the paper's editor in chief and publisher told me with a sigh of helplessness. The chiefs also felt helpless at seeing their own reporters become star guest-writers for other newspapers, under the motivations of earning extra income to supplement their petty salaries and of being pushed out by the supervising agency's vigilant control of their own papers. One of their reporters is a self-taught expert on the U.S. NBA games. He found his home base so small a pond, however, that he became a regular commentator on NBA games on a new sports channel of China's Central TV network.

These practices at Paper Y illustrate a unique pattern of flow in the "web of subsidies" within the media industry. That is, the "big papers" that are given a greater access to institutional and human resources under the commandist system find themselves "subsidizing" smaller, newly emerged papers that operate primarily in market conditions. In Paper Y's case, such subsidies took the form of a "brain drain" and freeloading of commodified information (Murdock and Golding 1977). Paper Y is an ideal organization to offer such subsidies in that it has human resources in reporting sports news but cannot utilize its human resources maximally due to tight control by its supervising agency. To Paper Y, having channels available for offering such subsidies may even be functional in releasing tensions between its journalists and the supervising agency. Journalists at Paper Y, therefore, may feel less deprived both professionally and financially. They find venues to report stories and to publish their articles; at the same time, they also receive payment for their reportage. As one reporter from Paper Y said in responding to my inquiry on their job satisfaction: "Paper Y is a nice place. You are not expected to do much here. Your pay is not high but decent, and for that amount of pay, you only need to work ten hours a week. In today's [City A], you cannot find any other place with this kind of combination. With all this free time, you can do many other things outside of the paper." Her colleague who was present during the conversation agreed with frequent nods of her head.

Weaving the web of subsidies constitutes the major portion of the improvised activities. It is both the goal and the substance of such activities. It originates from and reflects the source of real pressure on journalists and media organizations. At the same time, it also shows where the "center" of reform practices is located. Journalists' improvised activities are reconfiguring the social relationships based on which news is produced. Seeing and hearing the wheelings and dealings, one senses a bustling atmosphere in the media reforms. At the same time, one also senses the short-term and deal-based relationships produced. Still, these relationships provide early signs of alignment between media outlets and enterprises that could be a source of power that is, if not alternative to, at least somewhat distinct from that of the party hierarchy.

Reciprocity in Improvisation

While I was doing my fieldwork, an exposé of "the dark side" of the journalism profession came out. This book describes "paid journalism" (H. Wu 1995). The prevailing idea in City A at the time was that the community of Chinese journalists was suffering serious moral decay and was plagued by corruption. This exposé, in many people's minds, confirmed the impression that China's journalism reforms were "getting out of hand" (*luan*) and that media production was becoming a normless and lawless sphere. That is not my interpretation of the situation. As a matter of fact, in addition to the continued ideological control via the party apparatus and the bureaucratic control via the state regulatory agencies, such as the SPPA, other control mechanisms are present. One such mechanism consists of the norms and conventions the journalists share with their potential sources and sponsors.

A key to improvisation is building one's action on the norm of "reciprocity." In my fieldwork, I must take the opportunity to "reciprocate" in order to carry out my data gathering. Journalists apply this norm to managing their relationships with their potential sources and with the organizations to which they belong. Being able to "reciprocate" is an important indication of a social actor's status as a strategic player, that is, to being rationally calculating in choosing the means for a desired goal beyond a specific action setting. To reciprocate is to act based on "shared knowledge of perspectives of others and the interests underlying those perspectives" (Rucinski 1991:187). Such actions are always calculated within a shared interpretive framework (Berger and

Luckmann 1966; Goffman 1974). Numerous examples show the importance of this norm.

One day, I invited a seasoned young reporter from Paper X to join me for dinner. I told him that I wanted to "chat" with him on journalistic work. At the exact time of our appointment, he pulled up in a red Volkswagen. He carried a big sports bag in his right hand and a cellular phone in his left. Our conversation started with his hardware. He told me that when he bought this used car, his paper assisted him with an interest-free loan of 30,000 yuan (U.S. $8,000). The reason?

> Well, as reporters, we must be running around a lot. Sometimes, we need to get somewhere fast. Taking public transportation is out of the question because it's too crowded and too slow. How can we get timely news that way? We could take a taxi or one of our unit's cars. But our unit does not have so many cars. Sometimes, taxi drivers don't want to take you. . . . You know what [City A] taxi drivers are like. Our publisher basically said, "OK. I'll help you realize your dream of owning a car. The loan is interest free. If you take it, you must use the car to get news." It's a pretty good deal for both sides.

Similarly, to get wider and more timely coverage of breaking news stories, the paper supplies journalists with beepers and even gives some cellular phones, as was the case for my subject here. The beeper numbers of these selected reporters are printed on every issue of the newspaper under the name of "News Hotlines." The paper even designed a reward system (1,000 yuan for an especially big news story, 500 yuan for a big one, and so on) to encourage readers to tip their reporters about news. Do these measures actually work? In my interviews and my readings of the paper's yearbook, I encountered a number of stories of how the paper's reporters had beaten those at other papers in reporting unexpected news events.

This is one example of an intraorganizational manifestation of the reciprocity norm. This norm functions between a journalist and the newspaper organization at which the individual works. A different kind of organization-employee relationship could characterize reciprocity at this level. In my interviews with reporters from Paper Y, two of them almost used the exact words to express their frustration with the paper: "In this paper, you can't even make a long-distance call without getting permission first!" I had conversations with them separately. The story they told me was identical. Starting in 1994, due to a 13 percent decline in circulation and 40 percent increase in paper costs, Paper Y ran into severe financial difficulties. As a measure to "close the loopholes" in spending, the leadership decided to regulate the journalists' long-distance telephone calls. All the telephone sets with long-distance call access were concentrated in a few selected offices. A reporter who needed to make a long-distance call first had to fill out an application form and have the form approved by his or her department head. Although the reporters with whom I talked understood and accepted that every organization must have some managerial rules covering things such as costly long-distance calls, they felt "victimized" by the stiff managerial approach. They considered it vital to have unrestricted access to telecommunication channels to get timely news stories. The paper's managerial policies ought to facilitate the reporters' work and help them maintain a competitive edge in news coverage. Under what they considered "bureaucratic" management approach, they developed an ambivalence toward the paper. On the one hand, they felt frustrated over the lack of organizational support and a large enough news hole for them to become "big shots" in the profession. On the other hand, they were quite content to "stay put" with the paper because they had the benefit of working fewer than ten hours a week at a prestigious newspaper for about 1,000 yuan (roughly U.S. $120) a month.

The publisher and the editor in chief shared their journalists' understanding of the situation. Although they set up written policies restricting their reporters from writing for other papers, they told me, they did not want to enforce the policy seriously. They shared their reporters' frustration at not being able to print many newsworthy stories. They also appreciated the felt need of their journalists to have additional sources of income. Therefore, using the editor and publisher's own words, "We don't want to restrict our journalists too much, as long as they are not excessive."

Reciprocity is also a norm that characterizes how a paper or its journalists relate to other organizations or individuals. After Paper X started its weekly poll page, it allocated only an annual budget of 30,000 yuan (U.S. $8,000) for this page to operate. The paper had no polling capacity of its own. It had to contract polling agencies to conduct its polls or publish polls provided to it by commercial polling agencies. One day, when I was visiting the editorial office of this page, the editors were negotiating with a polling agency to conduct a poll for them. In my presence, a deal was struck between the two sides. The polling agency would conduct a poll with 1,000 randomly selected adult City A residents for 10 yuan (U.S. $1.20) per respondent, but the paper would provide all 1,000 copies of the questionnaire. The rate was far below the market level. The negotiation was taking place in a very informal atmosphere. The language used in the negotiation was simultaneously vague and specific. The polling agency claimed that, with that rate, they would not earn a penny. The only reason they would take on this project was for the newspaper to publish the results with an acknowledgment that their agency had carried out the fieldwork. City A by then was already crowded with various marketing research entities. This research agency was a latecomer and eager to establish some name recognition. The editor of the poll page, representing the paper in the negotiation, made an explicit promise that the agency's name would appear as stipulated. He did not specify, however, nor was he asked to specify, at which position on the page and in what type size or font the agency's name would appear. The manager from the agency, although promising quality control, did not specify how the agency would verify the results, nor was he asked to provide such specifications. The deal was struck with a handshake in front of one of the paper's deputy publishers, who gave his blessing. No paperwork was done, nor did anyone present ask for any paperwork.

I should make it clear that reciprocity here does not mean exchange interactions only, although such interactions best manifest the presence and actors' observations of the reciprocity norm. When the shared understandings of each other's perspective and the underlying interests were the basis for "good faith" negotiations, one party could reject the other party's offer without any harm being done. When an interaction failed because one party lacked "good faith" or an interaction was later reconstructed in a framework different from the original, the norm was considered violated. A couple of reporters told me, for example, about one reporter from a City A newspaper who wrote a piece for *Internal Reference,* a periodical circulated only among high-level party and government officials. The reporter in the story had joined a team of journalists to visit a northwestern province. On this "tour of duty," the local officials treated the large entourage of reporters with free transportation, lavish banquets, expensive departing gifts, and so on. After returning to City A, this reporter wrote a piece detailing the "extravagant treatment," criticizing both the local officials for providing the treatment and the reporters for accepting it and contrasting this treatment with the extreme poverty of the local peasants. My informants told me that they could not argue with this reporter on moral grounds, but they noted that he "was stinky" now in the journalism community because he had "betrayed" his peers. Similarly, those who push enterprises for financial deals also operate with a tacit agreement on the situation and their roles. Those who violated this agreement would see the collapse of one segment of their "web of subsidies," meaning they would not be able to develop any deal with the original partners or get exclusive information from the involved sources.

Reciprocity in improvised activities was revealed even more clearly in the source-journalist and sponsor-newspaper relationships. The extreme form is manifested in what has been called "paid journalism." In early August 1993, the Propaganda Ministry of the Central Committee of the Party and the SPPA joined forces with the *People's Daily,* the Xinhua News Agency, and the Ministry of Radio, Film, and Television to launch an unprecedented campaign against "paid journalism." No newspaper should seek financial sponsorship for its news or editorial page or section. No reporter or editor should solicit advertisement from a source. No newspaper should allocate advertising earning quotas to news and editorial departments. Things have changed somewhat since then.

Responses to this heavy-handed campaign, however, were varied. Each department in a paper, for example, was given a so-called independent budgeting right. It meant that a department would be allotted a fixed amount from the paper's overall budget. The department head was responsible for spending the money on journalists' bonuses, transportation, communication, compensation to contributing authors, and so on. This led each department to establish its own "small gold deposit" (*xiao jinku*) or private safe. In Paper V, every department has such a "gold deposit." If a news or an editorial department solicited sponsorship or advertisement for a given page, it would get a certain percentage of the commission fee, to be deposited in its "gold deposit." The advertising department would handle the actual transactions. The editorial department could distribute the money in its "gold deposit" to its members as additional bonuses; it could also use it to increase the rate of compensation to contributing authors, to organize department activities, and so on. One department head at Paper V said, "When our reporters' travel expenses can't be reimbursed by the paper, we reimburse them. We don't want to restrict our reporters." Journalists accept this organizational practice and continue to solicit ads and sponsorships for their own organizations. They share a clear understanding of the interests of the organization and its individual members and of the framework in which they could make a difference for both their organization and themselves. Similarly, the potential sources also understand the situation, and they continued to organize activities, news events, and press conferences and to send invitations to media organizations, frequently to individual reporters directly. The sources only changed the most blatant forms of their "subsidies." Now, instead of a "red packet" with a certain amount of cash, they reimburse the transportation and boarding expenses of journalists participating in their events, and they send material gifts to the journalists.

By practicing the norm of "reciprocity," journalists also develop a "web of facilitation." This term is used here to refer to something more sociological than the "web of subsidies." It refers to a particular mode of developing and using what Tuchman (1978) calls the "web of facticity." One journalist at Paper X, for example, told me that he and his colleagues found traffic police not very difficult to deal with, as most drivers in City A would claim. Very often, he could park his car in an illegal spot or make an illegal turn without receiving any fines. The reason? "We have cultivated a very good relationship with the city's traffic police." With this friendly relationship, he said, the reporters could move around and chase news quickly, despite the city's traffic nightmare.

In City A, I often heard journalists using the phrase "hao banshi," getting things done easily. They used this phrase when recounting whom they knew or who still "owed" them a favor. These people usually occupy some unique position or have access to those with direct control over vital resources such as transportation, communication, and capital. The journalists identify such professional "significant others" using phrases based on any kind of "special" prior contact, for example, being a relative, coming from the same city or province, having been to the same school, being a member of the same special project team, having had an important banquet together, having had a very memorable visit to a famous bar together, and so on. At this level, the fine distinctions that Western journalists and scholars tend to make, about reporters, sources, government officials and censors, all became blurred. Rather, all those involved were in the same social space to renew and strengthen their affective ties as well as to increase their deposits in the "savings account of favors." Getting things done was a means for such goals as well as a marker of this shared semiprivate social space, especially when those involved had to work out some "out of frame" (Goffman 1974) way of getting things done together. All these factors constitute the "web of facilitation"; they are situational and must be considered when improvising.

At Paper Y, according to the head of its advertising department, the major mechanism for attracting advertisers was to call upon the friends and friends of friends of department employees. That was also how the paper's circulation department facilitated circulation. Sometimes, a paper had to go an extra mile to extend such a "web of facilitation" to crucial areas. In order to gain active cooperation from the periodical circulation branch of City A Post Office,[14] for example, Paper Y offered the head of the branch a spot on its team visiting abroad. The paper's publisher told me: "We had to do that. Otherwise, they felt no obligation to improve our paper's circulation."

The necessity and the practice of establishing such a "web of facilitation" has led to specialization among journalists in "news net." Paper Y's specialty is covering sports. Its sports reporters each specialize in one sport: soccer, Ping-Pong, tennis, and so on. On the surface, such specialization is basically a news beat. In China, such specialization also means segmentation of the "news net" and of the "web of subsidies." When the reporter covering a beat was sick or not available for a story, the substitute reporter would have a very hard time getting information because he or she did not know the key sources or did not have a "savings account of favors" against those sources. In general, a journalist covering a beat establishes very close relationships with his or her sources (Meyers 1992), and it becomes very easy for the reporter to get inside information. This reporter also finds it very difficult to report stories critical of his or her regular sources because that would be construed as violating the shared trust and friendship held with them. Sometimes, a reporter would pass the information to a colleague, who would write the story. Most of the time, such stories would not be written.

Knowledgeable Actors

All these nonroutine activities are predicated on the condition that journalists as social actors develop their conceptions of the conditions of their activities and construct their discursive explanations or interpretations of their own activities (see Giddens 1984) through strategic uses of the available symbolic resources (see Pan 1997a).[15] One clear indication of Chinese journalists' knowledgeability is their extraordinary sensitivity to the symbolic markers of ideological legitimacy and cultural alternatives; they understand various key terms and symbolic expressions that can be used in their reform discourse to link their improvised news-making activities and the basic party press principles. Making such a link is a key step in legitimizing their nonroutine activities (see Berger and Luckmann 1966). Further, such knowledgeability means that Chinese journalists are able to reconstruct those "symbolic markers" of the party press institution in relation to the specific settings of their reform activities. I gathered evidence supporting this interpretation both from direct observation and from the circumstances of those observations.

My entry points to Paper X and Paper Y were opportunities for me to do some work for the papers based on my presumed knowledge of communication research and the media industry in the United States. My "subjects" were quick to recognize the cultural meaning of my "symbolic markers": I was affiliated with City A University, one of the most prestigious universities in China, and I had returned from abroad only recently with an advanced degree. Before I started my fieldwork, two of my journalist friends, both working for City A newspapers, warned me on separate occasions not to reveal my background as a researcher from abroad. I asked why that would be a concern. Remarkably, their explanations were identical: "If they know you just came back from abroad, they won't tell you anything." Taking their advice, I was prepared to reveal to my interviewees only my affiliation with City A University.

This scheme failed right from the beginning, however. On one cold afternoon in late January, I had just finished giving a group of sociologists at City A University a presentation on a survey study that I had worked on when a young man approached me with distinct eagerness. He introduced himself as a reporter from Paper X and told me that he had been intrigued by my presentation. To explain why, he took out a copy of the latest issue of Paper X and told me that he was one of the two editors of the special page on polls. With that introduction, I immediately became his source. He asked me a series of methodological questions related to interpreting survey findings, and he asked me to take a look at the paper and to give him my assessment of the reporting on surveys and polls as a form of journalism. When he learned that I was planning to visit his paper to interview some people there, he volunteered to help.

He was much more efficient than were my other informants. A week later, he called and told me that he had made all the arrangements for my visit. I went to his office in Paper X's building located in the southeastern corner of the city. The office was rather small, about 140 square feet. It contained four desks piled with old newspapers, magazines, opened letters, dictionaries, ashtrays, and a telephone. My informant showed me around the building, visited the other offices, and introduced me to other reporters and editors. When I was introduced to a young department head, he immediately presented his request in a no-nonsense style: "Teacher Pan, we need your help to design a market analysis. We know you are an expert in this area, so please don't say no." I was quite taken by their ability to make it plain to me that my need to interview them had created an opportunity for them to construct a reciprocity situation: I had been shown a gate into their "back region" (Ericson, Baranek, and Chan 1989) and a way to "earn" my access.

This eagerness to enlist me and their shrewdness in placing me in a situation of reciprocity are among the indications that the journalists were eager to tap into the symbolic resources not found in the traditional journalists' repertoire. In the "commandist system," the basis for legitimization of news and journalistic work consisted of nothing but the official interpretation of party policies and the official discourse on the tradition of "the revolutionary journalism" (see Tong 1994; T. Zhang 1992). Now, "audience needs," "market changes," "experiences from advanced foreign countries," and so on, could all become part of the basis for legitimizing certain practices.[16] The diversification of the symbolic resources is strongly associated with those in the cohort of journalists who entered the profession after the mid-1980s. One journalist from Paper X told me very proudly that most of his colleagues were in their mid-thirties or younger. Their new editor in chief was only thirty-three. They encountered an explosion of imported Western ideas while in college in the mid- and late 1980s. "Our knowledge base is very different from that of the old fellows," he said, "including those in your cohort, who were college students in the early 1980s. We call people in your cohort 'revolutionary old guards' [gemini lao ganbu]." This extremely self-conscious reporter claimed: "We are not limited by the old way of doing things. Frankly, we don't consider them as naturally given. I am interested in trying different things. That's what our party is doing, right? To reform, to do things no one has done before. People in my cohort have that edge."

I encountered numerous examples of journalists demonstrating both their knowledge of and their desire to know about journalistic practices in the West. Once after a working session on a readership survey, for example, a deputy publisher at Paper X asked me at the lunch table, "Now you know all about our paper. If you were to make a comparison, which American paper would it resemble?" Also at the lunch, this reporter-turned-manager asked me: "When you go back to the United States, would you please bring us market analysis materials by American papers? For example, USA Today, the New York Times. Or, better yet, such materials published by local metropolitan papers. We may find more similarities with them." On a different occasion, I was interviewing a seasoned reporter from the same paper in a hotel lobby. I asked him, "What is your ideal paper?" He asked me, "Are you asking me about my ideal paper in my ideal or my ideal paper in the present reality?" I was intrigued and said, "Both." He replied: "In the present reality, my ideal paper is our paper because it is the paper most appealing [to the market]. In my ideal, an ideal paper is a combination of the New York Times and USA Today. I'd like to have both the New York Times's authoritativeness and depth and USA Today's broad appeal and visual orientation."

Similarly, the editor in chief and the publisher of Paper Y frequently invoked their observations on foreign practices and their readings of some marketing and management books when explaining to me the measures and policies that they had decided on and implemented. Never in our conversations did they quote Marx, Mao, or the current party leaders, except Deng Xiaoping. Their symbolic resources, however, were much less diverse than those of journalists at Paper X and of the younger reporters and editors on their own paper. Although they were positioned much higher on the administrative hierarchy, and thus had more opportunities to visit abroad, to be exposed to government documents, and to meet with the high-level officials—whom they often referred to by first name (for example, Comrade Xiaoping) in their conversations with me—they were unable to drop references to Western media and events in the Western journalism profession as casually as did their younger colleagues. They showed, however, the same eagerness to learn about "market trends" and "audience needs." Similar to my experience at Paper X, when I was introduced to employees of Paper Y by a journalist friend, my informant in this paper, they also asked me to tell them about media operations and journalistic practices in the United States. Not long after our initial contact, they formally asked me to help them conduct a market analysis and organizational diagnosis. My mission, they told me, would be to discover what problems and opportunities they were facing and to provide specific recommendations to them on how to grasp the opportunities and to handle the problems.

Most of the younger journalists I encountered at these papers, the only exception being Paper U, had at least an undergraduate degree, and many of them even had graduate degrees, often from elite universities. Some of them had majored in journalism, but a majority of them had majored in other fields. Their credentials were quite different from those of the more senior journalists. In the older cohort, quite a few had worked as "amateur correspondents" (*yeyu tongxunyuan*) in local areas or work units or as bureaucrats in charge of party propaganda in local areas or work units. They tended to have a very different deposit of symbolic resources in their memories.

Paper U is the only party-organ paper that I examined. It recruits young people who worked as "amateur correspondents" or who just graduated from high school and sends them to City's Party College (*dang xiao*) to study for a period of time. They then return to the paper to work as journalists, while completing the requirements for a certificate equivalent to an undergraduate degree. These people were called "red kids" (*hong haizi*), a term reminiscent of "little red devils" (*hong xiaogui*) used during the revolution. A veteran journalist and department head at the paper said that the journalists who had gone through this process were "politically reliable" and better "tailored to the needs of the paper" than college graduates. He cited the paper's experience during the student uprising in 1989 as an example. During that time, he said, Paper U was the only paper in town that did not "commit political error." "We were under tremendous pressure. But our reporters stuck to the party's spirit." The only other organizations that have something similar to this recruitment venue are the *People's Daily* and Xinhua News Agency (to a lesser degree, the *China Daily*), which employ graduates of their own Journalism Institute and the Institute of Journalism Research affiliated with the Chinese Academy of Social Sciences.

Younger journalists also have knowledge resources to tap into for innovative news-making activities in their own work. Of the two young editors in charge of the poll-reporting page of Paper X, one has a degree in sociology and the other in demography. From their college curricula, they acquired the idea of the sample survey as a tool for data gathering. After becoming reporters, they realized that gathering data via surveys was not much different from the work of a journalist who observes an occurrence and interviews sources for information. One of them told me: "I know many Western media report polls frequently, particularly during elections. I want to make the sample survey a regular news-reporting tool and to make reporting of polls a regular feature of our paper." This young editor wrote a piece on reporting polls for the *Research Digest,* a newsletter circulated among the editorial staff of Paper X. In this short article, the author argues that polling is the best social science tool for bringing news closer to "truth" and objectivity. It is also a tool that enables newspapers to compete with television news.

During the time I was at Paper X, its poll page appeared once a week. The topics were all "benign" ideologically and politically. Examples include: "What books are [City A] residents reading?" "What are the experiences of becoming a father for the first time?" and "Who are the people whom today's youth admire most?" These topics were all carefully chosen not to reveal any hint of opposition to the official ideology. At the same time, the poll page showed its editors' innovative use of polls in news making: In every issue of this page, they printed a small box entitled "Poll Methodology," with a brief description of the sampling procedure, the mode of interviewing, and the margin of error. They also gave the page a catchy slogan: "We offer quantified facts to the public." In a recent book edited by the deputy chief editor of the paper, one of the editors of this poll page proudly quotes a professor at City A University as saying that Paper X's reportage of polls is "quite professional." This editor duly mentions that this professor has a Ph.D. in sociology from the University of Michigan.

A number of journalists expressed their acquiescence in the current situation and the progress in reforms. An illustrative case would be journalists' perceptions of and attitudes toward the issue of establishing a press law. Establishing a press law had been on the reform agenda for about fifteen years. During the latter half of the 1980s, it was a major issue of ideological conflict between the "conservatives" and "liberals" within the party and between the party and journalists (see Cheek 1989). The journalists that I talked to were ambivalent about this issue. Some of them felt that a press law would be irrelevant to their work because there were already other laws (for example, the legal stipulation on libel) and mechanisms to control journalistic work. They saw no need for another one. Many also felt that it was actually good not to have a press law under the current conditions because journalists would have more freedom to try new things without any codified rules to restrict their "reform" activities. The general consensus among those to whom I talked was based on two points: Nominally, they all agreed that eventually legal stipulations ought to be made to guarantee press freedom and to restrict the press from engaging in "illegal and unethical practices." Practically, they much preferred to deal with those reform activities that were doable and could bring immediate tangible results rather than those on "systemic change issues."

Very often, claims of ideological consistency with the party were expressed in a more pragmatic tone. When I was first introduced to the director of the news department at Paper X by my self-introduced informant, this young director expressed his welcome and concern to me. He said:

> We usually don't like to be in the spotlight. We are particularly anxious about being visited by people from abroad. We had sometimes been referred to by foreign correspondents as "an oppositional paper." That's just not true. We are not oppositional or even alternative to the party and the government. You can't reach that conclusion just because our paper is "hot" in the market. Saying that really puts us in a very difficult position.

From this complaint, he revealed to me both his sensitivity to the subtleties in the paper's political and ideological environment and his genuine belief that it was possible to be "hot" in the market and to "maintain consistency with the party," the dual requirements explicitly expressed in the official statements (Liang 1992). One of his associates elaborated on this: "How can a paper stand on its feet? To satisfy the 'two sides'—the officials and the public [er lao manyi—lao ganbu, lao baixin].[17] It's hard, but it's possible, and it's necessary." With journalists' frustration over having to "serve two masters" (Polumbaum 1990) in mind, I asked: "What if the two have different assessments of what you've done? Then which one would you choose?" He hesitated for only a second and then said, "The public [*lao baixing*], because our paper has to survive in the market." To substantiate his claim, he went on to give me the statistics showing how much their paper relied on newsstand sales and individual subscriptions. He contrasted that with party organs, which even today still rely primarily on institutional subscriptions or individual subscriptions paid for by work units as part of employees' fringe benefits.

To say that journalists today are in general more acquiescent toward the current situation as compared with those interviewed in the late 1980s by Polumbaum (1990) does not mean that they are more content with their working environment. Clearly, many journalists do feel that there is now a more open setting in which they can engage in innovative activities, ranging from innovative news-gathering techniques and writing styles to ways of connecting journalistic work with the other sectors of society. As one veteran reporter from Paper X said, "Job autonomy? I have complete autonomy. I can experiment with various kinds of news-gathering and -writing techniques. Of course, there are areas that I shouldn't get into. I don't want to get into them. There is no point." Obviously, he felt that in the local environment of his paper, he already had a sufficiently large space to explore. Many journalists from other papers expressed similar sentiments.

The space for innovative activities and the forbidden areas (*jin qu*) in news production are recognized simultaneously. Talking about press freedom, job autonomy, press law, institutional transformation, and so on, risks stepping on political land mines. The consequences of that can be grave, as practicing journalists have clearly seen since the Tiananmen incident. They recognize that and, consequently, would rather keep themselves occupied with exploring the safe domains. They also try to legitimize the party press system in new terms. One veteran editor from Paper U said: "This is the party's organ. It does not belong to you, nor does it belong to me. The party owns it. Of course, the owner wants to say whatever he wants. We are only working for him." A veteran editor from Paper W said: "All media belong to the party. The party is the boss, we are just employees. Employees take orders from the boss. There is nothing unusual about that." Paper V and Paper Z, because they are only nominally supervised by the supervising agencies (*zhuguan danwei*), practically operate as nonorgan papers. At these papers, journalists mostly work silently on their own assignments and rarely show up in their offices. When they do show up, their offices are filled with chitchat about buying cars, learning how to use computers, strange requirements by their children's kindergartens, outrageous price tags for some brand-name products, and so on. When I brought up issues like press freedom, press law, and system transformation in our conversations, the most common reaction was the question, "What's the use?" Then, the journalists would say, "What I am doing now is real." Clearly, journalists improvise their activities based on their knowledge of the institutional parameters and engage in discursive practices to legitimate their improvised activities with the officially recognized principles.

Discussion and Conclusion

In this chapter, I presented my interpretive account of how City A journalists improvise reform activities in news production. I organized my account around four major theoretical issues: the changing routines of news production through improvisation, the reconfiguration of the social relationships in news production through such improvised activities, the reciprocity norm that regulates improvisation, and journalists' strategic awareness of the institutional parameters for improvisation. This analysis shows that the social and institutional space opened up by the reform discourse remains limited and fragile. In this space, journalists must be able to link their activities to the official ideological principles. The strategy of making such linkages is to employ symbolic resources available to localize the setting in which journalists conduct their reform practices (Giddens 1984; Pan 1997a). Whenever such linkage fails, journalists must be able to modify their practices and to justify their modifications. Improvisation thus represents a unique mode of interaction between individuals' actions and the institutional locale of these actions. Journalists' improvised activities also help deconstruct and reconstruct China's journalism institution. Viewed in this theoretical context, my account certainly does not suggest a trajectory of reforms that can be characterized in evolutionary terms (see Giddens 1984 for a critique of the evolutionary mode of conceptualizing social change). Rather, my depiction shows the reforms to be a multifaceted dynamic of the commandist journalism institution, giving incentives to and incorporating nonroutine activities and to changing itself in China.

An empirically grounded premise for my study is that China's journalism reforms are being carried out under continued Communist control. By all accounts, the overall framework of the commandist media institution remains unchallenged or, rather, is excluded from being challenged (Yuan 1996). Given this precondition, the reforms are carried out as collaborative efforts involving both the journalists and the Communist control apparatuses (Pan 1998). They jointly explore what may work, that is, what market-related mechanisms and practices are justifiable within the party press framework and suitable for incorporation. The collaborative feature of the reforms became increasingly apparent after June 4, 1989. It is out of pragmatic necessity for both practicing journalists and the party apparatuses.

Such exploration is not guided by some known blueprint of a future system or journalistic institution. Further, journalists and the party bear very different orientations because of their different institutional roles (see Blumler and Gurevitch 1981; Polumbaum 1990), resulting in tensions that both motivate and constrain the collaboration. As a result, journalists design, implement, and justify their activities in a unique institutional locale that features rigidity, exclusion zones, and uncertainty. They have to be microsituational, opportunistic, and ideologically localized and particularized. These are the distinct features of improvisation. This chapter interprets my fieldwork observations to explicate the concept of improvisation as a key feature of China's journalism reforms. The concept helps us place some order on the seemingly chaotic and sometimes erratic reforms. It may also help shed some light on the swings back and forth between the loosening and the tightening of controls in the reforms (Chan 1995).

Journalists' improvised activities are changing the "map of reality" in China's journalism institution. They are also changing the "map of meaning" of journalism itself. To a large extent, the frequent shuttling of journalists among news making, advertising, public relations, business adventure, and political climbing has seriously affected the parameters that define "news" and "journalism." In this account, the trajectory of the changes associated with the reforms is much more murky or less directionally specific than other concepts, such as commercialization and marketization, would suggest. My analysis also suggests a path of change with a much less clearly defined pattern and destination than is implied by concepts such as "peaceful evolution." My analysis depicts a dynamic process of the reforms constituted by situated activities. Through these activities, the commandist system generates and incorporates some nonroutine activities. Along the way, the system changes itself. To this extent, I must agree with my journalist subjects that the political discourse on the principles of press freedom and the overall design of an "ideal media institution" has very limited relevance to what they have been doing. What they actually do and how they interpret what they do constitute the essence of the journalism reforms.

Although this chapter focuses on China's journalism reforms, my interpretation is cast in the broader theoretical terms of social change. The theoretical position that I have taken is that analyzing social change means examining the dynamic of social actors interacting with the existing institutions. These practices are situated in specific institutional locales. These practices are embedded with symbolic expressions that simultaneously "construct, deconstruct, and reconstruct" the existing institutions (see Leach 1976; Giddens 1984; Lincoln 1989), that is, the very institutional settings in which they are carried out. Placed in this framework, China's journalism reforms illustrate a unique pattern of social change. Analyzing journalism reforms helps to illuminate our understanding of this particular mode of social change.

Notes

1. This chapter is part of a larger project on China's journalism reforms. The fieldwork was partially supported by the New Recruit Research Fund from the Faculty of Social Science, the Chinese University of Hong Kong. The project was also made possible with institutional support from the Annenberg School for Communication, University of Pennsylvania, and the Institute of Sociology and Anthropology, Peking University. I wish to express my gratitude to both institutions and, in particular, to Dean Kathleen Jamieson of the Annenberg School for Communication. I also wish to thank Professors C. C. Lee and Mike Curtin for their thoughtful and detailed comments on an earlier version.

2. The predecessor of SPPA was the General Press Bureau under the central government, established on October 19, 1949. The agency was eliminated in 1952 as the party completed its construction of the commandist system (see Yu 1993).

3. All these figures come from *Chinese Journalism Yearbook* (1994, 1995). The specific figure for the profitable newspapers is hard to come by, partly due to the lack of a reliable mechanism for gathering such data. Three years ago, the officials from the SPPA put the figure of profitable newspapers at one-third of all registered papers (see Liang 1992). But the reliability of such an estimate is in serious doubt, not only because no number was ever presented but also because no authoritative accounting or classification frameworks have been established for describing the newspapers' financial status. Most of the newspapers in China still receive subsidies directly or indirectly in the form of state-owned office space, employee housing, equipment, and so on.

4. This paragraph is based on my paper on alternative symbolic resources and their uses in China's journalism reforms. For more complete arguments, see Pan (1997a).

5. For the purpose of protecting the anonymity of the journalists whom I interviewed and the media organizations that I visited, I will use City A to represent the city and the letters U to Z to represent the newspapers that I studied. Some materials that might lead to identification of the newspapers or journalists will be omitted or presented in summary terms.

6. I was told by various journalist friends that it would be very difficult for me to get inside any media organization because news organizations were considered highly politically sensitive. The situation became even more sensitive toward the last season of 1995 after Party Secretary General Jiang Zemin had made his "talking politics" speech.

7. Paper U is organizationally integrated with the city's only evening paper. Together, the organization's advertising revenue is 19.735 million yuan (about U.S. $2.47 million) (see Chen and Huang 1997). Based on my interview, about 60 percent of that figure came from the evening paper; Paper U by itself earned about 40 percent.

8. China's administrative hierarchy has four basic levels: *bu*, the ministry in the central government or its equivalent; *ju*, the department immediately under the ministries; *chu*, the departmental branch; and *ke*, sections in each departmental branch. This hierarchy is used to classify all organizational units. Each level is associated with specific authority and privileges. Applied to news media organizations, it means different levels of access to news sources and different degrees of authoritativeness. Formal central government activities, for example, such as National Congress meetings, presidential meetings with foreign heads of state, and so on, can only be covered by the journalists from the *bu*-level media. (This restriction has become more relaxed now.) International sports competitions, such as the Olympics, held overseas can only be covered by correspondents from the *bu*- or *ju*-level media organizations. This administrative hierarchy also means that officials of the central government and Party Committee, especially the officials of the Propaganda Ministry of the Central Party Committee, pay more attention to news coverage by the media at the *bu* and *ju* levels.

9. Any empirical study is limited by the cases selected. The issue of representativeness is not just a statistical matter of selecting a random sample, nor is it just a matter of empirical "external validity." Rather, it is also a theoretical issue of "constructing a case" that will situate and contextualize one's theoretical interpretations in concrete terms (see Ragin and Becker 1992). Applied to my study, an important consideration is whether I have chosen the cases that were born and continue to operate within the commandist system and at the same time have made significant moves into market. These are the cases that potentially provide the richest evidence of the unique mode of change that I intend to describe. The more traditionally influential papers, for example, the *People's Daily,* and the newly emerged commercial papers, for example, the *Shopping Guide,* will not serve my purpose. For my broader concerns, I wish to study those newspapers that fall into other cells of my three-by-two matrix of newspapers.

10. A similar practice was depicted in a recent case study of *Guangzhou Daily,* the party-organ paper of the capital city of Guangdong Province (Xie 1996). The newspaper recently was granted the permission to form the first "group corporation," meaning it received official blessing not only to publish additional officially registered newspapers and periodicals in addition to its main daily paper but also to diversify into other businesses, such as real estate, transportation, advertising, and so on.

11. Although China claims to have no censorship system, all media organizations are subject to two types of reviews, one internal and the other external. Usually, the internal review takes place before the publication. In a newspaper organization, a news

article is first reviewed by the head of the department responsible for the page on which the article is to appear; it is then reviewed as part of that page by the deputy chief editor, whose responsibility includes overseeing the page's production; and, finally, it is reviewed by the editor in chief or his or her substitute on duty on a particular day. For some important or in-depth reporting articles, the internal review process begins at the point of the article's conception. When a reporter conceives an idea for a big story, he or she must pitch the idea to his or her department head. Occasionally, the reporter could pitch the idea to the responsible deputy chief editor or even to the editor in chief directly, but that would be quite unusual and would reflect as well as cause bad feelings between the reporter and his or her department head. Typically, the department head would approve the idea and propose it in turn to the deputy chief editor. In exceptional cases, the editor in chief would need to approve a story proposal. The most important task of the three-layered internal review is to "keep the political gate" (*ba guan*), that is, to maintain political and ideological "correctness," or, to some, "safety." The external review is much less routinized. It is normally a postpublication review. NQW, the Department of Propaganda of the Party's Central Committee, the Ministry of Radio, TV, and Film, and the SPPA all have formed review groups that review the materials released by selected media outlets in China and present their findings to the decision makers in each of the agencies.

12. It is China's folk custom that elders give out small amounts of cash wrapped in red paper to children on Chinese New Year or on their birthdays. Many enterprises or organizations also pay journalists a certain amount of cash, placed in either unaddressed envelopes or wrapped in paper, as a gift. A cash payment of this type is called a "red packet."

13. The question asked here is much narrower than that concerning the impact of Tuchman's "web of facticity." With that concept, Tuchman (1978) is concerned with the processes of constructing social reality, that is, the processes through which "social facts" reported in the news and the empirical criterion employed by journalists to identify such facts are determined in various social relationships relevant to news production. In other words, those facts and principles are not determined by journalists or the news media in a context free of such social relationships. Editorial autonomy refers to the extent to which journalists make decisions concerning news production without any political or economic interference driven by the special interests of a particular party or organization.

14. In China, traditionally, all periodicals and newspapers were circulated via the post office. The Ministry of Posts and Telecommunications had a monopoly over the print media circulation. This monopoly was broken somewhat with the emergence of newsstands in major cities. Most newspapers, however, still rely primarily on the post office for their circulation. The SPPA forbids most party organs or organ papers to be sold on newsstands.

15. The concepts and theoretical arguments are more fully elaborated elsewhere (Pan 1997a). The types of symbolic resources and the patterns of using them in journalistic practices constitute an important part of our understanding of the journalism reform.

16. It is useful to note here that when "experiences from foreign countries" were referred to in official and nonofficial discourses, very often, two adjectives, "advanced" and "good," were used interchangeably, implying strongly both the linear evolutionary framework in comparing China with "foreign countries" and the value judgment of the result of such comparisons. Further, it was taken for granted that "foreign countries" here referred only to the advanced capitalist nations, primarily the United States.

17. The original phrase is "satisfying two 'olds,'" meaning the "old officials" and the "old one hundred family names," that is, the public. The term "old officials" here was used to refer to those conservatives within the party, represented by the retired octogenarians.

Bibliography

Anagnost, Ann Stasia. 1985. "Hegemony and the Improvisation of Resistance: Political Culture and Popular Practice in Contemporary China." Ph.D. diss., University of Michigan.

Bennett, W. Lance, Lynne A. Gressett, and William Halton. 1985. "Repairing the News: A Case Study of the News Paradigm." *Journal of Communication* 35:50-68.

Berger, Peter L., and Thomas Luckmann. 1966. *The Social Construction of Knowledge: A Treatise in the Sociology of Knowledge.* New York: Anchor.

Berkowitz, Dan. 1992. "Non-Routine News and Newswork: Exploring a What-a-Story." *Journal of Communication* 42:82-94.

Bocock, Robert. 1986. *Hegemony.* Chichester: Ellis Horwood.

Chan, Joseph Man. 1993. "Commercialization without Independence: Trends and Tensions of Media Development in China." In J. Cheng and M. Brosseau, eds., *China Review 1993.* Hong Kong: Chinese University Press.

———. 1995. "Calling the Tune without Paying the Piper: The Reassertion of Media Controls in China." In Lo Chi Kin, Suzanne Pepper, and Tsui Kai Yuen, eds., *China Review 1995.* Hong Kong: Chinese University Press.

Cheek, Timothy. 1989. "Redefining Propaganda: Debates on the Role of Journalism." *Issues and Studies* 25:47-74.

Chen, Huailin, and Huang Yu. 1997. "The Uneven Development in Mainland China Media Commercialization" ("Zhongguo dalu meijie shangyehua de feijunheng fazhan"). *Mass Communication Research* 53:191-208.

Chinese Journalism Yearbook Press. 1995. *Chinese Journalism Yearbook 1994.* Beijing: Chinese Journalism Yearbook Press (in Chinese).

———. 1996. *Chinese Journalism Yearbook 1995.* Beijing: Chinese Journalism Yearbook Press (in Chinese).

Chu, Leonard L. 1994. "Continuity and Change in China's Media Reform." *Journal of Communication* 44:4-21.

D'Andrade, Roy. 1986. "Three Scientific Worldviews and the Covering Law Model." In Donald W. Fiske and Richard A. Shweder, eds., *Metatheory in Social Science.* Chicago: University of Chicago Press.

Ericson, Richard V., Patricia M. Baranek, and Janet B. L. Chan. 1989. *Negotiating Control: A Study of News Sources.* Toronto: University of Toronto Press.

Fishman, Mark. 1980. *Manufacturing the News.* Austin: University of Texas Press.

Gandy, Oscar H. 1982. *Beyond Agenda Setting: Information Subsidies and Public Policy.* Norwood, N.J.: Ablex.

Gans, Herbert J. 1980. *Deciding What's News: A Study of CBS Evening News, NBC Nightly News, Newsweek, and Time.* New York: Vintage.

Geertz, Clifford. 1973. *The Interpretation of Cultures.* New York: Basic Books.

Gergen, Kenneth J. 1986. "Correspondence versus Autonomy in the Language of Understanding Human Action." In Donald W. Fiske and Richard A. Shweder, eds., *Metatheory in Social Science.* Chicago: University of Chicago Press.

Giddens, Anthony. 1984. *The Constitution of Society: Outline of the Theory of Structuration.* Berkeley: University of California Press.

Gitlin, Todd. 1980. *The Whole World Is Watching: Mass Media in the Making and Unmaking of the New Left.* Berkeley: University of California Press.

Goffman, Erving. 1974. *Frame Analysis: An Essay on the Organization of Experience.* New York: Harper and Row.

Gramsci, Antonio. 1971. *Selections from the Prison Notebooks.* Q. Hoare and G. Nowell Smith, eds. and trans. London: Lawrence and Wishart.

Hall, Stuart. 1980. "Encoding/Decoding." In S. Hall, A. Hobson, A. Lowe, and P. Willis, eds., *Culture, Media, Language: Working Papers in Cultural Studies, 1972–1979.* London: Hutchinson.

Hallin, D. C. 1986. *The Uncensored War: The Media and Vietnam.* New York: Oxford University Press.

Hu, Yaobang. 1985. "On the Party's Journalism Work" ("Guanyu dang de xinwen shiye: zai zhonggong zhongyang shujichu huiyi shang de jianghua"). Speech delivered at the Chinese Communist Party Central Committee Secretariat, February 8, and published in *People's Daily,* April 14.

———. 1996. Address at the *Liberation Daily,* published in *Journalism Front* (February):3–4.

Huang, Yu. 1994. "Peaceful Evolution: The Case of Television Reform in Post-Mao China." *Media, Culture and Society* 16:217–41.

Jiang, Zeming. 1993. "The Frontier of Propaganda and Thoughts Is Extremely Important for Our Party" ("Xuanchuan sixiang zhanxian shi women dang de yitiao jiqi zhongyao de zhanxian"). *Chinese Journalism Yearbook 1993.* Beijing: China Social Science Press.

Leach, Edmund. 1976. *Culture and Communication: The Logic by which Symbols Are Connected.* Cambridge: Cambridge University Press.

Lee, Chin-Chuan. 1990. "Mass Media: Of China and about China." In Chin-Chuan Lee, ed., *Voices of China: The Interplay of Politics and Journalism.* New York: Guilford.

———. 1994. "Ambiguities and Contradictions: Issues in China's Changing Political Communication." *Gazette* 53:7–21.

Li, Liangrong. 1995. "Reflection and Projection of the Fifteen-Year Journalism Reforms" ("Shiwu nian lai xinwen gaige de huigu yu zhanwang"). *Journalism University* (Spring):3–8.

Liang, Heng. 1992. "On Newspapers Getting into the Market" ("Lun baozhi zouxiang shichang"). *Reporters* 12:10–13.

Lincoln, Bruce. 1989. *Discourse and the Construction of Reality: Comparative Studies of Myth, Ritual, and Classification.* New York: Oxford University Press.

Liu, Jianming. 1991. *Macro Journalism [hongguan xinwenxue].* Beijing: Chinese People's University Press.

Liu, Weidong. 1993. "News Marketization and Policy Responses." *Journalism Knowledge* (November):15–17 (in Chinese).

Maltese, John Anthony. 1994. *Spin Control.* 2nd ed. Chapel Hill: University of North Carolina Press.

McManus, John. 1994. *Market-Driven Journalism: Let the Citizens Beware?* Thousand Oaks, Calif.: Sage.

Meyers, Marian. 1992. "Reporters and Beats: The Making of Oppositional News." *Critical Studies in Mass Communication Research* 9:75–90.

Murdock, Graham, and Peter Golding. 1977. "Capitalism, Communication and Class Relations." In James Curran, Michael Gurevitch, and Janet Woollacott, eds., *Mass Communication and Society.* London: Edward Arnold.

Pan, Zhongdang. 1997a. "Alternative Symbolic Resources and Their Patterns in Mainland China's Journalism Reforms" ("Zhongguo dalu xinwen gaige zhong fuhao ziyuan de tihuan ji xingtai"). *Mass Communication Research* 54:113–39.

———. 1997b. "Institutional Reconfiguration in China's Journalism Reforms." *Journalism and Communication Research* 3:62–80 (in Chinese).

———. 1998. "Venturing into Unknowns with Bounded Innovations: Institutional Reconfigurations in China's Journalism Reforms." Paper given at International Conference on Twenty Years of China's Reforms, Hong Kong, December 12–13.

Polumbaum, Judy. 1990. "The Tribulations of China's Journalists after a Decade of Reform." In Chin-Chuan Lee, ed., *Voices of China: The Interplay of Politics and Journalism.* New York: Guilford.

———. 1994. "Striving for Predictability: The Bureaucratization of Media Management in China." In Chin-Chuan Lee, ed., *China's Media, Media's China.* Boulder, Colo.: Westview.

Przeworski, Adam, and Henry Teune. 1970. *The Logic of Comparative Social Inquiry.* New York: Wiley.

Ragin, Charles C., and Howard S. Becker. 1992. *What Is a Case? Exploring the Foundations of Social Inquiry.* New York: Cambridge University Press.

Ransome, Paul. 1992. *Antonio Gramsci: A New Introduction.* New York: Harvester Wheatsheaf.

Rucinski, Dianne. 1991. "The Centrality of Reciprocity to Communication and Democracy." *Critical Studies in Mass Communication* 8:184–94.

Schudson, Michael. 1991. "The Sociology of News Production Revisited." In Michael Gurevitch and James Curran, eds., *Mass Communication and Society*. London: Arnold.

Song, Keming. 1994. "China's News Media Control System and the Responsibilities of the Editor-in-Chief of a Newspaper" ("Woguo xinwen shiye guanli tizhi he baoshe zongbianji zhize"). *Reporters* 2:7–10.

Sztompka, Piotr. 1993. *The Sociology of Social Change*. Oxford: Blackwell.

Tong, Bing. 1993. "Market Economy: A New Issue for Chinese Journalism" ("Shichang jingji: zhongguo xinwenjie de xin keti"). *Journalism Knowledge* (March):4–7.

———. 1994. *Main Body and Mouthpiece (Zhuti yu houshe)*. Henan: Henan People's Press.

Tuchman, Gaye. 1978. *Making News: A Study of Social Construction of Reality*. New York: Free Press.

Whyte, Martin. 1989. "Evolutionary Changes in Chinese Culture." In C. E. Morrison and R. F. Dernberger, eds., *Asia-Pacific Report 1989: Focus — China in the Reform Era*. Honolulu: East-West Center Press.

Williams, Raymond. 1973. "Base and Superstructure in Marxist Cultural Theory." *New Left Review* 82:3–16.

Wu, Guoguang. 1994. "Command Communication: The Politics of Editorial Formulation in the *People's Daily*." *China Quarterly* 137 (Summer):194–211.

Wu, Haimin. 1995. *Gold-Based Journalism (Jinyuan xinwen)*. Beijing: Huayi Press.

Xie, Jun. 1996. "The Significance of *Guangzhou Daily* Forming the First Newspaper Group Corporation in China" ("Guangzhou ribao zujian Zhongguo neilu shoujia baoye jituan de yiyi"). Paper presented at the Conference on Communication and Economic Development, Hong Kong, May 2–5.

Yu, Guoming. 1993. *An Examination of Chinese Journalism Institution — the Real World Motivating Forces and Future Direction of China's Journalism Reforms (Zhongguo xinwen shiye toushi — zhongguo xinwen gaige de xianshi dongyin he weilai zouxiang)*. Henan: Henan People's Press.

Yuan, Qingming. 1996. *The Existing Journalistic Views and News Media since China's Reform (Zhongguo gaigekaifang yilai di jiding xinwen guannian yu xinwenxue, xinwen meijie)*. Unpublished manuscript, Department of Journalism and Communication, Chinese University of Hong Kong.

Zelizer, Barbie. 1993. "Journalists as Interpretive Communities." *Critical Studies in Mass Communication* 10:219–37.

Zhang, Tao. 1992. *A History of Journalism in the People's Republic of China (Zhonghua remin gongheguo xinwen shiye shi)*. Beijing: Economic Daily Press.

Zhang, Xiaogang. 1993. "The Market versus the State: The Chinese Press since Tiananmen." *Journal of International Affairs* 47:195–221.

4

Chinese Communist Party Press in a Tug-of-War

A Political-Economy Analysis
of the Shenzhen Special Zone Daily

ZHOU HE

The Chinese Communist Party press is experiencing a tug-of-war, pulled in different directions by the forces of politics and those of an emerging market economy. Such a war, often unconsciously and involuntarily fought, is dragging the party press to unfamiliar terrain, shaking its traditional footing, commanding a new press configuration of politics and economics, and leading to new and ambiguous press roles.

This chapter explores the interplay of the often inherently antagonistic forces in the Chinese Communist Party press, focusing on the *Shenzhen Special Zone Daily*, a Communist Party newspaper based in China's first "capitalist lab." Using a political-economy perspective and a variety of research methods, this chapter examines this institution's management structure, intramedia competition, advertising operation, content, and the perspectives of journalists. Basing my argument on a five-mode tug-of-war conceptual framework, I maintain that the dynamics created by the war are gradually converting the party press into a "Party Publicity Inc."

Changing Reality and a Paradigm Shift

Despite its unquestionable political affiliation and manifest ideological orientation, the Chinese Communist Party press has undergone some gradual but significant changes.

FINANCIAL SELF-SUFFICIENCY

All the media organizations, run directly by the Communist Party or by various state offices, are voluntarily engaged in or forced into marketization. While playing the tune of the party-state, these organizations get only minimum or no subsidies from the party-state (Chan 1995; Hong 1998). Even such mouth-pieces of the Communist Party Central Committee as the *People's Daily* and Xinhua News Agency are pressured to be financially self-sufficient (He 1993a). As a result, a large portion of the major party-owned news organizations has become self-sufficient in one way or another.

EMERGENCE OF MEDIA EMPIRES

In the process of marketization, several party- or state-run media organizations have become financial giants, equivalent in wealth and financial power to some of their Western corporate counterparts. In 1997, for example, the *Xinmin Evening News* garnered RMB 613 million yuan (U.S. $73 million) in advertising revenue; the *Guangzhou Daily* under the Guangzhou Municipal Communist Party Committee made RMB 582 million yuan (U.S. $67 million) from its advertising revenue (Diamond 1997). In the same year, several party-owned newspapers, such as the *People's Daily,* the *Nanfang Daily,* the *Liberation Daily,* the *Beijing Daily,* and the *Shenzhen Special Zone Daily,* made huge revenues that ranged from RMB 100 million yuan (U.S. $12 million) to RMB 197 million yuan (U.S. $23.7 million) (Chen 1996). These media organizations are not only selling their readers to advertisers but also undertaking a variety of businesses, ranging from on-line data services to real-estate speculations (He 1993a; Chen and Lee 1998). In many ways, they are growing into "empires," similar to some of their Western counterparts in their early years of expansion.

A TREND TOWARD DEPOLITICIZATION

Although political propagation has remained the priority of the party press, there has been a trend toward depoliticization marked by soft ideological preaching (Lee 1994). The type of arm-twisting indoctrination typical of the party press for more than thirty years has gradually faded to secondary or tertiary places. On the rise has been what Chang, Wang, and Chen (1994) would call "social knowledge," which is more diversified in worldviews and softer on ideology. Another sign of depoliticization, if viewed in light of the entire press in China, is the dwindling position of the party newspapers in the industry relative to the growth of other types of publications. In 1978, party newspapers made up 76 percent of all the 186-strong newspaper industry, but in 1996 they accounted for only 17 percent of the 2,200-strong press (*Chinese Journalism Yearbook* 1997).

INCREASING RESPONSIVENESS TO THE AUDIENCE

The party press has become more responsive to the readers. It has increased the scope of coverage and provided information that may appeal to the audience, such as economic news, news on science and technologies, sports news, and social news. It has also extended its interaction with the audience through feedback and audience participation (Zhao 1998).

REDEFINED ROLES

Although the party leadership has consistently defined the party press as a mouthpiece of the party, media organizations and individual journalists have made sporadic efforts to redefine the roles of the press. In the late 1980s, according to several nationwide surveys, Chinese journalists downplayed the mouthpiece role and saw their most important roles as (1) an information provider; (2) a check on political power; and (3) an entertainment provider (People's University 1989; Journalism Research Institute and Capital Journalism Association 1988). Another national survey has found that Chinese journalists today variously regard the press's information role, correlation role, mouthpiece role, and "watchdog" role as most important (C. Chen et al. 1995). Although the "mouthpiece role" has been found to be reemphasized, other roles have remained fairly strong (Zhu et al. 1997).

ERODED PROFESSIONAL ETHICS

Professional ethics have been seriously eroded by the power of the profession, by money, or by a combination of the two. Journalists nationwide have been found to openly accept "payola," solicit bribes, trade news space for material benefits, speculate in stocks, publish paid news, or produce what Polumbaum (1994) calls "junk-food journalism" (see also He 1993a). Despite the central leadership's widely publicized campaigns against "paid news," journalistic ethics have continued to erode — and have become the thorniest issue in the press.

INCREASED NEWS HOLE AND ADVERTISING SPACE

In the past, only the flagship *People's Daily* published eight pages every day, and all other papers published only four pages or fewer. Today, eight to twenty-two pages have become the norm for even the municipal party newspapers. This increased news hole has demanded more content. On the other hand, the increased space has provided a vehicle for the party press to ride on the rapidly rising tide of advertising expenditures in the country, which have risen from RMB 73 million yuan (U.S. $8.8 million) in 1983 to RMB 46.2 billion yuan (U.S. $5.4 billion) in 1997 (*China Industry and Commerce Management Yearly* 1998).

ESCALATING COMPETITION

In a generally monopolistic media market where entry is strictly restricted for political reasons, an escalating competition has occurred both within and without the industry. The party newspapers now must compete not only with the increasingly popular electronic media but also with "nonparty newspapers" and with fellow party papers for circulation, advertising revenue, and even newsprint. The competition is so fierce in some cities with multiple media outlets that all competitors have felt the sting and have employed all kinds of promotional techniques, including kickbacks, free subscriptions, lottery drawings, freebies, free evening papers, and even administrative orders (He 1993a, 1995; Chan 1993).

ACCELERATED CONTROL–RELAXATION CYCLE

Although the cycle of intermittent control and relaxation has been a constant feature of Chinese politics and of the party press, the time span of this cycle has obviously shortened, and the scope of controls has been intensified in recent years. In the Mao era, this cycle occurred once every seven to eight years. In the post-Mao age, it happened about every two to three years. Over the past few years, this cycle has become almost an annual occurrence, affecting not only the press but also the normally more privileged circle of arts and literature (He 1994).

All these changes have gradually transformed the Chinese Communist Party press from a pure mouthpiece or "transmission belt" into a publicity enterprise of its own, driven as much by its own dynamics and momentum as by the visible hand of politics. The changes have also prompted a paradigm shift in the academia—from the Cold War perspective in the 1950s and the development-oriented paradigm in the 1970s to a search for new conceptual frameworks. From a sociological perspective, for example, Chang et al. (1994) have proposed a "social knowledge" model to replace the ideological propaganda model, suggesting that the news produced by the Chinese media should be viewed not as propaganda but as the basic knowledge needed for the building of a forced consensus in China. He (1993b) has proposed a central/market model that views the Chinese press as being driven by both bureaucratic controls and liberalizing market forces. Xue (1995) has developed a political-economic model to examine the interplay of politics and economics in the Chinese movie industry. Lee (1994) has also suggested the use of a political-economic perspective in the explication of the dynamics of the Chinese press. All these efforts seem to point to the need for a political-economy framework with which to examine the Chinese press as it struggles in the confusing and volatile game of balancing politics and economics.

Political Economy of the Chinese Party Press: A "Tug-of-War" Model

For decades, the political-economic perspective, which grows out of Marx's political economy, has been frequently used in the analysis of the capitalist media. In its simplest form, this perspective asserts that the mass media are part of the economic system within a political context. They are driven by market forces but are at the same time constrained by politics or "public intervention" (see Curran, Douglas, and Whannel 1980; Golding and Murdock 1996; Mosco 1996). In its more sophisticated form, it asserts that the mass media exist in a complex political-economic context and evolve from the past and, therefore, must be examined in a holistic and historical fashion; that the balance between capitalist enterprise and public intervention should find a central point; and that basic moral questions of justice, equity, and the public good must be engaged (Golding and Murdock 1996).

This perspective is apt to lead to empirically testable propositions about market determinations. It has the advantages of providing a broad and holistic picture of the dual dynamics that drive the mass media; explaining the broadly different stances various media organizations take toward audiences in the marketplace; linking the production of meaning to the exercise of power; and pointing out the political nature of communication, even though the ostensible driving force is economic.

However, the way this perspective is applied in the West is rather limited and insensitive to the interplay of politics and economics. Most of the research using this approach is more "economic" than "political" (Schudson 1991). For example, a seminal political economy study by Curran, Douglas, and Whannel (1980) of human-interest stories in the British popular press is a piece of market research, despite its disclaimer that those stories represent "reality in a form that

powerfully reinforces and complements the dominant political consensus articulated in its current-affairs coverage." Occasionally, such research goes to the
extreme of "political conspiracy," as shown in the propaganda model developed by Herman and Chomsky (1988).

This largely economic orientation seems to have stemmed from three factors. First, most of the scholars in this school are neo-Marxists and influenced
by the same forms of economic determinism inherent in traditional Marxist political economy. Second, as a breakaway approach from the classical liberal theoretical perspective that emphasizes the political function of the media, the
Marxist approaches naturally lean toward the opposite—the economic dynamics. Third, the Marxist approaches take for granted the Western democratic political framework, in which the interplay of politics and economics is not often
direct, ostensible, and conflicting.

If we shift our focus from the capitalist system to the contemporary Chinese "socialist" system, we find that the latter lends itself very well to a balanced *political-economic* analysis. In fact, the Chinese society today bears more
resemblance to the social settings based on which Karl Marx wrote his influential political economy than do most of the late capitalist societies in the West.
In today's China, politics and economics are too deeply intertwined to be
separated.

On the political side, the party-state exerts a tremendous influence on the
economy. First, it still owns a vital part of the economy, especially the giant
heavy-industry enterprises—despite a decade-long effort to develop township
enterprises, joint ventures, and foreign capital ventures and to privatize some
of the state-run enterprises. By orders, quotas, fiats, or other administrative
measures, the party-state and its representatives at various levels can directly
influence a vital part of the economy. Second, the state can direct the economy
by setting up development priorities and national projects, thus influencing the
allocation of economic resources. A good example is the "Three Gorges" dam
project, which will cost the country RMB 200 billion yuan (U.S. $24 billion)
and affect the entire economy. Third, the party-state controls all the major resources, ranging from land and minerals to energy. Any change in the pricing
of these resources can affect the operation of all economic sectors. Fourth, the
party-state owns and runs the entire financial system, thus controlling the capital needed for most economic activities. Fifth, the party-state regulates all the
economic activities in the country. Sixth, politics in China, in its broadest
sense, is pervasive. It has permeated the entire society after decades of politicization of everything—from governing to childbirth. Despite the recent

decentralization efforts by the government, the gigantic political web still exists and even extends to the enclaves of foreign ventures. Any economic activity can be easily turned into a political issue. Seventh, many politicians or offspring of the top politicians have turned themselves into businesspeople, and their businesses are actually based on their political resources.

On the economic side, the "socialist market economy" has developed in such a way as to be closely tied to the political system. First, it has not grown naturally from the bottom up but has been "imposed" by the leadership from the top down through often expedient economic reforms within a political framework that the leadership does not wish to change. Intrinsically, this "market economy" is incompatible with a political system built on the philosophy and logic of a centrally planned economy. Second, it coexists with a huge state-run economic sector and, therefore, has to deal with the bureaucratized state system all the time. Third, because of a constant worry that the "open door" will be someday shut, businesses often try to seek protection from various political forces. Fourth, because big money is usually made in areas in which the party-state controls the resources, such as land speculation and development, the trade between power and money has almost become a key to success in economic activities. Fifth, in the absence of a consensual order, compatible rules, and spiritual sustenance, the premature market economy is often chaotic, speculative, and shortsighted. It has the tendency to disregard any rule of game in its pursuit of a quick profit, thus conflicting with any regulatory power.

Because of this unique mesh of politics and economics in China, the two are often engaged in a pulling game, or what I would call a "tug-of-war." And nowhere is such a war more evident, fervent, and profound than in the Communist Party press. By nature, the party press is bestowed with an unambiguous political mission—serving as the party's voice to promote its interests, policies, and ideology (whatever it is now). However, for a variety of reasons, the most obvious of which is the budget burden (He 1993a), even the party press has been thrown out of the party-state budget and forced to survive in the market. In such a situation, the interplay of politics and economics becomes a major source of what Lee (1994) calls "ambiguities and contradictions."

This chapter uses the metaphor "tug-of-war" to conceptualize the dual dynamics that drive the Chinese party press today. It assumes a game in which each contestant vies to pull the other to its own domain. The constant contact, tension, pulling, and back-and-forth movement generate the major dynamics of the game. The motion of such a "war" varies from time to time and from place to place, and it changes in a dynamic way as the power of each side changes. Based on this basic assumption, five modes of the game are proposed to explicate how those two forces are interacting with one another in the Chinese party press.

1. Political dominance mode. In this mode, political interests dominate the game, while market forces (or economic interests) are trying to tug the rope to their side from within the other's territory, even though they are temporarily overpowered.
2. Political dominance with market momentum mode. In this mode, political interests have temporary dominance, but economic interests are gaining momentum and are pulling the opponent to their side.
3. Equilibrium. In this mode, both political and economic interests are a match, and a temporary equilibrium is struck.
4. Market dominance with political momentum mode. In this mode, economic interests have temporary dominance, but political interests are gaining momentum and are pulling the opponent to their side.
5. Market dominance mode. In this mode, market forces (or economic interests) dominate the game, while political interests are trying to tug the rope to its side from within the other's territory, even though they are temporarily overpowered.

These modes can be viewed both as the results of the tugging game and as the process of the tugging itself. If we freeze the game, we can view these modes as the temporary results of the game at that moment and locate the driving forces. However, when we view the game as a dynamic process, we can see that it constantly changes from one mode to another, depending on the strength of the contesting forces. Even when it reaches an equilibrium, the constant tension is still present, ready to change the balance at any moment.

The Case of the *Shenzhen Special Zone Daily*

With this conceptual framework in mind, this chapter zeroes in on one newspaper—the *Shenzhen Special Zone Daily* (*SSZD*). A case-study approach enables us to gather specific data at the institutional and individual levels, and, especially, to scrutinize the news production process from inside through observations and in-depth interviews. Several field trips to Shenzhen were taken in 1994, 1996, 1997, and 1999. The duration of the trips ranged from one day to one week. More than twenty staff members were interviewed.[1]

I have chosen the *Shenzhen Special Zone Daily* as the subject of study for three reasons. First, it is a typical party newspaper, owned and run by the Shenzhen Municipal Communist Party Committee. Second, perhaps nowhere in China is the interplay of politics and economics more evident than at this newspaper, which is located in China's earliest and most developed site of "capitalist experiment." Third, it is one of the country's top five profit-making newspapers and, therefore, is of tremendous importance in the party press. Fourth, because of its "avant-garde" status, the paper's development may well reflect where the Chinese Communist Party press is headed in the future.

MANAGEMENT: POLITICAL DOMINANCE WITH MARKET MOMENTUM

The management structure of the *Shenzhen Special Zone Daily* remains in many ways the model of a traditional Communist Party organ. At the same time, however, it is seriously challenged by emerging market forces.

The Institutional Structure

The basic institutional structure of the paper apparently has not changed much from the traditional setup. As is the case for most of the party newspapers in the country, its structure consists of two major divisions: the editorial division and the administrative/management division. The editorial division comprises the traditional departments, including a chief editor's office, a political news department, an economic news department, a reporting (general assignment) department, a sports department, and a photography department. What is somewhat different from a traditional establishment and many other newspapers is the elevated status given the societal news section, called the "societal page," which enjoys a quasi-department position in the institutional hierarchy. The administrative/management division is made up of the following departments: advertising, circulation, planning and finance, logistics, technical support, personnel, discipline commission, union committee, party committee, and journalism research. Within this dual structure, the editorial division enjoys much more power and importance than does the noneditorial part. This is evident in the editorial division's larger staff (more than 300 versus 190), higher rankings among the staff, and more involvement in the decision-making process.

Some signs, however, show that economic interests are gaining momentum. The paper is currently run by a director, not by an editorial board as most party newspapers are. The director is in charge of everything, in both the editorial division and the management division. The planning and finance department is frequently involved in decision making and is consulted on all business matters. This management system, according to several interviewees, is quite efficient editorially and financially. Signs also indicate a restructuring of overall management to enhance economic efficiency, whereby the director is assisted by a chief editor and a general manager, each responsible, respectively, for the editorial side and the management side of affairs. In the old days when the paper relied exclusively on state subsidies, editorial "correctness" was the primary concern, and the manager had only a marginal role to play in the media organization's decision-making process. Now, Dong Xiangling, director of the Planning and Finance Department, said that she had been more and more frequently involved in the decision-making process and had sat on the five-member committee that decided on the construction of the paper's lavish fifty-story office building. Since the completion of the office building in 1998, which stands as a glamorous landmark in the new downtown area of Shenzhen, the business side has gained more importance as it becomes imperative for the paper to cash in on its 600 million yuan (U.S. $75 million) investment by selling and leasing space in the building, of which the paper itself occupies only one-third.

Staffing

The staffing appears to be more influenced by the political system than by market forces at the top level. The main leaders of the paper, including the director and the top echelon of cadres, are appointed directly by the Municipal Communist Party Committee, which also determines the size of the staff (*bian zi*). All the staff, including those in the editorial departments, are treated as party cadres although they are paid under a journalism professional rank system rather than under a "cadre pay schedule" (Chen and Lee 1998).

However, some important changes have occurred in the hiring and firing of staff members below the top echelon. Employees, especially those recently hired, have been placed under a contract system. Under this system, the performance of all employees is evaluated every year. Those who fail the evaluation are given a three-month grace period. If they still cannot catch up, they will be fired. During my observation of the paper in 1996, two employees at the section level were fired because of their mediocre performance.

Incentive System

The incentive system is a combination of the "iron rice bowl" and the "performance bonus." Each staff member is paid a base salary according to his or her rank and years of service for the state. Every month, each editorial staff is given a quota of stories or photos to complete, and the quota is worth 1,300 points. Of these pieces, a certain number must be "star stories," which are rated by the paper's Journalism Research Institute. A middle-ranking journalist, for example, must produce two "star" stories each month. Any additional "star" story would be awarded a RMB 150 yuan (U.S. $18) bonus. At the end of each month, the paper would multiply the points assigned to each journalist by an index figure derived from the overall financial performance of the paper, which may range from 0.8 to 2. If the points are multiplied by 2, then the journalist would be paid RMB 2,600 (U.S. $270). The average middle-ranking journalist earns about RMB 4,000 to 5,000 yuan (U.S. $500 to $620) per month, of which more than half comes from bonuses. In addition, journalists enjoy subsidized housing and health care, as do all state employees. All those sources of income and benefits put journalists at the *Shenzhen Special Zone Daily* in the upper-middle class in Shenzhen, which is a high-salary and high-cost city in China. "We journalists are perhaps the best paid in the culture industry, next only to movie and singing stars," said one mid-level manager in the paper, who was paid RMB 10,000 yuan (U.S. $1,200) per month in 1999. "I can't spend all this money."

Financing

The paper is completely self-sufficient and making a good profit. More than 90 percent of the revenue comes from advertising and the rest from such small businesses as the printing plant. In 1998, its advertising revenue was RMB 380 million yuan (U.S. $47.2 million). Before 1994, it did not have to pay any tax. In 1995, it started to pay a 15 percent income tax, a 5.2 percent business tax, and a 17 percent asset appreciation. However, of all the taxes paid, 70 percent was refunded in the form of "propaganda costs" and "cultural funds."

Overall, the basic structure and management style are in what I call a "political dominance with market momentum mode." Obviously, the party's grip is firm at the top level of personnel. However, at the lower levels of the personnel management and in such areas as the incentive system and financing, practices of a market economy have crept in and are apparently gaining power. The management seems to be moving in the direction of establishing a "Party Inc.," which is self-financed and staffed by technocrats who work for the party boss to promote the party's interests — and to make a profit.

COMPETITION: MARKET DOMINANCE

Intramedia competition in Shenzhen is probably the most fierce and notorious in China. In a city of three million people (including two million of what is commonly called the "floating population"), there are eleven newspapers, twenty-eight magazines and journals, two television stations, at least two radio stations, and numerous movie and video theaters (see Cao 1995). In addition, all the Hong Kong media, especially the two television stations, Rupert Murdoch's Star TV, and the radio stations that spill their signals over the border, make up an uninvited but integral part of the Shenzhen media market.

In such a market, competition for audience "heads" and advertising money is fierce among all media and is especially "throat-cutting" between the *Shenzhen Special Zone Daily* and the *Shenzhen Commerce Daily (SCD)*. The *SSZD* is the party-organ paper, while the *SCD* is sponsored by the Municipal People's Government.

"The competition with the *Shenzhen Commerce Daily* has driven us nuts," said Zheng Hongyu, deputy director of the Chief Editor's Office, referring to a competition that caught the nation's attention and made the front pages of the Hong Kong press, which is well known for cutthroat competition. "We have been forced to join the devils [unscrupulous competitors]." The competition started in 1991 when the *Shenzhen Commerce Daily* was established by the Municipal People's Government so that it could have its own voice and also cash in on the lucrative media market. From the standpoint of the *SCD*, there was nothing wrong in a city like Shenzhen having two daily newspapers. In fact, most of China's major metropolitan cities and provincial capitals have more than one newspaper; Shanghai, for example, has the famous duo of the *Wenhui Daily* and the *Liberation Daily*. After all, the stated mission of the *Shenzhen Commerce Daily* was to cover economic news and activities related to the municipal government. Backed up by a cumulative investment of RMB 400 to RMB 500 million yuan (U.S. $48 to $60 million) over a five-year span, the *SCD* competed with the *SSZD* head-on from the outset.

Although the competition was waged in all areas, from content to advertising, the most fierce and controversial battle was fought over circulation. To expand its readership, the *SCD* employed a variety of strategies and techniques, such as setting up printing centers in four cities, including Beijing and Shanghai, to reach readers outside Shenzhen; expanding into Macao and Hong Kong; offering its *Shenzhen Evening News* for free to subscribers; holding prize-drawing competitions; occasionally offering free advertising space; giving kickbacks to advertisers or agents; and resorting to the administrative power of the government to impose subscriptions on subordinate offices and individuals. The most controversial strategy was the compulsory subscription imposed on parents of schoolchildren through the Municipal Education Administration. It was reported that schoolchildren had to produce a receipt showing their family held an *SCD* subscription before they could register and take classes. As a result of those aggressive promotional measures, the *SCD's* circulation rapidly climbed to more than 120,000 in Shenzhen alone. And its advertising revenue in 1997 reached RMB 97 million yuan (U.S. $11.6 million), which made it possible for the paper to build a lavish office tower.

Confronted by such aggressive competition, the *Shenzhen Special Zone Daily* reacted with almost exactly the same strategies and techniques — except for the overt arm-twisting compulsory subscriptions. It reinforced its interprovincial printing and distribution systems, extended its reach to Hong Kong, offered occasional free advertising space, and gave kickbacks. It established a sister paper, the *Eagle City Today,* and gave it to subscribers for free. It started a joint newspaper, the *Shen Sing Daily,* with the Sing Tao group in Hong Kong and bought a small specialized paper in Shenzhen. In fact, since 1997, *SSZD* has gradually built up a conglomerate of five newspapers and two magazines, for which it is awaiting official recognition. The *SSZD* sold its copies for RMB 0.5 yuan each while the cost was RMB 1.6 yuan. Furthermore, the paper occasionally offered an extra copy of the same paper to subscribers. During my field trip to Shenzhen in March 1996, I stayed with a friend, a professor at Shenzhen University, who subscribed to both *SCD* and *SSZD.* When we got two copies of the *Shenzhen Special Zone Daily,* I asked him what he would do with them. "I don't know," he answered. "I have nobody to send the extra copy to because everybody in this compound subscribes to the *Shenzhen Special Zone Daily.* Am I supposed to take a taxi and bring the extra copy to somebody on the other side of the town?"

This competition has undoubtedly wrought something positive. It has forced the two newspapers to improve their readability, timeliness, and scope of coverage. It has fostered a sense of competition among administrators and journalists. And it has made the papers more responsive to readers. The competition has been driven mostly by irrational market forces, however. Each paper could have established its own niche and shared a lucrative market that is fed by advertising money from around the country and from neighboring Hong Kong. But they both seem to have been engaged in a zero-sum game, trying to kill the opponent and take the entire pie. The competition has caused a tremendous waste of resources, especially of public goods, as in the case of the *Shenzhen Commerce Daily,* which uses a large sum of taxpayer money for its investment and operation. It has led to some unethical promotional techniques and has perpetuated them as legitimate practices. And it has created a vicious cycle that nobody knows how to break. "The more copies we print, the more money we lose," an executive editor at the *SSZD* said. "We could have been very profitable at the critical-mass point, about 200,000 copies a day, but we can't stop there."

ADVERTISING: AN UNEASY MONEYMAKER
IN A MARKET–DOMINANCE MODE

In 1998, advertising revenue at the *Shenzhen Special Zone Daily* reached RMB 380 million yuan (U.S. $47.2 million), making the paper one of the top five moneymaking papers in the country. This revenue also marked a new height in the paper's thirteen-year dramatic increase in advertising income, which went from RMB 400,000 yuan (U.S. $48,000) in 1982, to RMB 90 million yuan (U.S. $10.8 million) in 1992, to RMB 160 million yuan (U.S. $19.2 million) in 1993, and to RMB 310 million yuan (U.S. $37 million) in 1997.

By any standard, this would be an impressive economic performance. But Dan Ping, director of the advertising department, whose leadership had made all this possible, was extremely unhappy. In fact, when she was interviewed, she cried—in front of me, a stranger she had just met. "My job has completely burned me out," she said, "and has killed my husband." Dan's husband had died of a massive heart attack a few days earlier, and she thought that it was her demanding job that led to her neglect of her husband and eventually to his death. "I could have taken better care of him. I could have . . . ," she said, sobbing again.

Her job was not only demanding of her time but also of her psychology and morale, which it had wrecked. As the breadwinner of the paper and one of the few female executives in the country who managed such a large flow of money, Dan said she felt like a beggar. "I begged the editorial departments for more space," she said. "I begged the Municipal Administration of Industry and Commerce for faster approval of our ads. I begged our advertisers for business, and I begged our readers for a pardon when we occasionally carried a bad ad. I kowtowed to everybody everywhere [*dao chu ke tou*]."

After several years of an undoubtedly successful career, Dan Ping couldn't wait to quit her job. "If I were given a permission to go back to the editorial department [where she came from]," she said, "I would be out of here in ten minutes." She quit her job as the head of the advertising department and moved back to the editorial side in 1997, working as the paper's chief correspondent in Hubei Province.

Dan's experience highlights the tug-of-war between the politics and economics of advertising in a party newspaper, a war that is most conspicuously fought in (1) space and placement of advertising and (2) content of advertising.

Space and Placement of Advertising

In this area, the political interests of the party are naturally inclined to limit advertising space and restrict advertising to inconspicuous places, such as the inside or back pages. Despite the rapid development of advertising in China in recent years, the party apparatus from the top down still harbors a deeply rooted suspicion of the once "capitalist deceptive practice" and a worry that too much advertising would turn party newspapers into purely commercial papers, damage their authoritative status, and eventually change their basic mission. These concerns translate into several unwritten policies. Two of the most important ones are that advertising in party newspapers should not be excessive and that it should not be carried in places where important national or local political news should be.

On the economic side, the impetus of the market is to maximize profit. It strives for as much space for advertising as it can and puts advertising wherever it can make the most impact and profit. This impetus directly clashes with the political interests.

In this battle, the market forces appear to have been on the winning side at the *Shenzhen Special Zone Daily*. As the market expands in Shenzhen, the demands and needs for advertising have steadily driven the advertising space up in the paper, from a very minimal amount in 1982 to half of the twenty-two weekday pages at present. In 1998, the average daily advertising space reached more than seven pages, including the four-page editions on Saturdays and Sundays. Advertising has also won the right to appear on the front page and in full pages inside and on the back.

However, some of the last political defense lines have remained fairly firm, making the lives of people like Dan Ping difficult. In the battle for space, advertising has apparently hit the ceiling. Dan Ping said the paper could not carry any more ads, or "leaders in Beijing would speak up." The paper has made some attempts to expand its advertising space but has found out that 50 to 60 percent of the total space is the ultimate limit. To make full use of the 50 to 60 percent hole, the paper's leadership has set up fixed space for advertising every day, and the advertising department has been required to fill up the hole — no more and no less. Moreover, the paper cannot add any page unless approved by the Press and Publication Administration in advance. This type of control, said interviewees in the department, has made their job a mission impossible and has put them in constant conflict with the editorial departments. "I cannot control the flows and ebbs of advertising," said Dan Ping. "So, every time there is more advertising and a request for a larger display by advertisers, I would beg the chief editor and editors of the pages for some special treatment. And I am tired of begging."

Another remaining political territory is the restriction on front-page advertising. Despite the encroachment onto front pages by advertisements over the years, advertising today can appear only at the bottom of the front page and can take only one-fourth of the page. The *SSZD* made two attempts to carry a full-page ad on the front page in 1987, the first such attempts in the country, and it was severely criticized by leaders both in Beijing and in Shenzhen. Ever since then, the paper has made no attempt to test the boundaries and has no plan to do so in the near future.

Content of Advertising

Political and administrative controls appeared to dominate the game in the area of advertising content. By state regulations and laws, advertisements for eleven categories of consumer products and services, as well as comparative and educational advertisements, must be subjected to censorship by a designated independent review board made up mostly of officials from the Administration of Industry and Commerce. Ideologically incorrect, factually deceptive, and morally unhealthy advertisements are forbidden (Cheng 1996).

The *Shenzhen Special Zone Daily* apparently has followed those rules closely. Every day in the reception room of the advertising department, there are long lines of advertisers or their representatives. They are held up because the staff for the newspaper need to check their IDs; their letters from the work units; their "medical advertisement certificate," if they are involved in medical products; and, most important, their certificates of approval from the Administration of Industry and Commerce. Ads created by the paper's own staff also have to be sent to the censors. The process takes from a few days to two weeks.

Ads that are not subject to outside censorship are scrutinized by the advertising staff of the paper. This caution is exercised for two political considerations. First, because of the paper's status as an institution of the party, anything it publishes can be taken as representing the authoritative voice of the party and can have serious political ramifications. Second, if anything goes wrong because of the ads, the blame is usually placed on the paper—not on the advertisers.

One incident has made the advertising staff particularly wary of what is advertised. Before the Chinese Lunar New Year in 1996, a travel agent placed an ad in the paper for train tickets out of Shenzhen, which were in great demand. Everything was checked up by the staff, and the agent was found to be legitimate. But right before the holiday season, the agent disappeared with deposits from several hundred customers. Customers were outraged not only because their money had been ripped off but also because they had lost valuable time in purchasing the tickets that would take them home from the city of migrants for the traditional family reunion. Scores of these customers surrounded the paper's office building, demanding compensation and tickets and denouncing the party newspaper for cheating its readers. "At one point," Dan Ping recalled, "there was almost a riot." The crowd was appeased only when Dan went out and begged for a pardon, promising to compensate them for their losses and to buy train tickets for them through the newspaper's connections.

Dan and her staff feel that censorship of ads is necessary to protect the paper's customers. However, the liability placed on the paper and the amount of work censorship creates for the staff are simply too much to handle.

Despite all the political considerations and constraints, especially those on the content, advertising at the *Shenzhen Special Zone Daily* appears to be in an increasingly dominant position. Internally, it is given an increasingly high priority. For example, on March 26, 1996, the advertising department managed to add an eight-centimeter ad across the front page, pushing the ad space up to almost half of the front page. Externally, some constraints are likely to be loosened. In fact, the country's regulations on advertising have softened with regard to ideology expressed in advertising. Following the *Guangzhou Daily*, the *SSZD*'s equivalent, which obtained the right to add pages as needed, the *SSZD* has been given the power to control its pages. For everybody, it seems, the power of advertising dollars is too strong to resist.

THE NEWSPAPER CONTENT: A SOCIALIST FACE WITH A CAPITALIST BODY

Wu Songying, director of the *Shenzhen Special Zone Daily*, described his paper this way: "Our first and second pages are planned economy, but the rest is all market economy." This remark, made in a private conversation, seemed to capture well the mix of the paper's content and the driving forces behind.

Indeed, the paper is profoundly torn by the efforts to sustain a "socialist face" and the needs to nurture a "capitalist body." As the designated publicity outlet for the Shenzhen Municipal Communist Party Committee, it has—and takes it as its responsibility—to carry out the publicity work for the party. But as a financially independent enterprise, it is forced to ride on the tide of the marketplace, trying to appeal to the largest common denominator and, more important, to attract advertisers. This dual mission, which is contradictory enough in and by itself, is further compounded by two unique factors: the country's first "capitalist" experiment in Shenzhen and the city's proximity to Hong Kong. As the first city to experiment with a market economy, the city's leadership is keenly aware of the scrutiny by the central leadership and by those in other cities and provinces. And their worry is not unfounded. Over the past twelve years, three publications in Shenzhen, including the well-known *Shenzhen Youth Daily,* have been closed by the central leadership for their alleged "bourgeois liberalism." In no other city have so many publications been shut down. In such a situation, there is a need to keep a more politically correct face so as not to be accused of being capitalistic. At the same time, from a regional political point of view, there is also a need to justify the success of the experiment so as to protect the benefits derived from measures of a market economy.

On the other hand, because of the proximity to Hong Kong, there is the imperative to be more "capitalist" than its inland counterparts to appeal to the large number of investors and tourists from Hong Kong and to the general population that has been directly exposed to Hong Kong's free media, especially the electronic media.

The Content

To examine the content of the paper, two techniques were used: a traditional analysis of the subjects covered by the paper and an analysis of frames. The traditional analysis was designed to examine what was covered. Based on previous studies of the Communist press (see, for example, Chang, Wang, and Chen 1994; He 1988; Lee 1981; Roxburgh 1987), twenty-one subject categories were developed (see table 4.1 for the list of categories). These categories included not only those commonly used in the analysis of the Communist press but also five new ones: special economic zone issues; corruption; socialist spiritual civilization; media; and Hong Kong, Macao, and Taiwan issues. The new categories were created to accommodate the changing Chinese press and the unique characteristics of the *Shenzhen Special Zone Daily*.[2]

Because the purpose of this study was not only to examine what was covered but also to investigate how things were covered as a result of the tug-of-war between political interests and market forces, an analysis of frames was conducted. Unlike the traditional classification of "tones," which is too simplistic and insensitive, especially to the subtle changes in the Chinese press, the framing analysis could be useful in detecting the "persistent patterns of cognition, interpretation, and presentation, of selection, emphasis and exclusion, by which symbol-handlers routinely organize discourse" (Gitlin 1980:27). Because what was examined was the entire news and nonnews presentation in the *Shenzhen*

Special Zone Daily, not individual events or issues, three general frames (or metaframes) were developed along the line of the broad approach to the analysis of television news taken by Iyengar (1991). The frames were orthodox, modified orthodox, and unorthodox. Basically, the orthodox frame reflects a worldview that sees things mainly in these terms: socialism is better than capitalism; the Communist Party is the savior of China; anything good comes out of socialist spiritual civilization or the "Lei Feng" spirit; democracy in the West is hypocritical; crimes in China are rare and are severely punished by the effective legal system; corruption is rare and is often disclosed and punished; sports are a demonstration of a country's political power, and sports victories bring honor to the motherland; disasters are rare and are often occasions on which heroism demonstrates itself; the economy is developing healthily under the competent leadership of the Communist Party; and political stability is perpetual. The modified orthodox frame is similar but lower pitched and devoid of some of the blatant political and ideological innuendos. The unorthodox frame reflects a pluralistic and matter-of-fact worldview, devoid of the high- and low-pitched political and ideological allusions.

I picked a week of the *Shenzhen Special Zone Daily* and its supplement *Eagle City Today,* March 22 to 28, 1996, as the sample. The unit of analysis was each story, illustration, and photograph. This week was selected to coincide with my second round of field observations and interviews. By analyzing the content together with observations and interviews, I expected to understand not only the expressed content but also the processes, logic, and reasons behind it. In addition to the analysis of this week's content, I examined 248 stories deemed by the editors to be the best of 1994 and compiled by them into a book entitled *A Moment in History: A Selection of 1994 News Stories in the* Shenzhen Special Zone Daily (Journalism Institute of the *Shenzhen Special Zone Daily* 1995).

The content of the *Shenzhen Special Zone Daily* during the sample week was found to be something of a mosaic. Coverage of the active economy in Shenzhen made up the largest portion of it, accounting for 21 percent of the 815 items. Other major parts of the mosaic were international events and China's diplomatic endeavors (14 percent); sports (11 percent); activities in science, technology, education, arts, and culture (9 percent); and events in Hong Kong, Macao, and Taiwan (7 percent). Coverage of political activities made up only 6 percent of this picture. Even when all the politics-related categories (such as socialist spiritual civilization, crime/law, model/hero, corruption, military, and special zone issues) were pooled together, they constituted only 18 percent of the constructed reality (see table 4.1).

Table 4.1. Shenzhen Special Economic Zone Daily: *Subjects and Frames of Stories during a Sample Week in 1996*

Subject and Frame	Orthodox		Modified Orthodox	Unorthodox	Unidenti-fiable	Row Total
Economy	93	(55%)	21 (13%)	42 (25%)	11 (7%)	167 (20.5%)
International and foreign relations	57	(51)	16 (14)	34 (31)	4 (3)	111 (13.6)
Sports	21	(24)	10 (11)	42 (47)	16 (18)	89 (10.9)
Science, technology, education, arts, and culture	39	(53)	15 (21)	7 (10)	12 (16)	73 (9.0)
Hong Kong, Macao, and Taiwan	43	(77)	6 (11)	6 (11)	1 (2)	56 (6.9)
Life experience	22	(46)	14 (29)	7 (15)	5 (10)	48 (5.9)
Politics	46	(98)	1 (2)			47 (5.8)
Spiritual civilization	40	(100)				40 (4.9)
Environment	13	(38)	10 (29)	8 (24)	3 (9)	34 (4.2)
Crime/law	23	(68)	7 (21)	4 (12)		34 (4.2)
Human interest	2	(9)	3 (14)	9 (41)	8 (36)	22 (2.7)
Public welfare and health	14	(74)	2 (11)	1 (5)	2 (11)	19 (2.3)
Model/hero	12	(100)				12 (1.5)
Information and how-to			1 (9)	1 (9)	9 (82)	11 (1.3)
Social issues	1	(9)	1 (9)	9 (82)		11 (1.3)
Disaster	8	(80)	1 (10)	1 (10)		10 (1.2)
History	3	(33)	1 (11)	2 (22)	3 (33)	9 (1.1)
Media	8	(89)	1 (11)			9 (1.1)
Corruption	5	(100)				5 (0.6)
Military	5	(100)				5 (0.6)
SEZ issues	3	(100)				3 (0.4)
Total	485	(56.2)	110 (13.5)	173 (21.2)	74 (9.1)	815 (100%)

$X^2(60, N = 815) = 340, p < 0.001$; Cramer's $V = 0.37$

By the pure number of items, it appears that market forces were triumphant, tilting the constructed reality toward economic activities and events that would appeal to the marketplace. However, when the display and length of the stories were examined, the picture was different. Political news and related items were all displayed in prominent places, usually on the first three pages, whereas other types of news were placed inside. Because the *Shenzhen Special Zone Daily* was printed on a four-page fold, this placement was especially important. When the first page was picked up, the reader was likely to read the four pages in the same section—simply for the convenience of it. The political stories were also usually much longer than other types of stories. For example, on March 22, 1996, the paper carried the full text of a report by Tian Jiyun, Vice Chairman of the Standing Committee of the National People's Congress, which took up almost the entire second page. Another political story on March 24, 1996, which was about Foreign Minister Qian Qichen's speech in Hong Kong on Taiwan independence activities, ran from the front page to the third. On the same day, the full text of the decision by the National People's Congress on amending the country's criminal code took up the entire second page.

When the frames of the stories were analyzed, the greater tugging force of political interests was even more evident. Of all the stories and illustrations, 56 percent used the orthodox frame, and 14 percent used the modified orthodox frame. Only 21 percent of the stories, mostly about economics, international affairs, and sports, adopted an unorthodox frame (see table 4.1). Even in stories about corruption and disasters, where an unorthodox frame was most likely to be used, the frame was predominantly orthodox, emphasizing the rarity of official corruption and the effective enforcement of law or discipline, and the heroism in disasters—although many of them were manmade.

If the reality as presented during the week of March 1996 was constructed unconsciously by a diverse group of journalists with different personal agendas, professional norms, and perceptions, the reality of 1994 was consciously reconstructed by the paper's top journalists to represent what they called "a moment in history." In this reconstructed "ideal-type" reality, economic activities also made up the largest part (36 percent of 248 stories). However, unlike the picture of 1996, government politics constituted the second largest segment (9 percent). When all the politically oriented segments (spiritual civilization, model/hero, special zone issues, crime/law, and corruption) were pooled together, they made up an even larger portion of the picture (30 percent). Given the much greater length and more prominent placement of these stories, they undoubtedly overpowered any other competing forces to dominate the game (see table 4.2).

The analysis of frames also shows that political considerations overpowered market forces. Of the 248 stories, 61 percent were projected through the orthodox frame and 23 percent through the modified orthodox frame. Only 15 percent used the unorthodox frame, which was a smaller percentage than that during the week of 1996. As in 1996, the unorthodox frame was employed more in the area of economy than in any other area. In politics, none of the stories used the unorthodox frame, although one-third of them were projected through the modified orthodox frame.

Table 4.2. Shenzhen Special Economic Zone Daily: *Subjects and Frames of the Best Stories in 1994*

Subject and Frame	Orthodox	Modified Orthodox	Unorthodox	Row Total
Economy	38 (42%)	27 (30%)	25 (28%)	90 (36.5%)
Politics	14 (67)	7 (33)		21 (8.5)
International and foreign relations	11 (65)	4 (24)	2 (12)	17 (6.9)
SEZ issues	16 (94)	1 (6)		17 (6.9)
Spiritual civilization	17 (100)			17 (6.9)
Model/hero	12 (86)	2 (14)		14 (5.6)
Science, technology, education, arts, and culture	8 (62)	5 (38)		13 (5.2)
Social issues	3 (25)	7 (58)	2 (17)	12 (4.8)
Sports	7 (64)	1 (9)	3 (27)	11 (4.4)
Disaster	9 (90)		1 (10)	10 (4.0)
Hong Kong, Macao, and Taiwan	7 (88)		1 (12)	8 (3.2)
Media	3 (43)	2 (29)	2 (29)	7 (2.8)
Human interest	1 (25)	2 (50)	1 (25)	4 (1.6)
Crime/law	1 (33)	1 (33)	1 (33)	3 (1.2)
Corruption	1 (33)	2 (66)		3 (1.2)
Environment			1 (100)	1 (0.4)
Total	151 (60.9)	58 (23.4)	39 (15.7)	248 (100%)

$X^2(30, N = 248) = 77, p < 0.001$; Cramer's $V = 0.39$

The Making of the Content

Through observations and in-depth interviews, I made a special effort to check how the traditional measures of political control worked and in what ways they were challenged by market forces. As previous studies show (see He 1993a, 1996; Polumbaum 1990), controls over the party press in China were exerted primarily in the following forms: (1) legal controls through such measures as registration and licensing of news organizations; (2) financial controls over the budget and resources; (3) control over the personnel, especially the executives; (4) suppression and withholding of sensitive or "inappropriate" information; (5) "voluntary" submission of copies of important stories for preview; (6) post-view by party apparatus, such as the propaganda departments; (7) direct interference by leaders; and (8) self-censorship established through training and organizational culture.

It was found that most measures of political control over the content remained fairly strong despite challenges from market forces. Particularly strong was the direct interference from the local party leaders. Almost every day, some interviewees said, reporters and editors would get calls, internal documents, and memos, announcements, or canned stories from various leaders on the municipal party committee. As one senior editor aptly put it: "Our first and second pages are given to the municipal party committee for free. The leaders can do whatever they wish with those pages."

I sat in a prepublication meeting held by the paper's managing editors. The gatekeeping process at this meeting was illustrative of what went on behind the manifest content. The meeting held on Monday, March 25, 1996, was a typical example of the routine daily meetings convened to decide what would go into the paper the next day. Attending the meeting were managing editors from the departments of economic news, political news, reporting, and photography and from the editorial board and societal issue page. A deputy chief editor presided. The meeting started with a rundown of the stories and photos available for the next day. As editors finished their "menus," they noticed that there was not enough space for all the stories because of a larger volume of ads. An additional front-page ad, eight centimeters high, was to be run across the page for the People's Construction Bank, and the fourth and sixth pages were both "washed out" by ads. "Must be the result of some hard pushing by the Advertising Department," one editor said. All editors sighed but let it go, as if they had been through this all the time.

Then the group approved a story on intellectual property that had been previewed by the Municipal Commission on Protection of Intellectual Property. There was no discussion of the story nor any sign of unhappiness about the preview and the long time it had taken. The group quickly passed several economic stories and photos on "spiritual civilization"—some good deeds by citizens, improvements in service, and "model workers"—apparently two regular categories on the diet. As the discussion of items from the departments was about to end, the deputy editor asked: "Were there any other political activities at the municipal party committee?" He was pleased when the editor from the Political Department assured him that all the political activities were covered.

The deputy chief editor brought up his items: a commentary handed down from the Municipal People's Congress in session, which is a "must" on the front page; an article sent by the Municipal Inspection Bureau (jan cha ju), to be published on any page where space was available; and two articles about the meeting on the work of special economic zones. The only thing he was not pleased about was an announcement that the Public Security Bureau wanted published on the front page. The editor said, "I told them that it couldn't be done because the municipal party committee would criticize us if we did so."

The editors killed only one story idea: three photos on the "Russian Water

Ballet," because the photos were too "commercial," even though they might appeal to the readers. The only complaining party at the meeting was the editor from the societal issue page. For a month, she said, her page had been "washed out" by news on meetings and then by advertisements. She put up a lengthy elaboration on a story about "wage-earning" farmers and finally got it in.

Two Important Events

Two other events were also illustrative of the pulling forces of politics and economics on the content of the paper. One was a series of articles written and ordered by Li Youwei, former Secretary of the Shenzhen Municipal Communist Party Committee, on the advantages of the special economic zone. The other was a series of installments reporting on the fate of a corrupt government official.

Starting in 1993, Hu Angang, member of the Research Team on the State of the Nation under the Chinese Academy of Sciences, which is the top leadership's think tank, challenged the legitimacy and usefulness of the concept of the special economic zone (SEZ). He argued that the SEZs had outgrown their mission of experiment in a market economy and that their continuing existence could only widen the gap between privileged areas and the rest of the country. He even accused special interest groups in the SEZs of trying to keep their monopoly and special privileges through what he called "payment of political and economic rent." For a time, there were rumors that Hu's remarks were a trial balloon from the top leadership, which was planning to eliminate the SEZs. In June 1995, Li Youwei published a lengthy article in the *Shenzhen Special Zone Daily* to rebut Hu's views. He also instructed the *SSZD* to publish a series of articles in defense of the SEZs. Regardless of what he and his subordinates said in their strongly worded and emotional rebuttals, the fact that he used a local party newspaper to square off against a presumed theorist for the central leadership was of great significance. It symbolized a new twist in Chinese politics that featured a conflict between the central leadership and the local officials whose power base grew with the economic power in the regions they ruled. It also showed that regional politics was so deeply entangled with local economic interests that the *Shenzhen Special Zone Daily* served both as an instrument of the Shenzhen Municipal Communist Party Committee and as a spokesman of the giant "Shenzhen Inc." Concerned about the ramifications of such a debate, the central party leadership soon issued a stern order to end it, saying that it was inappropriate for local leaders to use local media outlets to challenge theorists working for the central leadership (Cheng 1995).

A series of stories about the corrupt government official was published in 1994 and 1995. It was a tremendous hit in Shenzhen. When the story was run, *SSZD* circulation skyrocketed, and copies were sold out the moment they hit the streets. What made this series a scoop was not its timeliness or newsworthiness but the way the story was framed and written. It was about Wang Jianye, the country's most serious embezzler up to that time, who had stolen RMB 15 million (U.S. $1.8 million) in two years. Numerous news stories were published in the local and national press when Wang, a middle-ranking official with the Municipal Planning Bureau, was arrested. The series, titled "A Homeless Soul," framed the saga as, in one critic's words, "a compassionate and heartbreaking love story" between Wang and his mistress, who would die for each other with or without money and who actually faced death smiling in each other's arms when Wang was executed. Never before had such a "humanistic" frame been used in the Chinese Communist Party press to depict a "renegade corrupted by the decadent bourgeois ideology." The reaction from readers was a combination of curiosity, excitement, anxiety (as the trial went on), and empathy. "Every day, I received scores of phone calls from readers," said Yang Liguang, author of this series. "In the course of writing the story, I felt I was carried away by the person of Wang. So were the readers." Not surprisingly, such a series was not well received by the leadership. The municipal propaganda department called at once and sent a circular to the newspaper, saying that the series did not adequately disclose the evil inside Wang. However, the top municipal leaders didn't say anything, nor did the newspaper leadership. "They were certainly unhappy," Yang Liguang said of the city leaders, "but they restrained themselves from criticizing the series in public for they feared to offend a huge audience or to create a forbidden-fruit effect." By the time of my interview with him, nothing had happened to the author. In fact, Yang, a member of the National Writers Association, was promoted to the position of deputy managing editor of the *Eagle City Today*. His manuscript of the Wang series was sent to an auction agent, who said he had confidence in selling it for RMB 1 million yuan (U.S. $83,000).

My content analysis, interviews, and observations all suggest that the paper's content and much of the news-making process fall into the political dominance mode. Most of the politically oriented stories are prominently displayed and of great length. Moreover, the majority of the stories depict a constructed reality in orthodox or modified orthodox frames. In the news-making process, as demonstrated by the prepublication meeting, political considerations outweigh economic and "commercial interests" most of the time. Regional politics also add some new force to the already strong political side.

The pulling and struggling forces of the marketplace, however, are also noticeable, as shown in the wide range of subjects covered, the great amount of economic news, and the appearance of a small but evident proportion of stories using the unorthodox frame. Most important, an unorthodox presentation of a corrupt official eludes punishment primarily by riding on public pressure from the readers' market.

THE JOURNALISTS: IN THE MODE OF POLITICAL DOMINANCE WITH MARKET MOMENTUM

The journalists at the *Shenzhen Special Zone Daily* are an interesting group, made up of three layers of people. The first layer consists of the veterans who arrived in Shenzhen when the special economic zone was just established. Many of them, such as Dan Ping and Yang Liguang, came from arts or literature backgrounds. The second layer consists of graduates from such major journalism programs as the Chinese Academy of Social Sciences, Fudan University, and the People's University. They came to Shenzhen primarily for personal reasons, one of which was a spouse's urban residency. The third layer consists of the "gold rushers," mostly recent college graduates on a quest for better career and monetary opportunities.

In any case, most of the journalists are self-selected and highly motivated. Many of them are talented, well versed in local news, and up to speed with the latest world developments. A young reporter interviewed for this study, for example, knows far more about the Internet than do most American college students.

Confined by political controls over the party newspaper and limited by a local media market, however, these journalists have found it extremely difficult to become top-notch in their field in China—if they should ever wish to. On the other hand, they find the thriving and chaotic economic market in Shenzhen offers a tremendous temptation to use their social networks in legal or illegal business deals. They have seen people become millionaires overnight. They have heard, very often on their jobs, windfall stories. And, more important, they have often come across opportunities to get rich through the connections they have established.

Caught between their jobs and these temptations, the journalists have found themselves tugged by a variety of forces. The pulling effects of politics and economics are particularly noticeable in these areas: (1) career choices; (2) ethics; and (3) the journalist's role.

Career Choices: To Stay or Not to Stay

In a city of enormous wealth that has been built on investment from around the country and by privileged policies of the central government, getting rich over-night is no fantasy. These talented and well-educated journalists at the *SSZD* apparently are constantly bothered by the thought that they may be able to make it financially, just as others do. In fact, when they look for role models and success stories among colleagues on the paper, they often see or are told about in-house legends such as the following:

> Story 1: A financial news reporter established a rapport with a corpora-tion in Hainan Province by writing several positive stories about it. In return, the corporation offered him an opportunity to purchase 100,000 shares of stock at RMB 1 (U.S. $0.83) each. When the cor-poration went public, the value of the stock skyrocketed. Colleagues estimated that the shares he held were worth RMB 10 million (U.S. $8.3 million).

> Story 2: A reporter was given some stock options after covering exten-sively some big corporations in Shenzhen. He made about RMB 1 million (U.S. $83,000) overnight when he sold the shares.

> Story 3: An editor, who quit his job as a journalist following the Tianan-men Square incident in 1989, signed a contract to run a resort and became CEO of that lucrative business. It was believed that he also owned several restaurants in Shenzhen and was a multimillionaire. Despite the tremendous losses this person suffered in his business expansion during the economic downturn and financial crisis in Asia between 1997 and 1998, he is still regarded as a legend.

> Story 4: An economics reporter covered the urban housing develop-ment beat for some time. Because of this close connection, the city's urban residential housing authorities allocated a four-bedroom apart-ment in the city's best location to the *SSZD*, specifically designated for that reporter.

> Story 5: An arts editor developed an interest in the stock market when it was first established in Shenzhen. After several years of following the market, he became an expert and was hired as a highly paid guest anchor for Shenzhen Television's weekly stock exchange program.

> Story 6: A police beat reporter once covered a case of police brutality in which a man was beaten to death. When he came back to write the story, he received a call from the police warning him of serious con-

sequences if he published it. He backed off. After this case, he developed a close relationship with the police and eventually was hired as the manager of a company run by the police.

Because of these stories and the ubiquitous influence from the marketplace, journalists at the *SSZD*, like everybody in government office, are tempted by the idea of leaving their journalism jobs and "jumping into the commercial ocean." In their fantasized career moves, surprisingly, political or organizational loyalty is rarely an important consideration. In fact, I have never heard anybody talk about loyalty to the party's propaganda work or to the paper in any reference to a possible job change. What does figure in the calculation are, primarily, economic factors: income, job security, pension, health insurance, and housing. The major reason why many *SSZD* journalists stay with the paper is the job security, the fairly high income the paper provides, and housing benefits that make them part of the city's upper-middle class. As one reporter said, "It is certainly exciting in the 'ocean,' but it is also very dangerous there."

Ethics

While journalism ethics has become a major issue nationwide and a focal point in the central leadership's latest round of tightened controls over the press, journalists at the *Shenzhen Special Zone Daily* do not seem to see it as a serious problem.

This feeling appears to stem from three factors: ambiguous codes of ethics; acceptance of the law of value exchange in a market economy; and comfortable incomes and benefits at the *SSZD.*

Several journalists said that they never had a clear and specific code of ethics. In their training, journalistic or otherwise, very little had to do with journalistic ethics. In the institutions where they worked, rarely was there any clear guideline or definition of ethical journalism. Many felt that in a society where human relations are extremely important and are often lubricated by such symbolic gestures as dinners, gifts, and favors, the line of ethical practice is extremely difficult to draw. One journalist, for example, said that because of his job, he was very frequently taken to dinner and, in turn, gave dinners, and that he occasionally got gifts from contacts. "Where should I draw the line?" he asked. "And in what way can I be ethical without offending my contacts?"

In a market economy that has grown almost overnight from scratch, the free exchange of value—or of anything—seems to have become a social and cultural norm in Shenzhen. At the extreme end of the scale is the notion that everything, from power to human bodies, can be traded for its market value. Such a notion is not a rare and despised deviance in Shenzhen. Some influence of this notion on journalists seems to be unavoidable. Indeed, when interviewed, some journalists demonstrated a callousness or even an indifference to ethical issues. One journalist said that when ethics in other professions and overall social morals are lacking, it is meaningless to talk about journalism ethics.

Overall, I have found that "foul play" is far less rampant at the *SSZD* than at some of the national news organizations. A major reason is that journalists are paid fairly well and enjoy many fringe benefits, including housing. "We are not so desperate as our impoverished colleagues in Beijing," said Hu Zhimin, then associate director of the Journalism Research Institute of the *SSZD*. Another reason is that when serious ethical problems are found, journalists at the *SSZD* can be fired far more easily than can journalists in Beijing. Furthermore, the economic "biggies" in Shenzhen, who have the resources to wrap up good "red envelopes" (with cash payments), do not have to subject themselves to the power of a local newspaper. Rarely, said some interviewees, do companies give out "red envelopes." The normal gifts are small souvenirs or small product prototypes.

The Journalist's Role

In September 1994, when I gave a talk comparing Chinese and Western journalism to a sizeable group of *SSZD* journalists, including some of the executive editors, I refrained from being too outspoken or too critical of the Chinese press system at the beginning, lest I embarrass my hosts and offend the audience. During the break in the two-hour talk, however, my hosts told me that I could say whatever I wanted to and that nobody would be offended. I then went on with a more detailed comparison and pointed out some of the fundamental problems of Chinese journalism, including the ill-defined role of the press. From the enthusiastic response at the question-and-answer session, the lingering exchange of ideas that continued well after the talk, and from the fact that I was invited to give another talk, I sensed a rekindled interest in the role of the press among *SSZD* journalists. Obviously, they appreciated genuine press freedom (socialist or capitalist), they would like to be a watchdog on power, and they wanted to be able to provide information the way they liked it to be.

This interest, however, appears to be subdued in their routine work as journalists. There is a sense of being hapless, hopeless, and helpless. These journalists are harnessed and frustrated by the omnipresent political constraints while becoming more cynical about ideology and their profession in the face of the increasingly strong market forces. "The era of journalists being crownless kings is over," said Yang Liguang, the journalist who wrote the series, "Homeless Soul," about a corrupt official. "Today, it is equally difficult to cover the economically powerful."

Illustrative of the plight of journalists covering the "rich," or what Bagdikian (1983) calls "sacred cows," was a clash between an *SSZD* journalist and members of an extravagant wedding party. On January 15, 1994, a motorcade—made up of a Lincoln limousine, six Mercedes-Benzes, and a convertible with several camcorders on it—ran through the thoroughfare of Shenzhen and caused a curious commotion among pedestrians. When the wedding motorcade, reportedly "more extravagant than a motorcade for a president," arrived at a luxurious hotel, an *SSZD* photographer who happened to be there took a few pictures. He was immediately surrounded and harassed by a group of young men from the party, who "each carried a cellular phone in hand." Even after the reporter showed his press card he was still forced to expose his film. The *SSZD* published a story the next day, saying that "journalists at this paper have never experienced such a rude act before." The paper also held a public discussion, which was framed more in terms of the good tradition of frugality than of press freedom or journalists' right to cover events that take place in public premises.

Since that incident, journalists at the *SSZD* have not encountered outrageous harassment of that nature. However, they feel that their hands are tied when it comes to exposure of social problems in either the economic or political realm. "We can't do anything about the 'big tiger' [corrupt high-ranking government officials]," said a managing editor who used to run the social issues section. "As a result, we turn to the petty 'flies' [low-ranking officials]." He showed some pride and excitement when he talked about two major scoops under his leadership in 1998: one about a gun-waving policeman who threatened to kill security guards and a passing district attorney for being denied access to a private property, and the other about an abusive tax collector who intentionally crashed a car a second time when damage payments were demanded from him. But he admitted that those were trivial things as opposed to the rampant corruption among the government officials and that he or his colleagues could do little about major wrongdoing in society.

Because of incidents such as the outrageous harassment by the wedding party and many more in the political realm, most journalists interviewed feel that the power of journalists is gone. To them, being a journalist is just like being an employee in a company. "You do whatever your boss tells you to do," said a journalist. Indeed, as the party press is being gradually depoliticized, so are journalists rapidly deideologized. The zeal for an ideal (which used to be the realization of Communism in the world), the mission of being a critic of social evils, and the desire for reforms, all of which manifested themselves powerfully in the 1989 Tiananmen movement, seem to have faded away, at least among a large proportion of journalists.

Journalists apparently have begun to settle, though rather reluctantly, for a new role: being the publicity officer for the "Party Inc." This new role is different from the traditional propagandist role in several ways. It is not so ideologically driven. The main mission is to promote the image of the party and to justify its legitimacy rather than to brainwash or impose an ideology on the audience. From a mission like this, the new role that follows demands that image promotion be voluntarily accepted by the audience. Therefore, it requires the employment of appealing and engaging techniques, such as readability, broad scope of coverage, and some sense of impartiality. This role does not require complete ideological loyalty and commitment to the party-state from journalists. It is embedded in a financially self-reliant entity, and, therefore, must incorporate profit-seeking considerations into the publicity operation.

Clearly, the journalists are still confined by the political system — probably even more so than before, though in a different way. However, the influence of the market is getting stronger and stronger, as shown in the stories of the journalists' moneymaking role models, their unconventional attitudes toward ethics, and their acceptance of a new role. As the party's depoliticization goes on and personal mobility increases, the notion of *da gong zai* (a migrant or mobile worker) may get more embedded in the definition of the once glamorous and ideologically driven profession.

Discussion

This chapter has attempted to analyze one case of the Chinese Communist Party press. I have concentrated on the interplay of politics and economics, two major driving forces behind the party press. Through the use of a five-mode conceptual framework of a tug-of-war, I have shown that the two types of forces stand off against each other in different ways at different levels. In terms of advertising operations and competition mechanisms, market forces are obviously on the winning side, dragging an avant-garde of the party press well into the terrain of an emerging market economy. In the area of management, political controls remain tight at the top level, but market forces are gaining momentum and are gradually pulling the system toward a more profit- and economics-conscious establishment. This market influence on newspaper management is particularly strong in such areas as financing, hiring, and firing of employees and in the internal incentive system. At the individual level, journalists are found to be mobile psychologically, physically, and ideologically. They have developed an attitude toward professional ethics that is noticeably influenced by market forces, and they have begun to settle for the role of "hired" party publicity officers. The only area in which political interests remain an overmatch for market forces is in the content and much of the news-making process. Even there, however, some gradual changes are taking place. The scope of coverage is noticeably larger, covering not only publicity-oriented subjects but also subjects that would interest readers in an expanding market. More important, the orthodox framing of reality, which sees the world mostly through the old political lenses, is being complemented by modified and unorthodox frames.

Compared with the study by White (1990) of Shanghai's reform media in the 1980s, this study has found some continuities as well as new developments and dimensions. The emerging trend of depoliticization of media content in Shanghai reported by White has been found to be more obvious and stronger in Shenzhen. The experimental nature and limited scope "open" recruitment of journalists in Shanghai has been well established, with the papers in Shenzhen implementing an over-the-board contractual system for all journalists except for the top leaders. The Shanghai Party newspapers could hardly rely on advertising revenue for a living in the 1980s (the *Liberation Daily* and the *Wenhui Daily* have since become two of the country's most profitable newspapers). In Shenzhen in the 1990s, the two party state-run papers have made a fortune out of advertising revenues, which provided more than 90 percent of the *Shenzhen Special Zone Daily*'s income. More important and also absent, unnoticed, or hidden beneath the surface in the Shanghai media as observed by White were such elements as the bonus-oriented incentive system, the weight of economic considerations in *SSZD* operation and structure, the tough intramedia competition, the dilemma of the advertising operation, the notion of "hired guns" (or *da gong zai*), and the increasing significance of business management.

Clearly, this chapter shows that the pulling forces of politics and economics have changed the internal and external configuration of a party newspaper toward what I call a "Party Publicity Inc." Such an "Inc." takes it as its main job publicizing the party's policies and interests. However, unlike the old propaganda instrument served by the party press for decades, the new "Inc." is oriented more toward promoting the image of the party and justifying its legitimacy than toward ideological brainwashing and conversion. More important, as an "Inc.," financially responsible for its own survival, it operates in many ways more like a business entity than like a purely party-paid organ, subject as much to economic pressure as to political influence. The "Inc." needs to attract the ideologically disenchanted audience by softening its publicity messages (or separating such messages from other information) and providing a wide range of information to respond to market demands. Although such an "Inc." owes its existence to party affiliation and is directed by party-appointed executives, it is increasingly staffed by "hired" technocrats whose ideology, interests, and loyalty may differ from those inherently demanded by the party press.

This gradual movement toward a "Publicity Inc.," as manifested in the *Shenzhen Special Zone Daily,* apparently reflects a natural trend to which the party press must adapt itself. Since the end of the ideologically charged Cultural Revolution, the Communist Party leadership has gradually and reluctantly given up full ideological indoctrination (Dittmer 1994), viewing it as both a lost battle and a crusade incompatible with the market-oriented and pragmatic economic reforms. In fact, the leadership and the entire party membership have been confused about what ideology to adhere to in the midst of frequent outpouring of a de-Maoist undercurrent, the reinterpretation of Marxism, and the introduction of capitalist economic mechanisms. In the early 1980s, Zhao Ziyang, then premier of the State Council, decried the circumstance that only a handful of people in the party genuinely understood Marxism and socialism. Concerned about further confusion and a complete ideological breakdown, former paramount leader Deng Xiaoping decreed at the outset of the economic reforms that the party should engage in no "theoretical debate" about whether the reforms were socialistic or capitalistic (*xing she hai shi xing zi*). Although ideological rhetoric has remained in the official political discourse and sporadic campaigns with ideological undertones have occurred, such as the 1996 campaign initiated by General Secretary Jiang Zemin to "underscore politics" (*jiang zheng zhi*), these campaigns have mainly served the purpose of political struggle, not genuine ideological indoctrination. For the leadership of the Communist Party, the most important thing is to justify its mandate, maintain its rule, and keep the country in "stability and unity."

On the other hand, the Chinese people have been undergoing a progressive deemphasis of ideology. Two generations of Chinese have been through numerous ideological campaigns, and, consequently, the Chinese have grown fed up with the arm-twisting indoctrinations and hypocrisy of those preaching the Communist ideology. The younger generation has grown up in the reform era and, with the party relaxing its political work in schools, has never been seriously exposed to any fixed set of ideological doctrines. Furthermore, many people have grown disenchanted with ideology and alienated by political suppression, such as the crackdown on the 1989 Tiananmen movement, and by the commercialism that has swept the nation. For Chinese, any ideological propagation is not only irrelevant but also dangerous, as it has the potential to resurrect the "bad old days" from which they have tried so hard to break off.

This changed reality has propelled the party press to descend from an ideological highland to a pragmatic publicity plateau, and it has made such a move possible. After the party cut the "milk supply" to the party press, that press had to do what was necessary and possible to transform itself into a moneymaking and publicity-oriented enterprise in one form or another. Although the *Shenzhen Special Zone Daily* is in the avant-garde of this transformation, it apparently represents a trend among the party press. Indeed, a "Party Publicity Inc." is perhaps where the Communist political system and the increasingly capitalist economy in China, two inherently antagonistic forces, can find some middle ground and strike a balance—no matter how transient that balance may be. This trend appears more universal and inevitable if we look at the changes in some similar systems. In Taiwan, for example, the Kuomintang (KMT, or the Nationalist Party) has run a similar propaganda system for decades. Like the Communist system in the mainland, this system has lost much of its credibility and a tremendous amount of money, thus becoming an unbearable liability on the Kuomintang. In the early half of 1996, the KMT tried to reorganize the system, merging some publications and cutting others (Lee 2000). The direction in which the KMT's culture-propaganda system is moving is undoubtedly a "Party Publicity Inc.," although it bears noticeable differences from the mainland Chinese version. In Russia, the once ideologically charged press has failed to pull itself out of the ruins of a collapsed Communist system and has become neither an important political force nor a viable business. One obvious reason is that the Russian press has not worked out the conflict between market forces and the legacy of a propaganda machine through the trial-and-error operation of a "Publicity Inc.," which can provide the time and mechanisms to soften high-pitched propaganda and to accumulate financial resources for a more substantial transformation.

The prototype of a "Party Publicity Inc.," as represented by the *Shenzhen Special Zone Daily,* is, of course, immature and vexed by many problems. One of the major problems is the danger of abrupt changes in politics wrought by either the central or the local leadership, or both. As the recent history of the cycle of alternate control and relaxation by the party leadership has shown, every time there was a political crisis (such as the Tiananmen movement in 1989) or a serious internal political struggle, the party press would again be tightly controlled and used as a loaded political weapon. The derailment of the decade-long press reforms and the repoliticization of the press in the wake of the Tiananmen movement was a good example. Provincial and local party media organizations need to serve both the big boss in Beijing and the local party leadership. As the economy rapidly develops in such privileged areas as Guangdong, Shanghai, and Shandong, the power base of the local party leadership has grown tremendously. Very often, the local party leadership has interests that conflict with those of the national party leadership. As a result, political clashes take place. In those clashes, the local party press may be employed to serve the local boss against Beijing. This scenario, which has already been seen in Shenzhen, is even more likely in the post-Deng era in which leaders lack charisma or absolute power to rule the country effectively from Beijing. In either case, expedited repoliticization would hurt the party press's credibility, disenchant the audience, and break the fragile and transient accommodation of both political and economic interests under a "Party Publicity Inc." After all, political interests in the party press—and even in the *Shenzhen Special Zone Daily*—are still an overmatch for economic interests in several key areas. Although it is unlikely that the country and the party press will turn back to the ideologically charged era prior to the economic reforms, the danger of repoliticization is clear and present. And any tilt to the political side would change the momentum and balance of power in the political-economic tug-of-war, making it more difficult for the market forces to come in and assist with the reconfiguration of a "Party Publicity Inc."

Another major problem is the chaotic, cutthroat, and often wasteful competition between party-run and state-run news organizations and among the party press. Under the current licensing system, the media market is fairly restricted, with entries being carefully screened and selectively granted by various party and government offices, such as the party propaganda apparatus and the government press and publication bureaus at various levels. Theoretically, media organizations that cater to their specified audiences should enjoy a virtual license to print money, as in the case of broadcast media in the United States. This is especially true with the party press that enjoys a monopoly in providing political and general information. In reality, however, the organization and division of labor in the industry are not so well mapped out and implemented. Attracted by the increasingly lucrative media market, with growing advertising expenditures and higher demands for information and entertainment, and prompted by the desire to have their own publicity outlets, government offices and state-run enterprises of various kinds have flocked into the media market and created their own media outlets, using one legitimate reason or another to obtain the required licenses (see chapter 2 in this volume). The dramatic growth in the number of newspapers in the country over the past decade is a good indication of the trend. Although licensed for a specialized segment of the market, many of the media outlets encroach on one another's territories and even on the party press's monopolistic turf. In addition, a great number of existing media outlets, especially publications, have tried to expand their turf by beefing up their weekend editions and inserts. For a time, many supplementary publications surpassed their master publications to such an extent that the State Press and Publication Bureau had to step in and penalize some of the most outrageous ones. Furthermore, it has become almost a common practice for periodical and book publishers to contract out their registration numbers to freelancers to do whatever they think will make a quick profit.

All this has created an entangled web of competitors, some obvious and others hidden. Because the media system in China is set up to reduce redundancy and minimize competition, there is a lack of effective rules to regulate this unexpected fierce competition. There is no rule to level the ground of competition so that all media outlets, party and nonparty, large and small, can compete on an equal footing. Very often, the big party newspapers are in a disadvantageous position for competing commercially with the "small papers" (mostly tabloids) because they operate under a different set of rules. There is no rule on how much taxpayer money can be used as start-up capital to overpower the competitor (as in the case of the *Shenzhen Commerce Daily*). And there is no rule governing who should bear the responsibility for wasting the public's money in senseless competitions and for saving public institutions from the possible resultant bankruptcy. In such a situation, competition among media outlets is inevitably chaotic and wasteful. How the Chinese Communist press gets out of the vicious and wasteful competition, as seen in Shenzhen, will tremendously affect the formation and operation of the "Party Publicity Inc." More important, how willing the party is to bail out losers in the competition—and in what ways—will remain a thorny issue for the "Party Publicity Inc."

As for eroded journalistic ethics, the "Party Publicity Inc." is obviously not the sole solution. The problem can be fairly well solved only when the moral standards of the entire society change in favor of ethical practices. Nevertheless, this chapter suggests that a financially healthy "Party Publicity Inc.," such as the *Shenzhen Special Zone Daily,* can partially alleviate the problem by paying journalists comfortably and penalizing wrongdoing severely.

After this discussion, an ultimate question arises: Where will the Chinese Communist Party newspapers go from here? Could they transform themselves again from "Publicity Incs." into powerful independent newspaper chains, on par with some of their counterparts in the West, if the party is out of the picture one day?

To this question, Hu Zhimin, the former associate director of the Journalism Research Institute at the *SSZD,* responded by citing a Chinese proverb: "If the skin is gone, where can the hair stick?" (*Pi zhi bu cun, mao jiang yan fu?*).

Notes

I wish to thank Xiang Liping for her valuable assistance and all of the people at the *Shenzhen Special Zone Daily* for sharing their thoughts with me.

1. The results of the interviews reported in this chapter reflected what this author thought were representative views or views on the interviewees' specialized areas. The identified sources were all interviewed through the official channel after this author obtained a written official permission from the director of the *Shenzhen Special Zone Daily.* They were notified of the nature of the research and knew that their views would be reported in research publications. Identities of sources who were not interviewed through the formal channel were withheld.

2. As a metropolitan newspaper in Shenzhen, the *SSZD* devoted a significant amount of coverage to the success of the zone, the problems of such zones, its driving-engine role in the country, the "radiating effects," and policies on special economic zones. Although some of the issues could have been categorized as either economic or political, they were separately classified to demonstrate the self-justification role of the paper and the regional political interest. The paper also devoted sizeable coverage to what is called socialist spiritual civilization in China, a buzzword phrase for activities that represent an uplifting, selfless, generous, friendly, and altruist spirit. This category was coded separately from the category of models and heroes that involved activities of groups or collective units. As corruption became so rampant that the government had to wage continuous campaigns against it, more and more stories about official corruption, a taboo area in the past, found their way into the paper. Official corruption, which may not always be legally punishable, is distinguished from other crime and law issues. Hong Kong, Macao, and Taiwan issues, to which the *SSZD* devotes three-fourths of a page every day, were neither purely domestic nor purely foreign; they were given a separate category. Another category was created for coverage of media activities that could be both political and economic at the same time.

Bibliography

Bagdikian, Ben H. 1983. *The Media Monopoly.* Boston: Beacon Press.

Cao, Yu. 1995. "Shenzhen xinwen chuban ye de xiangchuang yu pinggu" ("The State and Appraisal of the Press and Publication Industry in Shenzhen"). *Journal of Shenzhen Special Zone Daily* 3:29–30 (in Chinese).

Chan, Joseph Man. 1993. "Commercialization without Independence: Media Development in China." In Joseph Cheng, ed., *China Review 1993.* Hong Kong: Chinese University Press.

———. 1994. "Calling the Tune without Paying the Piper: The Reassertion of Media Controls in China." In Joseph Cheng, ed., *China Review 1995.* Hong Kong: Chinese University Press.

Chang, Tsan-kuo, Chin-Hsien Chen, and Guoqiang Zhang. 1993. "Rethinking the Mass Propaganda Model: Evidence from the Chinese Regional Press." *Gazette* 51(3):173–79.

Chang, Tsan-kuo, Jian Wang, and Chi-Hsien Chen. 1994. "News as Social Knowledge in China: The Changing Worldview of Chinese National Media." *Journal of Communication* 44(3):52–69.

Chen, Huailin. 1995. "The Trend of Commercialization in the Chinese Media." Paper presented at Conference on Chinese Press, June, Wuhan, China (in Chinese).

———. 1996. "On the Uneven Development of the Marketization of the Chinese Press." Paper presented at Conference on the Present Status and Development of Chinese Press Management, March, China (in Chinese).

Chen, Huailin, and Chin-Chuan Lee. 1998. "Press Finance and Economic Reform in China." In Joseph Cheng, ed., *China Review 1997.* Hong Kong: Chinese University Press.

Cheng, Hong. 1996. "Advertising in China: A Socialist Experiment." In Katherine Tolland Frith, ed., *Advertising in Asia: Communication, Culture, and Consumption.* Ames: Iowa State University Press.

Cheng, Ying. 1995. "A Heated Debate on the Fate of Special Economic Zones." *The Nineties Monthly (Jiu shi nian dai)* (Hong Kong). October, 49–53 (in Chinese).

China Industry and Commerce Management Yearly. 1998. Beijing: China Industry and Commerce Press (in Chinese).

Chinese Journalism Yearbook. 1997. Beijing: Chinese Academy of Social Sciences Press (in Chinese).

Curran, James, A. Douglas, and G. Whannel. 1980. "The Political Economy of the Human-Interest Story." In Anthony Smith, ed., *Newspapers and Democracy.* Cambridge: MIT Press.

Diamond Information Enterprise Co., Guangzhou. 1997. A report on the monitoring of advertising in the Chinese press (in Chinese).

Dittmer, Lowell. 1994. "The Politics of Publicity in Reform China." In Chin-Chuan Lee, ed., *China's Media, Media's China.* Boulder, Colo.: Westview.

Gitlin, Todd. 1980. *The Whole World Is Watching: Mass Media in the Making and Unmaking of the New Left*. Berkeley: University of California Press.

Golding, Peter, and Graham Murdock. 1996. "Culture, Communications, and Political Economy." In James Curran and Michael Gurevitch, eds., *Mass Media and Society*. 2nd ed. New York: Arnold.

He, Zhou. 1988. "Changes in the Soviet Concept of News—to What Extent and Why?" *Gazette* 42:193–211.

———. 1993a. "Press Freedom in China: Past, Present and Future." Proceedings of the 1993 Conference of Chinese Communication Research and Education: Journalism and Communication Research on Mainland China. Taipei, Taiwan: Research Center College of Communication, National Chengchi University.

———. 1993b. "The Need for a New Perspective in Studying the Chinese Press." Panel paper presented at the annual convention of the Association for Education in Journalism and Mass Communication, Kansas City, Kansas.

———. 1994. "Alternating Control and Relaxation: A Vicious Cycle the Chinese Press Cannot Break." *Hong Kong Economic Journal,* December 2 (in Chinese).

———. 1995. "Ferocious Circulation Wars in the Chinese Press." *Hong Kong Economic Journal,* December (in Chinese).

———. 1996. *Mass Media and Tiananmen Square*. New York: NOVA Science Publishers.

Herman, Edward, and Noam Chomsky. 1988. *Manufacturing Consent: The Political Economy of the Mass Media*. New York: Pantheon.

Hong, Junhao. 1998. *The Internationalization of Television in China: The Evolution of Ideology, Society, and Media since the Reform*. Westport, Conn.: Praeger.

Huang, Yu, and Xu Yu. 1996. "Towards Media Democratization: The Chinese Experience and a Critique of the Neo-Authoritarian Model." Paper presented at the annual conference of the International Communication Association, May, Chicago.

Iyengar, Shanto. 1991. *Is Anyone Responsible? How Television Frames Political Issues*. Chicago: University of Chicago Press.

Journalism Institute of the *Shenzhen Special Zone Daily*. 1995. *A Moment in History: A Selection of 1994 News Stories in the* Shenzhen Special Zone Daily. Shenzhen: China Youth Publishing House (in Chinese).

Journalism Research Institute of Chinese Academy of Social Sciences and Capital Journalism Association. 1988. *People's Appeals and People's Expectations*. Beijing: Journalism Research Institute (in Chinese).

Lee, Chin-Chuan. 1981. "The United States as Seen through the *People's Daily*." *Journal of Communication* 31(4):92–101.

———. 1994. "Ambiguities and Contradictions: Issues in China's Changing Political Communication." In Chin-Chuan Lee, ed., *China's Media, Media's China*. Boulder, Colo.: Westview.

———. 2000. "State, Market, and Media: The Case of Taiwan." In James Curran and Myung-Jin Park, eds. *De-Westernizing Media Studies*. London: Routledge.

Mosco, Vincent. 1996. *The Political Economy of Communication*. London: Sage.

People's University Public Opinion Research Institute. 1989. "A National Survey of Journalists' Attitude toward Journalism Reforms." In Chen Chongshan et al., eds., *A Perceptive View of Media Effects in China*. Shenyang: publisher unidentified (in Chinese).

Polumbaum, Judy. 1990. "The Tribulations of China's Journalists after a Decade of Reform." In Chin-Chuan Lee, ed., *Voices of China: The Interplay of Politics and Journalism*. New York: Guilford.

———. 1993. "Press Commercialism and the Breakdown of Journalism Ethics in Mainland China." Paper presented at the International Conference on Chinese Communication Research and Education, July, Taipei, Taiwan.

———. 1994. "Between Propaganda and Junk-Food Journalism: Exploratory Terrains in Mainland Chinese News Coverage." Paper presented at the annual conference of the Association of Education for Journalism and Mass Communication, August, Atlanta.

Roxburgh, Angus. 1987. *Pravda: Inside the Soviet News Machine*. New York: George Braziller.

Schudson, Michael. 1991. "The Sociology of News Production Revisited." In James Curran and Michael Gurevitch, eds., *Mass Media and Society*. New York: Arnold.

White, Lynn. 1990. "All the News: Structure and Politics in Shanghai's Reform Media." In Chin-Chuan Lee, ed., *Voices of China: The Interplay of Politics and Journalism*. New York: Guilford.

Xue, Ting. 1995. "A Political Economy Analysis of Chinese Movies (1979–1994)." Master's thesis, Chinese University of Hong Kong.

Yu, Xu. 1993. "Professionalization without Guarantees: Changes in the Chinese Press in the Post-1989 Years." *Gazette* 53:23–41.

Zhao, Yuezhi. 1998. *Media, Market, and Democracy in China: Between the Party Line and Bottom Line*. Urbana: University of Illinois Press.

Zhu, Jianhua, David Weaver, Ven-hwei Lo, Chongshan Chen, and Wei Wu. 1997. "Individual, Organizational, and Societal Influences on Media Role Perceptions: A Comparative Study of Journalists in China, Taiwan, and the United States." *Journalism and Mass Communication Quarterly* 74(1):84–96.

5

Seeking Appropriate Behavior under a Socialist Market Economy

An Analysis of Debates and Controversies
Reported in the Beijing Youth Daily

STANLEY ROSEN

More than a decade after the military crackdown in and around Tiananmen Square, one of the more surprising developments has been the continuing growth of the Chinese media. Back in 1979, China had only 186 newspapers, with the number rising rapidly to 1,574 by 1986. By 1993, the total had reached 2,000, and by early 1996, there were 2,235 openly circulated newspapers in China. There seems little doubt that this expansion is closely related to China's march toward a "socialist" market economy. As late as 1988, there were 407 party-organ newspapers (*jiguan bao*), constituting 25 percent of the openly circulated papers. From the late 1980s to 1996, however, a perceptible shift appeared, so that of the more than 600 new papers entering the market during these years, 70 percent did not even receive government subsidies. Such papers were compelled to appeal to readers if they were to survive (Lin 1997:68–69). By 1995, there were 128 officially registered evening papers; the public's interest can be gauged by noting that 90 percent of their subscribers are individuals, not units, and that often the largest part of their income is derived from advertising (*China News Analysis* 1995:1–2). The most popular newspapers in Beijing, Shanghai, and Guangzhou, based on consumer spending, are all evening papers.

This growth in the popular press has clearly come at the expense of the more rigidly controlled "party" or "official" press. Despite some attempts at expansion and streamlining, newspapers like the *People's Daily* (*Renmin ribao*), *Guangming Daily* (*Guangming ribao*), and *Economics Daily* (*Jingji ribao*) have been unable to compete with city dailies for individual subscribers or advertising dollars (Bacani and Law 1996:32). Statistical data from the Newspaper and Periodicals Circulation Bureau of the Ministry of Posts and Telecommunications show that most newspapers have been losing subscribers since January 1989, with the average decline nationwide about 35 percent. The major nationally circulated papers (many of which have a built-in cushion because of institutional subscriptions) have declined on average 30 percent, although some of them have declined by more than 50 percent. In 1993, of the 20 national papers considered particularly important, only one increased circulation (by 0.7 percent); the large majority of the others declined by more than 10 percent. In 1994, none of the 20 papers increased circulation, and the average decline was 13.7 percent. Provincial and municipal party organs have had similar declines (Li 1995). At the same time, however, as one recent national survey of the reading habits of Chinese citizens from 1978 to 1998 noted in its analysis of newspaper circulation, the reform period has witnessed the increasing voice and influence of provincial and subprovincial papers at the expense of central organs (Kang, Wu, Liu, and Sun 1998).

The increasing importance of market dynamics, combined with political decisions made in the aftermath of Tiananmen, has also had an important effect on the kinds of discussions and debates one now finds in the Chinese media. Following the Thirteenth Party Congress of October 1987 and prior to June 1989, China was a very lively place for intellectual discussion and contention. There was, by today's standards, a surprising amount of official tolerance toward those questioning China's past, present, and future. The most obvious example was the six-hour documentary shown twice on Chinese television in 1988 entitled *River Elegy,* which attacked some of the major icons of Chinese civilization, including the Great Wall, the image of the dragon, and the Yellow River. There were also debates in the press and before large audiences on university campuses over the best way for China to become democratic, whether a "neoauthoritarian" model (à la South Korea, Singapore, and Taiwan) or a more direct, Western-derived model best fit China's conditions. Conservative Party leaders, to be sure, were unhappy about this openness, but the policy at that time — under Zhao Ziyang's stewardship — was to discourage the Communist Party from interfering in academic and cultural debates. And there were newspapers such as the *World Economic Herald* (*Shijie jingji daobao*) in Shanghai —

banned in April 1989—that were more than willing to push the envelope (Rosen 1996a).

Following Tiananmen, a decision was made to control political life and strictly limit academic debates that might have political implications. The overriding emphasis was placed on maintaining stability. As part of the government's new strategy, the public was offered a more varied cultural life, albeit of a nonthreatening nature. Along with the sharp increase of karaoke bars and discos came an explosion of tabloid newspapers and sensationalistic magazines, all of which was further fueled by the elimination of state subsidies and the necessity for all cultural organizations to adjust to the new requirements of the market. This new competitive environment for media products has brought forth television programs and newspapers—such as *Focal Point Inquiry* (*Jiaodian fangtan*) and *Southern Weekend* (*Nanfang zhoumo*)—that have won broad popular approval by emphasizing investigative journalism and the exposure of corruption. Such investigative journalism has become successful enough to yield a number of popular books that recount their experiences and reprint the original stories (Liang 1998; Li and Sun 1998; Wang 1998). Thus, while one no longer expects to find leading intellectuals engaging in freewheeling academic debates with obvious political implications in today's Chinese newspapers and magazines, there does appear to have been an increase in discussions of wider and more immediate societal interest. If, as Zhang Xiaogang and others have argued, China's transition to the market has produced a duality of formal and informal roles for the press—all media are required to adhere to the official propaganda line formally, while journalists informally attempt to free themselves from state control as their media seek liberties in the marketplace—one can expect over time to see the promotion of debates on controversial or cutting edge issues even in "official" publications, as such publications attempt, in an era of declining circulation, to distinguish themselves from their more rigid brethren. Indeed, Zhang sees press debates as a substitute for public forums, enabling citizens to identify their interests, form groups, and raise demands, and he urges the Chinese media to continue to sponsor these debates as an important way to foster the growth of democracy (Zhang 1993; Schell 1995; Lee 1994).

While the study of press debates in a relatively closed society can provide valuable information on public attitudes not readily available from other sources, most often the purpose of these debates, it should be remembered, is didactic, that is, to direct the public by means of an open press discussion to the one right answer. Where there are several competing potential right answers, containing apparent conflicts over core values, press debates can be used either to reconcile the conflict for the public or, more subtly, to promote one core value over another. Even debates on topics that are relatively free from party attention will likely have a particular editorial spin. For example, in the debate over "appropriate" images for women, and the benefits and costs of being a "strong woman" (*nu qiang ren*), there was a divergence between popular women's magazines that often focused on the unhappy family life resulting from too much success outside the home, and Women's Federation magazines, which stressed the positive aspects of being a strong woman (Rosen 1994). Perhaps the most open discussions appear in internal journals, albeit within rather restrictive guidelines. *Neibu wengao* (*Internal Manuscripts*), the internal edition of the party's foremost ideological journal, *Qiu Shi* (*Seeking Truth*), will often present articles by local party officials with divergent viewpoints, or present a range of opinions on an issue in a single article. Since this journal is available in most Chinese libraries, it provides valuable information on contentious issues within the party to an informed and interested public. On the other hand, newspapers of record like the *People's Daily* will seldom offer debates; their role is to inform the public *after* an authoritative decision has been reached.

Arguably, the most *interesting* case of an official newspaper that has transcended its origins is the *Beijing Youth Daily* (*Beijing qingnian bao*), the organ of the Beijing Municipal Party Committee's Communist Youth League. Starting as early as January 3, 1989, the *Beijing Youth Daily* has been a pioneer in packaging [*baozhuang*] the news by assigning responsibility for individual pages to subeditors, who then plan the layout of the entire page. Over time, the reader could look forward to special sections each week, for example, on "The News of the Week" (on Tuesdays, beginning in 1993), on "Literature, Culture and Sports" (on Thursdays), or on "Youth Weekend" (on Saturdays, beginning in 1992). To remain relevant for its youthful and increasingly "hip" readership, new sections on computers and automobiles were added as regular weekly features, as was a public opinion poll on an issue of general interest. At the end of January 1994 the newspaper was divided into two sections, and in July it expanded to a daily (Qiu 1995:77).

As part of its strategy for success in a crowded marketplace of declining newspaper subscribers, the *Beijing Youth Daily* began to pursue stories that had elicited wide public interest or concern and that raised important questions about the future role of the country's key institutions and core values under the impact of a market economy. It was not uncommon for the newspaper to dispatch a reporter to a distant province to investigate a story that had created particular interest in a local provincial paper. They also proactively solicited and published submissions from the public as part of an ongoing debate over the new phenomena that had arisen (Yu 1995; Zheng 1994).[1] Their emphasis on investigative reporting and consumer issues won them high praise in public opinion polls. For example, in a survey commissioned by the Central Propaganda Department, the Public Opinion Research Institute of Chinese People's University examined the attitudes of readers toward newspapers with a national circulation, concluding that the *Beijing Youth Daily*'s approval rate among the public was "far higher" than the average for national (*quanguoxing*) papers. In terms of content, the average approval rate for national papers was 56.3 percent; for youth papers the average was 59.1 percent; and for the *Beijing Youth Daily* it was 78.7 percent. Of particular interest in the current market economy, the trust expressed for advertisements in the *Beijing Youth Daily* by its readers was 56.8 percent; by contrast, only 22.9 percent of the total national sample expressed their trust in newspaper advertisements. Overall, the *Beijing Youth Daily*'s 84 percent approval rating far exceeded the general approval rating of 61 percent for the nation's major papers (Yu 1995). In 1994, the average circulation for each issue of the *Beijing Youth Daily* was 151,822, placing it fourth in Beijing among daily newspapers, behind only the *Beijing Evening News,* the *Beijing Daily,* and the suburban edition of the *Beijing Daily* (*Zhongguo xinwen nianjian* 1995:845–46).[2] By 1996 the circulation had climbed to 192,300 (*Zhongguo chuban nianjian* 1997:16).

The success of the *Beijing Youth Daily* and the strategy used to achieve its current recognition have been widely reported in the Chinese press. The paper has for a number of years walked a fine line, testing the limits of investigative reporting and consumer advocacy, more than once incurring the ire of propaganda department officials.[3] The titles of several recent articles from Chinese professionals writing on journalism provide a good picture of the *Beijing Youth Daily*'s image: "*Beijing Youth Daily:* The Newspaper that Refuses to Behave" and "*Beijing Youth Daily:* Eight Strengths and Five Shortcomings to Avoid" (Yu 1995; Sun 1995). In a sense, as the latter report perhaps inadvertently brings out, some of the newspaper's strengths are also potential weaknesses. For example, the newspaper is highly praised for its exposés, in October 1994, on county-level corruption in education and, in December 1994, on health hazards of the pork sold in the Beijing market. In the latter report, particularly, the paper is commended for educating the public and winning the trust of the masses.

By contrast, the newspaper has been criticized for pursuing and writing about unusual events or current trends "even if they do not promote socialist spiritual civilization," for becoming too excited when tracking down a story and publishing an account before all the facts are in, and for going well beyond the bounds of a local paper and reporting on international events without approval from propaganda organs. A good example of the latter sin is the paper's coverage of American arms sales to Taiwan in September 1992, which China clearly viewed as a violation of two Sino-American joint communiqués. Particularly upsetting to the authorities was the interview the newspaper conducted with a USIA representative from the American Embassy. Not only was the interview unauthorized, but it was viewed as allowing the Americans to present their version of events, in competition with China's official propaganda organs. An example of overly enthusiastic reporting was the coverage of testing of urine samples of Chinese athletes at the 1994 Asian Games in Hiroshima, making it appear that the Japanese had in some way tampered with the sample of one of the Chinese athletes. Here they violated the strictures from the State Commission on Sports not to report independently on any controversial or sensitive issues until a conclusion had been reached by the Executive Council of the Asian Games (Sun 1995). It is therefore not surprising, as will be discussed below, that the *Beijing Youth Daily* provided the most detailed and balanced reporting on the "Ping-Pong controversy" at the Hiroshima games.

The *Beijing Youth Daily*'s success, particularly the trust it had earned for its consumer protection work, ironically became the source of the newspaper's biggest challenge in the summer of 1996. Although it is beyond the scope of this chapter, this controversy is nevertheless illustrative of many of the points noted above. It suggests the dangers facing a newspaper that has successfully carved out a market niche by winning the trust of consumers, while offending powerful interests unaccustomed to being publicly challenged.

Briefly, on June 5, 1996, the *Beijing Youth Daily* reported that, in Anhui Province, three young girls—aged five, four, and one—had died of poisoning after drinking a popular children's beverage produced by Wahaha, a large state-owned enterprise in Hangzhou. Given page-one coverage in its popular "Newsweek" section, complete with endearing pictures of the one- and four-year-olds before the incident, the newspaper provided detailed information from the local public security bureau on the sequence of events before and after the incident. The report continued, rather chillingly, by noting that although the incident had occurred over a month earlier, virtually no one in Beijing was aware of it. Moreover, Wahaha was still among the best-selling brands of children's drinks in the capital. The report concluded in a typically provocative manner, pointedly stating that the key problem was that even now it was still difficult to determine how the toxin had entered the Wahaha beverage, certainly raising questions about the culpability of the drink company (*Beijing Youth Daily,* June 5, 1996:1; *Ming bao,* August 21, 1996).

After this story appeared, Wahaha soon discovered that the Chinese masses were no longer purchasing the drink, one indication of the national influence of the newspaper. The company, interestingly, seemed not to relish confronting the popular newspaper in the court of public opinion, but rather criticized the *Beijing Youth Daily* in an internal publication, arguing that the report was unfounded and had caused them to incur huge losses. At the same time, they used their bureaucratic clout to protest at the higher levels of the party and government. The Central Propaganda Department immediately ordered the *Beijing Youth Daily* to stop publication for realignment. An investigation showed that the report was correct, but the company still argued that the contamination occurred after the beverage had left the factory. Although the newspaper was supported by the Beijing Municipal Party Committee and the Central Propaganda Department rescinded its order, the *Beijing Youth Daily* was still held accountable for breaking two "press rules." First, the media can cover civil or criminal cases before a ruling is given by a judicial organ only if they have special permission; and second, no newspapers are allowed to carry reports provided by reporters of other press units in other localities. After several months, a Hong Kong source reported that the newspaper's director (*shezhang*), Cui Enqing, was to be replaced by someone sent from the *Beijing Daily.* Two years previously, the editor in chief, Chen Ji, had also been suddenly removed, allegedly because the leadership was dissatisfied with the newspaper's performance.

Recent Debates in the *Beijing Youth Daily*

For the purposes of this chapter I have chosen to focus on one aspect of the *Beijing Youth Daily:* the use of debates to generate discussion on contentious issues. While less "sensational" than their muckraking activities, and less likely to incur official displeasure, these debates are very helpful in understanding current developments in Chinese society and at least some of the range of opinions that exist on these issues. I will look at four prominent debates covering the period from October 1994 to June 1995, all of which address the general question of appropriate behavior under a market economy. They reflect the growing pains of a nation not only seeking to chart its future but also, to the dismay of many in the older generation and the party leadership, beginning to question and reinterpret its past. At the same time, the manner in which these debates are shaped reveals, to some extent, the editorial line of the newspaper. The four debates to be discussed are as follows:[4]

1. The He Zhili–Koyama Chire 1994 Asian Games Ping-Pong Debate
2. The Wang Dingding Good Samaritan Debate
3. The Yang Bailao–White-Haired Girl Reinterpretation of the Past Debate
4. The Fang Min State–Private Enterprise Communist Party Role Debate

THE HE ZHILI–KOYAMA CHIRE
1994 ASIAN GAMES PING-PONG DEBATE

Even during the Maoist period, sports stars had fame and popularity in China. Ping-Pong champion Zhuang Zedong, for example, helped promote the Mao cult by attributing his success to the Chairman's writings. Later, he was reportedly in line for a position as Minister of Culture if the "Gang of Four" had prevailed. China's opening to the outside world, the decline of political zeal, and the headlong rush toward a consumer economy have made sports stars more popular than ever. The National Basketball Association Game of the Week, broadcast with a Mandarin voice-over, and Italian League soccer games are among the most watched programs in China. In 1992, the Chinese government allowed the formation of homegrown professional soccer and basketball leagues across the country, leading to local fan clubs and Chinese stars. But the government, anxious to provide nonthreatening outlets to entertain the public while wary of providing any source of uncontrolled mass allegiance, has moved cautiously. Sporting events, particularly when China is facing a foreign opponent, have the potential to be volatile. In 1985, for example, Beijing fans rioted after the Chinese national team lost to Hong Kong during the early elimination rounds of the 1986 World Cup. The episode, in which cars were set ablaze and several police officers were injured, became known as the "May 19 Soccer Incident" (Tempest 1996).[5]

In this context, the victory of Koyama Chire in the women's table tennis singles tournament at the 1994 Asian Games in Hiroshima takes on added meaning. If this were merely a case of a Japanese opponent triumphing over China's best players it would still have attracted a good deal of attention in China, but the result in this sports event cut much deeper. Koyama Chire is Chinese and, under her original name—He Zhili—had been a star of the Chinese team until 1987. As the *Far Eastern Economic Review* noted when covering this story, He Zhili's decision to change both her country and her name came after being ordered by her coach to lose a match at the 1987 New Delhi world championships so that her teammate could advance to the finals. Defying the coach, she won both her semifinal match and the world championship. As a result, she was accused of having committed "a serious error" and, by her own account, was severely restricted in her athletic career from then on. Although she was a top-seeded player in women's Ping-Pong, her coach barred her from competing in the 1988 Seoul Olympics (Kuhn 1994).

This was not the end of the story, however. She married a Japanese engineer, moved to Japan, and changed her name and citizenship. As the 1994 Asian Games were about to begin, Koyama, seemingly past her prime at age thirty—most Chinese athletes are forced to retire from competition at age twenty-five to provide opportunities for the next generation—vowed to teach her former teammates a lesson. Her performance was as good as her word. She created a sensation, as one Chinese newspaper reported, by defeating in one day Chen Jing, the women's singles champion in the 1988 Seoul Olympics, in the morning; Qiao Hong, the women's singles champion at the Fortieth World Table Tennis Championships, in the afternoon; and Deng Yaping, the women's singles champion in both the Forty-first World Table Tennis Championships and the 1992 Barcelona Olympics. The televised images of Koyama in her Japanese colors, standing triumphantly on the winner's platform as the Japanese flag was raised behind her and the Japanese national anthem rang out, flanked on each side by the Chinese superstars who had finished second and third, was simply unendurable to many Chinese back home (Ye 1995). Almost immediately, He/Koyama was denounced in the Chinese press as a traitor to her motherland. As one reader put it, "The moment Ms. He Zhili . . . appeared on the awards platform under the Japanese flag, I felt as nauseated as though I had found a fly in a savory dish of food" (*Beijing Youth Daily,* November 7, 1994:1).[6]

The most extensive discussion—and apparently one of the few that offered a more balanced approach—appeared in the *Beijing Youth Daily.* The series began on October 18, 1994, five days after Koyama's victory, with an article by He Dong raising the issue of nationality and suggesting that "even the notorious and scabrous Maradona, who has been selling himself to foreign teams . . . to make more money, and who has been a constant source of . . . scandals" must still be admired and respected for unconditionally performing for Argentina whenever there is a major international soccer competition. An editor's note pointed out that Koyama's actions had already polarized Chinese citizens, with many people agreeing with He Dong that Koyama's success was a "betrayal," although others had argued that too much was being made of what was essentially an athletic contest. Readers were encouraged to send in their responses, and the series continued until October 31, at which point the editors offered a summary of the debate; however, because letters continued to arrive after that date, an additional recapitulation was offered on November 7 (*Beijing Youth Daily,* October 18:1, October 20:2, October 23:2, October 24:A2 and B1, October 25:2, October 27:4, October 31:1, and November 7:1, all 1994).

There were several related issues at the heart of the discussions. Certainly there was the question of the relationship between sports and patriotism, as well as between sports and ethics. Also addressed, however, was the conflict between individualism and collectivism, specifically, whether one should be obedient to authority and, to Koyama's critics, whether a nation's interests should come before personal revenge. For Koyama's supporters, perhaps the key point was that the relationship between the individual and the state must change to reflect the movement of the country to a market economy, with its emphasis on competition. Some readers noted the existence of a so-called overseas legion, referring to dissatisfied Chinese stars who had left the country and now were competing for other nations against China, and that, in fact, the Koyama case was part of a much larger and more complex problem.[7] Nevertheless, despite the loss of many star athletes and the admission that when Chinese played each other in international matches coaches were given the authority to dictate winners and losers, ostensibly to ensure more medals for China, there were contributors who seemed to feel that self-assertive individualism was as great a sin as lack of patriotism. One letter chastised Koyama, suggesting that if "you had waited your turn, certainly your coach would have later arranged for your teammates to let you win. Of course you wanted to be the world champion, but did you think that others didn't have big ambitions as well?" (Kuhn 1994).

It was clear from some of the contributions that Koyama's victory, as well as her actions during the matches, stirred up deep-seated patriotic and/or nationalistic feelings. For example, several complained about Koyama's use of the Japanese term *yoshi* (meaning "good" or "well done") whenever she had made a particularly good shot. For one reader, the raising of the Japanese national flag in honor of Koyama's victory brought on thoughts of Chinese collaborators during the Second World War.

In their summation, the editors noted that the 180 submissions were evenly divided between those that supported He Dong's original article and those that opposed it. In their own conclusion, however, the editors left no doubt where they stood. While acknowledging that Koyama had good reason to rebel against an outdated system of personnel control in sports, it was at the same time suggested that, because her attack fell upon "Chinese national sensibilities," she had actually invited the indignation and censure that followed. To the editors, the debate showed how "patriotism and nationalist sentiment still constitute the most important spiritual force . . . of a nation." Any nation, they argued, which loses that spiritual resource will enjoy no respect in the world. They also noted favorably how, despite value changes that have followed the establishment of a market economy, these changes have not diminished "the unflagging patriotic sentiments and intense national self-esteem of the Chinese nation." They closed by calling for in-depth education in patriotism, suggesting that there is no conflict between enhanced patriotism and the cause of reform and openness.

In their final recapitulation of November 7, they acknowledged but downplayed the fact that the viewpoints presented "differed widely and even ran counter to each other," arguing that the more important point was that the majority expressed strong patriotic sentiments. As they put it, "[A]n intrinsic sentiment common to all the different viewpoints is concern for China, anxiety for China, and love for China." They divided the letters into three types. The first type, based on "simple and unsophisticated national sentiments," condemned Koyama outright for playing against her motherland. The second type reflected on the reasons Koyama had to "challenge" her former teammates in such an intense manner and viewed the entire affair as a tragedy shared by all. Finally, Koyama's supporters emphasized her courage and determination and felt that, having been wronged by her coaches, she was perfectly justified in pursuing her individual goals, and that sports should not be politicized. Interestingly, most of those who took this position were young cadres and students in colleges and middle schools. Finally, they closed by reiterating that "national sentiment and patriotism are essentially the most instinctive and basic sentiments of human beings" but that, given the enormous changes going on in China in terms of the relationship between the individual and the state, educators in patriotism will have to move beyond merely appealing to the emotions and the self-evident truths of the past if they want to remain successful.[8]

THE WANG DINGDING GOOD SAMARITAN DEBATE

Wang's Predecessors: Zhang Hua and Zhang Haidi
The Wang Dingding case is only one recent example of the problems Good Samaritans, activists, and labor models have faced since the end of the Cultural

Revolution. Following that most ideological and fervent of post-1949 political campaigns—and the regime's own disavowal of its ends and means—there was widespread disillusionment regarding open-ended political commitments and a pronounced cynicism toward those that claimed or appeared to perform good deeds. The Chinese press frequently offered accounts of unpleasant incidents, such as, for example, crowds of bystanders heckling PLA soldiers rescuing injured citizens. Letters to the editor in newspapers and magazines offered individual testimony from those who had suffered abuse by "doing the right thing." Appeals to engage in selfless behavior, to emulate Lei Feng and "serve the people," not only went unheeded, they often invited the ridicule of those who remained idealistic and committed to "Communistic" behavior.

Given the inhospitable environment for "models" in the reform period, the press has attempted at various times to resocialize youth into once again fostering a Communist value system. One of the most widely publicized cases—both in China and abroad—was the Zhang Hua case in 1982 (Rosen 1995). The Zhang Hua case is important because it revealed the extent to which pragmatic materialism had affected student attitudes and governed the relationship between individuals of "unequal value." Perhaps it was human capital/rational choice theory taken to its logical extreme. Briefly, Zhang was a twenty-four-year-old medical student in Shaanxi Province who leaped into a night-soil pit to rescue a sixty-nine-year-old peasant from drowning. However, along with the peasant, Zhang was overcome by methane fumes and died in the hospital after a passing dairy worker rescued him in turn. Posthumously hailed as a national hero for his selfless act, Zhang was the subject of an extensive media campaign—including the obligatory diary excerpts—launched by China's major newspapers. He was portrayed as a university student and party member who admired Lei Feng and had interests beyond his own professional success.[9]

While most discussions followed the usual practice of merely enumerating in glowing terms what other university students could learn from Zhang Hua's lofty ideals, Shanghai's *Wenhui Daily* tried a different, and in retrospect fatal, approach. Noting almost casually in an editors' note that "we may occasionally come across some objection" when learning from advanced elements, the editors published a letter from a Hangzhou youth who argued against the behavior of Zhang Hua, calling it an emotional act that, in fact, damaged the long-term interests of the state. For a young student with much to contribute to the Four Modernizations, in whom the state had already invested heavily, to risk his life for an old peasant was "to exchange gold for the same amount of stone." A forum under the title "Is It Worthwhile for a University Student to Risk Death to Save an Old Peasant?" was started, presumably to refute the Hangzhou youth's objection. Unexpectedly, 1,600 letters were received within a few days, with the dissenter garnering embarrassingly robust support. Although the Zhang Hua study campaign limped along until the end of the year, and the infidel duly made a self-criticism under pressure, it seems clear that most college students found Zhang Hua's sacrifice both tragic and foolhardy.[10]

The Zhang Hua case also is representative of an additional phenomenon common in reporting on model personages and model behavior, one familiar to reporters and assumed by the general public, that is, the exaggeration of the positive and the removal of the negative. Zhang Hua was promoted in the press as a model party member, as one who took the emulation of Lei Feng as his highest ideal. Skepticism among the public that Zhang Hua was an aberration and completely unrepresentative of "real" people was countered when one hundred students from the same PLA medical college which had produced Zhang became national models for rescuing more than a dozen tourists who had fallen off a cliff. This "proved," according to the arguments of political work cadres, that there was in fact a widespread "spirit of socialist humanism" among youth (Xinhua 1984). Ironically, interviews with reporters (personal interview 1990) who investigated and wrote about the Zhang Hua case provided a much more interesting picture of the "real" Zhang. When they visited his university, they discovered that his classmates were very upset about the way the posthumous case to honor Zhang had been conducted. They agreed that Zhang was an exemplary individual, widely liked and respected, and fully capable of making his sacrifice. What they objected to was the characterization of Zhang as a Lei Feng–like "docile tool" of the party. The real Zhang was far less obedient. Against university rules, for example, he had a girlfriend. On a number of other issues, he was frequently at odds with the school leadership. His independent nature made him, in some ways, the antithesis of the Lei Feng model. Of course, none of this could ever be officially reported.

Even the most important youth model since Lei Feng—wheelchair-bound Zhang Haidi—who became a national model in 1983, was not all she seemed to be. Having been denied schooling because of her disability, press reports noted how, through self-study, she scored an impressive four hundred points on the university entrance examination. Zhang had spent twenty of her twenty-eight years either in bed or in a wheelchair, her paralysis the result of a failed operation. Despite her disability, she constantly went out of her way to help others in need. Her success was a rebuke to all those, like Pan Xiao, who had asked publicly in the pages of *Chinese Youth* (*Zhongguo qingnian*) back in

1980, "What Is the Meaning of Life?" Zhang Haidi's answer, not unlike the official view of Zhang Hua's sacrifice, was that "the meaning of life lies in making contributions, not in making demands."[11]

While most reporters offered the Zhang Haidi story straight, Liu Binyan, then one of the most widely respected journalists in China, emphasized Zhang's independence and her very un-Lei Feng-like unwillingness to do as she was told in his long account in the *People's Daily*. In an interview several years later (personal interview 1988), he related to me how he had been criticized for writing that article and how, after further investigation, he had discovered various anomalies in the official account of Zhang's life. For example, her score of four hundred on the university entrance examination was, in fact, the result of adding together the two hundred points she had received on each of the two occasions she took the exam; her frequent depression had led to an unreported suicide attempt; and so on. When these discrepancies became known, her backers in Shandong Province quietly toned down their hagiographic campaign.[12]

The Wang Dingding Case

By the time the "Wang Dingding phenomenon," as it came to be called, took place in January 1995, the level of public suspicion regarding Good Samaritans and their reported deeds was quite high (*Beijing Youth Daily*, March 29, 1995:2). The basic facts of the case, as reported in the press, are clear. An eighty-four-year-old woman was knocked down by a bicyclist in Taiyuan city, Shaanxi Province. Wang Dingding, a member of the Communist Youth League, saw what had happened and immediately took the old woman to a hospital to have her fractured wrist set and then took her to another hospital for X rays. That evening, Wang's mother took the woman into her home for the night. The next day, when the old woman's relatives came to get her, Wang Dingding and his family escorted the woman to a hospital, and Wang's mother paid two thousand yuan in hospitalization fees on behalf of the woman's family.

The controversy began when the woman's family insisted that Wang Dingding and his girlfriend must have been responsible for the accident, while Wang Dingding's family protested his innocence. Wang said simply that the old woman seemed very pitiable, and they had only wanted to do a good deed. The Great Wall Radio Station and the *Taiyuan Evening News* initiated a discussion and provided continuing coverage of this story. One young person reportedly sent 250 yuan to the station, suggesting it be passed on to the old woman. He claimed he was, in fact, the guilty party, but did not have the courage to come forward. The *Beijing Youth Daily* sent a reporter to investigate and offered the views of a lawyer, noting that his comments were "quite representative" of the public. He said, "I've read all the reports on this incident. I maintain that the person responsible is none other than Wang Dingding. Why? Wang Dingding took the old lady to the hospital, then took her to his home to spend the night, and paid 2,000 yuan on her behalf. Would he do all those good things if he hadn't knocked her down? Who'd believe that? Are there good people like that in society today? It's a sure thing he knocked her down." Indeed, even the 1,854 yuan which had been left from the 2,000 yuan Wang's mother had paid the hospital was pocketed by the old woman's family.

The top leadership of the municipal and provincial party committees was unwilling to let the matter rest with such an unsatisfactory conclusion. They took part in radio discussions and organized public seminars to promote spiritual civilization, revolutionary values, and a proper outlook on life. Wang Dingding's employer conferred on him the title "Excellent Communist Youth League Member," and Taiyuan city nominated him "Activist in the Construction of Spiritual Civilization." The press forum concentrated generally on the issue of whether it was possible to be a good person. A number of contributors gave examples of how good people are frequently wronged, and how they themselves have been warned to be careful in helping others, since such selfless behavior could easily cause them unwanted problems. One person noted that if you see fighting on the street and you try and stop it, you simply end up being "grilled and interrogated at the police station." Another participant lamented the apathy displayed by the public when someone is in trouble. He admonished those who rationalize their lack of public spiritedness by arguing that "thousands of years of humanist spirit were destroyed overnight by the Cultural Revolution" or that "moral decline is the inevitable price of economic advance" to "stop evading the issue." The newspaper noted that most people in Taiyuan still had doubts, and that the matter had yet to be settled, but they concluded on a relatively optimistic note. They suggested that the public's perception was gradually shifting. If indeed Wang Dingding is really so willing to help others and nurses no grudges or regrets after being wronged, then this is most unusual in today's social atmosphere, and he is truly remarkable and should be set up as a model for conscious emulation.

THE YANG BAILAO—WHITE-HAIRED GIRL REINTERPRETATION OF THE PAST DEBATE

It is interesting to see the effect the market economy has begun to have on issues that have long been accepted among party members and many ordinary citizens as key verities of the Chinese Revolution. In 1995, to commemorate the fiftieth anniversary of China's defeat of Japan, the well-known revolutionary folk opera, *The White-Haired Girl,* was revived and performed in many parts of China. The response, particularly from young people, was both unexpected and disturbing to political educators and to anyone else who had long found in the opera a microcosm for the necessity of the Chinese Revolution.

The White-Haired Girl was composed and first staged in the Communist base areas during the Chinese Civil War (1927 to 1949), and tells the story of Xi'er, the daughter of poor peasant Yang Bailao. Yang is unable to pay his debts to tyrannical landlord Huang Shiren and is tricked by Huang's evil caretaker, Mu Renzhi, into selling Xi'er to Huang to cancel the debts. Xi'er is taken away by Huang and his henchmen, whereupon Yang Bailao commits suicide in remorse. After Xi'er is raped by Huang, she escapes into the mountains where years of hardship turn her hair white. She returns to human society only when the People's Liberation Army liberates the region and Huang Shiren is executed.

The controversy over *The White-Haired Girl* began when the Beijing Municipal Party Committee received a letter from Yang Jinxue, a forty-year-old worker, expressing great concern over comments he heard from young people at performances of the opera. His letter noted that "Many young people don't know who Yang Bailao and Xi'er were, and those who do say, '[I]t was only right and proper that Yang Bailao should pay up his debts, and there was nothing reprehensible in Xi'er paying up for her father.'" The letter was critical of today's younger generation as being primarily concerned with food, clothing, and consumption and who "know nothing about the old society and sneer at revolutionary traditions." Yang urged the party's propaganda departments and youth league organizations to concentrate on educating young people in China's revolutionary and patriotic traditions (*Beijing Youth Daily* June 12, 1995:1).

The *Beijing Youth Daily* interviewed the letter-writer, Yang Jinxue, and, for contrast, a twenty-year-old garment designer about what the opera meant to them. The designer had seen the opera, as had most Chinese in their twenties and thirties, when she was young, but had declined an invitation to see it again. Her complaints were considered representative of those of other young people. She argued that the opera was too old and uninteresting, that the old society is irrelevant to the present, that the heavy-handed political message turned people off, that her generation doesn't have much of a sense of history, and that debts must be paid. Although she agreed that Huang Shiren was indeed too vicious and cruel, she saw no basic difference between Huang's pressing for a payment of a debt in the old society and her own urging of her friends to return money they owed to her. She compared the highly successful Puccini opera *Madame Butterfly,* with its eternal, romantic theme, to the limited historical view of *The White-Haired Girl.* She also noted that she had eagerly seen the American film *True Lies* several times in succession.

The following installment in the series consisted of an interview with the director and performers of the opera, who tried to explain the background to the story and the nature of class society. They too were dismayed that youth saw no difference between landlord-peasant relations in a feudal society and contractual relations in a contemporary market economy. Even those who did acknowledge the difference could not see how the past had any impact on their lives today. The performers proposed that, as in the past, the drama be brought into factories, villages, and schools and that student tickets be subsidized (*Beijing Youth Daily,* June 19, 1995:1). Unlike the two debates discussed above, however, and despite the *Beijing Youth Daily*'s prominent placement of the conflict as the lead story, with pictures, in two separate issues, this discussion died out quickly. There indeed appeared to be little interest in a revival of *The White-Haired Girl* among China's youth.

In a rather fascinating way, however, there seemed to be more discussion in the Hong Kong press over the revival of the opera than there was in China itself. The China-watching journal *Open* (*Kaifang*) ran a special series on the increasing polarization between rich and poor in China, noting, in ironic contrast to the response in the mainland, that the story of Huang Shiren and Yang Bailao was being repeated again in China. Quoting reports from the mainland, they suggested that when peasants today were shown the opera they identified with Yang Bailao and felt that they, too, suffered exploitation, even wondering whether they should join the Eighth Route Army. At the same time, others openly suggested that it was logical for Xi'er to become Huang Shiren's concubine rather than to marry her own boyfriend, a poor peasant who had no money at all (Cai 1996). An article in the magazine *Contending* (*Zhengming*), on the other hand, tied the revival of *The White-Haired Girl,* along with other works associated with the Maoist period, such as *The Red Lantern* (*Hongdeng ji*) and *The Golden Road* (*Jinguang dadao*), to an attempt of the ultraleft to restore their golden age (*Zhengming* November 1995:88–89).

THE FANG MIN STATE–PRIVATE ENTERPRISE
COMMUNIST PARTY ROLE DEBATE

The debates over Wang Dingding and *The White-Haired Girl* were fairly typical of debates in the Chinese press, even including those prior to the reform period. The most obvious attribute shared by these debates is their didactic nature; they were intended to present to the newspaper's readership the proper way to behave. The debate over He Zhili's behavior was subtler in that there was no unequivocal determination of right and wrong presented. Even here, though, the newspaper made sure to emphasize that the majority of the submissions from readers, regardless of their views, "expressed strong patriotic sentiments." The "Fang Min Storm" (*Fang Min fengbo*), as *Beijing Youth Daily* called it, raised much more sensitive political questions, with important implications for the future of some of China's key institutions. The issues at the heart of the Fang Min case addressed the relative importance of state and private enterprises; the role of the Communist Party, if any, in the new, large private concerns; and whether party members should have less freedom to change jobs than do ordinary workers. Although the newspaper's own spin on the case could be seen clearly from the manner in which their two articles were written, the discussion offered valuable information on a subject seldom covered in the open press, and one which is likely to assume far greater importance as China's reforms continue. Among other insights, the reports showed how private enterprises, particularly those run by party members and former military personnel with good connections, were able to use their flexibility and quick reaction time to move into new, untapped markets and accumulate large amounts of capital. They also revealed how different social and bureaucratic interests interpreted this case in a manner that best furthered those interests.

The case was introduced in an editorial note in the first article. On November 19, 1994, Fang Min, Secretary of the Party Committee at the Xinjiang Number 3 Construction Company—a key building enterprise in the Xinjiang Autonomous Region—who had been nominated by the Party Committee of the autonomous region for training as a member of the Third Echelon of future leaders of the country, formally submitted her resignation to the head company of the autonomous region's construction companies. On the same day, she signed an agreement with the Xinjiang Guanghui Group of Enterprises to go and work as the group's deputy general manager and to concurrently take charge of party affairs. The head company's leadership tried repeatedly to persuade her to stay, but Fang Min balked, insisting that she wanted to explore a new path for party work in private enterprises. Prior to this, Fang Min had many times exchanged opinions with upper-level party organizations and had written long letters explaining her motives. Twenty-six days later, the Party Committee and Committee of the Congress of Workers and Staff at the autonomous region's head company made a decision to dismiss Fang Min from her positions as secretary and member of the Number 3 Construction Company's Party Committee and, on the administrative level, to strike her name from the company's rolls. The *Beijing Youth Daily*'s first story asked: "Should Fang Min's name have been stricken from the rolls?" (*Beijing Youth Daily,* February 15, 1995:2).

The key issue raised for discussion was whether Fang Min should be regarded as a party secretary or as an ordinary working person. The answer to that question would help determine whether her "job-hopping" (*tiao cao*) should be seen as a "walkout" or as acceptable labor mobility. The first article contained five interviews, all conducted in Beijing; three of the five interviewees were senior officials of ministries concerned with this case.

Not surprisingly, the three ministerial officials—from Construction, Labor, and Organization—offered very different interpretations of Fang Min's actions. The official from the Ministry of Construction argued that Fang Min should first be regarded as a party secretary and that she is, therefore, subject to organizational principles and party discipline. Since she left her party post prior to gaining approval to do so, her actions weakened the party's "fighting strength" and set a bad example for others. He noted that some veteran Communist cadres, after retiring, had been engaged by private enterprises to serve as key workers in party affairs. The difference with Fang Min was their more advanced age and retired status and the fact that their new employment had received approval from the party.

By contrast, the official at the Ministry of Labor supported Fang Min's decision. He argued that private ownership serves as a useful and necessary supplement to public ownership, and that it is playing an ever greater role. Since publicly owned enterprises already possess a strong party organization and many party cadres, it should be quite easy to replace Fang Min with a leader of equal quality. It doesn't matter whether one does party work in a publicly owned or a private enterprise, the same fundamental interests—those of the party and the people—are being served. When balancing the two options, one should choose the option most beneficial to the party's construction. Since the party organization is weak in private enterprises, Fang Min's decision to extend the party's power to these previously neglected units is a correct one.

The chief of the Propaganda Section of the Research Department at the Ministry of Organization took a middling position, arguing that it was unrealistic to offer any final conclusions at this point, since the Fang Min case represented a new phenomenon occurring under new circumstances. His ministry had already begun to study the question of how to strengthen party leadership over nonstate enterprises and how to view the mobility of party cadres, but the state had as yet produced no clear policies. He did note that cases similar to Fang Min's had already occurred in the open cities in the coastal areas and at the Capital Iron and Steel Factory, without provoking any major repercussions.

The final two interviewees, both of whom supported Fang Min, were a professor who was a leader in the field of administrative management and a female manager of a company. After explaining the formal rules on talent mobility among administrative personnel, the professor argued that talent belongs to the state, not to any individual unit, and Fang Min's decision was not taken out of selfish motives but out of a desire to explore new paths. She had "walked out" because her unit refused to approve a transfer through regular organizational channels, leaving her no other recourse. The female executive said that she would also take the same road as Fang Min, given the opportunity.

A month later, the *Beijing Youth Daily* ran a follow-up story in which they noted the responses their readers had had to the first article. Some readers had felt that the entire Fang Min affair had been a public-relations ploy on the part of the private enterprise, while others wondered whether Fang could be successful in her new job. To answer those questions, the newspaper dispatched a reporter to Xinjiang to conduct interviews with those involved in the case (*Beijing Youth Daily,* March 15, 1995:2).

The party secretary of the head company that had supervised Fang Min's work unit initially rejected a request for an interview. Only after intervention from the Propaganda Department of the regional Party Committee did the party secretary agree to answer some questions. He still insisted, however, that the issue was not Fang's departure but the fact that she had left without obtaining approval from the party organization. Since she had violated organizational principles, she had to be dealt with according to organizational principles. The deputy chief of the Propaganda Department, who had arranged the interview, offered a different interpretation, suggesting that, despite his own views that private enterprises were part of the socialist economy, some people persisted in arguing that they were capitalist by nature.

The *Xinjiang Economic News* had given prominent space on its front page to the Fang Min affair in January, with a lengthy report entitled "Should She Have Job-Hopped?" Ten days later, they published another article entitled "I Am Shocked that Fang Min Did Such a Thing." The article was accompanied by an editorial note claiming that the paper had received numerous readers' letters after publishing their initial story and had chosen to publish this one written by Ma Changguo, a veteran worker at the Number 3 Construction Company, where Fang had been party secretary. Ma had written:

Fang Min, who bore the title of Secretary of the Party Committee at a large state-owned enterprise, threw aside the work entrusted to her by the party, abandoned more than ten thousand employees, and left without a by-your-leave to join a private enterprise, triggering powerful repercussions at the Number 3 Construction Company, producing an extremely bad impression, and causing uncalled-for damage to the party's reputation. . . . These years, state-run enterprises are facing a re-orbiting as well as increasingly sharp competition, making their work more and more difficult. Did she leave because the work was difficult? If that is the case, I see her action as the same as deserting before a battle.

The visiting *Beijing Youth Daily* reporter went to see Ma Changguo to get more details on the case, only to find that Ma had in fact not written the letter; the letter had been written by a reporter. Ma had aired his views at a cadres' meeting, saying that there were rumors that Fang Min had left because she would be paid 4,000 yuan a month at a private company. This was causing strong repercussions among the masses. If she wanted to further her career, why not do it at the state company rather than going to a private enterprise? When a local reporter came to ask about Ma's views, Ma said that he didn't know what was actually going on, but that Fang should at least have handed in her resignation before leaving. When the Beijing reporter informed Ma that Fang had indeed written a letter of resignation before leaving, Ma said that no one had ever told him that. Since a search for the editor of the *Xinjiang Economic News* proved fruitless, additional information on its role in the affair could not be obtained. Workers interviewed at the Number 3 Construction Company said that if the party leadership had simply let her go they would have assumed she had left because of work requirements, and that would have been the end of it.

A visit to the Chairman of the Board of Directors at the Guanghui Group—where Fang was now employed—provided some interesting information regarding private companies and how they become successful. Guanghui had started with 3,000 yuan less than six years earlier and now possessed more than 200 million yuan in fixed assets. To counter some rumors about the manner in which Guanghui had succeeded, the Chairman discussed how the company had taken advantage of the market and had launched three major campaigns. At first, the company acted as an agent for other businesses but, after accumulating some capital, they launched their first campaign.

After some analysis they determined that Xinjiang was backward in food, beverages, and entertainment, so they set up the poshest karaoke bar and restaurant in Xinjiang, taking the lead in this field. In the course of operating the restaurant, they learned about Xinjiang's petroleum resources and trade, and, after more analysis, they started their second campaign and went into the oil trade. Then they learned that they had no import-export rights because they were a private enterprise, so they joined with the China International Enterprises Corporation in Beijing and cooperated on the basis of their respective strengths. In 1992, they did more than 88.7 million U.S. dollars' worth of bulk trade, equal to more than one-sixth of Xinjiang's total value of bulk trade. In 1993, there was an upsurge in real-estate business nationwide, but it had bypassed Xinjiang. Guanghui leaped into the market and started construction on the first two residential complexes in Xinjiang. The profit made from that venture provided an excellent foundation, and they have also now become the largest manufacturer in the granite and marble industry in the northwest.

Following such economic successes, they decided that they needed work on "rear-area construction," to establish "an intrinsic and extrinsic image for the enterprise as a whole." One of Guanghui's special features is its large number of party members and demobilized army men; seven of the company's eight board members are party members. Their experience in the army has made them particularly aware of the importance of ideological and political work, hence the appointment of Fang Min.

Fang Min herself was still agitated over the rumors questioning her motives. She noted that she used to make more than 20,000 yuan at the Number 3 Construction Company and was secretary of a Party Committee responsible for more than 10,000 employees. Since Guanghui had only a few hundred employees, she argued that there was no justification for saying her objectives were money and power. As the first Party Committee secretary in Xinjiang to come to a private enterprise from a state-run enterprise, she viewed herself as a pioneer, and she hoped that rules and regulations governing such personnel transfers would be drafted in the future. She also dismissed the rumor that she was so daring because she had backing from some high-ranking party secretary in Xinjiang, noting that her problems had come about precisely because she didn't have any important party backing. Fang concluded with the hope that cases of discrimination against private enterprises will not continue to occur, and the *Beijing Youth Daily* report concluded that, even after the Fang Min case dies down, the questions that it has raised will remain profound and far-reaching.

Conclusion

As China continues to move toward a market economy, one would expect the contradictions faced by the press, particularly those media required to provide ideological and political guidance, to intensify. Faced with declining circulation and increasing competition, the party announced in 1995 that promotion for its publications would be "market-oriented," while at the same time arguing that party organs such as the *People's Daily* are of such "national importance" that their fortunes should not be subject to the whims of the market (*China News Analysis* 1995). The *Beijing Youth Daily,* as a "local" organ now responsible for its own profits and losses, by contrast, has been permitted to adjust its format and content repeatedly to appeal to a wider market. Every day, since July 1, 1995, one of its eight pages has been devoted to a special topic; on Wednesdays, the paper expands to sixteen pages, with four pages each on computers and automobiles (Qiu 1995). Moreover, the paper's editors periodically choose a "hot point" (*redian*) and cover the subject in depth with a series of six articles.

The debates discussed above—all of which address new phenomena which have arisen under the impetus of a market economy—provide a reasonable overview of the interests, methods, and style of the *Beijing Youth Daily*. They also reveal how public opinion is shaped in a closed society. Just as with public opinion polling in China, in which only "acceptable" findings can be printed in the widely circulated open press, debates and discussion forums are expected to conclude in a manner which promotes the current policies of the government (Rosen 1989). In this regard, the *Beijing Youth Daily*'s promotion of patriotic values and public-spirited behavior is unexceptionable. Even their support for labor mobility and an expanded role for the party in the private sector, while more contentious, still falls within the parameters of current party initiatives. What has made this newspaper more lively and worthier of attention than virtually all of its competitors has been its initiative in tracking down controversies on issues of broad public interest (for example, the He Zhili–Koyama Chire case) or of great importance to understanding social, political, economic, or cultural change in China (for example, the Fang Min case) and then providing detailed coverage of these cases.[13] At the same time, the *Beijing Youth Daily*'s recurring problems and leadership changes will likely have some effect, at least in the short term, on the paper's willingness to take on controversial topics. Reportedly, since the Wahaha incident, the newspaper's staff has been more scrupulous in adhering to the "rules." Moreover, prior to the October 1996 party plenum, Jiang Zemin issued a stricter party line to the news media and propaganda organs. In a speech given at the *People's Daily* which the newspaper carried the next day, along with three photos of Jiang, those working in the media were told to be "loyal to Marxism, loyal to the party, and loyal to the people." Although there was no elaboration of these slogans, foreign analysts tied Jiang's media concerns to the recent turmoil at *Beijing Youth Daily* (*China News Digest* 1996). Should the paper need more detailed guidelines, the report on the *Beijing Youth Daily*'s strengths and weaknesses cited in the introduction, with its specific analysis of "good" and "bad" articles carried in the paper, has useful reference value. That report concluded that newspapers need to know when to "grasp" a story and when to let go, offering four principles as guidelines. First, is the story congruent with the major programs of the party and the government? Second, is it beneficial to the interests of the party, the government, and the people? Third, is it in keeping with the party's policy on journalism and propaganda discipline? Fourth, is the information accurate? (Sun 1995). It will be interesting to see whether the newspaper's balance between the interests of "Marxism, the party, and the people" undergoes any pronounced shift.

Notes

1. The *Beijing Youth Daily* also prepared posters to advertise its new image and even produced a series of books under the overall title *"Beijing Youth Daily* Phenomenon Study Series."* This includes, *inter alia, Women* (1996a) and *Xinwen* (1996b).

2. *Beijing Youth Daily* appears six days a week, with a weekend edition, while the *Beijing Evening News* and *Beijing Daily* publish 365 days a year.

3. According to interviewees there, the newspaper has been criticized for, among other things, reporting on airline hijackings to Taiwan and covering the murder of Taiwan tourists at the Qiandao Lake resort in Zhejiang Province. In both cases, the newspaper repeatedly ignored warnings to cease such coverage, and both cases led to personnel changes. For a list of guidelines on how newspapers should report on specific areas considered sensitive—for example, corruption, natural calamities, migrant workers, prostitution, enterprise reform, stock markets, and international news—provided at a July 1994 meeting by Qiao Shi, see *China News Analysis* (1995:6–7).

4. For translations of many of the articles from these debates, see Rosen (1996b).

5. This incident is also depicted in the *River Elegy* documentary as an example of weakness in the Chinese national character.

6. For some of the earliest attacks on He Zhili, see *Yangcheng Evening News,* October 14, 15, and 16, 1994 (all page 3).

7. Indeed, the presence of Chinese athletes playing for other countries against China has been noted in the foreign press.

Kuhn (1994), quoting the *China Sports Daily,* says that more than six hundred Ping-Pong players have left China in search of better prospects. A more detailed report appeared in *Culture and Life* (*Wenhua shenghuo bao*) No. 67, May 1991, and was later translated in Mao (1994). The story discussed the success of both coaches and players abroad. Ironically, there was a reverse spin on the story, which detailed how foreign countries—primarily in Europe and Japan—were setting regulations to prevent the overseas Chinese from dominating the sport in these countries. In a further irony, China was universally praised for its "internationalism," allowing its players to play elsewhere, but there was concern that the national pride of these other countries would be hurt. The story was filled with patriotic rhetoric, informing readers that despite their current stay abroad, the hearts of these players remained in China. In a final irony, He Zhili's mother told correspondents that despite her marriage to a Japanese, "He was trained in China and still has a Chinese heart, and she would never play against China."

8. The story continued into 1995 with interviews with He Zhili, in which she argued that her actions were misunderstood, and with her chief opponent, Deng Yaping. See, for example, *Beijing Youth Daily,* January 28, 1995 (2); *Beijing Youth Daily,* February 9, 1995 (1); and *Beijing Youth Daily,* February 16, 1995 (4). The story was also widely reported in the Hong Kong press. See *Trend (Dongxiang),* May 1995 (74–75), and *Outpost Monthly (Qianshao yuekan),* February 1995 (82–83) and April 1995 (49–51). Interestingly, He was supported by her hometown paper in Shanghai, while Deng Yaping's critical comments were published in Beijing. When in the summer of 1995 I visited the Sports Middle School, from which He had graduated, I found strong support for her among the leading school officials.

9. In the *Guangming Daily,* for example, thirty-nine stories on Zhang Hua appeared between October 7 and October 30, 1982, and ten stories between November 2 and November 28, 1982.

10. Several foreign academics teaching in China at the time told me they queried their own students about Zhang Hua's sacrifice, but they found few if any who said they would have risked their lives to try to save the life of an elderly peasant. When asked whether they would have done so if their university president had been in the peasant's place, they were much less certain.

11. On Zhang Haidi, see Rosen (1995:22–23). On the Pan Xiao discussion forum, see Seybolt (1981). For a comparison between the Pan Xiao discussion and the 1960 discussion entitled "What Is the Ideal Life of a Revolutionary Youth?" see Ownby (1985). Ironically, interviewees responsible for the Pan Xiao discussion have informed me that Pan Xiao's letter was actually a composite, pasted together from two separate letters the magazine had received.

12. Zhang's suicide attempt is also reported in *Zhengming,* July 1983 (58–59).

13. In picking only four debates and covering only a limited time period, I am greatly shortchanging the range of the *Beijing Youth Daily*. It contains an abundance of information, for example, on popular culture, including extensive reviews of Chinese and foreign films. One interesting article compared Forrest Gump with Ah Q. Also included are essays by respected academics on more esoteric subjects. Moreover, the paper frequently "scoops" the competition. When film director Zhang Yimou angrily withdrew his film from the Cannes Film Festival in 1999, the *Beijing Youth Daily* gave Zhang a forum in which to express his opposition to Western demands on Chinese films. See *Beijing Youth Daily,* April 19, 20, and 21, 1999.

Bibliography

Bacani, Cesar, and Law Siu Lan. 1996. "Vanguard of a Free Press? China's For-Profit Dailies Edge Out Party Organs." *Asiaweek,* January 5, 32.

Beijing Youth Daily (Beijing qingnian bao). 1994, 1995, 1996, and 1999.

Beijing Youth Daily and other periodicals. July 1996.

Cai, Yougmei. 1996. "Huang Shiren, Yang Bailao de gushi chongyan" ("A Revival of the Story of Huang Shiren and Yang Bailao"). *Kaifang zazhi (Open Magazine)* (Hong Kong) (February):34–36.

China News Analysis. 1995. "The Press and Its Market after the Fourth Plenum." No. 153, March 15, 1.

China News Digest. 1996. Global News, No. GL96-141, September 30.

Dongxiang (Trend). 1995. Hong Kong (May):74–75.

Guangming ribao (Guangming Daily). October and November 1982.

Kang, Xiaoguang, Wu Yulun, Liu Dehuan, and Sun Hui. 1998. *Zhongguo dushu toushi: 1978-1998 dazhong dushu shenghuo bianqian diaocha (A Perspective on the Reading Habits of the Chinese: An Investigation of the Changes in the Reading Habits of the Masses from 1978-1998).* Nanning: Guangxi Educational Press.

Kuhn, Anthony. 1994. "Ping-Pong Politics: Table-Tennis Mutiny Spurs Sports-Ethics Debate in China." *Far Eastern Economic Review,* December 8, 44–45.

Lee, Chin-Chuan, ed. 1994. *China's Media, Media's China.* Boulder, Colo.: Westview.

Li, Dongsheng, and Yusheng Sun, eds. 1998. *Jiaodian fangtan jingcui (Focal Point Inquiry in a Nutshell).* Beijing: People's University of China Press.

Li, Yongjiao. 1995. "Zhongguo baokan dazhan" ("The Great War of Newspapers and Periodicals in China"). *Guangjiaojing yuekan (Wide Angle Monthly)* (Hong Kong) (October):32–36.

Liang, Jianzheng, ed. 1998. *Jiaodian fangtan: cong linian dao yunzuo (Focal Point Inquiry: From Concept to Realization).* Beijing: Xuexi Press.

Lin, Mu. 1997. "Zhongguo baoye: zouxiang jituanhua" ("The Chinese Press: Moving Toward Institutionalization"). *Xin Shiji (New Century).* June 6, 68–71.

Mao, Yan, trans. 1992. "Chinese Players in Foreign Robes." *China Now* 141 (Summer): 16–17.

Ming bao, Hong Kong. August 21, 1996. Trans. in Foreign Broadcast Information Service Daily Report, China, 174 (on-line).

Ownby, David, ed. 1985. "Changing Attitudes among Chinese Youths: Letters to *Zhongguo qingnian." Chinese Sociology and Anthropology* 17 (4) (Summer).

Qianshao yuekan (Frontline Monthly), Hong Kong. February and April 1995.

Qingnian bao (Youth News), Shanghai. January 28 and February 16, 1995.

Qiu, Qiren. 1995. "'Beijing qingnian bao' cong xingshi dao neirong de gaige jiqing" ("From Form to Content: The Fervor of Reform at *Beijing Youth Daily").* *Ming Pao Monthly* (Hong Kong) (September):77.

Rosen, Stanley. 1989. "Public Opinion and Reform in the People's Republic of China." *Studies in Comparative Communism* 22 (2–3): 153–70.

———. 1994. "Chinese Women in the 1990s: Images and Roles in Contention." In Maurice Brosseau and Lo Chi Kin, eds., *China Review 1994*. Hong Kong: Chinese University of Hong Kong Press.

———. 1995. "Prosperity, Privatization, and China's Youth." *Problems of Communism* (March–April): 1–28.

———. 1996a. "China since Tiananmen Square." *The World and I* (April):36–43.

———, ed. 1996b. "The Controversy Caused by a Loss in Ping-Pong and Other Debates on Chinese Society Highlighted in the Chinese Press." *Chinese Education and Society* 29 (3) (May–June).

Schell, Orville. 1995. "Maoism vs. Media in the Market-Place." *Media Studies Journal* 9 (3) (Summer):33–42.

Seybolt, Peter J., ed. 1995. "'What Is the Meaning of Life?' Selections from *Zhongguo qingnian.*" *Chinese Education,* 14 (4) (Summer).

Sun, Shikai. 1995. "*Beijing qingnian bao:* ba chang yu wu jie" (*Beijing Youth Daily:* Eight Strengths and Five Shortcomings to Avoid). *Zhongguo baokan yuebao* (*Chinese Newspapers and Periodicals Monthly*), June 6, 17–19.

Tempest, Rone. 1996. "China's New Public Passion." *Los Angeles Times,* April 25, A1, 8.

Wang, Huaqiao, ed. 1998. *Zhenshi de yanshuo: touguo 'Nanfang zhoumo' kan zhongguo* (*The Truth in Words: Looking into China by Penetrating 'Southern Weekend'*). Beijing: Zhongguo chengshi chubanshe.

Women changshi le shenma (*What We Have Tried*). 1996. 2 vols. Beijing: Culture and Arts Press.

Xinhua. February 25, 1984. Reprinted in Foreign Broadcast Information Service Daily Report, China, February 28, 1984, K6–8.

Xinwen zhoukan sanji tiaoyue (*Newsweek Triple Jump*). 1996. Beijing: Culture and Arts Press.

Yangcheng Evening News, Guangzhou. October 14, 15, and 16, 1994.

Ye, Yonglie. 1995. *He Zhili fengbo* (*The Furor over He Zhili*). Xining: Qinghai People's Press.

Yu, Guoming. 1995. "Bu anfen de '*Beijing qingnian bao*'" ("*Beijing Youth Daily:* The Newspaper that Refuses to Behave"). *Beijing qingnian gongzuo yanjiu* (*Research on Youth Work in Beijing*) 8–9 (August–September):19–20.

Zhang, Xiaogang. 1993. "The Market versus the State: The Chinese Press since Tiananmen." *Journal of International Affairs* 47 (1):195–221.

Zheng, Xingdong, ed. 1994. *Xinwen chongji bo: Beijing qingnian bao xianxiang saomiao* (*News in Attack Waves: Describing the Beijing Youth Daily Phenomenon*). Beijing: People's University of China Press.

Zhengming (*Contention*), Hong Kong. July 1983 and November 1995.

Zhongguo chuban nianjian 1997 (*Chinese Publications Yearbook*). 1997. Beijing: Chinese Publications Yearbook Press.

Zhongguo xinwen nianjian (*Chinese Journalism Yearbook*). 1995. Beijing: Chinese Journalism Yearbook Press.

6

The Nature and Consequences
of China's Unique Pattern
# of Telecommunications
Development

Daniel C. Lynch

The Chinese telecommunications system has developed with exceptional rapidity since the mid-1980s, even as the central party-state has lost a significant degree of control over almost all forms of information flowing into and through Chinese society.[1] Yet ironically and mistakenly, most specialists on Chinese "thought work" (*sixiang gongzuo*), or propaganda, have focused their research on the *mass* media (television, radio, film, and print) not considering *tele*-communications (telephone, fax, e-mail, and the Internet) as constituting significant components of the thought-work enterprise. The reason is that, historically, China's telecommunications networks were not, in fact, typically used for propagandistic purposes, but were instead used almost exclusively to coordinate the activities of a sprawling bureaucracy and a planned economy.[2]

Today, however, everything has changed, and anyone seriously interested in understanding China's economy, society, culture, and politics must come to terms with the significance of the country's telecommunications development—both quantitatively and qualitatively.[3] Why has telecommunications capacity expanded so rapidly? What is the relationship between this expansion and the overall line of reform and opening since 1978? How does the nature of China's telecommunications development fit into broader patterns of change in the other forms of thought work explored elsewhere in this book? What will be the consequences of China's unique pattern of telecommunications development for the country's future?

Before trying to answer these questions, it is important to recognize that the messages sent throughout a society through its telecommunications system can be every bit as propagandistic—able to convey meaning—as messages sent via television, newspapers, and the other mass media. Even messages that appear on the surface to be apolitical may be subtly restructuring the political culture in ways whose importance is likely to become clear only over a long period of time.

Harold Lasswell, a pioneer in the study of communication effects, defined "propaganda" as "the control of opinion by significant symbols, or, to speak more concretely and less accurately, by stories, rumors, reports, pictures, and other forms of social communication." Propaganda, in the broadest sense, "is the technique of influencing human action by the manipulation of representations. These representations may take spoken, written, pictorial, or musical form. . . . [B]oth advertising and publicity fall within the field of propaganda" (Severin and Tankard 1988:103–4).

All organizations, groups, and individuals within society are predisposed to create and circulate persuasive messages in support of their interests, whether their interests are narrowly political in nature, economic, or even "public." There is, of course, substantial variation in degree of message politicization— including the extent to which a message directly supports or subverts the political system. At the same time, not all communications messages *are* propagandistic: Many are created purely to coordinate action and are thus relatively prosaic in nature. Probably most telecommunications messages fall into this category, with telephone calls and faxes usually being used to arrange meetings, give instructions, and acquire highly specific information. (E-mail and the Internet are, of course, much more problematic in this regard.) But even if only 5 percent of a society's telecommunications messages are genuinely propagandistic in nature—and possibly political—as long as the proportion does not decrease, in situations in which the total volume of telecommunications messages expands (as in China), the absolute number of propagandistic messages must also increase. This fact is crucial because it implies that a significant degree of control over thought work is being taken from the state by individuals and groups in society. With increasing frequency and effectiveness, "unauthorized" and nonofficial groups and individuals can generate and circulate their own propagandistic messages, even if typically they use their telephones and fax machines for more mundane purposes.

At the same time, telecommunications are rapidly merging with the mass media in nature and function—most obviously in the form of the Internet. In China, general access to the Internet was inaugurated in late 1994, and the number of subscribers has increased exponentially every year since (see table 6.1).

Companies macromanaged by the Ministry of Information Industries (MII) *xitong* now provide cable television services in many locales, although still not on a large scale (Interviews 131, 132, 134, 141, and 144; Xu 1994).[4] Moreover, the *People's Daily*, Chinese Central Television (CCTV), and numerous other mass media organizations make extensive use of satellites and other telecommunications technologies to manage their transglobal operations. Fax machines are now virtually ubiquitous in urban China's larger firms, government departments, and other organizations. They can be, and are, used to disseminate newspaper and magazine articles as well as more prosaic messages. In short, the technology-driven blurring of the traditional distinctions between telecommunications and the mass media promises to move telecommunications even closer in nature to "classical" thought work.

But even traditional technologies such as the telephone can play important roles in diffusing the innovations and new ideas first adopted by society's "opinion leaders" from the mass media and then conveyed to increasingly wider audiences (Rogers 1995). Sometimes individuals and groups use telecommunications technologies actively and consciously to hasten the diffusion of innovations; sometimes they do it passively and unconsciously. Under Mao Zedong, who ruled China from 1949 to 1976, the central party-state exerted a great deal of control over the "multistep flow" of innovations and ideas by mandating that grassroots-level units frequently convene small study groups to "discuss" central propaganda—carefully imparting the correct "spin" to the masses (Whyte 1974). Now, however, the Center can neither completely control the symbols that the mass media—including foreign media—create and circulate in China, nor can it prevent individuals in formerly isolated work units from discussing the new media content with interlocutors across town, in other parts of China, and even abroad. The new values, perceptions, and ideas acquired interpersonally and from the radically changed "symbolic environment" can now much more easily and quickly be spread throughout society as a result of telecommunications development and the government's loss of control over telecommunications content.

Telecommunications therefore become crucial to the formation of transorganizational and transregional social networks and groups in China, a society that before 1978 was highly cellularized in structure (Shue 1988). People were isolated from each other in workplaces and locales, and China's rudimentary telecommunications network served only to send orders and information up and down vertical bureaucratic hierarchies. The prereform telecommunications network was not designed nor did it function to link individuals, organizations, and groups horizontally. Today, however, the multicentric, automated network rapidly taking shape is shattering this decades-old (even centuries-old) pattern of local isolation and establishing conditions for the development of a cross-hatching "societal *xitong*," linking individuals, organizations, and groups throughout the country with each other and with people abroad.

The implications of this development are potentially profound, even though very difficult to specify. Telecommunications development will obviously facilitate the formation and functioning of all manner of new social networks and groups. Some of these networks and groups will probably adopt antiregime stances, whether as civil society associations promoting democracy, new religious organizations such as the *Falungong,* criminal gangs, or even revolutionary movements (Su 1992; Sun and Wu 1993). Of course, telecommunications development will not be the only factor determining whether such groups will appear and what their social impact will be. Nor will telecommunications development necessarily be the most important factor. But it will be one very important facilitative factor—part of a larger picture—and seriously complicate the central party-state's efforts to maintain control over society and proactively pursue its long list of social goals.

The Pattern of China's Telecommunications Development

In shorthand terms, China's telecommunications development has been fast, fragmented, and commercialized. Rapid technological dissemination, administrative fragmentation, and the highly market-oriented nature of the country's telecommunications development have all contributed to a sharp decline in the Center's difficulties controlling thought work—in interaction with changes in the mass media system (Lynch 1999). Increasingly, message sources are proliferating, message creators are becoming more commercially oriented, and messages from abroad are circulating in ever larger numbers.

As suggested by table 6.1, China has experienced nothing short of a telescoped telecommunications revolution since just the mid-1980s, both in terms of quantity and quality (Zhao and Liu 1994). On average, every urban household owned a telephone by 2000, and every rural household was expected to own a phone by 2020 (Interviews 103 and 114; McGregor and Keller 1993).

Table 6.1. Key Indicators of Telecommunications Development, 1970–1996

Year	Telephones per Capita	Long Distance Calls per Capita	Mobile Cellular Subscribers	Paging Service Subscribers	Fax Machines	Faxes Sent
1970	0.003	0.10			83	
1978	0.004	0.19			1,484	
1985	0.006	0.36			1,266	139,242
1986	0.007	0.39			1,341	145,119
1987	0.007	0.47			1,413	152,101
1988	0.009	0.58			1,876	176,177
1989	0.010	0.70			2,600	241,457
1990	0.011	1.02			3,826	555,481
1991	0.013	1.49			6,183	968,834
1992	0.016	2.45	176,943	2,220,000	9,410	1,712,182
1993	0.022	4.28	638,268	5,614,000	12,276	2,706,055
1994	0.033	6.32	1,567,780	10,330,000		3,423,700
1995	0.048	8.37	3,629,416	17,392,000		4,423,080
1996	0.058	10.41	6,852,752	25,362,000		5,650,000

Sources: *China Statistical Yearbook,* 1997, 1990, 1988.

In fact, in every major category, China's telecommunications capacity has been expanding with astonishing rapidity, facilitating, among other things, an amazing fifteenfold increase in the number of long-distance telephone calls per capita each year between 1989 and 1996. Nor does this rapid growth show any sign of abating. Each year, the MII revises upward its projections for various targets of telecommunications development. For example, in 1991, the ministry projected that China would have 48 million exchange lines in place by 2000; in 1994, it projected 140 million lines; and in 1996, it projected 170 million lines. Similarly, the number of telephones per 100 people was expected in 1991 to reach 3 by 2000; in 1994, the figure was raised to 8 per 100; and in 1996 it was increased to 10.5 per 100 ("Urban Residents" 1991; "Report Views" 1994). Of course, there is significant inequality in distribution of telecommunications capacity, with the big urban areas enjoying the greatest capacity and the fastest growth. In 1996, China's 360 million urban residents had access to 55 million telephones, a ratio of 1 phone for every 6.5 people. But in the countryside, 864 million Chinese citizens shared a mere 15 million telephones—about 1 phone for every 57.5 people. Still, rural residents' access to telecommunications facilities was increasing rapidly, transmitting the revolution in symbol-dissemination to the countryside (*Zhongguo tongji nianjian* 1997).

Yet despite this celeritous growth, telecommunications still constitutes a costly bottleneck in the Chinese economy. The country's transformation into a market-oriented system has been unexpectedly fast, and annual growth rates were perennially in the 8 to 12 percent range until the Asian economic meltdown in 1997 and 1998. Fixed telephone density remains very low in China despite rapid growth because growth started from a very low base. However, fortunately for China, the telecommunications revolution arrived at a propitious historical moment: precisely the time cellular telephony was taking off worldwide. As a result, China has been able to leapfrog past some of its telecommunications bottle-necks by developing—frequently, importing—advanced mobile telephone and paging capacity. Table 6.1 reveals the amazing growth of this capacity. In five years from 1992 to 1996, mobile cellular subscribers grew 38.7 times, whereas paging services also increased by 11.4 times. A figure of 6.9 million cellular sub-scribers in 1996 was expected to increase to 18 million by 2000. When Xining, Qinghai, inaugurated services in March 1994, all of China's provincial capitals had at least one mobile cellular service ("Cellular Mobile Phone Calls" 1994). Meanwhile, the ranks of the 25.4 million pager owners in 1996 were expected to increase to an amazing 100 million by 2000—nearly 8 percent of the population. People from all walks of life in China increasingly use pagers as substitutes for per-sonal telephones. A friend or colleague dials the paging service and requests a return call, which the recipient makes a few minutes later from a public phone.

Mobile telephone and paging services exemplify the important qualitative improvements in China's telecommunications system that are laying the groundwork for establishment of a high-capacity, digital, broadband network that could become the envy of some countries that are economically more ad-vanced but that are hamstrung by high "sunk costs" in copper wire networks. In China, optical fiber transmission networks are disseminating rapidly, along with automated switching technology. A national trunk transmission network consisting entirely of optical fiber was expected to link all provincial capitals and 80 percent of prefectural-level cities—domestically and internationally—by 2000 (Interview 114). Already by the mid-1990s, some 86 percent of the telecommunications network was automated (that is, users required no opera-tor intervention to complete calls), with the figure approaching 100 percent in large cities (Interview 132; Weinstock et al. 1994). Residents of more than 850 Chinese cities could make direct-dial, automated calls to nearly 200 countries and regions around the world, as well as to each other ("Telecommunications Minister" 1994). All major cities were expected to be linked into this auto-mated network by 2000 (She and Yu 1993). No other country's telecommuni-cations system will ever have developed as rapidly, both in terms of overall capacity and degree of technical sophistication.

These developments present direct challenges to the Center's control over thought work because messages sent via optical fiber are extremely difficult to intercept, while automated switching implies, by its very nature, the absence of operators who can (regularly) eavesdrop on conversations or "pull the plug" during a regime-threatening emergency. Even during the political crisis of 1989, the regime was apparently unable to stop the flow of faxes and telephone calls into and through China by shutting down the national telecommunications grid. Long-distance calls originating domestically and abroad "increased abruptly" in the week after June 4, and while the call-completion rate fell, this was simply because of an "overloading of the operating capacity of telecommunications facilities," not because the facilities themselves were shut down ("China's Posts and Telecommunications" 1989). The switching was automatic and highly decentralized, so the authorities in Beijing could do little to prevent news of the killings on the edges of Tiananmen Square from spreading widely throughout urban China.

Message-Source Pluralization

Telecommunications technologies have combined with several administrative variables to cause a multiplication in the number of points at which the Center must exert power or authority to control the flow of propagandistic communications throughout society: message-source pluralization. Most important administratively is the fact that telecommunications service providers are not classified bureaucratically as part of the propaganda *xitong,* the system to which the central party-state assigns primary jurisdiction over thought work. While newspapers, television stations, radio stations, and other mass media outlets are all parts of this system, telecommunications service providers are organized under the finance and economics *xitong.* At the same time, policing telecommunications networks is primarily the responsibility of the public security apparatus, which itself is part of yet another *xitong.* The rationale for classifying telecommunications as essentially an instrument of economic management rather than propaganda is simply that, historically, China's telecommunications networks were used only to convey technical orders down and administrative information up bureaucratic hierarchies, not to transmit cross-regional or cross-*xitong* messages that would normally be considered propagandistic. Telecommunications networks were also considered to be mere carriers of messages—like roads, railways, and canals—rather than originators of messages. At best, they were thought of as being only passive components of the overall thought-work enterprise.

The result of this historical legacy is that the vast majority of the documents and instructions issued by the party's Central Propaganda Department (CPD) to mass media outlets do not usually reach the hundreds of official and semiofficial companies and organizations that supply the Chinese public with telecommunications services. Consequently, the CPD has little or no direct influence over these units, despite the fact that they are rapidly merging with the mass media (or taking on their character) to provide the public with obviously propagandistic messages — for example, in the form of Internet services. A major restructuring of the *xitong* system would be required before the CPD could easily and systematically influence telecommunications units' operations, but no such restructuring was under discussion as of mid-1998 (Interview 78).

Not only does the propaganda *xitong* suffer from limited influence over telecommunications flows; ironically, even the Ministry of Information Industries itself has little influence over telecommunications development at the provincial level and below, with what lingering influence it does have continuing to decline. This fact is unusual from a comparative perspective, because, as the geographer Ronald Abler points out, "[T]hroughout history, telecommunications industries and services have never diffused; they have always been deliberately expanded by strong centralized authorities" (Abler 1991). Telecommunications have traditionally been considered classic public goods that the market would not supply in the absence of direct government provision or a guaranteed monopoly. It was this sort of thinking that convinced the Chinese Communist government to establish a Ministry of Posts and Telecommunications (MPT) in the early 1950s to plan the nation's telecommunications development in a centralized, authoritative way. In 1958, however, during the Great Leap Forward, most of the MPT's key decision-making powers were decentralized to the localities, which afterward became responsible for planning regional telecommunications development. This policy line lasted until 1961, when economic retrenchment forced a recentralization. But in 1971, during the chaos of the Cultural Revolution, the MPT was completely dissolved and merged into a new Ministry of Communications dominated by the People's Liberation Army (PLA). The MPT was reestablished in 1973, but authority over telecommunications development was again decentralized to the provinces and below. The legacy is one of a very weak bureaucracy struggling to manage the development of a modern social function that, in other societies, very strong bureaucracies (or strong parastatal firms) have managed (Zita 1987).

The serious central budget deficits evident in table 6.2 reinforced the tendency toward decentralization within the MPT system and precluded the possibility of restoring significant powers to the central ministry. Partly to avoid having to fund the telecommunications expansion considered necessary to support the "four modernizations," the Center decided formally in 1978 to grant provincial telecommunications bureaus independent accounting status, along with the rights to retain significant portions of their revenues for reinvestment and to seek other sources of investment. In 1980, this line was taken a step further when the State Council adopted the policy of "developing intracity telephone service with intracity telephone revenue." All municipal telecommunications revenue (except for taxes) would be retained by the local service providers, and they would be given the responsibility of designing local telecommunications development plans (Zita 1987; Tan 1994; Ure 1994). As a result, the overall proportion of telecommunications investment originating at the Center decreased from 60 percent in 1983 to less than 9 percent in 1989 (Lin 1993a).

In fact, by the late 1980s, the MPT's responsibilities had largely been confined to managing the national trunk network (the linkages above the provincial level) and international connections. This was no small responsibility, of course — involving the construction of nationwide optical fiber, microwave,

Table 6.2. Central Government Budget Deficits, 1978–1996

Year	Revenue	Expenditures (100 million yuan)	Balance	Deficit/ Revenue
1978	1,132.26	1,122.09	10.17	—
1979	1,146.38	1,281.79	(135.41)	0.118
1980	1,159.93	1,223.83	(68.90)	0.059
1981	1,175.79	1,138.41	37.81	—
1982	1,212.33	1,229.98	(17.65)	0.015
1983	1,366.95	1,409.52	(42.57)	0.031
1984	1,642.86	1,701.02	(58.16)	0.035
1985	2,004.82	2,004.25	0.57	—
1986	2,122.01	2,204.91	(82.90)	0.039
1987	2,199.35	2,262.18	(62.83)	0.029
1988	2,357.24	2,491.21	(133.97)	0.057
1989	2,664.90	2,823.78	(158.88)	0.060
1990	2,937.10	3,083.59	(146.49)	0.050
1991	3,149.48	3,386.62	(237.14)	0.075
1992	3,483.37	3,742.20	(258.83)	0.074
1993	4,348.95	4,642.30	(293.35)	0.067
1994	5,218.10	5,792.62	(574.52)	0.110
1995	6,242.20	6,823.72	(581.52)	0.093
1996	7,407.99	7,937.55	(529.56)	0.071

Source: China Statistics Yearbook, 1997:247.

and satellite grids—and the MPT took up the responsibility with enthusiasm, successfully building an impressive and well-functioning network within a very short period of time. But the key point remains that, at the provincial level and below, the MPT—and its 1998 successor, the MII—very quickly became virtually powerless to influence telecommunications development at the local level except insofar as central intervention was necessary to insure nationwide intercompatibility of technical standards. In fact, most multinational telecommunications equipment providers asserted in interviews that the central ministry "doesn't even have a clue" about the telecommunications development plans of most locales, let alone enjoy significant influence over them (Interviews 110, 114, 116, and 121).

This picture of MPT/MII weakness should be modified, however, in the light of two important considerations. First, the MII continues to preside over a nationwide revenue redistribution system that "requires" richer provinces to transfer portions of their telecommunications revenue to poorer provinces (Ure 1994).[5] For example, Guangdong Province is "required" to give a certain (unspecified) percentage of its revenue to the MII in Beijing, which uses the money to help fund the development of telecommunications in poor provinces such as Xinjiang, Gansu, and Ningxia. This redistribution system is completely distinct from the national taxation system; it is a purely intra-*xitong* system managed by the MII. The effect is to *reduce* MII influence over telecommunications development decisions in the richer provinces while *strengthening* the central ministry's influence over decision making in the poorer provinces. The more profound effect, of course, is to spread the difficulties of thought-work management from the richer areas capable of developing telecommunications autonomously to the poorer areas in need of assistance. Often, the poorer areas are precisely the regions where thought work must be most assiduously controlled because they are populated by potentially restless minorities. The dilemma lies in the fact that those minority groups are more likely to stay satisfied if their economic situation improves, which can only happen in the presence of sustained telecommunications development.

The MII also continues to enjoy veto power over extremely large telecommunications investments that provinces and localities—even the wealthier ones—are proposing to make. Precisely what the cutoff point is at which MII approval must be secured is not a figure that any officials were willing to divulge; apparently it varies by province, personality factors, and other considerations. In general, however, the figure "does get a bit higher each year," implying a steady continuation of the decline in central authority over local telecommunications investment plans (Interview 132). Of course, the MII does enjoy the authority to veto telecommunications projects that would result in local or provincial systems becoming technically incompatible with the national network and international gateways. It can also in general assert a vague, macroregulatory authority to ensure that components of the China-wide network support the integrated development of the nation's overall telecommunications grid. But the grand development strategy is developed at the State Council level, with the MII acting essentially as an agent overseeing implementation of the State Council's will.

The decentralized nature of planning and investment in telecommunications is most evident in the cellular telephone industry, whose celeritous growth is discussed above (see table 6.1). While the MPT, with the assistance of Ericsson and Motorola corporations, played an essential role in developing the technical basis for nationwide roaming capability, almost all of the initial infrastructural development of the cellular industry came as a result of local- and provincial-level initiatives. (The MPT did supply poorer regions with investment funds and presumably advice through the centralized redistribution scheme.) Crucial to cellular telephony's decentralized development pattern was the fact that the State Radio Regulatory Commission (SRRC) — the government body responsible for allocating those segments of the electromagnetic spectrum not controlled by the PLA — is itself independent of the MPT/MII and highly decentralized. At the provincial and local levels, the SRRC tends to be completely supportive of regional efforts to develop cellular and other telecommunications services, even when the result is serious spectrum interference problems with neighboring jurisdictions (Huang 1993; "Control of Telecommunications Market" 1993).

The SSRC's relative autonomy is, like the MPT/MII system's general decentralization, an administrative legacy of the prereform period. Yet another important prereform period legacy that contributes to fragmented management and message-source pluralization is the tendency begun in the 1950s for bureaucratic systems to establish their own, "private" telecommunications networks — rather than to rely on the MPT's public network — to fulfill their internal telecommunications needs (Oksenberg 1974; Zita 1987). The most important of these networks are the ones belonging to the PLA and certain energy and transportation ministries. These bureaucracies have always required relatively advanced and reliable telecommunications capabilities to coordinate their far-flung activities, and they could not rely on the rudimentary MPT system to satisfy their needs. Telecommunications were sufficiently important to the military and to the energy and transportation ministries that they decided to build their own networks.

Consequently, by 1993, of China's 32 million telecommunications lines, an extraordinary 12.74 million (40 percent) belonged to these independent bureaucracies, and only the lines of the PLA and the Ministry of Railways enjoyed formal interconnection capability with the MPT's 19.26 million public lines (L. Xie 1993; Zita 1987). The bureaucracies owning private networks would not even rely on the MPT for transprovincial telecommunications; instead, they constructed their own long-distance trunk networks (He 1994). Even provincial and local government bureaucracies established their own private networks, and they remain central to their operations today. For example, in Shanghai, as of 1992, there were 92 private networks being used by various branches of the municipal government, and an additional 125 networks were being used by field offices of national ministries (Ding 1994).

It was widely recognized by the early 1990s that the existence of these private networks constituted an enormous waste of scarce societal resources. The telecommunications needs of the PLA and government ministries could have been much more efficiently supplied by a centralized MPT, perhaps in the form of dedicated lines carved from an improved public network. Under the planned economy, however, efficiency was not the primary concern; even today, for the PLA and many ministries, efficiency is not usually a major concern. On the other hand, making money *is* a major concern, and because the private networks are wasteful and underutilized, the introduction of a market economy in the mid-1980s created pressures and incentives for the PLA and the ministries to open up their private networks to public use. The pressures came primarily from heavy institutional users of the public system who were dissatisfied with the MPT's service; the incentives, obviously, arose from the income to be generated by supplying services to dissatisfied units for a fee.

In October 1992, Minister of the Electronics Industry Hu Qili formally mooted before the State Council the idea of linking the underutilized private networks into alternative public networks. Hu suggested two networks, each to be run by a separate company affiliated with the now-defunct Ministry of Electronics Industry (MEI). The first company, Liantong (Unicom), or "the United Telecommunications Company," would provide alternative long-distance services to the Chinese public; it was expected to become "the MCI of China." The thinking behind Liantong was simply that competition in the telecommunications industry would stimulate the MPT into providing better service. It would also keep Liantong running efficiently. The second company,

Jitong, or "the Auspicious Telecommunications Company," would concentrate on providing "value-added services," such as electronic data transfer, e-mail, video-on-demand, and Internet access. Despite fierce opposition from the MPT, the State Council approved the creation of Jitong in June 1993 and of Liantong in December 1993. These decisions—which resulted both from centralized, rational calculation and from the high bureaucratic status and political skills of Hu Qili—clearly held the potential to fragment management of telecommunicated thought work even further, since now there would be at least three service providers at each level of the governmental hierarchy (Interview 131; He 1994).

But one of Hu Qili's key selling points in convincing the State Council to approve the new networks' creation was that Jitong, in particular, could strengthen state management of the macroeconomy by supplying the Center with a constant stream of on-line information concerning customs receipts, the money supply, and other pertinent information. At the same time, the new networks would support the transition to a "socialist market economy." In principle, the MPT system could do the same, but it was highly bureaucratized and sluggish when it came to innovation and as of 1993 was bloatedly over-staffed with smugly self-satisfied mandarins. In April 1994, however, the MPT's longtime minister, Yang Taifang, retired and was replaced by an energetic but poorly connected engineer named Wu Jichuan—a man whom most foreign observers predicted would never be able to compete with the more senior and better-connected Hu Qili in the MPT-MEI bureaucratic struggle, which rapidly become white-hot (Interviews 121, 131, 144).

Over the course of the next four years, however, Wu confounded his critics not only by vigorously pursuing the continued development—quantitatively and qualitatively—of the MPT's service provision, but also by repeatedly blocking the efforts made to get Liantong and Jitong get off the ground. Liantong and Jitong needed to secure access to the MPT's public network to attract customers, but Wu and the MPT constantly delayed and prevaricated in round after round of negotiations, infuriating MEI officials (Interview 131). Eventually, MEI chief Hu Qili himself (apparently) hit upon a risky strategy: convince the State Council to establish a Telecommunications Commission higher in rank than both the MPT and MEI and therefore empowered to establish a more level playing field. In the end, this strategy backfired spectacularly, and in March 1998, the State Council *did* establish a new superministry: the MII. Both the MEI and MPT were formally abolished, but what, in fact, happened was that the MPT simply changed its name to MII and absorbed the now-defunct

MEI. The MPT's old headquarters in Beijing became the MII's new headquarters. The first Minister of Information Industries was none other than Wu Jichuan, and the chagrined Hu Qili went on to other work (Lynch 1999).

In name, at least, this bureaucratic reorganization did not alter the central government's commitment to introducing horizontal competition into the telecommunications industry at all levels of the hierarchy (central, provincial, and local), and both Liantong and Jitong continue to exist, at least as of this writing. Officially, the MII—like the MPT before it—is under orders to "separate regulation from management," so it is possible the new superministry will come to resemble a neutral regulatory body and that Liantong and Jitong will still have a future. Wu Jichuan probably feels much less threatened by their existence now that Hu Qili is out of the picture. However, all of this is pure speculation, and in any case the Asian economic crisis resulted in most major structural reforms in China being put on hold in 1998. Early in 1999, however, it was revealed that the MII telecommunications system would be broken up and managed by regional providers, along the lines of the 1984 AT&T breakup in the United States. But whether this plan (which had been discussed for years) will ultimately be implemented remains to be seen. In any case, the MII does not enjoy any more authority over local telecommunications strategic development than did the MPT. Obviously, any breakup of the public network would further fragment telecommunications management. Hence, the general trend toward highly decentralized telecommunications regulation and operation in China will continue and probably even intensify.

Marketization of Message Orientation

In the early 1980s, the central party-state adopted the policy line of eventually making China's telecommunications service and equipment providers (along with most other state-owned enterprises) "responsible for profits and losses" (*zifuyingkui*). In reality, the telecommunications companies are, as a result of this reform, much more responsible for profits than for losses, and none of the basic providers in the MII system has ever gone bankrupt and ceased operations. Service and equipment providers in the poorer regions are, as explained above, subsidized though an intra-*xitong* revenue-redistribution scheme and probably also from local tax revenues. But still, the fact that telecommunications unit personnel now exercise a significant degree of control over how unit revenues are spent—and can use some unit income to improve their own material living conditions—creates strong incentives to cater to market demands for better services and equipment. These demands are fueled by the rise of collective and private enterprises throughout the new market economy, and by the fact that the vast majority of state-owned enterprises in all industries are now "responsible for profits and losses." The transfer of effective *economic* (as opposed to *legal*) property rights to firm income thus interacts with administrative fragmentation to stimulate the further dissemination of both basic and advanced telecommunications equipment and services, which stimulates the economy but confounds the state in its efforts to maintain control over thought work (Interview 132; Barzel 1989; Kornai 1992).

Unlike in the mass media, telecommunications has also witnessed a significant, if still limited, *legal* privatization in certain sectors since the early 1990s. The "Provisional Arrangements for Approval and Regulation of Decentralized Telecommunications Services," promulgated by the State Council in November 1993, explicitly permit both state-owned and collective enterprises to offer the public telecommunications services, provided that the enterprises first obtain licenses from the MPT/MII (Interview 132; Wang 1993). It is particularly noteworthy that "collective" firms are allowed to enter the telecommunications business, because in the Chinese political economy at the turn of the century, "collective" is often—though not always—little more than a euphemism for "private."

Collective and private firms concentrate on the provision of specialized, high-profit services such as mobile cellular, paging, on-line information, and VSAT linkages.[6] (Only the MII is forced to supply loss-leading services such as basic telephony in the poorer villages.) So many collective and private firms had entered the telecommunications market by the mid-1990s that the SRRC in Beijing was forced by problems of signal interference to start regulating more rigorously the assignment of spectrum space (Wang 1993). It only cost about 1 million yuan (U.S. $120,187) to set up a paging station serving one thousand subscribers, an initial investment that could be recouped in a year (Lin 1993b). As a result, an enormous array of companies entered the paging and mobile cellular markets, usually in alliance with territorial-level government bodies. Other companies began supplying a large variety of on-line information that included everything from pornography to weather forecasts, a "burst of value-added services" regarded by multinational telecommunications analysts as the verge of a takeoff into exceptionally rapid growth by 1995 (Interviews 102, 103, 114, and 122). About one thousand VSAT networks were in operation as early as mid-1993, a figure expected to increase tenfold by the year 2000 (Interview 147; Yao et al. 1993; "Spokesman Gives Update" 1993). All of these services increased the Center's challenges in maintaining control over thought work, but their provision evolved logically from the economic and administrative reforms of the 1980s.

One of the most colorful examples of the effective economic privatization of telecommunications service provision can be found on the streets of Guangzhou. At least in the densely populated downtown area of this hyper-commercial southeastern city, the residents of about every fifth household or store have pulled their private telephones out onto the sidewalk and placed them on stands, inviting passersby to make calls for a fee. These phones are most certainly not the public phones run by the MII system, the residents insist, implying that the public phones are inferior. These phones are privately owned and operated. Apparently, the residents do not require—or do not bother to obtain—a license for providing basic telecommunications services to the public. It also seems unlikely that they pay taxes on the income gained from providing these services. Only in Guangzhou, it should be noted, was this phenomenon evident.

This sort of entrepreneurial telecommunications service provision stimulates the MII to become more responsive to its customers, fueling the further spread of information and symbols outside of state control. A similar sort of phenomenon occurred right after the founding of Liantong and Jitong in 1994. In the early 1990s, the MPT required applicants for telephone service to pay a deposit equal to several hundred U.S. dollars and to pay it up to a year before service provision would actually begin. Naturally, MPT units retained the interest on these deposits, and thereby increased their income, without providing their customers with anything in return other than the privilege of having their names put on a list. Moreover, it is alleged, prospective customers would also often have to offer MPT officials bribes in exchange for this privilege. But from 1994 to 1995—the year after Liantong and Jitong were founded—both the wait for and the cost of basic telephone service fell sharply in the big cities, even though the two new service providers had not yet begun operations (Interview 132).

The beneficiaries of commercialization and competition are obviously not only the providers of telecommunications services—whether in the state, collective, or private sector—but also individuals, groups, and organizations in Chinese society at large. Their increasing access to relatively low-cost telecommunications services not only improves the efficiency of their businesses and the quality of their daily lives, but also allows them to take from the state a significant degree of control over thought work. Simply put, if the people choose, they can now use telecommunications services to transmit not only prosaic messages but also propagandistic messages, whether created anew or re-circulated after acquisition from the rapidly changing mass media environment. As a result, the commercialization of telecommunications service provision combines with fragmented management and technological advance to strengthen society vis-à-vis the state in the ongoing, all-important struggle to control thought work.

Message-Source Globalization

The data presented in table 6.1 reveal in a striking way the likelihood of significant thought-work globalization via telecommunications in the years following China's spring 1989 political crisis. Probably most important in this regard is the exponential increase in long-distance telephone calls per capita between 1989 and 1996. While most of these calls are probably devoted purely to facilitating economic cooperation among firms and firm subsidiaries in Guangdong and Hong Kong, many are routed through Hong Kong from and to destinations abroad (including Taiwan), and they clearly hold the potential to act as conduits of propagandistic messages.[7] Two other especially noteworthy pieces of data are the rapid dissemination of fax machines and the sharp increase in the number of fax messages sent between 1989 and 1993 (the last year fax machines were counted). Scholars and commentators have made much ado about the role of fax technology in informing dissidents throughout China about the declaration of martial law in Beijing on May 21, 1989, and about the Tiananmen massacre the night of the third to the fourth of June. The data presented in table 6.1 reveal that 2,600 fax machines were in use throughout China in 1989, a figure that increased at least five times by the end of 1993. But all informants at multinational telecommunications firms insisted that the 12,276 fax machine figure for 1993 vastly understated the true number of machines in use even at that early date because a registration system that the Center introduced in the aftermath of Tiananmen disintegrated within a year. By the mid-1990s, anyone could purchase a fax machine and simply plug it into the telephone jack in his or her wall (Interviews 102, 103, 110, 114, and 122). Thus, availability of technology is interacting with administrative disarray and the increasing income produced by economic growth to facilitate the importation of information, ideas, perceptions, and values from abroad.

The 2.7 million fax messages sent in 1993—eleven times the figure of 1989—is also considered likely to be an underestimate, because China's telecommunications companies have no reliable way of knowing which entries on a phone bill represent telephone calls and which represent fax messages. Presently, most international fax messages that China sends and receives are probably designed to support business activities concentrated in the Pearl River Delta, just as in the case of phone calls. But should a new political crisis break out, perhaps in conjunction with the implementation of state-owned enterprise reform (which will produce massive unemployment), Chinese dissidents (both at home and abroad) will be in a much better position than even in 1989 to exchange their ideas and criticize the government. They will also find it much easier to mobilize and coordinate protest activities, making use of bases both at home and abroad.

Arguably the most important development in the globalization of Chinese thought work—or at least the development with the most profound long-term potential—is the linking of the country to the Internet, a process which began in earnest only in early 1995. Worldwide, the number of computers (as opposed to individual users) connected to the Internet increased 51 times between 1990 and 1995, from 130,000 to 6.64 million (Markoff 1995). But except for a few dedicated linkages between research institutes in China and both Europe and the United States, China was not an early participant in this rapid growth. Part of the problem was technological/economic—there were simply too few computers in the country to support Internet access—and part was bureaucratic and political: The MPT was struggling with the MEI to maintain control over computer networks (and the value-added services they would support) but faced little incentive to provide the public with Internet access because it faced no competition.

In July 1993, however, in conjunction with the debate over whether the State Council should approve Liantong and Jitong, the MPT unveiled China-pac, a computer-based telecommunications network suitable for data transmission, e-mail, and other value-added services that initially linked thirty provincial capitals and the city of Chongqing. There were, at first, some 5,500 domestic ports, and subscribers could (in theory) make connections to external networks through international gateways in Beijing and Guangzhou ("Opening of Public Switching Data Network" 1993). However, MPT subdivisions demanded exorbitant rates for access to the outside world; for example, the Beijing Telecommunications Authority charged U.S. $5,000 per month for a dedicated line to the United States (Zheng 1994). As a result, there were few takers, and the MPT *xitong* missed an outstanding opportunity to secure the advantages of early market entry and keep potential competitors out.

In 1994, when the MPT lost its monopoly over computerized telecommunications networks, the door to the Internet opened wide. First, the State Council approved Jitong's proposed "Golden Bridge" project, among whose services would be Internet access. Second, two educational networks were formed, one under the aegis of the State Education Commission (SEC), the other under the Chinese Academy of Sciences (CAS). The SEC's China Education and Research Network (CERNET) was expected eventually to link hundreds of thousands of scholars and students at universities all over China with their counterparts in the outside world, especially in Hong Kong, Taiwan, and the United States. The CAS network was similar but would link more senior scholars and researchers. Almost immediately, Jitong articulated as one of its primary missions the merger of CERNET and the CAS network under Golden Bridge, so that a unified second, larger network could eventually be formed to counterbalance the MPT's Chinapac (Interviews 122 and 141).

Under the pressure of competition from Jitong and the educational providers, the MPT finally began to promote expansion of Internet usage via Chinapac late in the winter of 1995. To stimulate interest, subscribers were granted free access for several months beginning in February, with the result that already four hundred individuals and units (all located in Beijing) had opened MPT accounts by mid-April. By the end of 1995, access had spread to most major cities, with *New York Times* sources estimating that anywhere from 30,000 to 100,000 Chinese individuals had secured Internet access (Interview 134; Tacey 1995; Faison 1996). These figures increased exponentially, so that 2.5 million Chinese citizens enjoyed Internet access by the end of 1998, a figure expected to rise to six million by 2002 (Interviews 79 and 80). The most active users were students, professors, and businesspeople involved in external trade and investment—opinion leaders who would undoubtedly convey new ideas, values, and worldviews to ever wider circles of the Chinese population.

Administrative management of the Internet, though fragmented horizontally, is centralized vertically in Beijing. That is, regardless of the service to which an individual or unit seeks to subscribe, approval must come from the relevant central agency in Beijing. For example, potential Shanghai subscribers to the MII's Internet service can submit applications in Shanghai but must obtain approval from the MII before receiving an account. This practice is consistent with the maintenance of MII authority over all transprovincial and international long-distance telecommunications services. But its primary function appears simply to be to route revenue to the MII, not to control the content of e-mail or what external Web sites people can access—though that is done too, of course (with mixed results). The MII can deny accounts to suspected "bad elements," but once individuals and units secure accounts, the MII and other central agencies can no more easily monitor e-mail than they can telephone calls or faxes (Interview 122).

In one key respect, the Center appears to be holding the line on thought-work globalization: It continues, largely successfully, to prevent foreign multinationals from owning and/or operating any component of the Chinese telecommunications system. (The same holds true for the mass media.) To be sure, Beijing welcomes with open arms foreign investment in the manufacture of telecommunications equipment and the provision of consulting services on network management (Interview 103; L. Xie 1993). But it repeatedly reiterates a firm opposition to foreign ownership of or control over telecommunications networks, primarily, it appears, because of a fear that if foreign interests secured control over the nerves of thought work, China's national security (broadly defined) could come under serious threat. Foreigners and media interests in Hong Kong and Taiwan might use their control over telecommunications networks to supply Chinese cable television subscribers with pornography, news, and other "spiritually polluting" and "bourgeois liberal" satellite TV and videotapes. The United States and its allies could penetrate the Chinese telecommunications system to pursue "peaceful evolution" and undermine the "people's democratic dictatorship." Thus, while foreign telecommunications executives appear convinced that it is "only a matter of time" before China allows them to own and operate domestic networks, Chinese leaders insist that this will never happen and have held their ground on this point consistently for years (Interviews 102, 103, and 132; "Overseas Firms" 1993; Hong 1993; State Science and Technology Commission 1994).

Belated Efforts to Regulate Telecommunications Flows

During the summer of 1993, the Center launched a large-scale crackdown on all manifestations of undesirable thought work, a campaign whose best-known component abroad was a new set of restrictions on ownership of satellite dishes. But the crackdown was (and remains, as of this writing) far more extensive and significant than restrictions on satellite dishes, and it includes efforts to eliminate from the so-called cultural market such "cultural trash" as pornography, politically incorrect books and magazines, and "crass," "feudal superstitious," and "spiritually polluting" films and television programs (Lynch 1999).

Curiously, though, the crackdown did *not* initially encompass China's telecommunications networks. The reasons are complex. First, as explained above, China's telecommunications networks were, until recent years, simply too underdeveloped to be used for anything other than technical and administrative purposes. The perception of telecommunications as "nonpropagandistic" in nature persists despite a rapidly changing reality. Even the managers and personnel of telecommunications companies share the misperception that telecommunications are fundamentally nonpropagandistic, or they at least exploit the misperception in pursuit of their personal interests. For example, one informant argued vigorously that telecommunications service providers should not be required to take on the burden of stopping people from using telecommunications networks to transmit pornography and that certainly they should not be incorporated into the propaganda *xitong* so that the central party-state could more easily control thought work:

> Pornography and counterrevolutionary spiritual products are everywhere, but not every unit can be a part of the propaganda *xitong*. Should the transportation departments become part of the propaganda *xitong*? Should they be held accountable when bad people use the roads and railways to transport pornography? (Interview 131)

To most people in the telecommunications business, keeping pornography and other undesirable cultural products out of the "symbolic environment" is a problem for the police and other departments charged with regulating book, periodical, and videotape markets. It would certainly be *mafan* (trouble) if the telecommunications units started having to play a role. But in this regard, the State Council assigned the Ministry of Public Security (MPS) and the Ministry of State Security (MSS) joint responsibility for "safeguarding computer information systems," including value-added telecommunications, on March 1, 1994. "No organization or individual may use computer information systems to engage in activities that endanger national or collective interests, as well as the legitimate interests of citizens," the decision specifies ("PRC Regulations" 1994). Implementing this decision will certainly require cooperative efforts on behalf of both the security ministries and the telecommunications service providers. And indeed, as telecommunications continue to merge with the mass media in nature and function, the need for such cooperation will of necessity increase if the Center hopes to retain its desired degree of control over thought work.

The rapidity of China's communications revolution makes it even more difficult for Beijing's leaders to adapt to the challenges presented by the Internet and other high-tech telecommunications than it is for the leaders of other countries. Even the United States finds it difficult to deal with hackers, child pornographers, spammers, and other Internet abusers—and Americans invented the Internet. For China's leaders, the Internet's challenges are nothing short of bewilderingly difficult to grasp. After all, only two decades ago, China was hopelessly backward technologically in all but a few specialized spheres. Now, perhaps four million of its citizens sign on regularly to the Internet.

Only in early 1996 did the Chinese authorities seem finally to wake up and grasp the significance of the Internet, if not necessarily the entire telecommunications threat to state control over thought work. On February 1, 1996, the State Council promulgated a new set of regulations governing Internet service provision aimed primarily at limiting the number of providers to the then-current four: the MPT, the MEI, the SEC, and the CAS (Faison 1996). These regulations resembled an autumn 1993 initiative to force China's new suppliers of other kinds of value-added services to register with the MPT, an effort that most observers attributed to the MPT's desire to profit from the services rather than to control content (Wang 1993). However, the 1996 Internet regulations do specifically address the thought-work problem by expressly forbidding use of the Internet to transmit pornography and other content "that may hinder public order," including political information sent into the country by dissidents living abroad. At least, it appeared, the propaganda *xitong* was stepping in and exerting influence over what formerly was exclusively the turf of the telecommunications' *xitong*. This trend has continued and intensified, even though telecommunications organizations such as the MII are still not classified as part of the propaganda *xitong*. Late in the summer of 1996, the government began trying to block access to external Internet Web sites supplying news and pornography, and ever since it has maintained a blacklist of banned sites (Interview 176). During the May 1999 anti-American demonstrations that followed NATO's bombing of the Chinese embassy in Yugoslavia, China at various times completely shut down external Internet access, though the precise reasons are unclear (Interview 180).

All these efforts have been sporadic and only partially effective, raising the question of whether the Chinese state possesses the techno-administrative capacity to control the dissemination of Internet (and other telecommunications) information in a sustained way, over the long haul. Specifically with regard to the Internet, one foreign specialist asserted that "they don't know how to control it, and they don't even know they don't know how to control it" (Interview 157). Similarly, an MEI official admitted that "neither the Ministry of Public Security nor anyone else in China currently possesses the technology to police today's telecommunications networks because they're too sophisticated" (Interview 144). Foreign and Hong Kong telecommunications equipment providers believe that technology will soon become available to monitor or staunch the flow of value-added telecommunications flows "to a degree." For example, it might be possible to use "firewall" technology to completely shut down the transmission of all video messages into China during an emergency. But this technology will be "extremely expensive" even assuming it works, and it is far from clear that Beijing would be able to afford it or absorb it in the next decade or so, given China's general level of technological backwardness.

The high cost of interdicting advanced telecommunications flows interacts with the fragmented nature of China's telecommunications system (technologically and administratively) to make stopping the circulation of heterodox messages supremely difficult. The net result of the installation of highly decentralized automated switching equipment and optical fiber transmission systems is a continuing increase in the number of points at which "bad" messages must be intercepted if the central party-state is to prevent them from "poisoning" the minds of the people. Internet access is restricted to a few nodes and can therefore more easily be controlled, but that is not the case with telephone and fax transmissions. Within about two decades, the Chinese state will likely find itself in a position in which it can still, indeed, monitor individual messages—for example, the messages sent and received by known dissidents—but not *all* messages, the messages sent by the vast majority of the population. The implication is that, clearly, thought work will become progressively more difficult to control, and ideological authoritarianism will be challenged to its roots.

The Sociopolitical Implications of Beijing's Declining Control

A society's communication patterns are embedded in larger cultural contexts and as a result do not usually determine political outcomes unilaterally. But changing communication patterns can render current political orders unstable, increasing the costs of maintenance and reducing the costs of change. Even in this situation, though, the outcome of the changes is not easily predicted; specifically in the case of China, more liberal and open communication flows will not necessarily lead to democratization. They will, however, make it significantly more difficult for the state to sustain authoritarian rule.

For example, liberalized communication flows seem very likely to contribute to the development of so-called genuine public opinion. All of the important Chinese leaders who spoke at the National Conference on Propaganda and Thought Work in January 1994 made a special point of calling on the Communist Party to "correctly guide public opinion" (*Quan Zhongguo* 1994). Not until the crisis of 1989, it seems, did China's leaders come to realize with a shock that the Chinese people were capable of generating a genuine *public* opinion, not in the sense of aggregates of individuals holding secretly to their views, but rather in the sense of "people recognizing a problem, producing conflicting ideas about what to do, considering those alternatives, and trying to resolve the matter by building consensus for a line of action" (Price 1992). Members of society in alliance with disaffected elements of the party-state were clearly doing just that in the spring of 1989, and China's repressive leaders recognized the ominous link between autonomous generation of public opinion and reduced prospects for continued authoritarian rule.

But telecommunications development does not necessarily lead automatically to the development of a liberal public sphere, the rise of a civil society, and democratization. Certainly it facilitates such an outcome, but that is only one of several possible effects of telecommunications development on society:

- Telecommunications development may facilitate the formation of transregional and even transnational criminal organizations. Already this phenomenon is plaguing China, as gangsters selling drugs, guns, and prostitutes make ready use of cellular telephones and other advanced telecommunications technologies. Frequently, their partners are based in Hong Kong, Macao, Taiwan, and abroad (Su 1992; Sun and Wu 1993).
- Telecommunications may strengthen national unity by creating horizontal linkages across regions and *xitong*—the "societal *xitong*" concept discussed above. Again, there is evidence that this phenomenon is also taking root in China as the market economy becomes increasingly institutionalized. For example, new political parties suddenly blossomed throughout urban China in the fall of 1998 after word leaked out that the leadership was contemplating political reform. (Subsequently, the parties were crushed.) Similarly, the anti-American demonstrations of spring 1999 spread much more quickly than probably would have been possible in the absence of horizontal telecommunications linkages now in place as a result of fifteen years of development.

- On the other hand, telecommunications can also facilitate national disintegration. This effect is more subtle, but no less real. People enter into specialized networks distinct from and divorced from the larger society. They go about their business, making money, enjoying their lives, and pursuing their personal goals, oblivious to the goals of "strangers" and the state. They can much more easily "tune out" state messages when the communications system becomes more horizontal in nature and no longer exclusively vertical. The result is a collective of people living in the same territory, but disunited: leading different lives and pursuing different interests; helping people with whom they have *guanxi*, but ignoring (at best) others. In a national crisis, the Chinese people might or might not "hang together."

- Finally, telecommunications facilitate the massive importation of "global culture," including everything from popular music to the deeper values of individualism, hedonism, and self-actualization that originated in the West a few centuries ago and subsequently swept the world. Here, the Internet is especially important, but e-mail, faxes, and telephone calls also convey values and information into China from abroad.

Of course, it is possible that telecommunications actually play a relatively passive role in these processes, and that the "big media" of television, film, radio, and print remain far more important. Perhaps telecommunications facilitate the further dissemination of new values and worldviews, but usually these values and worldviews are acquired from the mass media, or interpersonally. In this view, telecommunications remain relatively unimportant in the thought-work enterprise, and China's leaders are correct in their assessment that telecommunications are far less serious a threat to their control over thought work than are the other media, which therefore demand far more serious attention and stern treatment.

But in the end, this view seems likely to be dangerously mistaken. Telecommunications' social effects have always been underestimated, both by scholars and public figures alike. The Internet seems finally to be waking the world up to the socially transformative potential of telecommunications development. But it still remains very, very difficult to predict exactly how telecommunications will change a society like China's. Will they facilitate democratization, or render the society crime-ridden and even less civil, less likely to be characterized by the trust and sense of community that democratization requires? Will telecommunications development knit the country together in a societal *xitong*, or fragment it into self-interested *guanxi* networks pursuing their selfish interests—also inconsistent with democratization? Only the passage of time can provide answers to these questions, but it is certain that telecommunications will play an increasingly central role in China's sociopolitical development. Fifty years from now, historians may be shaking their heads in bewildered wonderment at how twentieth-century analysts could have so blithely overlooked telecommunications' enormous social importance.

Notes

1. In this chapter, the terms "central party-state" and "the Center" refer to the Beijing-based, higher-level networks and hierarchies charged with the overall task of managing all forms of propaganda. The composition of these networks fluctuates, but they always include officials at the ministerial and vice-ministerial levels in the governmental Ministry of Information Industries, Ministry of Culture, and State Press and Publications Administration, as well as in the party's Central Propaganda Department. Other ministries and organizations become important in managing propaganda flows during campaigns. (For details, see Lynch 1999.) That the central party-state has lost a significant degree of control over thought work is an assertion supported by the countless complaints of high-ranking propaganda officials that the media are now saturated with vulgarity, violence, inanity, and "feudal superstition," much of which originates abroad. (See the speeches collected in *Quan Zhongguo* 1994.)

2. But communications scholars in general have tended to ignore telecommunications. See Sinha (1994) for a thoughtful examination of this phenomenon.

3. Examining these developments is, of course, the purpose of this chapter, which is based on extensive reading of documentary materials from 1993 to 1999, and on eighty interviews with people knowledgeable about the Chinese media system, conducted in Beijing, Guangzhou, Kunming, Hong Kong, Taipei, Los Angeles, Washington, and New York. The interviews are numbered 101 to 180 in the text. Not everyone interviewed is cited specifically in this chapter, but the observations of all informants helped structure the author's thinking about telecommunications in China. The most pertinent observations came, of course, from informants working specifically in China's telecommunications companies investing in China. But even informants in other media industries and the Chinese Communist Party's propaganda apparatus shared extensive knowledge about how the telecommunications sector has developed, functions, and is managed in China. Informants could not be selected at random; they were selected on the basis of availability. Guarantees of anonymity increased their willingness to talk, and their comments were mutually reinforcing and consistent with the written record, suggesting little or no systematic bias.

4. The term *xitong* denotes a vertical bureaucratic hierarchy.

5. The term "requires" appears in quotation marks because compliance is not always effectively enforced.

6. "VSAT" is an acronym for "very small aperture terminal." VSATs are satellite-based, dedicated networks that link the offices of multinational corporations, banks, airlines, and other business and government organizations whose activities are scattered across large territories. The *People's Daily (Renmin ribao)* makes extensive use of VSAT technology, as does the Xinhua News Agency.

7. During the mid-1990s, before the Asian economic meltdown, at any given moment during peak periods on business days, some 15,000 telephone calls were being made from Hong Kong to China or vice versa (Clifford 1994).

Bibliography

Abler, Ronald. 1991. "Hardware, Software, and Brainware: Mapping and Understanding Telecommunications Technologies." In Stanley D. Brunn and Thomas R. Leinbach, eds., *Collapsing Space and Time: Geographic Aspects of Communication and Information*. London: HarperCollins Academic.

Barzel, Yoram. 1989. *Economic Analysis of Property Rights*. New York: Cambridge University Press.

"Cellular Mobile Phone Calls Available in Qinghai." 1994. Xinhua News Agency, April 3. Trans. in *FBIS Daily Report (China)*, April 5, 80–81.

Chen, Yunqian. 1993. "Driving Forces Behind China's Explosive Telecommunications Growth." *IEEE Communications Magazine* (July):20–22.

"China's Posts and Telecommunications Have Returned to Normal." 1989. *Zhongguo Xinwenshe*, June 19. Trans. in *JPRS Telecommunications Report*, July 18, 1.

Clifford, Mark. 1994. "Communications: China Calling." *Far Eastern Economic Review*, March 31, 56–58.

"Control of Telecommunications Market Strengthened." 1993. Xinhua News Agency, September 13. Trans. in *FBIS Daily Report (China)*, September 14, 43.

Ding, Lu. 1994. "The Management of China's Telecommunications Industry: Some Institutional Facts." *Telecommunications Policy* 18 (3):195–205.

Faison, Seth. 1996. "Chinese Cruise Internet, Wary of Watchdogs." *New York Times*, February 5, A1 and A3.

He, Fei Chang. 1994. "Lian Tong: A Quantum Leap in the Reform of China's Telecommunications." *Telecommunications Policy* 18 (3):206–10.

Hong, Wen. 1993. "Official Cited on Telecommunications Investment." Xinhua News Agency, May 10. Trans. in *FBIS Daily Report (China)*, December 9, 41–43.

Huang, Jie. 1990. "Bringing Order to the Radio Dial." *Beijing Review*, January 22–28, 37–38.

Kornai, Janos. 1992. *The Socialist System: The Political Economy of Communism*. Princeton: Princeton University Press.

Lin, Sun. 1993a. "Funding Telecommunications Expansion." *China Business Review* (March–April):31–33.

————. 1993b. "Mobile Communications Takes Off in China." *Telecom Asia* (April): 86–88.

Lynch, Daniel C. 1999. *After the Propaganda State: Media, Politics, and "Thought Work" in Reformed China.* Stanford, Calif.: Stanford University Press.

McGregor, James, and John J. Keller. 1993. "AT&T, China Set Broad Pact for Phones, Gear." *Wall Street Journal,* February 24, A3.

Markoff, John. 1995. "AT&T May Have Edge in Future On Line." *New York Times,* August 21, C1 and C4.

Mufson, Steven. 1996. "Chinese Protest Finds a Path on the Internet." *Washington Post,* September 17, A9.

Oksenberg, Michel. 1974. "Methods of Communication within the Chinese Bureaucracy." *China Quarterly* 57 (January/March):1–39.

"Opening of Public Switching Data Network Report." 1993. Xinhua News Agency, August 31. Trans. in *FBIS Daily Report (China),* September 14, 24.

"Overseas Firms Cannot Manage Communications." 1993. Xinhua News Agency, May 10. Trans. in *FBIS Daily Report (China),* May 11, 37.

"PRC Regulations on Safeguarding Computer Information Systems." 1994. Xinhua News Agency, February 23. Trans. in *FBIS Daily Report (China),* March 24, 34–36.

Price, Vincent. 1992. *Communications Concepts 4: Public Opinion.* Newbury Park, Calif.: Sage Publications.

Quan Zhongguo Xuanchuan Sixiang Gongzuo Huiyi Wenjian Huibian. 1994. Beijing: Xuexi Press.

"Report Views Telecommunications Usage Nationwide." 1994. Xinhua News Agency, February 5. Trans. in *FBIS Daily Report (China),* February 9, 29–30.

Rogers, Everett M. 1995. *The Diffusion of Innovations.* 4th ed. New York: Free Press.

Severin, Werner J., and James W. Tankard Jr. 1988. *Communication Theories.* 2nd ed. New York and London: Longman.

She, Qijiong, and Yu Renlin. 1993. "Telecommunications Services in China." *IEEE Communications Magazine* (July).

Shue, Vivienne. 1988. *The Reach of the State: Sketches of the Chinese Body Politic.* Stanford, Calif.: Stanford University Press.

Sinha, Nikhil. 1994. "Telecommunications Capabilities and Development: Towards an Integrated Framework for Development Communication." Paper presented at the Pacific Telecommunications Council Conference, Honolulu, January.

"Spokesman Gives Update on Satellite Communications." 1993. Xinhua News Agency, October 20. Trans. in *FBIS Daily Report (China),* October 21, 27.

State Science and Technology Commission. 1994. *A Guide to China's Science and Technology Policy: White Paper on Science and Technology, No. 5.* Trans. in *JPRS China Science and Technology Report,* April 8, 1, 50–53.

Su, Xiaokang. 1992. "The Dabbling Civil Society" ("Bandiaozi de shimin shehui"). *Democratic China (Minzhu zhongguo)* 11 (August):1–3.

Sun, Hui, and Wu Mengshuang. 1993. "Underground Criminal Societies Rapidly Expand Their Influence." *Society* 105 (October):47–48. Trans. in *JPRS China Report,* March 22, 1994, 34–36.

Tacey, Elizabeth. 1995. "Threat to Limit Internet Access." *South China Morning Post,* May 25, 10.

Tan, Liangjun. 1994. "Challenges to the MPT's Monopoly." *Telecommunications Policy* 18(3):174–81.

"Telecommunications Minister on Improvements." 1994. Xinhua News Agency, January 12. Trans. in *FBIS Daily Report (China),* January 13, 15.

"Urban Residents Increasingly Installing Private Telephones." 1991. Xinhua News Agency, December 8. Trans. in *JPRS Telecommunications Report,* December 26, 14.

Ure, John. 1994. "Telecommunications, with Chinese Characteristics." *Telecommunications Policy* 18(3):182–94.

Wang, Yanrong. 1993. "Radio Stations to Be Surveyed, Registered." Xinhua News Agency, May 28. Trans. in *FBIS Daily Report (China),* June 7, 29.

Weinstock, Jordan, Greg Apostolous, and Chen Yunqian. 1994. "Fiber Optics Networks in China's Drive for Economic Development." Paper delivered at the Pacific Telecommunications Council Conference, Honolulu, January.

Whyte, Martin King. 1974. *Small Groups and Political Rituals in China.* Berkeley and Los Angeles: University of California Press.

Xie, Jiangfa. 1993. "Years of Deficits in Perspective, Solutions." *Economic Theory and Economic Management* (*Jingji lilun yu jingji guanli*) 6(28):26–31.

Xie, Liangjun. 1993. "Telecommunications Expansion Unabated." *China Daily (Business Weekly),* February 21, 8. Reprinted in *FBIS Daily Report (China),* February 23, 38–39.

Xu, Yang. 1994. "Fresh Bid to Switch Viewers On to Cable TV." *China Daily,* March 22, 3. Reprinted in *FBIS Daily Report (China),* March 24, 36–37.

Yao, Yan, Cao Zhigang, and Yu Renlin. 1993. "R & D Activities on Wireless Systems in China." *IEEE Communications Magazine* (July):30–33.

Zhao, Di Ang, and Liu Junja. 1994. "Telecommunications Development and Economic Growth in China." *Telecommunications Policy* 18(3):211–15.

Zheng, Cindy. 1994. "Opening the Digital Door: Computer Networking in China." *Telecommunications Policy* 18:236–42.

Zhongguo tongji nianjian (China Statistical Yearbook). 1988–97. Beijing: National Statistical Bureau. Published annually.

Zita, Ken. 1987. *Modernizing China's Telecommunications.* London: Economist Intelligence Unit; Hong Kong: Business International Corporation.

7

The Media and the Legal Bureaucracy of the People's Republic of China

TAHIRIH V. LEE

I n the People's Republic of China (PRC), the texts of major national statutes (*falu*) and regulations (*guiding*) are published in the primary Chinese Communist Party newspaper, the *People's Daily* (*Renmin ribao*). These publications are official not only in the sense that their contents contain officially enacted laws, but also because the newspaper is operated by the government of the PRC and the government intends, by publishing these laws, to send particular signals to the public that can be referred to in official discourse as authoritative. Other transmissions by the print and broadcast media which are related to law are orchestrated by the government and are designed to send official signals that carry authoritative weight. Such transmissions come in a wide variety of formats, from comic books to television programs to newspaper articles to treatises. They cover a wide variety of legal topics, but they have as their common purpose the communication of official interpretations of the law and reports about the implementation of law. What emerges in this chapter is the authoritative nature of media transmissions related to law.[1] This authority does not derive from a single entity within the bureaucracy overseeing media transmissions, but rather from the conformity produced by a kind of self-censorship by all of the organs orchestrating media transmissions.

Under pressure from market forces, the mass media in China have undergone a transformation. Have the changes wrought by market forces undermined the authority of the transmissions about law by the state? To answer this question, this study undertakes a discursive analysis of sample transmissions of the state-run news agency Xinhua; two major legal newspapers run by branches of the Ministry of Justice; and other materials generated by governmental offices of the PRC, such as popular and internal party treatises. It uses two such samples, each of which touches on the subject of Hong Kong: one sample of several dozen transmissions from 1984, and another sample of several hundred transmissions from 1995 through the first half of 1996. These media transmissions interpreted and amplified the relevant law in ways that signaled, by the mid-1990s, a major policy governing law in Hong Kong: control of the PRC central government over "political" matters and a new sharing of control over "economic" matters by both the PRC central government and local entities officially recognized by the government. This pattern remained consistent through the changes in format of the media transmissions heralded by the commercialization of the mass media by 1995 and 1996.

The Bureaucracy's Use of Media to Propound PRC Law

The pattern of using media to implement law began with the earliest activities of the Chinese Communist Party (CCP). As it built itself earlier in the century, the infant CCP took advantage of the capabilities of the new electronic media of the 1920s and expanded the scope of the state-run media as it was then constituted under the Guomindang government. The CCP focused on solidifying its control of the press, radio, and film, and on sending messages through these media which showed its solidarity with the people. To these ends, in the 1930s, a vibrant period for both the press and for Shanghai's film industry, the Chinese Communist Party ran its own newspapers (MacKinnon 1997; Liu 1966) and organized China's first film society. In the 1930s and 1940s, Communists produced films designed to show the party's patriotism by emphasizing its anti-Japan stance. By 1953, the Chinese Communist Party had banned foreign films and turned China's film industry into a mouthpiece for Soviet and Chinese Communism (Dissanayake 1988:161–63; Vogel 1980:83–84; Clark 1988:177–80). At the same time, the party closed or assumed control of the radio stations and of the hundreds of newspapers that had flourished in Shanghai and Canton and other cities during the Republican era. In the 1940s and early 1950s, these publications publicized the party's widely heralded efforts to give land to poor farmers (Liu 1966:12; Vogel 1980).

During the important political movements of the 1950s and 1960s, the party used the media under its control to attempt to influence public behavior. Mao Zedong and other top leaders sent signals through the press and radio to political activists about whom to target, how vigorously to implement party programs, and which sanctions to mete out to those who resisted. Cadres at the local level followed the instructions they received through the media to enforce central campaigns through personal contact with the people in their jurisdiction. Personal contact with the "masses" was the path to membership in the party for youthful recruits, and Mao Zedong relied on young activists to carry out his most radical programs, such as land reform and the purges of 1966 to 1968 (examples are clearly documented in Vogel 1980). In official terms, the central leadership, by the end of the 1970s, had a commitment to "mass participation and mass control," which it accomplished through "communication with the masses" directly by media or by way of cadres informed by media (Li 1980:42).

With the advent of the legalization campaign initiated at the Third Plenum of the Eleventh Party Central Committee Meeting in 1978, all media channels were enlisted in the dissemination of the party's new optimistic views about law and of news about the party's mounting achievements in building a legal system. Beijing's major publishing houses, even the Foreign Languages Press, churned out compilations of the statutes, simplified explanations of statutes, and comic books to help citizens identify their new legal rights. The *People's Daily* became the primary vehicle for publishing the full texts of statutes enacted by the National People's Congress. The *People's Daily* also took on the task of publishing official versions of legislative history, official interpretations of the statutes, reports of current bills under consideration by the National People's Congress and by congresses below it, and notices of new policies of central administrative agencies. The government founded specialized legal newspapers, what is now the national *Legal System Daily* (*Fazhi ribao*) and regional versions such as the *Shanghai Legal System News* (*Shanghai fazhi bao*). These journals published legislative history, official interpretations of statutes, reports of bills, and notices of administrative policies which were either not published elsewhere, and therefore were the only versions of these statements available to judges, or were replicas of the documents that the CCP sent to all judges in the PRC for study in Tuesday afternoon "political study" (*zhengzhi xue*) sessions.

The party leaders in the late 1970s used the media to publicize the law because few lawyers or other legal professionals had survived the Cultural Revolution to serve as intermediaries between the central leadership and the masses. Yet, even after the number of lawyers in the PRC grew to exceed ninety thousand in 1996, the central government's program to use mass media to communicate official policy and discourse about law to the masses showed no signs of abating. The Ministry of Justice is the central government executive agency in Beijing that oversees the nationwide effort to educate the public about central law and policy. Apart from operating at least half a dozen law schools in major cities throughout the PRC, the ministry sponsors a variety of less specialized legal education programs, such as lecture circuits into remote areas by junior law professors. In October 1995, attorney Zhang Yong (1995), Deputy Division Chief of the Publicity Department of the Beijing Bureau of the Ministry of Justice, described his job as helping to formulate a five-year plan for the education of ordinary people (*laobaixing*) about the 152 laws that will be enacted in the PRC in the next five years. That job entailed organizing "special legal lectures for top Chinese leaders," "[e]xamining and approving textbooks of specialized law which are edited by other government branches," and supervising the production of *Communication of Promotion of Mass Legal Education Magazine*. From Zhang's career path thus far, propaganda work in the mid-1990s appeared to be plentiful enough to offer the loyal and energetic a fast track to prominence in the PRC government. At the tender age of thirty, he had already obtained a Master of Law degree, interned in a law firm, interned as a judge, worked his way up through three positions in the Ministry of Justice, and published eight articles, one entitled "Mass Legal Education: A Tough Job in China" and another entitled "The Key to Public Legal Education Lies in Persistence and Implementation."

Television and film contribute to the promotion of official views of the legal system. One example of an audiovisual production aiming to publicize an official interpretation of law was a television program aired in Shanghai in 1993 called *Society's Classics* (*Shehui jingzhuan*). It featured a segment called "Law's Letterbox" (*Falu xinxiang*) in which a lawyer from the Number 10 Law Firm of Shanghai answered questions about law submitted to the program by viewers. One question was in reaction to a story the program had run earlier about a woman who abused her child, accompanied by gruesome photos. The viewer asked if there were any regulations prohibiting child abuse. The lawyer responded that there were some relevant Shanghai regulations which implemented the prohibitions in the national criminal and marriage laws.

One striking feature of the bureaucracy's use of media to run the legal system is the splintered nature of governmental control over media transmissions. All of the central ministries—the State Council Information Office, the CCP Central Committee General Office, the CCP Central Propaganda Department, and the CCP Central Politics and Law Commission—each have responsibilities for orchestrating print or video transmissions about law. For example, the Ministry of Justice and the CCP's Central Politics and Law Commission supervise the publication of the *Legal System Daily*. In another example, the Ministry of Civil Affairs and the State Council Information Office are in charge of developing a television series to commemorate the tenth anniversary of the promulgation of the Organic Law on Villagers Committees. The CCP Propaganda Department regularly issues joint documents with central ministries, though it does not participate in the issuance of the most important documents concerning economic matters. Beginning in the mid-1990s, the most important policy documents on economic affairs emanated from the People's Bank, the Ministry of Foreign Trade and Economic Cooperation, and the Economic Planning Commission.

Some law-related media transmissions outside of Beijing are overseen by lower-level branches of the central ministries or the CCP Central Politics and Law Commission. The *Shanghai Legal System News* is published by the Shanghai Bureau of Justice, which is an arm of the Ministry of Justice, and is overseen by the Shanghai Politics and Law Committee, an arm of the CCP Commission (Chen 1991:348–49; Gelatt 1987:217, 231).[2] Even transmissions overseen by subcentral bodies do more than simply print the party's latest interpretation of law. They also report on bills currently under review by subcentral congresses. The *Shanghai Legal System News,* for example, published a report about a bill under consideration (March 25, 1996, 1). It is a bill proposing implementing legislation for two national real-estate laws under consideration by the Shanghai People's Congress.

The State Council articulates law without formal enactment in the "documents" (*wenjian*) issued by party organs and the central ministries and agencies. Those internal documents (*neibu wenjian*) that are "secret" are not released to anyone outside the party, while others which are for public consumption (*zhongyao wenjian*) are released directly to all judges and law professors, to a selected group of law firms and consulting firms, and to the public through the print and broadcast media. The variety of channels through which law is disseminated in the PRC allows the party to target different audiences, both within and without Chinese officialdom, in part to tailor its interpretations of the law to the intended audience, in part to withhold information successively from larger segments of the population. The interpretations intended for high-level party members are enacted and published in the media less frequently than are the interpretations destined also for low-level party members, which in turn are published in the media less frequently than are the interpretations destined also for groups within the public at large. The "secret" or "classified" (*neibu*) documents circulated internally within the Chinese Communist Party contain official interpretations of the law that are intended only for party members. The legal interpretations intended for Chinese audiences outside of China and foreign audiences are published in overseas arms of the party press agency and by the Foreign Languages Press in Beijing.

Another striking feature of the role of media in China's legal system is the bureaucracy's dependence on it to express official views of law both within and without the bureaucracy itself. In the PRC, disseminating messages from the center through centrally orchestrated media to broad swaths of the population is a method of communicating to the public central interpretations of law. This method of official communication is designed to accomplish a variety of goals: to educate the public about the correct interpretations of the law, to legitimate the government by portraying the government as reinforcing widely held public values, and to enforce the law by persuading the public about the merits of adhering to the correct interpretations of the law and threatening forced reeducation if these interpretations are not adhered to. The PRC government has, over the past several decades, built a vast program for using the media to communicate with the public about central law and to shape public behavior in conformity to that law. But the state-run media also send orders to officials lower down in the administrative hierarchy. The legal newspapers communicate official delegations of legislative authority by notifying local governments about their authority to enact implementing regulations for specific statutes or policies. When the *Legal System Daily* (1995a) published a notice of a new policy by two central departments, for example, it authorized all local governments to draft implementing measures for it.

Judges and bureaucrats throughout China rely on, and are dependent on, frequent communications of uncodified policy from the central leadership, who occupy the top party positions and the top executive positions of president, premier, and vice premier, who head the sixty-some administrative ministries and agencies headquartered in Beijing. Each court in the four-tiered court system of the PRC is formally linked to the Chinese Communist Party through three separate yet mutually reinforcing mechanisms. One is the practice of recruiting judges from the ranks of the party and the People's Liberation Army. Another is the use of weekly study sessions for judges similar to those held for all government officials and teachers at every level. At these sessions, judges and law professors study the important secret documents during some of their weekly staff meetings every Tuesday afternoon (J. Zhao 1996). This weekly practice makes PRC judges more likely to study the party's or central administration's documents than the formally enacted statutory law. Meanwhile, filing cabinets full of published regulations in the chambers of the most sophisticated courts in China collect dust. A third mechanism is a procedure called "adjudication supervision" or "trial supervision" (*shenpan jiandu*), which permits certain officials to reopen an otherwise final civil or criminal judgment. Each court must work with these officials, who are designated by the party through the Standing Committee of the People's Congress at the same level as the court. The prospect of any judicial decision being reopened by proven party loyalists subjects judges to pressures to implement central policies in their decisions (Woo 1991). In a comprehensive examination of the Supreme People's Court since the legalization campaign began in 1979, Susan Finder (1993:145, 222) concludes that in all of its work the court is subject to party leadership. The court implements Central Political-Legal Committee and other party initiatives and clears important policy decisions and other critical decisions with the party leadership.

In China, the party permits and encourages the public to contact the press in order to give the party feedback about its policies and to report transgressions of the law (Polumbaum 1994b). The editors of the *People's Daily* are known to be among the conduits to government for support of local causes. An American journalist (Lawrence 1996) reported the story of a forty-six-year-old local party boss and farmer from northeastern China near the Russian border whose village employs him as a full-time lobbyist in Beijing. As part of his lobbying efforts, Tian Chunshan visited editors of the *People's Daily*.

The media function in lieu of legal professionals as authoritative interpreters of the law in China. The relative dearth of lawyers makes them insufficient vehicles for disseminating official interpretations of law. The relatively low status of legal scholars in the PRC further undermines their ability to contribute authoritative interpretations of the law. Courts take cognizance of academic articles on relevant legal issues, but they do not accord them as much weight as Supreme Court opinions or party documents. Such extensive reliance on mass media to transmit interpretations about the law exerts an impact upon China's legal system. According to Victor Li (1980:33–37), while the capabilities of media allowed them to disseminate the law widely, a laudable goal, the limitations of media simplified the message about law that could be transmitted. As he concludes, the law speaks directly to the general public through the mass media. The use of this channel affects the language of the law, which must be stated in simple colloquial terms rather than technical jargon. The specific rules cannot be very detailed or complicated, since the mass media can convey only broad ideas. By using the mass media to communicate legal norms directly to the public, China in effect has taken a path to overcoming the public's ignorance of the law that we in the United States have rejected. China does not subscribe to the legal fiction that everyone knows the law, but instead has carried out a massive program of public education about the law. The scope of this program is as overwhelming in Chinese terms as the number of lawyers is astounding in American terms (Li 1980:33–37).

Judges add little to this process of disseminating the law. It is not just the practice of adjudication supervision that limits their impact, nor the absence of a doctrine of *stare decisis,* which would make the rulings of judges binding on parties to cases in lower courts. These alone do not explain all of the forces which limit the role of judges in the legal bureaucracy of the PRC. The allocation of the power to appoint judges further undermines the ability of judges to make law in China. The party leaders at each administrative level, not the courts, appoint the most powerful judges in China, that is, each court's president; these presidents, in turn, nominate for appointment all the judges in their courts, with the People's Congress at each level given authority to approve the appointments. This makes courts beholden to local political interests and lessens their interest in following judicial precedent. Even the Supreme People's Court, which sits atop the national court system, does not appoint judges and has been relatively powerless to change the appointment process. The court came closest to influencing appointments when it submitted to the National People's Congress draft legislation for upgrading the professional standards of the judiciary, one of the provisions of which attempted to shift the power of appointment to the court system. The NPC passed the law in 1995 after dropping the provision (M. Zhang 1995).

The State Council, the party's Central Propaganda Department, and the party's Central Politics and Law Commission exert a unifying force on the media transmissions related to law, but there appears to be no coordinator of the three. Far from presenting the staff of the Ministry of Justice's propaganda departments with opportunities for developing maverick interpretations of the law, this legal education program is highly official and is linked to the top leadership by the oversight of the State Council. Not only do the dictates of the State Council constrain the legal interpretations of the Ministry of Justice, but the ministry also coordinates its legal education work with the party's Central Propaganda Department, as do other ministries in Beijing. So dependent is the PRC government on media transmissions of its laws and policies that the most powerful people in the PRC are directly linked to those in charge of the state-run media.[3]

Tension between Commercialization
and the Legal Bureaucracy

Despite the enormous amount of control the PRC central government exercises over China's far-flung media industry, maintaining that control is a perennial problem for lawmakers. Not all media transmissions in the PRC have been pure expressions of central policy and legal interpretation. Some have been mixed with personal expressions of renegade zeal, as were articles published in the *World Economic Herald*, the *People's Daily*, the *Guangming Daily*, and the *Beijing Daily* in the spring of 1989. Judy Polumbaum (1994b) ably demonstrated in the mid-1990s that the central government does not exert complete control over the press in the PRC.

The most potent liberator of the media industry from government control has been the pressure exerted by the market forces that have gained strength in China since the late 1970s. As it launched its legalization campaign, the party began loosening its control over the media. In 1978, it permitted officially recognized "mass organizations" and work units to publish their own newspapers, so long as they registered with the government. These newspapers were censored by local party propaganda departments and subject to being "shut down by the state at any time" (Polumbaum 1994b). In the 1990s, another genre of newspapers cropped up outside the aegis of the party. Called "small newspapers" (*xiaobao*), by the mid-1990s these enjoyed a broad-based circulation in major cities and formed a prominent part of popular urban culture.[4] Elites in China consider them "trash." Some are tabloids run by rumormongers eager to make a yuan at the price of people's reputations (Huang 1996; Polumbaum 1994a).

Speaking about the latest incarnation of this popular brand of journalism, film director Huang Jianxin (1996) says that "everyone fears the press" in the PRC because it is viewed as corrupt enough to blackmail people and to ruin their reputations. So widespread is the perception of a terrorizing tabloid press that citizens are using the new Administrative Litigation Law to combat the use of the media to defame people (Josephs 1993; Polumbaum 1994b). In a notorious example of this, a woman filmed in a candid shot by director Zhang Yimou during the filming of *The Story of Qiu Ju*, released by Sony Pictures in 1992, sued Zhang in a PRC court for defamation because the film included several seconds of allegedly unflattering footage of her eating cotton candy. The problem, according to her, was that the footage showed a mole on her face. The court dismissed the case on the ground that Zhang did not profit from the footage (B. Zhao 1996).

There has been a gradual commercialization of media generally in the PRC, with the result that now not just the press, widely acknowledged in the 1990s to be commercialized (MacKinnon 1997), but also television and film productions, too, survive by stimulating consumer demand. The legal education program of the Ministry of Justice by 1995 had become more high-tech and more oriented toward entertainment than when it began in 1980. The Ministry assigned four of its five bureaus jurisdiction over a different medium or media industry: (1) legal publications (newspapers and books); (2) audiovisual productions; (3) entertainment programs; and (4) companies that produce publications and videos for both domestic sale and for export. A fifth bureau was responsible for investigating law enforcement (Y. Zhang 1995). As of 1994, the PRC government began to permit the country's 684 television stations to sell segments of time to advertisers, and their audiences have blossomed to approximately 600 to 800 million television viewers and more than one million satellite dishes. With increased competition from one thousand cable channels in the PRC and a surge in viewer demand for entertainment, programs which aim to amuse, such as game shows, situation comedies, variety shows, and music videos, are a staple of evening television (Waters 1994). In 1982, the film *Yamaha Fish Stalls* was the first of a new film genre in the PRC which aimed purely to entertain. With funding flowing in from Hong Kong, these films flourish today, despite a crackdown in the fall of 1989 that lasted for several years. These films include scenes of petty urban crime, snappy and sarcastic dialogue, and juvenile delinquents and drug addicts. A few, such as the films of Huang Jianxin, are set in contemporary China. They reflect not the party line so much as widespread alienation and cynicism, "mindless bureaucratic stagnation," and the disillusionment of the masses with politics (Pickowicz 1994:78–80; Steger 1996).

The processes of "commercialization" and "privatization" have done more than give rise to alternatives to the state-run media (see chapters by Pan and He in this volume); they have also changed the form and content of the state-run media transmissions. Even such "big newspapers" (*dabao*) as the regional legal newspapers have become at least to some extent self-supporting and partially sensationalized in order to attract readers. The government's pledge to end subsidies of all newspapers is certainly a step in this direction (Polumbaum 1994a). A general shift in emphasis toward commercial viability in the media and a general increase in demand from the public for entertainment, variety, and sophistication are driving both the state-run and the privately run media to enliven their format and content. This shift is accompanied by an intense competition for readership, which spurs an effort to remain commercially viable, relevant, and attractive to the public.

It is tempting to conclude that current trends toward "commercialization" and "privatization" spell the end of any role by the media in China's legal system. Does not attention to entertainment and aesthetics preclude attention to transmitting official messages? Does not financial independence inevitably weaken ties to the government? Because the answer to both queries is "not necessarily," it would be a mistake to rule out the media as continuing to play an integral role in China's legal system in the early twenty-first century.

The "privatization" and "commercialization" of media do not preclude their transmission of official interpretations of the law. On the contrary, new trends in the state-run and quasi-state-run media appear to be strengthening their ability to communicate official messages about law. Through market competition, the media that innovate, such as the *Beijing Youth Daily* run by an officially approved mass organization and therefore not directly by the government, have gained newfound influence (see Stanley Rosen, "Seeking Appropriate Behavior under a Socialist Market Economy," in this volume). While the PRC central government does not orchestrate the content or form of semi-privately run media, orchestrated messages may be continuing behind the cover of more commercial-looking and commercially run state-run media. The new look of all media transmissions could encompass a movement underground, so to speak, of the party and its methods of sending messages about law to the public. In this scenario, the party would attempt to camouflage its control behind different formats or tones than it has used in the past. In Russia, even after its political system had moved away from totalitarianism and toward democracy, Yeltsin's government continued to "manage information" and attempted to centrally control the mass media, television in particular (Polumbaum 1994b). Despite new vehicles, the essential ingredient for sources of law remains intact: the continued dissemination of the attitudes toward law that the party deems correct for lower levels of cadres and for the masses.

Nor does the loosening of financial control over media preclude their transmission of official interpretations of the law. There are degrees of censorship, and in the PRC the degree of control by the party over the content of publications and broadcasts ebbs and flows (Polumbaum 1994b). Members of the party cannot agree on how tightly to control the press, even after the move toward financial independence of newspapers is well under way, and yet this lack of consensus apparently has not yet removed from the party the prerogative to tighten control. Despite the commercialization of China's media, the

United States nongovernmental organization Freedom House concluded in 1996, after a survey, that the PRC was one of the four countries whose government exercised the tightest control over its country's media. That year, President Jiang Zemin launched an internal party drive to require those in charge of broadcasting, theater, cartoons, films, and the publication of fiction to issue guidelines about how the creators of their products could make them "more Chinese" (Mufson 1996).

The more heavy-handed the censorship, the closer the censorship approaches orchestration, where presumably conditions are ripe for sending official interpretations of the law through the press and radio and television broadcasts. It is difficult to say, in the abstract, where on this spectrum the government ceases to send official messages about law. The innovations in format and content heralded by commercialization do not, however, necessarily lessen the authoritativeness of the media messages about law. It might be possible for control over certain kinds of transmissions to remain tight, while others are freer, as occurred in China under Guomindang rule. Media transmissions of matters that are politically sensitive, which might include anything related to China's legal system, might continue to be orchestrated, while others are given more freedom. Polumbaum (1994b) has shown that in the 1980s a few private newspapers did comment on political subjects but that in the 1990s the PRC government has generally prohibited the media not operated by the state from expressing opinions about anything officially viewed as having "political" importance.

Hong Kong as a Case Study

The two samples are taken from the *Legal System Daily;* the *Shanghai Legal System News;* United States government translations of Xinhua press and television transmissions from September 1995 through May 1996; and the party-run English-language newspaper *China Daily* from January 1995 through June 1996. The two samples were published about twelve years apart. This time gap allowed conclusions to be drawn about the changes in content and format brought by the privatization and commercialization of the state-run media.

The two samples of newspaper articles and official broadcasts reveal that even the more commercialized media of the PRC of the mid-1990s continued to channel to the public official messages about legally correct behavior and about the achievements of the PRC in building its legal system. The media also continued to use simple language and avoided elaborate explanations. Though format and content changed under the impact of the commercialization of

China's state-run media, this trend did not appear to have weakened the media's role in transmitting law.

To the English-speaking world, notably Hong Kong, the United States, and the United Kingdom, the Xinhua news service annually sent dozens of articles about Hong Kong laden with the legal terminology developed in the PRC's legal framework for the Hong Kong Special Administrative Region (SAR). Many of the articles on Hong Kong that appeared in the *China Daily* from March 1995 through April 1996 were Xinhua press releases and not bylines, which means their content was tightly controlled by the party. This control also showed in the repetition of themes and vocabulary from article to article. As a further sign of control, the set of themes mirrored the list of items on the agenda for discussion in Beijing by the Sino-British Joint Liaison Group. The items covered included the following (Xinhua 1995f): international rights and obligations, air services agreements and arrangements with Taiwan, protection agreements, surrender of fugitive offenders, mutual legal assistance in criminal matters and the reciprocal recognition and enforcement of judgments in civil and commercial matters, civil service matters, defense and public order, franchises and contracts extending beyond 1997, sewage disposal and investment promotion, localization of laws, adaptation of laws, the court of final appeal, the implementation of the provisions of the Joint Declaration relating to the right of abode in Hong Kong after 1997, visa abolition agreements, retirement protection and social welfare.

Which laws lay behind this publicity effort? The PRC government set the parameters for the rule of law in Hong Kong with constitutional and international legal instruments that are written, formally enacted, and recognized as both in the PRC and in the international community. Thus, in 1982 the PRC enacted a constitution which created an administrative unit called the Special Administrative Region. The Special Administrative Region is not to be confused with the Autonomous Region (Tibet and Mongolia), which is provided for in Articles 112 through 122 of the PRC Constitution, or with the Special Economic Zone (Shenzhen, Zhuhai, and Hainan), which enjoys no constitutional status; it is, rather, a creature of the State Council, the PRC's executive organ. In 1984, the governments of the PRC and Great Britain negotiated an agreement providing for the transfer of sovereignty over Hong Kong from Great Britain to the PRC on July 1, 1997. As signatories to this Joint Agreement, the PRC and Britain registered it with the United Nations pursuant to the United Nations Charter, whereby the agreement became an official source of international law under the charter. In accordance with the agreement, in

1990 the National People's Congress adopted a constitution for Hong Kong called "The Basic Law of the Hong Kong Special Administrative Region of the People's Republic of China" (hereafter referred to as the Basic Law). The adoption of this law came seven years before the PRC was to assume sovereignty over Hong Kong and before the law went into effect.

Although these legal instruments laid the blueprint for Hong Kong's legal system after 1997, their mere existence ensured neither their acceptance nor their effect, and their terminology was not detailed, self-defining, or defined in the legal instruments. Nor was the status of the Basic Law settled. On the mainland, it was a national statute (*falu*), while in Hong Kong it served as the supreme law, the constitution against which the validity of official acts could be judged (Basic Law, Article 158). The bulk of the law on Hong Kong appeared in the wake of these documents, the fruits of a publicity campaign to legitimate and amplify the enacted law. The PRC State Council's Foreign Ministry engineered the campaign and pointed it toward the populations of the PRC, Taiwan, Hong Kong, Britain, and the United States. The PRC policies on Hong Kong's integration into the PRC, as publicized in the media, aimed to facilitate not only the acceptance of the legality of the Joint Agreement and of the Basic Law by people and governments both in mainland China and overseas, but also the acceptance of Beijing's evolving interpretations of those laws. The media transmissions on Hong Kong contained elaborations on the questions left unanswered in the two legal documents and, in an incremental and evocative way, laid out the PRC government's official interpretations of important terms in those documents. In other words, the media provided authoritative keys to unlock the meaning of the legal documents.

Virtually all of the transmissions in the sample focused on either the legal status of Hong Kong or on the nature of the transition of Hong Kong to Chinese sovereignty. Like the *Legal System Daily,* the *China Daily* dwelt on the legal status of Hong Kong and the nature of Hong Kong's transition to SAR status, although unlike the Chinese-language paper, the English-language paper highlighted the mutual economic interests between Hong Kong and the PRC and the economic advantages for Hong Kong of becoming a part of the PRC. The disparate emphases of the two groups of transmissions suggests that PRC lawmakers continued to direct carefully the interpretations that the media disseminated, because their difference can be explained by the different educational tasks that needed to be accomplished in Hong Kong and abroad from those necessary in mainland China. Hong Kongers and overseas Chinese needed to be assured that the change of sovereignty would not hurt Hong Kong, while mainlanders were already convinced that Hong Kong's reunion with China would benefit the country.

THE STATUS OF HONG KONG AFTER JULY 1, 1997

Some of the most important questions left unanswered under the terms of the legal instruments revolve around the status of the Hong Kong Special Administrative Region. The arrangement under the PRC Constitution, the Joint Declaration, and the Basic Law outlines in only broad terms the bounds of autonomy to be enjoyed by Hong Kong. The Joint Declaration and the Basic Law contain a promise that Hong Kong is free to remain capitalist and autonomous until the year 2047, and a provision that Hong Kong as a Special Administrative Region of the PRC will enjoy "a high degree of autonomy," except in "foreign affairs" and "national security" (*China Daily* 1993a; Ghai 1993:19). More specific provisions provide for an independent tax system, the continued circulation of the Hong Kong currency, autonomy in levying customs duties, independent membership in the General Agreement on Tariffs and Trade/World Trade Organization, and an independent judiciary with the power of "final adjudication" (Campbell 1993). These provisions did not clarify, however, how closely connected to the PRC the Hong Kong Special Administrative Region would be. By inventing a new term, the Special Administrative Region, the drafters of these legal documents avoid being specific about the connection because Hong Kong cannot be analogized to recognizable political units such as the protectorate, the province, the federated state, or the allied state.

The centerpiece of the media effort to set out the status of Hong Kong is the official moniker "One country, two systems," coined by the PRC government in 1984 to describe the imminent relationship between the PRC and Hong Kong. Since then, the term has appeared in official PRC pronouncements on a regular basis and was codified in the Basic Law in 1990. Notwithstanding the six-year lag in codifying that term and its lack of statutory or judicial definition, the repeated dissemination through the media of "One country, two systems" and similar terms and phrases gave them a life of their own, a life that formal enactment alone probably could not have given them. This kind of publicity makes the laws more self-enforcing than they otherwise would be.

Under the terms of PRC domestic law, Hong Kong's status is both independent from and subordinate to the PRC central government. On the one hand is the provision in the Joint Declaration that Hong Kong would maintain political and legal autonomy and the Basic Law's provision that Hong Kong will enjoy "a high degree of autonomy" except in "foreign affairs" and "national security." On the other hand is the Basic Law's subordination of Hong Kong in its requirement that the legislature of Hong Kong report all its legislation to the National People's Congress Standing Committee in Beijing, which puts the Hong Kong legislature on the same footing as the provincial people's congresses on the mainland, and the Basic Law's provision that the National People's Congress Standing Committee may invalidate legislation by Hong Kong's legislature that the Standing Committee deems to conflict with the Basic Law or subsequent legislation passed by the National People's Congress for application in Hong Kong (Zhou 1993).

The terms used to lay out these limitations in the Basic Law were even broader than those used in the Joint Declaration, and the drafting of each document gave rise to fears in Hong Kong that the language chosen would defeat the promises of autonomy for the Hong Kong SAR sounded in the PRC media. A survey of Xinhua press releases and televised speeches in January and February 1984, during the negotiation of the Joint Declaration, reveals the beginning of a concerted PRC government effort to clarify anticipated contradictions between these promises and the language of the law by assuring that Hong Kong will remain autonomous in virtually every way after 1997. At this time, the assurances came in the form of promises of the continuity of Hong Kong's "political, economic, social, and legal systems." The broad language and the inclusion of the terms "political" and "legal" evoked images of legislators and judges in Hong Kong making law without approval from Beijing.

During the fourteen-month period from March 1995 to May 1996, the media coverage of the status of Hong Kong and the impending takeover was substantially larger than it had been eleven years earlier. The *Legal System Daily* frequently devoted one of its four pages to coverage of Hong Kong, Taiwan, and Macao and did not limit its Hong Kong coverage to that page. Hong Kong occasionally even made the front page. Throughout the sample period, at least sixty-four articles about Hong Kong were published in that newspaper alone.

With the expansion of media coverage of Hong Kong from 1984 to 1996 came a change in the language used to discuss Hong Kong's status after 1997. The language became more repetitive, forceful, and liberally sprinkled with phrases from the Basic Law. From December 1995 to March 1996, three phrases were especially prominent: "Hong Kong people governing Hong Kong," "A high degree of autonomy," and, by an overwhelming degree, "One country, two systems." Despite their lack of self-definition and their ambiguity, the almost daily repetition of these phrases lent them an emphatic and reassuring quality. Their multiple invocations punctuated not just single editions of a newspaper, but single pages of a newspaper, and even single articles (Fang 1995a; Rui and Fang 1996; Shen 1996; Luo 1996).

The moniker "One country, two systems" appeared on average more than once a month in the *China Daily* in 1995 and 1996. The term refers to a policy under which the PRC promises to preserve Hong Kong's capitalist system even while absorbing it into socialist China. In its media appearances, the term was labeled a "concept" that people needed to understand better, as in one newspaper article which promoted a TV miniseries on the ground that it "will help people understand the concept of 'one country, two systems'" (Xinhua 1995h). The media response to the very problem it had identified was to explain the phrase in only general terms. In the bulk of its media treatment in the two samples, the moniker was simply associated with "stability," "independence," and "prosperity" and linked with the language from the Basic Law which granted Hong Kong "a high degree of autonomy."

The elaboration in the press of this statutory language in the mid-1990s continued to depict Hong Kong under PRC rule as maintaining the independence it had enjoyed under British rule. Then-premier Li Peng, for example, stated in a major speech that the SAR's high degree of autonomy specified in the Basic Law must be "fully guaranteed," and both central government departments and localities would not be allowed to meddle in the autonomy. Li's words were echoed in the PRC press by lesser officials, who stressed the phrases "high degree of autonomy," a lack of "interference" by the central government in Hong Kong affairs, and "the social system and way of life will remain basically unchanged." In other transmissions, however, there was new stress on an increase in independence for Hong Kong, particularly in its judiciary, because of the institution of the Court of Final Appeal in Hong Kong (for example, Xinhua 1995a). This new theme appeared notwithstanding the continuing emphasis elsewhere in the media on continuity and the perpetuation of the same level of independence enjoyed under British rule.

The independence of Hong Kong and its status as an entity separate from the PRC repeatedly appeared as elements of Hong Kong's status as an SAR. The separateness of Hong Kong from the PRC was emphasized in announcements about differences between the currencies of the two places (Liu and Yang 1996). Separation was also evoked by mentioning the international status of Hong Kong citizens and by discussing the fact that they would use a different passport from those used by mainland residents (Xinhua 1995d).

Between 1984 and 1996, the type of autonomy promised to Hong Kong in the PRC media changed. While media transmissions in 1984 had stressed the promise of both political and economic autonomy, by 1996 the PRC media stressed mainly the economic autonomy of Hong Kong after 1997. In an interview published by *Ta Kung Pao* in Hong Kong, for example, Premier Li Peng declared that "Hong Kong will maintain its status as an economic center, trade center, financial center, and shipping center," but left out mention of its legal or political status. This phrase was repeated by PRC media throughout 1996, as were other phrases which also sounded a new emphasis on economic autonomy. Prominent among other phrases were "preserve its capitalist system" and "the current social and economic systems in Hong Kong and Macao will remain unchanged." Laundry lists of specifics on autonomy appeared in the PRC press from which were conspicuously absent any assurances about political or legal autonomy. One example is the following: "Factors that have promoted Hong Kong's economic success, such as a highly open economic system, free movement of personnel, cargo and capital, low tariffs, sound legal institutions and scarce governmental intervention will be preserved in Hong Kong after 1997" (Xinhua 1996b). Another such example read: "Except for foreign affairs and defense, which will be handled by the central government, everything else will remain the same: the legal system, the existing lifestyle, the currency, the economic and financial policies, and so on" (Xinhua 1996f).

On the other hand, such promises of an autonomous economy were coupled with reports about the union of Hong Kong's economy with that of the PRC. These stressed the growth of trade and investment between the two and the mutuality of their economic interests, with respect, for example, to United States trade sanctions and to foreign investment in China. Hong Kong was portrayed as the ideal "bridge" between the PRC economy and the rest of the world.

What is more, by 1996 the PRC media were sending messages which undermined the earlier promises of political autonomy. By then, the earlier promises had faded into assurances of "self-rule," with hints that Beijing would select this "self." Although top leaders reiterated that the PRC would not send a single official to assume office in Hong Kong, nor would it take a cent from Hong Kong, numerous media transmissions indicated that the concept of self-rule for Hong Kong meant rule by loyalists to Beijing. The official media published explicit admonitions against Hong Kong becoming a "political center." The official media went so far as to issue warnings of a PRC military and police presence in Hong Kong before the handover (Xinhua 1996c, 1995h).

Media transmissions also confirmed the administrative and legal unity of Hong Kong and the PRC, with signals both explicit and subtle. As an example of a more direct signal of this unity, it was proclaimed that the Basic Law would be valid not only in Hong Kong but also in the whole country and that all provinces and cities and all people in the mainland must abide by the Basic Law as it related to Hong Kong.[5] This is particularly apparent in the official reports about the Preliminary Working Committee and the Hong Kong Special Administrative Region Preparatory Committee, two bodies established by the PRC central government to implement the provisions of the Basic Law which gave the PRC central government supervisory authority over the making of law in Hong Kong. Such reports repeatedly linked these bodies with the phrase "Hong Kong people ruling Hong Kong." The reports also emphasized that these bodies were representative of Hong Kong's citizenry, using with particular frequency the phrase that both bodies included "people from all sectors and circles of Hong Kong." The transmissions confirmed that the Committee by 1995 was already reviewing Hong Kong legislation for consistency with PRC national law and by early 1996 was already taking steps to select the first governor and the first legislature of the Hong Kong Special Administrative Region (Xie 1995; WuDunn 1993). The message that the Preparatory Committee represented Hong Kong citizens and already possessed the power to choose Hong Kong's chief executive and legislators and to nullify Hong Kong law made the Preparatory Committee the primary vehicle for Hong Kong's "self-rule." Making the committee the focal point for representative lawmaking was tantamount to nullifying the then-current Legislative Council in Hong Kong, which, since Governor Patten's reforms in 1992 and 1995, became more directly elected by the citizens of Hong Kong. The identification of the Preparatory Committee with "self-rule" softened the promises of political and legal autonomy made in the Joint Declaration and the Basic Law.

Another question about the legal status of Hong Kong is how foreign it is to the PRC. Under PRC domestic law and international law, the extent to which Hong Kong will be considered foreign to the PRC after July 1, 1997, is unclear. On the one hand, PRC law currently classifies contracts involving at least one party from Hong Kong as "foreign economic contracts" for the purposes of applying PRC law (Lin et al. 1993:13–14). In addition, official sources refer to Hong Kong investment and trade with the mainland as "foreign" (Sun 1996). Under the Basic Law, Hong Kong continues to impose its own customs duties and to retain its membership in the General Agreement on Tariffs and Trade/World Trade Organization. On the other hand, in the Basic Law, China's central government expresses the view that Hong Kong is historically, ethnically, and culturally a part of China and that, therefore, under international law, its citizens are rightful subjects of China. The elements in the Basic Law which preserve Hong Kong's status as separate from the PRC may be a pragmatic measure designed to preserve Hong Kong's links to international trade networks, but they raise domestic and international law questions about the extent of Hong Kong's assimilation into the PRC.

PRC media coverage of Hong Kong in the PRC in 1996 responded to these questions left open in the enacted law by assuring Hong Kong citizens that they would retain all of the economic advantages of foreigners (Xiao 1995). The PRC media also repeatedly transmitted images of Hong Kong as falling within the boundaries of the PRC. To send a signal of Hong Kong's assimilation into the PRC, articles about Hong Kong in the *Legal System Daily* did not appear on the "international" page, and some reported official rebukes of foreign countries for "meddling" in Hong Kong's affairs. One report stressed the purely internal, domestic nature of election reform in Hong Kong during the few years immediately preceding 1997. Another report publicized a request of the PRC Foreign Ministry that all consulates in Hong Kong declare that Hong Kong is a "part of China's territory" and obtain its approval to continue operating in Hong Kong after 1997 (Li 1996). The language in dozens of declarations of the autonomy and prosperity in Hong Kong's future implied that Hong Kong was already part of the "nation" of the PRC. Qian Qichen, a vice premier and the chair of the Preparatory Committee, addressed the NPC with these words: "Love for the country coincides with love for Hong Kong, and the interests of Hong Kong people coincide with those of the state and nation. Only under such conditions can we do a good job of recovering Hong Kong." The inclusiveness of this language makes Hong Kong into a domestic part of the PRC, while the invocation of the emotional language of "love" harks back to the intensely ideological days of the late 1950s and late 1960s when independence on any level was subversive.

Likewise, Jiang Zemin in the televised speech declared that

> the [Preparatory] Committee should rely on *uniting all forces that can be united, that is, should unite the vast numbers of patriots.* The fundamental law for doing a good job is, without saying, the Basic Law. It must be observed not only by the people of Hong Kong, but also in handling affairs in the hinterlands that are related to Hong Kong. There should be no doubt as far as this is concerned. *This is not only a matter of concern of the people of the whole country, but also a genuine concern of the international community.* (Italics added)

The final sentence quoted here from Jiang's speech implies that Hong Kong is already part of the "whole country" of the PRC. By dividing the world into two parts, called "the whole country" and "the international community," Jiang forces the listener to decide into which part Hong Kong falls, knowing the listener is precluded from choosing "the international community" under the terms of the PRC Constitution, the Joint Declaration between the PRC and Britain, and the Basic Law. With the language about "uniting . . . patriots," Jiang sends several signals at once. "Patriots" creates an image of Hong Kong citizens as party loyalists, exactly the image of Hong Kong's "self" that the party positioned itself to create and support by providing for avenues of party political and legal oversight in the Basic Law. As mentioned above, this is an image that softens the guarantees of political and legal autonomy to Hong Kong that the PRC media publicized in 1984, just before the Joint Declaration with Britain was signed.

In the same breath, the language of unity connotes the willingness of the party to use force against Hong Kong if its full cooperation is not forthcoming. "Unity" in the PRC media since at least the mid-1980s is a code word for the party's program for handling internal, geographically based threats to its authority. The central leadership emphasizes unity in its statements, programs, and laws which target groups with reputations for ignoring central dictates, namely non-Han peoples, overseas Chinese, prosperous Chinese within the PRC, and non-Communists within the PRC. Many of these groups are concentrated in particular geographic areas—the non-Han peoples in Tibet, Inner Mongolia, and in the western provinces of Xinjiang, Yunnan, and Gansu; the prosperous Chinese in the southern and eastern coastal provinces of Jiangsu, Zhejiang, Fujian, and Guangdong; and the overseas Chinese in Taiwan and Hong Kong. The "unification" campaign that has been under way since the mid-1980s is an example of a central program that stresses unity for the territory-based groups of PRC entrepreneurs, ethnic minorities, and overseas Chinese. The campaign sends a two-pronged message. It stresses, first, that disunity will not be tolerated. But it also attempts to depict the regional diversification of China's economy as a problem that only the central government can solve. The "economic gaps between regions, nationalities, economic sectors and groups have widened," declared the head of the Department of United Front Affairs (He 1993). Despite the conciliatory images projected in the media transmissions about unity, in selected circumstances, the central government has backed up an emphasis on unity expressed in law with military action, as it has several times in Tibet since the 1950s. The media efforts to portray Hong Kong as in the same classification as Taiwan and Tibet signals that the CCP's military policy toward these areas is similar.

THE NATURE OF THE TRANSITION

Questions involving the nature of the transition of power over Hong Kong remained unresolved in the legal documents. The Basic Law lays out a structure for Hong Kong's government that preserves the four branches of the colonial government, namely the executive, legislative, administrative, and judiciary. But would the PRC begin before the handover to replace Hong Kong's current officials in any of these branches with people loyal to the PRC and to change their procedures? Would the PRC establish a new court of final appeal for Hong Kong? The Basic Law authorizes the Standing Committee of the National People's Congress to void laws enacted in Hong Kong that conflict with the Basic Law. Did this power extend to the laws of Hong Kong enacted before the handover? Even before July 1, 1997, did Hong Kong's government cease to enjoy some of the perquisites of power it enjoyed before the Joint Declaration was signed, such as the power to draw up its annual budget, which were nonetheless not explicitly prohibited by the Joint Declaration or by the Basic Law?

The official news reports in the sample sent out a resounding "yes" to all of these questions. Dozens of transmissions either in Chinese or English discussed the transition by highlighting the importance of loyalty to the PRC government on the part of Hong Kong officials. A telling example is the use of the term "patriots" in a way which links the concept to obedience to central PRC policy (Lin 1996). "Love" of the "motherland and Hong Kong" was another catchphrase that appeared frequently in press reports in the mid-1990s to stress the importance of fealty to Beijing. "A sense of responsibility for both the country and Hong Kong residents" was used to convey this desirable attitude (Xinhua 1995e). The term "stability" appeared often in contexts which made it clear that Hong Kong civil servants did not have the autonomy to challenge central policy. Even explicit admonitions were sent through the PRC media before the handover to Hong Kong civil servants "that their job is to perform duties according to the law or government directions" (Xinhua 1996d). Dozens more transmissions reported on the steps already taken by the PRC government to instill in Hong Kong officials the practices of mainland China's bureaucracy. Such practices included the use of Chinese by judicial officials and civil servants (Xiao 1995c; He 1995).

The sample contains dozens of transmissions about the initiatives of the PRC central government to prepare Hong Kong's legal system for its official incorporation into the PRC on July 1, 1997. Featured among them were summaries of the reports from the subcommittees of Beijing's Hong Kong Special Administrative Region Preparatory Committee and from the Sino-British Joint Liaison Group, which had completed a comprehensive review of Hong Kong's laws a year and a half before the handover. Themes of hard work, efficiency, and timely completion of delegated tasks dominated these articles and conveyed a sense of confidence in the PRC's commitment both to the rule of law and to the reassertion of sovereignty over Hong Kong (Lian et al. 1996). The PRC central government publicized its denunciation of the most sweeping law enacted by the Hong Kong Legislative Council before 1997, the Hong Kong Bill of Rights (Xinhua 1995g). Other articles described significant input by the PRC government into the short-term fiscal planning for Hong Kong's government and the selection of the SAR's governor and legislators. For example, one outlined PRC principles to guide the current joint Sino–British efforts to set the budget for Hong Kong's government for 1998 and 1999 (Fang 1995b). These reports signaled that the vague exhortations in the Joint Declaration to cooperation laid the groundwork for a curtailment of the colonial government's budgetary power.

By attempting to lay to rest questions arising out of the legal framework of the Hong Kong SAR with broad assurances of decisive and aggressive action by the PRC government, the PRC media signaled both the legitimacy and the supremacy of PRC central law over Hong Kong. The domestic and international press reports of Chinese blood spilled in and near Tiananmen Square at the hands of the People's Liberation Army intensified pressure on the PRC government to instill confidence in its ability to preserve Hong Kong's economic success and the rule of law there. The PRC press reports since 1989 show that the government staked its domestic and international reputation on the transition of Hong Kong to PRC sovereignty.

Not only did the sample of media transmissions about Hong Kong serve as sources of official interpretations of the legal framework for the Hong Kong SAR, but these transmissions functioned as fully a part of the PRC legal system, notwithstanding their still foreign target. They attempted to portray the Chinese government as more successful than Britain in its efforts to build a legal system for Hong Kong. Many of the transmissions about the transition period in Hong Kong ring with nationalism, as if the central government were attempting to stir the sentiments of its readers that create a sense of solidarity between the PRC central government and Hong Kong Chinese (Ren 1996; Zhao and Li 1995). Some articles aired the pain of China's experience with British colonization (Zhou 1996).

An example of such reporting was the treatment of the British government's role in the transition. When Britain was mentioned, it was as a troublesome coauthor of the system that would ensure Hong Kong's autonomy. Such evocations implied that, if British officials failed to consent to the PRC's plans for Hong Kong, Hong Kong's autonomy would be in jeopardy. Dozens of reports portrayed British officials as meddlers who refused to cooperate with the PRC in its efforts to create a smooth transition. Many focused on Governor Patten's reform of the procedures for electing the Legislative Council in 1995. But such portrayals faulted Britain for other aspects of its participation in the transition, such as the negotiations over the Basic Law and its implementation. These portrayals emanated from the mouths of the top leadership. Li Peng, for example, declared through an English translation that resolving differences with the British over the Court of Final Appeal "was rather tough" (Xinhua 1995b). Admonitions alternated with expressions of good will and renewed commitment to strengthen cooperation.

Some reports focused on the celebration of the handover in a way that suggested that a sense of success and euphoria about the event was building during the transition period. Much was made, for example, of the preparations for the ceremony that would mark the return of sovereignty at midnight on June 30, 1997. Elaborate measures included the distilling of a wine in mainland China to be decanted and drunk only during the ceremony (Wan 1996). The imposing electronic clock provided by the PRC government to perform the "countdown" (dao jishi) in minutes to midnight, June 30, 1997, conspicuously placed in Tiananmen Square, was reported in the legal newspapers in 1995 (Zhao and Li 1995). In another angle on Chinese nationalism, some official articles reported on various social problems plaguing Hong Kong, thus highlighting the failures of British rule and implying its illegitimacy. Among the blots on colonial Hong Kong was the difficult condition of women. They were underemployed (Xiao 1995d) because of unfair discrimination against them (Wen 1996). The health and socialization of women in Hong Kong was suffering (Tai 1996). Because women were smoking more than before, they were resisting proper socialization (Peng 1995). Hong Kong was also failing its youth, as evidenced by the spread of drug use and sales among them (Xue 1995; Su 1995b). Hong Kong's education system was failing its students. Not only were school-age children committing suicide (Sun 1995a), but Hong Kong schools did not measure up to those in the PRC either in academic rigor or in the promotion of morals (Sun 1995b; Lin 1995c).

Other problems highlighted in the legal newspapers were rising unemployment (He 1995b), pornography (Su 1995a), and crime. Crime in Hong Kong was on the rise, as suggested in transmissions which cited a growth in the number of robberies in Hong Kong (Xing 1995a) and cases of laundering money (Xing 1995b). Statistics peppered some of the articles, giving an impression of alarming numbers of criminals in Hong Kong. One story, for example, noted that Hong Kong police arrested more than 1,800 illegal employers in a single month (Xiao 1995b). Some reports described various ways in which the police force of Hong Kong was unable to cope with the current scope of criminal activities there (He 1995a; Su 1996). Others stressed the high degree of organization of criminals in Hong Kong.

In developing this theme, the official newspapers attempted to lower expectations about the takeover by portraying the PRC as inheriting a legion of problems created and left to fester by its predecessors in Hong Kong. The implication was that Britain's poor governance left a legacy that might mar the new Hong Kong SAR despite the carefully crafted legal framework. Several of the articles highlighted disturbances associated with Hong Kong's outcast populations. The Vietnamese refugees whom the Hong Kong government had housed for years in giant detention facilities were a source of social and political trouble for Hong Kong, in the PRC portrayals, and their presence in Hong Kong was solely the fault of the British colonists (Fang 1996; Xu 1996). One article used the alarming term "rebellion" (*baoluan*) to describe the protests by Hong Kong's Vietnamese refugees in May 1996. Another article described bungled attempts by Great Britain to deal with Hong Kong's homeless population. Another article described a recent succession of incidents of "uncivilized behavior" by passengers on buses, men who beat up bus drivers badly enough to send them to the hospital for treatment. "Concerned public figures" urged the Hong Kong government to quickly adopt measures to curb similar violent conduct (Sun 1996). The articles either showed the current Hong Kong government unresponsive to serious problems or showed the top PRC leadership united with "all sectors" of Hong Kong against Great Britain and the current Hong Kong government in their concern about the problems and their demands for solutions. In a similar vein, the spotlight was thrown on Hong Kong's fiscal problems, such as overspending by the colonial government (H. Xin 1995), its difficulty collecting taxes (Lin 1995a), and dysfunction in its regulatory system (F. Xin 1995).

Other problems highlighted in the PRC press included defects in Hong Kong's legal system (A 1995b) and police corruption (Xiao 1995a). Even the reports that focused on laudable traits of the Hong Kong police force mention larger problems that formed the backdrop to police work, such as a growing prison population (Zheng 1996), a mounting caseload for the police in recent years (Lin 1995b), and the lack of safety in the workplace (Mai 1996). A host of official transmissions in 1995 and 1996 rang with a heady, nationalistic tone and projected a sense that Hong Kong was already a part of China. One such article summarized the evaluations of six hundred of Hong Kong's laws by the Legal Sub-Group of the Preliminary Working Committee for setting up the Preparatory Committee of the Hong Kong Special Administrative Region. The headline depicted the Committee as on a "Course of Glory and Responsibility" and on a "Mission" (Fang 1995a). Other articles aimed to stir nationalistic sentiments by portraying the transition of sovereignty over Hong Kong as a return to the "motherland" rather than a takeover by the PRC. China's central legal daily pursued this campaign with phrases full of forceful and grandiose sentiments, such as, "The return of Hong Kong eliminates imperialistic, colonial invasion of oppression left on the minds of the Chinese people, the product of a great historical event" (Zhou 1996). The term "patriots" and the phrase "love the motherland" punctuated a variety of articles and broadcasts on Hong Kong, and, in at least one, Hong Kong law became a metaphor for British imperialism (He 1995).

Pains were taken to distance Hong Kong from its British colonial past. One Xinhua transmission reported that "[t]he Cultural Panel made proposals on the . . . tackling of colonialist influence." Another report stated that "with the Chinese as their main body, [Hong Kong entrepreneurs] widely assessed the situation and made the wise decision to go into the manufacturing industry." Hong Kong's success cannot be attributed to "colonial influences. . . . Since the late 1970s, forces pushing Hong Kong's economic development have come mainly from the Chinese mainland" (Xinhua 1996a). Some PRC media transmissions acknowledge positive aspects of Hong Kong's colonial past and present, primarily its economic success. But they attributed it to the growth of the PRC's economy and to PRC policies. They portrayed the removal of British rule as a blessing for Hong Kong's economic future and depicted the assimilation of Hong Kong into the PRC as an opportunity for ethnic unity and an expression of the self-reliance and self-strengthening of the Chinese. When Xinhua touted the economic advantages of the integration of Hong Kong with the PRC, or described Hong Kong as poised for economic growth, it credited the Basic Law and PRC policies for laying out a democratic and scientifically optimal blueprint for Hong Kong's prosperity. The Basic Law was portrayed as designed to ensure a "rosy" or "bright" future for Hong Kong.

IMPACT OF COMMERCIALIZATION ON TRANSMISSIONS
RELATED TO HONG KONG

The Hong Kong SAR is governed by broadly worded legal enactments and yet is a centerpiece of the PRC government's vision for China's prosperity at the dawn of the twenty-first century, and, as such, it is a subject of intensive government regulation. The rule of law in Hong Kong epitomizes two important litmus tests of the PRC government's legitimacy in the 1990s: its ability to distinguish itself from foreign influences, and its aptitude for regulating capitalist markets. The law related to Hong Kong is a decade and a half old and is experimental in the sense that it is connected with international legal instruments and overseas Chinese.

Despite its novelty within China, PRC law on Hong Kong has received the same treatment at the hands of the legal bureaucracy as have the rest of the matters dealt with by law in the PRC. The state-run media funnel messages to the lower levels of the bureaucracy and to the public, messages which are designed both to clarify the party's current interpretations of the law and to make the rudiments of the law more available and self-enforcing. The latter function of media transmissions on legal subjects sometimes requires simplification to the extent that interpretations of the law are obfuscated. To that end, the media send double messages. The messages relay both the likely continuity of Hong Kong's independence and its discontinuity with its liberation from an overweening, cloying British rule. Media messages also emphasize at the same time Hong Kong's separateness from mainland China and its gradual merging with it. The intended impact of these contradictory signals is not to clarify legal terminology, but to assuage fears about the meaning of the legal terms.

Commercialization spurred some changes in the format and content of the media transmissions about law since the early to mid-1980s. The media language about and formats for Hong Kong law became livelier and more varied. The entertainment value of media transmissions appeared to gain importance, even in those media that remain tightly controlled by the government. Attention was paid to creating variety in the formats of the articles about Hong Kong, in an apparent attempt to attract readers. Photographs, eye-catching typeface styles for article titles, and artistic graphics all featured more prominently in the latter sample. Variations in typeface carried political significance as well. The legal newspaper articles on Hong Kong in that sample came in three varieties of typeface, with the boldest reserved for the most authoritative pronouncements. The articles on the front page of the *China Daily* tended to contain more than one theme, suggesting greater importance, while articles further back in the publication tended to revolve around a single theme, suggesting lesser importance.

The adaptation of law-related transmissions to the demands of the marketplace did not sacrifice faith to official interpretations of the laws. There were three pieces of evidence to this effect. First, as the official PRC coverage of Hong Kong grew between 1984 and 1996, its content became more oriented toward economic incentives for Hong Kong citizens to trust the Basic Law. The prominence of the economic theme, an important mark of PRC central policy in the 1990s, signaled the authoritativeness of these transmissions. Second, each item in the sampler filled in a gap in the formal law, a function of the media in other areas of PRC law. They did this by expanding upon the domestic impact of constitutional and international legal instruments, two relatively new subjects for the official media of China, and yet by 1996, they did so in a way that closely tracked the functions of the official media transmissions about other types of law in the PRC. Third and finally, the transmissions about Hong Kong reported on the achievements of the PRC government in its efforts to build a legal system that would accommodate Hong Kong.

Has commercialization affected the transmissions about law in any way? Yes, but not in a way that shows that the legal bureaucracy has relinquished its use of media to transmit official policy about law. Rather, the change is a shift toward making the format of the transmissions more appealing without sacrificing the authoritativeness of the content. It is a window on how the bureaucracy has been forced to adapt to market pressures, an environment in which it must compete with a growing number of claims on the attention of the Chinese public. The trend toward entertainment in the official media did not seem to necessitate a loosening of state control over the messages sent. The language about Hong Kong became more repetitive, technical, and emotionally charged, and the English-language transmissions about Hong Kong stressed the economic benefits of submission to the Basic Law. The transmissions about Hong Kong continued, however, to portray the Hong Kong Special Administrative Region as economically both independent and dependent and as politically and legally dependent on Beijing. Despite the enhanced appeal of the vehicle, the pervasiveness of economic incentives in the newer samples confirms that the official media did not stray from party policy, which showed increasing stress on economic incentives in other areas of law.

Conclusion

The state-run media are vehicles for informing the population of China about official interpretations of the law. The PRC government refers to this process as "education." Propaganda departments at every level of the bureaucracy are responsible for this. The forty-some central ministries, the Information Office of the State Council, the General Office of the CCP Central Committee, two CCP commissions, and their branches at lower levels are all engaged in the business of producing media products which convey messages about law. These institutions use media instruments from print, radio, television, video, and cinematographic film for communicating both with government officials and the public. Judging from the size of the enterprise, the lawmaking bureaucracy of China heavily depends upon the media to do its job. This relationship between media and law in the PRC is not unlike those in the former Soviet Union and in Taiwan until 1987, where state-run media transmitted official policy to the public. It is perhaps true, however, that nowhere else in the world today is a media industry so heavily engaged in the business of transmitting governmental views about law as in the PRC. In the United States, home to perhaps the largest media industry, the government does not even publish its own statutes and judicial opinions, but contracts with private companies to handle this job. Given the rarity of any mention of government in the work of social scientists who study the dissemination of information in the United States, the United States government appears to play a relatively minor role in the dissemination of official interpretations of United States law. Prominent studies of the dissemination of information and knowledge in the United States contain virtually no mention of government (Havelock 1969, 1973; Rogers 1995; Oleson and Voss 1979; Crane 1972). Other prominent publications on the subject approach an analysis of the role of government in only general terms (Reingold 1979; Dupree 1979).

From the mid-1980s through the mid-1990s, despite the heavy reliance of the bureaucracy of China on mass media to transmit official interpretations of the law, there was no single government body to oversee the production of all media transmissions related to law. This splintering of authority over the media did not, however, lead to the introduction of unorthodox or maverick interpretations of the law into media transmissions, except for a brief period in the aftermath of the Tiananmen Square crisis. The willingness of those who orchestrated and produced media transmissions to practice self-censorship may be a key to the consistency of the official interpretations of law communicated in the state-run media. Apparently in response to increased competition for readers from independent media, the orchestrators of the official media adapted their style of communicating official interpretations of the law to the new demands of the market. Changes in the technological means of communication have not made the bureaucracy less dependent on the media to communicate its interpretations of the law.

Electronic telecommunications are on the rise in China, but the impact that their proliferation may exert on the control by the PRC's lawmakers over the implementation of law is difficult to ascertain. Law scholars at Beijing University are developing on-line computer databases, which they advertise for sale to foreigners, but which thus far are not available in all law firms or law schools in the PRC. As of the fall of 1996, the Chinese Law Research System (*Zhongguo falu jiansuo xitong*), produced out of Beijing University, contained statutes, regulations, and explanations enacted by the NPC and the NPC Standing Committee, or issued by the State Council, the Ministries, the Supreme People's Court, or the Supreme People's Procuratorate. If these databases continue to be limited to statutes and regulations, their main effect may be to make PRC law more transparent. If they become avenues for disseminating commentaries and reports on the law, however, they may weaken the persuasive impact of state-sponsored vehicles for legal commentary and reporting.

Even if the impact of images about the law that emanate from the state weakens, the official lawmakers of the PRC may benefit in another way from the advent of electronic dissemination of images about law in the PRC. If the lawmakers continue to desire the flexibility in articulating the law that they have enjoyed since the founding of the PRC, then in principle, electronic media transmissions of law should serve the central government better than broadcast or print media transmissions. Broadcasts leave a less permanent public record than print transmissions do, and electronic media leave a less permanent record than broadcasts do. The freer the government is from being held to a public record of its law, the greater its flexibility to change the law.

It is too soon to tell whether a partial shift away from orchestration toward censorship will broaden to encompass the entire media and make all of the media more independent of the party. If that were to happen, the media might play a less important role in the legal system. Run by people who are not necessarily party members, and sending messages that do not carry official authority, popular media not orchestrated by the party are less plausibly part of China's legal system or sources of law. Although the government would censor them, censorship need mean merely that these media avoid broadcasting prohibited subjects, rather than that they broadcast officially approved messages. The pattern of censorship begun by the Guomindang during the Republican era and continued in Deng Xiaoping's People's Republic prohibits private media from broadcasting messages on subjects which the government has reserved for itself. Under this type of censorship, the private media presumably enjoy wide latitude on preapproved matters.

Although China's media industry handles perhaps more government legal business than media elsewhere, it is possible that the law-related content of media elsewhere is growing. A panel entitled "The Blurred Boundary between Law and Popular Culture," presented at a conference on "Picturing Justice: Images of Law and Lawyers in the Visual Media," sponsored by the University of San Francisco School of Law, identified a trend in the United States of a "growing interdependence of popular culture and official legal proceedings" and explored the ways in which this conjunction had "altered how law is practiced" in the United States. (This view was expressed in a brochure published before March 1996 by the University of San Francisco School of Law.) With the White House's mounting sophistication in manipulation of the media in the United States in recent years (Stephanopolous 1999; Hitchens 1999), it is not far-fetched to interpret the connection between media transmissions and the administration's policy on law-related matters as growing more intimate. It remains to be shown whether the PRC government's influence over its media has served as a model for governments other than those dominated by a single political party, such as the USSR or Taiwan.

Notes

1. I would like to thank Professor Chin-Chuan Lee for inviting me to participate in this project and for bringing together a variety of highly accomplished scholars with a great deal to learn from one another. I collected the hundreds of articles used in this study with the able assistance of Helen Chae and Zhao Jianzhuang. The translations of all Chinese language materials used, unless otherwise noted, are my own.

2. For a brief description in English of the Central Committee's Politics and Law Commission and the Politics and Law Committees, see Baker 1996:17–19, though Baker mistakenly names the Shanghai Politics and Law Committee as the publisher of the legal newspaper.

3. The vice president of the central ministry of foreign affairs, Zhou Nan, was also the chief of the Hong Kong bureau of the Xinhua News Agency, the official mouthpiece of the party in Hong Kong and the PRC government's premier representative there before the selection of Tung Chee-hua as chief executive of the Hong Kong Special Administrative Region (SAR) in 1996. Until then, Zhou Nan was the Chinese

equivalent of Governor Christopher Patten. So important a figure was he that he agreed in 1996 to remain in this post until 1999 in a bid to help minimize the disruption attending Hong Kong's transition to Chinese sovereignty (Shen 1996). See Chan and Lee (1991:49–63) for the role of Xinhua in Hong Kong's political transition.

4. The term "small newspapers" was coined as early as 1917 in Shanghai, where the genre was born. At that time, the term reflected both the short length of the pieces published and the amusing nature of their content. Although many of the papers specialized in popular topics of particular interest to Shanghainese of the time, such as late Qing art, the Guomindang feared the potential of these papers for political resistance and enacted regulations that limited their content to simple and trivial topics such as celebrity gossip and that prohibited them from publishing articles on foreign or domestic affairs (Qin 1993).

5. A more subtle message was voiced in the observation that throughout the forty-year existence of the PRC's ceremonial government building, the Great Hall of the People, each PRC province, autonomous region, and municipality has had a room there named after it (Zhao and Feng 1996). Hong Kong was not given a room but used the Guangdong room.

Bibliography

A, San. 1995a. "Heichi heibaozha zaiji, qinxiong fan quankao 'wodi'" ("Secret Eating and Secret Bomb Detonation, Seizure of Violent Criminals Totally Dependent on 'Groundsleepers'"). *Legal System Daily,* November 26, 4.

———. 1995b. "Xianggang de lushi tousu zhidu" ("Hong Kong's System of Lodging Complaints against Lawyers"). *Legal System Daily,* December 3, 4.

Baker, Philip. 1996. "Party and Law in China." In Leslie Palmier, ed., *State and Law in Eastern Asia.* Aldershot: Dartmouth Publishing.

Campbell, David. 1993. "Economic Ideology and Hong Kong's Governance Structure after 1997." In Raymond Wacks, ed., *Hong Kong, China and 1997.* Hong Kong: Hong Kong University Press.

Chan, Joseph Man, and Chin-Chuan Lee. 1991. *Mass Media and Political Transition: The Hong Kong Press in China's Orbit.* New York: Guilford.

Chen, Yuan. 1991. *East-West Trade: Changing Patterns in Chinese Foreign Trade Law and Institutions.* New York: Oceana.

Clark, Paul. 1988. "The Signification of Cinema: The Foreignness of Film in China." In Wimal Dissanayake, ed., *Cinema and Cultural Identity: Reflections on Films from Japan, India, and China.* Lanham, Md.: University Press of America.

Crane, Diana. 1972. *Invisible Colleges: Diffusion of Knowledge in Scientific Communities.* Chicago: University of Chicago Press.

Dissanayake, Wimal. 1988. "Chinese Cinema." In Wimal Dissanayake, ed., *Cinema and Cultural Identity: Reflections on Films from Japan, India, and China.* Lanham, Md.: University Press of America.

Dupree, A. Hunter. 1979. "The National Academy of Sciences and the American Definition of Science." In Alexandra Oleson and John Voss, eds., *The Organization of Knowledge in Modern America, 1860–1920*. Baltimore: Johns Hopkins University Press.

Fang, Jin. 1995a. "Guangrong, wush de licheng—xianggang tebie xingzhengqu chou weihui yuweihuiyuan man wancheng shiming" ("The Course of Glory and Responsibility—the Members of the Preliminary Working Committee for Setting up the Preparatory Committee of the Hong Kong Special Administrative Region Fully Complete Their Mission"). *Legal System Daily*, December 10, 4.

———. 1995b. "Liangru weichu fang wei genben." *Legal System Daily*, December 3, 4.

Fang, Wen. 1996. "Zhigang yue nan chuan min wenti ze zai gangying" ("Problem of Stagnant Harbor Teeming with Southern Boat People Fault of British Hong Kong Government"). *Legal System Daily*, May 19, 4.

Finder, Susan. 1993. "The Supreme People's Court of the PRC." *Journal of Chinese Law* 7:145.

Gelatt, Timothy A. 1987. "Legal and Extra-Legal Issues in Joint Venture Negotiations." *Journal of Chinese Law* 1:217.

Ghai, Yash. 1993. "The Constitutional Framework." In *Hong Kong in Transition: Problems and Prospects*. Hong Kong: Faculty of Law, University of Hong Kong.

Havelock, Ronald G. 1969. *Planning for Innovation through Dissemination and Utilization of Knowledge*. Report to the U.S. Department of Health, Education, and Welfare, Office of Education, Bureau of Research, Center for Research on Utilization of Scientific Knowledge, July.

———. 1973. *The Change Agent's Guide to Innovation in Education*. Englewood Cliffs, N.J.: Educational Technology Publications.

He, Delong. 1995. "Xianggang falu zhongwenhua renwu fanzhong richeng jin" ("The Translation of Hong Kong Law into Chinese Is a Task Whose Urgency Brings a Strenuous Schedule"). *Legal System Daily*, November 19, 4.

He, Deyou. 1995a. "Xianggang jingcha duojuzhai" ("Hong Kong Police Debt Mounts"). *Legal System Daily*, October 1, 4.

———. 1995b. "Xianggang: shiye lukengao, 'tiefanwan' chixiang" ("As the Rate of Unemployment Rises, 'the Iron Rice Bowl' Becomes Popular"). *Legal System Daily*, October 1, 4.

He, Jun. 1993. "The Party to Unite All Social Sectors in Unification Drive." *China Daily*, November 4, 1.

Hitchens, Christopher. 1999. "I'll Never Eat Lunch in This Town Again." *Vanity Fair*, May, 72–80.

Huang, Jianxin. 1996. Speech, Walker Art Museum, Minneapolis, April 12, observed by the author.

Josephs, Hilary K. 1993. "Defamation, Invasion of Privacy, and the Press in the People's Republic of China." *UCLA Pacific Basin Law Journal* 11:191–220.

Lawrence, Susan V. 1996. "Speaking Up for Their Rights." *U.S. News and World Report*, June 10, 50–52.

Li, Victor Hao. 1980. *Law without Lawyers.* Boulder, Colo.: Westview.

Li, Yi. 1996. "China Asks All Consulates in Hong Kong to Sign Agreements." *Hong Kong Economic Journal,* January 20, 19. Trans. into English as "Beijing Asks Hong Kong Consulates to Sign Status Agreements," *FBIS-CHI-96-014,* January 22, 85.

Lian, Jintian, Liu Siyang, and Zhao Xinbing. 1996. "Li Ruihuan tong gang'ao diqu zhengxie weiyuan zuotan" ("Li Ruihuan Holds Informal Talks with Members of the Hong Kong–Macao Area Government Joint Committee"). *Legal System Daily,* March 12, 2.

Lin, Hua. 1995a. "Xianggang de chaoji 'dagong huangdi'" ("Hong Kong's Super 'Work Emperors'"). *Legal System Daily,* September 3, 4.

———. 1995b. "Xianggang de fuzhu jingcha" ("The Auxiliary Police of Hong Kong"). *Legal System Daily,* October 1, 4.

———. 1995c. "Xianggang juban gongde xinweichan yundong guli zhongxiaoxue shengmen aihu gongwu" ("Hong Kong Conducts Movement to Promote Public Morality and Faith, Urge High School and Elementary School Students to Love Household and Public Property"). *Legal System Daily,* December 10, 4.

———. 1996. "Gangren zhigang bixu yi aiguozhe wei zhuti" ("Hong Kong People Ruling Hong Kong Must Put Patriots in the Main Part"). *Legal System Daily,* March 3, 4.

Lin, Huichen, Xu Shiqiu, and Peng Yuezhong, eds. 1993. *Shewai jingjifa jilun (General Discussion of the Foreign Economic Contract Law).* Beijing: China University of Politics and Law Press.

Liu, Alan P. L. 1966. *The Press and Journalism in Communist China.* Washington, D.C.: Advanced Research Projects Agency, United States Department of Defense, June.

Liu, Zaiming, and Fan Yang. 1996. "Hong Kong Will Benefit from China's Prosperity; Capital Flight Unlikely—Notes on Visit to Beijing at the Beginning of the Ninth Five-Year Plan," Part 8 of 8. *Wen Wei Po,* January 22, A2. Trans. as "Hong Kong: Economic Problems of Concern to Hong Kong Reviewed," *FBIS-CHI-96-021,* January 31, 91.

Luo, Baowen. 1996. "Yao ba jiang zhengzhi de yaoqiu luoshi dao lingdao ganbu zishen jianshe he budui gexiang jianshe zhong qu" ("We Need Leading Cadres, Departments, and Troops to Individually Establish Explanations of Government Requirements"). *Legal System Daily,* March 12, 1.

MacKinnon, Stephen R. 1997. "Toward a History of the Chinese Press in the Republican Period." *Modern China* 23:3–16.

Mai, Li. 1996. "Baoxian nujingjiren shoupian, daitu lesuo bucheng sipiao" ("Female Insurance Manager Deceived, Ruffians Extort but Do Not Rip Up the Receipt"). *Legal System Daily,* March 3, 4.

Mufson, Steven. 1996. "Can Soccer Boy Kick Evil Cartoon Influences Out of China?" *St. Paul Pioneer Press,* October 15, 1D.

Oleson, Alexandra, and John Voss, eds. 1979. *The Organization of Knowledge in Modern America, 1860–1920.* Baltimore: Johns Hopkins University Press.

Peng, Hui. 1995. "Xianggang de ren shou baoxian" ("Insurance for Hong Kong Smokers"). *Legal System Daily,* March 26, 4.

Pickowicz, Paul G. 1994. "Huang Jianxin and the Notion of Post-Socialism." In Nick Browne, Paul G. Pickowicz, Vivian Sobchack, and Esther Yau, eds., *New Chinese Cinemas: Forms, Identities, Politics.* Cambridge: Cambridge University Press.

Polumbaum, Judy. 1994a. "Striving for Predictability: The Bureaucratization of Media Management in China." In Chin-Chuan Lee, ed., *China's Media, Media's China.* Boulder, Colo.: Westview.

————. 1994b. "To Protect or Restrict? Points of Contention in China's Draft Press Law." In Pitman B. Potter, ed., *Domestic Law Reforms in Post-Mao China.* Armonk, N.Y.: M. E. Sharpe.

Qin, Shaode. 1993. *Shanghai jindai baokan shilun (A History of Shanghai's Modern Press).* Shanghai: Fudan University Press.

Reingold, Nathan. 1979. "National Science Policy in a Private Foundation: The Carnegie Institution of Washington." In Alexandra Oleson and John Voss, eds., *The Organization of Knowledge in Modern America, 1860–1920.* Baltimore: Johns Hopkins University Press.

Ren, Jia. 1996. "Xianggang qingnian minzu yishi zengqiang" ("National Consciousness of Hong Kong Youth Strengthened"). *Legal System Daily,* March 10, 4.

Rogers, Everett M. 1995. *Diffusion of Innovations.* 4th ed. New York: Free Press.

Rui, Mu Lai Di, and Fang Jin. 1996. "Qian Qichen jiu minzhu he xinxin wenti fabiao yijian" ("Qian Qichen Expresses His Opinions about Democracy and Faith"). *Legal System Daily,* March 25, 1.

Shehui jingzhuan: falu xinxiang (Society's Classics: "Law's Letterbox"). 1993. Television show viewed by the author in Shanghai, PRC, June 22.

Shen, Fang. 1996. "Mianxiang gangren, jisi guangyi" ("Turn in the Direction of Hong Kong People, Let Us Pool Our Ideas"). *Legal System Daily,* April 21, 4.

Shen, Xiaohong. 1986. Director of the Council for International Educational Exchange Nanjing University program. Interview with the author, August 11, New Haven, Conn.

Steger, Kate. 1996. Speech at Walker Art Museum, Minneapolis, April 12.

Stephanopolous, George. 1999. *All Too Human.* Boston: Little, Brown.

Su, Ming. 1995a. "Xianggang wang jiao zhankai dasao huang erbai seqing zhaopian bei chaichu" ("Hong Kong Wang Jiao Launches a Massive Sweep in which 200 Pornographic Photographs Are Destroyed"). *Legal System Daily,* October 1, 4.

————. 1995b. "Xianggang yixie qing shaonian beibi canyu fandu" ("Some Hong Kong Youths Forced into Drug Trafficking"). *Legal System Daily,* December 3, 4.

————. 1996. "Xianggang jingfang caiqu daguimo xingdong, beihuozhi xiao daoban guangpan wodian" ("Hong Kong Police Adopt Large-Scale Activities, Capture the Den Where Stolen Booty Was Hidden"). *Legal System Daily,* March 10, 4.

Sun, Hong. 1996. "Five-Year Plan Benefits Hong Kong." *China Daily,* February 26, 5.

Sun, Taihui. 1995a. "Xianggang jiaoyushu zhaokai yantaohui fenxi yuanyin" ("Hong Kong Education Officials Convene Conference to Analyze the Causes"). *Legal System Daily,* November 26, 4.

————. 1995b. "Xianggang ruguo bunuli jiu hui bei chaoguo" ("Hong Kong, If Not Hardworking, Can Be Surpassed"). *Legal System Daily,* November 26, 4.

————. 1996. "Xianggang sishou renyuan bei dashijian songchu youguan renshi huyu gangfu yuyi zhongshi" ("Hong Kong Company Personnel Hit in Incidents Send Relevant People to Appeal to the Hong Kong Government to Attach Importance to Them"). *Legal System Daily,* May 12, 4.

Tai, Hui. 1996. "Xianggang nuxing ran aizibingdu zhe zhengduo" ("Hong Kong Women Catching Chinese Mugwort Virus on the Rise"). *Legal System Daily,* May 12, 4.

Vogel, Ezra F. 1980. *Canton under Communism.* 2nd ed. Cambridge, Mass.: Harvard University Press.

Wan, Yuelin. 1996. "Wei xianggang huigui zuguo tezhi xiqing jiu" ("Motherland's Wine Made Specially for Happy Celebration of the Hong Kong Handover"). *Legal System Daily,* February 25, 4.

Waters, Katherine. 1994. "Media Expands to Satisfy Chinese Appetite." *China Information Bulletin* 5 (December):2.

Wen, Xin. 1996. "Xianggang jiuye funu rengshou qishi" ("The Employment of Women in Hong Kong Still Suffers from Discrimination"). *Legal System Daily,* March 10, 4.

Woo, Margaret Y. K. 1991. "Adjudication Supervision and Judicial Independence in the PRC." *American Journal of Comparative Law* 39.

WuDunn, Sheryl. 1993. "China Raises Ante over Hong Kong." *New York Times,* April 1, A7.

Xiao, Qiao. 1995a. "Liangming xianggang jingyuan beipanxing wunian" ("Two Hong Kong Policemen Sentenced to Five Years"). *Legal System Daily,* November 26, 4.

————. 1995b. "Xianggang daji laogong heishi" ("Hong Kong Assaults Labor Black Market"). *Legal System Daily,* December 3, 4.

————. 1995c. "Xianggang jiangwei gongwuyuan kaishe zhongwen keicheng" ("Hong Kong in Future Will Offer Civil Servants Chinese Language Courses"). *Legal System Daily,* November 12, 4.

————. 1995d. "Xianggang nuxing jiuye nan" ("It's Difficult for Hong Kong Women Seeking Employment"). *Legal System Daily,* March 26, 4.

Xiao, Sun. 1995. "1997 Brings New Era in HK." *China Daily Business Weekly,* November 13, 1.

Xie, Liangjun. 1995. "Deleting of Hong Kong Legislation Stirs Concern." *China Daily,* July 19, 1.

Xin, Fan. 1995. "Xianggang: Jinqian yu falu xiangdou" ("Hong Kong: Money and Law in Tension"). *Legal System Daily,* November 12, 4.

Xin, Huo. 1995. "Gangfu caizheng yusuan zhichu piangao, shibi yingxiang xianggang" ("Hong Kong Government's Budget Deficit Too High, Will Affect Hong Kong's Smooth Transition"). *Legal System Daily,* March 26, 4.

Xing, Wang. 1995a. "Xianggang de shijie an zengjia" ("Number of Hong Kong's Cases of Professional Robbery Rises"). *Legal System Daily,* December 10, 4.

————. 1995b. "Xianggang 'xiheiqian' anjian jizeng" ("Number of Cases of Laundering Money on the Black Market in Hong Kong Soar"). *Legal System Daily,* October 1, 4.

Xinhua. 1995a. "Basic Law Ensures Rosy Future for HK." *China Daily,* April 4, 1.

————. 1995b. "HK Advisors Welcomed." *China Daily,* April 29, 1.

————. 1995c. "HK Panels Deliver Final Suggestions." *China Daily,* December 11, 4.

————. 1995d. "HK's Passport to the World." *China Daily,* November 16, 2.

————. 1995e. "Hong Kong Talks End on Good Terms." *China Daily,* December 16, 2.

————. 1995f. "Joint Group Discusses HK Issues." *China Daily,* November 3, 1.

————. 1995g. "Ministry Clarifies Japan, HK Stance." *China Daily,* November 15, 2.

————. 1995h. "TV Program to Show Change in Hong Kong." *China Daily,* April 5, 2.

————. 1996a. "HK People Make Own Success." *China Daily,* "Opinion" Section, April
11, 4.

————. 1996b. "Lu: HK to Stay Successful." *China Daily,* May 31, 1.

————. 1996c. "PLA to Guard HK's Stability." *China Daily,* March 16, 2.

————. 1996d. "Preparatory Committee Seeks Advice in Hong Kong." *China Daily,*
April 12, 2.

————. 1996e. "State to Ensure Democratic HK: Lu." *China Daily,* June 12, 2.

Xu, Yang. 1996. "Ministry Spokesman Condemns HK Riots." *China Daily,* May 15, 1.

Xue, Yuan. 1995. "Xianggang qingshaonian lanyong yaowu quxiang 'sanhua'" ("The
Trend of Hong Kong Youth Substance Abuse"). *Legal System Daily,* March 26, 4.

Zhang, Min. 1995. "Justice Zhang Min on China First Judge Law." *China Law Update,*
June 25, 12–13.

Zhang, Yong. 1995. Speech, Minneapolis, October.

Zhao, Bin. 1996. Interviews with the author, University of Minnesota Law School,
Minneapolis, February 12–14.

Zhao, Jianzhuang. 1996. Interview with the author, Professor Henan Cadre College of
Politics and Law, Minneapolis, November.

Zhao, Wei, and Li Nanling. 1995. "Xianggang, jinru huigui daojishi" ("Hong Kong
Enters the Countdown to the Handover"). *Legal System Daily,* March 17, 2.

Zhao, Xinbing, and Feng Xiuju. 1996. Xinhua report of January 18. Trans. into
English as "PRC: Lu Ping on Post-1997 Hong Kong Self-Government," *FBIS-
CHI-96-013,* January 19.

Zheng, Yu. 1996. "Xianggang jianyu renman weihuan" ("Hong Kong Prisons Full of
Prisoners"). *Legal System Daily,* March 3, 4.

Zhou, Wei. 1993. "The Sources of Law in the SAR." In *Hong Kong in Transition: Problems and Prospects.* Hong Kong: Faculty of Law, University of Hong Kong.

Zhou, Xingbao. 1996. "Xuexi qianchi xie xinbian" ("Washed White as Snow of the
Former Humiliation and Writing a New Chapter"). *People's Daily* (overseas edition), July 20, 5.

8

When Capitalist and Socialist Television Clash

The Impact of Hong Kong TV on Guangzhou Residents

JOSEPH MAN CHAN

M edia effects have been at the core of empirical communication research since the early twentieth century. Mass media were at first
generally considered to be very powerful in changing the audience's cognition, values, and even behavior (for example: DeFleur and Ball-
Rokeach 1982; Petty and Priester 1994). This "powerful effects" perspective
later gave way to the "limited effects" model as variables such as reference
groups, selective perception, level of involvement, and socioeconomic status
were found to have intervening influence. Mass media came to be viewed more
as a reinforcing than a change agent. As promulgated by the uses and gratifications approach to the study of media effects (Katz, Blumler, and Gurevitch
1974; Blumler 1979; Rubin 1994), the audience was reconceptualized as being
composed of active rather than passive media consumers. Reception studies
done in the tradition of cultural studies also came to recognize the activeness of
the audience and the polysemy of content (Morley 1992; Liebes and Katz
1990). In spite of such findings, more researchers have begun to argue that it is
wrong to assume media effects can be ignored, even though the dominant ideological model may be simpleminded.

Empirical studies in the last two decades have witnessed the rediscovery of
media effects. More attention has been paid to the significant impact of mass
media at the organizational, institutional, and cultural levels (McQuail 1994;
Turner 1990). The differential access to media has been shown to result in
"knowledge gaps" between the more and less educated (Tichenor, Donohue,

and Olien 1970). Mass media can have important effects on people's picture of the world as well. One of the most researched concepts is the agenda-setting function of mass media (McCombs and Shaw 1972; McCombs 1994), which refers to the media's ability to define the salience structure of issues among the public. Another set of studies grouped under cultivation analysis (Gerbner and Gross 1976; Gerbner et al. 1994) has found that television can have long-term effects, such as the shaping of viewers' worldview. The studies pioneered by Noelle-Neumann (1984) suggest that the media can affect the climate of opinion to the extent that it may result in a "spiral of silence."

An enduring concern in the study of media effects has been the relatively weak causal linkage between media exposure and impact. Most of the studies are correlational in nature, thus stopping short of establishing causality. While some experiments can firmly establish the causal connection, it is doubtful whether their results can be generalized to a natural setting. The quasi-experimental design in a field setting as explicated by Cook and Campbell (1979:78) appears to strike a good balance between establishing the need for causality and that for generalizability. The design employed in this survey is called the "post-test-only design with nonequivalent groups," whose lack of pretests is compensated by intergroup comparability.

This project studies how the capitalist television from Hong Kong may have an impact on the socialist city of Guangzhou. While it continues the tradition of using the survey method to study the impact of television on individuals' attitudes and values, it extends the scope of media effects to media use and media evaluation. The quasi-experimental design also separates it from the many correlational studies of the past. That the capitalist television input is external and alien to the socialist system within which the survey was done helps to isolate the cause.

Cultural Metropolitan Domination

The effects of cross-border television are often examined on two fronts: (1) institutional influence, in regard to industrial configuration, media ownership, content, organization, and production logic; and (2) reception influence, as reflected in audience viewing behavior, media evaluations, tastes, attitudes, values, and social perceptions (Elasmar and Hunter 1996). While this chapter will touch on the institutional impact of Hong Kong television on Guangzhou, its primary focus is on the reception end.

The study of transborder communication is often informed by the concepts of media imperialism (Boyd-Barrett 1977; Lee 1980; Schiller 1991), media internationalization (Chan 1994), and cultural globalization (Robertson 1992; Featherstone 1990; Tomlinson 1991). Cultural globalization treats the world as the unit of analysis and stresses the autonomy of the processes integrating the world as a whole. The notion of media imperialism captures the unbalanced flow of information across nations as a result of inequity in the international economic and political order. It is a particular pattern of media internationalization, which refers to "the process by which the ownership, production, distribution, or content of a country's media is influenced by foreign media interests, culture, and markets" (Chan 1994:71). Missing from this definition is the concept of media consumption, which, I think, should have been included as well. In other words, the consideration should be how the audience in a country is affected by foreign media in terms of media consumption; evaluation, as well as cognitive and value changes, form an integral part of media internationalization. The present research can be viewed as an empirical study in this area.

At the time of conducting the survey on which this chapter is based, Guangzhou and Hong Kong were under Chinese and British rule, respectively. The flow of information between these cities can arguably be qualified as "international" communication. Just three hours away from each other by train, Hong Kong and Guangzhou also constitute a metropolitan duo. This is particularly true in light of the reunification of Hong Kong with China in 1997, thus bringing the two cities within the same national boundaries. Considerations such as these have led me to search for a "middle-range" concept that can better capture the Hong Kong–Guangzhou relationship than the foregoing "global" concepts. However, it should be added that Hong Kong will continue to be distinguished from socialist China as a capitalist city by virtue of China's policy of "one country, two systems" toward Hong Kong.

What appears to be more relevant to this study is the concept of metropolitan domination, related to the "central place theory" in urban sociology and geography, which explores the "centrality" of cities in the formation of urban systems (Presto 1991). Cities are regarded as "central places" if they provide surplus goods and services to dependent cities or "deficit places." "Auxiliary" places are those that are neither clearly central nor deficit. Tokyo, London, New York, Shanghai, and other cosmopolitan cities all appear to play such a central role in their respective countries. Neighboring and even some far-off cities are heavily under the cultural spell of these urban centers.

Observations as such have led me to define metropolitan domination as the subordination of one place to an urban center as a result of unequal distribution of resources between the two places, be they economic, political, or cultural in nature. Resource gradients between two places do not necessarily result in a domination structure contingent upon the degree of free flow of goods, services, and information, as well as the physical, linguistic, and cultural distance between the two places. In general, higher freedom and affinity will more readily result in one place dominating the other. While affinity is more or less a constant, the two major effective variables affecting the domination structure are the level of free flow and the resource gradients. In other words, the direction of domination may be reversed as freedom of exchange and patterns of resource distribution change. Domination can take place in the realms of economy, polity, and culture, states that interact to determine the resultant pattern. Of particular interest to this chapter is cultural domination as reflected in television.

To understand the relationship between Guangzhou and Hong Kong, we have to examine how they differ in economic strength and media richness. Hong Kong, a global financial and trade center, boasted a per capita income of about U.S. $16,000 in 1993 when this survey was conducted, whereas Guangzhou had a per capita income of about U.S. $3;000 the same year.[1] Hong Kong had a population of six million, which was about twice that of Guangzhou. Hong Kong is a regional center of telecommunications and audiovisual productions (To and Lau 1995; Chan 1996) exporting movies and television programs to many parts of the world. In 1996, its television industry consisted of four terrestrial channels, four regional satellite services, and a twenty-channel cable network. Guangzhou's television industry, among the most developed in China, had two provincial channels, one municipal channel, and two cable networks in the same year. As a whole, Guangzhou's television is limited to the provincial level, whereas Hong Kong is a regional or global player. Since the reform era began, Hong Kong investments have poured into Guangdong, which has become economically dependent on Hong Kong. A common aspiration for Guangdong residents is to visit Hong Kong, which is generally perceived to be economically and culturally more advanced. The above gaps between Hong Kong and Guangzhou, perceived and real, are expected to result in the dominance of Hong Kong television culture. In sum, drawing on the studies of media effects and transborder communication, this chapter aims to study the impact of Hong Kong television on Guangzhou.

Uneven Accessibility to Hong Kong Television

Xenophobic and antiforeign in general outlook, China has been taking a cautious approach to foreign culture (Liao 1990). It carefully controls the inflow of all foreign media, including books, newspapers, radio, terrestrial television, and satellite television. The propaganda mission of the Chinese Communist Party (CCP) is to cultivate socialist values and weed out bourgeois influence. Cultural protectionism ebbs and flows as China takes its political turns (Chan 1994). It peaked during the Cultural Revolution, when China was dissociated from the world. Any exposure to foreign media was suspect and subject to political scrutiny. Foreign influence virtually came to a halt. China's cultural protectionism subsided as it began its reform and open-door policy in the early 1980s. Limited foreign media products are officially allowed to enter China if they abide by restrictive rules and quotas.

Unofficially, foreign culture has been flowing into China via spillover and media piracy during the reform era (Chan 1994). Geographical proximity and industrial competitiveness have rendered Hong Kong the most important source of spillover, particularly for the area of Guangdong, resulting in what may be called a puncture in China's shield of cultural protectionism. China bans any unauthorized reception of cross-border television signals, including those from Hong Kong. Technically speaking, it is illegal for Guangdong residents to receive Hong Kong television. However, people have defied the ban and set up antennae and cable networks to carry Hong Kong programs. All this has been happening as Chinese media go through a commercialization or marketization process which results in a tug-of-war between ideological control and profit motive (Chan 1993; Lee 1994; Chen 1998; He 2000). Tension as such has enabled the Chinese media to improvise media reforms and use party rhetoric and other symbolic resources to justify the introduction of unorthodox journalistic practices (Pan 2000).

In the 1980s, Guangzhou antennae facing Hong Kong popped up, on and off, in tandem with the oscillations in the city's and China's political moods. The antennae, for instance, were dismantled when the authorities launched campaigns against "spiritual pollution" (1983), "bourgeois liberalization" (1986), and "peaceful evolution" (1989) or when central leaders were to visit Guangdong.[2] They mushroomed again as the momentum of the campaigns waned. Initially, most antennae were owned by individual households or buildings. Later, work units and residential compounds set up large reception dishes and rudimentary cable networks to carry Hong Kong television as a benefit for their members or as profit operations. In some counties in the Pearl River Delta, the networks are run by local governments that collect installation and maintenance fees from the cable subscribers.

Residents who are not served by cable networks do not have regular access to Hong Kong television. However, they can watch Hong Kong television on occasions when domestic Chinese channels carry Hong Kong programs. While Guangdong TV rarely carries Hong Kong programs on its Mandarin Lingnan Channel,[3] it often features entertainment programs such as drama series and movies on its Cantonese-speaking Zhujiang TV channel, whose target area is the Pearl River Delta in the vicinity of Hong Kong.

At the time of the survey in mid-1993, formal and official cable TV in Guangzhou was being constructed. The rudimentary networks that carried Hong Kong television could only unevenly cover Guangzhou, thus dividing the audience into two groups: one with full access to Hong Kong television and the other without. This makes Guangzhou an ideal site for investigating the effects of transborder capitalist television on a socialist society.

While the alien nature of Hong Kong television will help isolate the cause of effects on Guangzhou residents, it is a natural laboratory for observing how socialist and capitalist television may fight out as they meet. We can hypothesize that when capitalist and socialist television cultures meet in a socialist marketplace, the entertaining qualities of capitalist television will be more readily recognized than will its informational attributes. This discrepancy may be the result of the structural differences between a capitalist and socialist television system. The key function of capitalist television is to entertain, whereas that of socialist television is to "educate."

An analogous situation existed between East and West Berlin before German reunification. But political control in East Berlin was so tight that it was impossible for outside researchers to conduct audience surveys to investigate the impact of television from West Berlin. East Germany collapsed so quickly in the midst of an "instant glasnost" (Willnat 1991) that no survey plans, to my knowledge, were implemented. In contrast, state control in Guangzhou was relaxed to the extent that a sizable portion of the population had full access to Hong Kong television and that surveys could be conducted if the proper arrangements were made. Other studies have examined the influence of foreign television that is receivable on an occasional basis and at a general level in the context of China (Chu and Ju 1993; Pan, Chaffee, Chu, and Ju 1994; Lull 1991). This study is unique in that it focuses on the specific impact of Hong Kong television, which offers a regular choice for many of its neighboring audience members.

Methods and Analytical Strategies

This study is based primarily on a representative survey of Guangzhou citizens living in the districts of Zhuhai, Dongshan, Liwan, and Yuexiu. These four districts were selected because they constitute the traditional geographical core of Guangzhou, where most of the urban population lives. Omitted were newly developed districts, such as Tianhe and Baiyun, whose population is scattered over vast semirural areas, rendering the survey interviews excessively costly.

The survey was commissioned to a social research company owned and operated by teachers at a major Chinese university. They were responsible for sampling, pretesting, and interviewing. Recruited from among the students at the university, the interviewers were trained by research assistants from Hong Kong, who were also responsible for data input and quality checking.

The sample was generated first by drawing a random sample of 1,500 people, aged fifteen or above, from a computerized roster of all residents registered with the government. A breakdown of the resultant sample by district was found to approximate the proportions of actual district populations. Stratified by districts, the sample was systematically selected at equal intervals to yield an initial survey sample of 979.

The face-to-face questionnaire survey was carried out in August and September of 1993. Out of the potential respondents, there were ninety rejections, sixty-three unreachables (due to repeated absences), eighty who had moved, and fifty-eight with unclear addresses. Excluding those who had moved and those with unclear addresses, the final survey sample size was 841. Given 688 successful interviews, the study has a response rate of 81.8 percent.

To supplement the survey data, I conducted in-depth interviews with more than fifteen Chinese television practitioners, policy regulators, scholars, and market researchers in Guangzhou and Hong Kong from 1993 to 1996. These interviews contributed to my understanding of the industrial background of Guangzhou's television and the institutional impact of Hong Kong television. Documents and published material related to the theme of this chapter were also analyzed.

As mentioned earlier, there exist two audience groups in Guangzhou: one with full access to Hong Kong television and the other without. The former could watch both entertainment and information programs produced in Hong Kong, whereas the latter could watch Hong Kong entertainment programs only when they were carried by the domestic channels on an occasional basis.

The survey showed that the group with most access to Hong Kong television (62.2 percent) was about twice the size of the other group (37.8 percent). A systematic comparison of the socioeconomic statistics of the two groups shows no significant differences. As Cantonese is comprehensible to about 97 percent of the population, physical accessibility to Hong Kong television appears to have demarcated one group from the other. This turns the survey into a quasi-experimental design (Cook and Campbell 1979), with the sector accessible to Hong Kong television as the "experimental" group and the other sector as the "control" group. Comparing these two groups in terms of reception, tastes, and attitudes will therefore serve to test the impact of Hong Kong television on Guangzhou residents.

Impact on Viewing Patterns

The program menu available to each group makes an immense impact on their viewing patterns. The program menu of the group without Hong Kong television is restricted to Chinese channels, including the Beijing-based national Chinese Central Television (CCTV), Guangdong Province's Zhujiang TV and Lingnan TV, as well as the municipal Guangzhou TV. In addition to these Chinese channels, the group with access to Hong Kong television can tune in to television based in Hong Kong, including the Cantonese TVB Jade and ATV Home, the English TVB Pearl, and ATV World. Some can even receive Star TV, a regional satellite TV service from Hong Kong.

Table 8.1 shows the most-watched television channel of the respondents in both groups. In the group without Hong Kong television, Zhujiang TV, primarily a Cantonese service that caters to the audience of the Pearl River Delta, is the most popular among all the Chinese channels (53 percent), followed by

Table 8.1. The Most Watched TV Channel by Access to Hong Kong TV

TV Channel	HK TV Receivability		
	Yes (%)	No (%)	Difference (%)
Chinese TV			
CCTV	5.3	8.5	-3.2
Lingnan TV	2.0	7.5	-5.5
Zhujiang TV	11.2	53.0	-41.8
Guangzhou TV	6.1	31.0	-24.9
HK TV			
TVB Jade	56.4	—	—
ATV Home	12.8	—	—
Others	6.2	—	—
	100.0%	100.0%	
	(N = 358)	(N = 200)	

Question format: Which is your most watched TV channel?

Table 8.2. Chinese TV Exposure by Hong Kong TV Receivability:
"Frequent" or "Very Frequent" Exposure

TV Channel	HK TV Receivability		Difference (%)
	Yes (%)	No (%)	
Chinese TV			
CCTV	16.2	27.1	–10.9
Lingnan TV	14.6	37.1	–22.5
Zhujiang TV	35.2	77.4	–42.2
Guangzhou TV	36.1	71.3	–35.2
HK TV			
Jade	80.9	—	—
Home	72.6	—	—
Pearl	35.1	—	—
World	25.0	—	—
Star TV	24.8	—	—

Minimum subsample size = 230

Question format: How often do you watch the following TV channels? The response is a five-point Likert scale, beginning with "very frequently" and moving through "frequently," "occasionally," and "rarely" to "extremely rarely."

the city channel of Guangzhou TV (31 percent). The Mandarin Lingnan TV (7.5 percent) and CCTV (8.5 percent) are far behind in popularity. This viewing pattern shows that Guangzhou residents, like their counterparts in other nations, prefer television services that are culturally akin and informationally more relevant. Given enough time, it is possible for the municipal Guangzhou TV even to surpass the provincial Zhujiang TV in popularity. Zhujiang TV and Guangzhou TV owe part of their popularity to their strategic inclusion of Hong Kong television programs and production formats.

The competitive edge of Hong Kong television is clearly visible in the viewing pattern of the group with most access to Hong Kong television, which finds TVB Jade the most attractive (56.4 percent). The distant second and third are ATV Home (12.8 percent) and Zhujiang TV (11.26 percent). Grouping the channels by origins, Hong Kong television outperforms the Chinese channels in popularity by a ratio of about 3:1 (75.4 percent versus 24.6 percent), lending support to the notion of metropolitan domination.

The relative positions of the Chinese channels in the group with access to Hong Kong television are similar to those observed in the group without, but they have become much subdued in absolute terms. The subdued effect appears to be the most visible in the cases of Zhujiang TV (–41.8 percent) and Guangzhou TV (–24.9 percent). The impact on CCTV (–3.1 percent) and Lingnan

Table 8.3. Correlation between Exposure to Chinese TV and Hong Kong TV in the Group with Access to Hong Kong TV

HK TV	Chinese TV			
	CCTV	Lingnan	Zhujiang	Guangzhou
Jade	–0.22***	–0.19***	–0.20***	–0.10*
Home	–0.14**	–0.13**	–0.13**	—
Pearl	—	—	—	—
World	—	—	—	—
Star TV	—	—	—	—

Minimum subsample size = 292
*p ≤ 0.05   **p ≤ 0.01   ***p ≤ 0.001

TV (–5.5 percent) is virtually negligible. The implication is that those Chinese channels that possess greater popularity will lose a higher proportion of the audience when Hong Kong television first becomes available.

Table 8.2 further illustrates the impact of Hong Kong television on the viewing habits of Guangzhou residents, who were asked to rate the frequency of their viewing of each television channel, using a five-point Likert scale ranging from "very frequent" to "very infrequent." The scale is collapsed into three categories for analysis. While the hierarchy of channel popularity is similar to that indicated in table 8.1, Guangzhou TV and ATV Home are found to have exposure comparable to Zhujiang TV and TVB Jade, respectively.

Table 8.3 shows the correlation matrix of exposure to various television channels in the group with access to Hong Kong television. It is noticeable that exposures to TVB Jade and ATV Home correlate negatively with exposures to virtually all the Chinese channels. This speaks to the general domination of viewers by Hong Kong programs. TVB Jade is evidently the most dominant force, followed by TVB Home. A comparison of the sizes of the correlation coefficients indicates that Guangzhou TV is the most competitive in facing up to the challenge of Hong Kong television. This is a logical outcome, as Guangzhou TV tends to carry more Hong Kong programs and to adopt a more localized and entertaining approach to programming.

Impact on Evaluations of Hong Kong and Chinese TV

The evaluation patterns of television remain relatively stable in a closed system. The introduction of programs that are different in type, quality, and origins, however, will likely result in changes in the evaluation patterns, as the new elements upset the existing equilibrium by providing new standards for comparison and even a modified frame of reference. Specifically, the exposure to television programs from Hong Kong is expected to affect the audience's evaluation of domestic television. Implied by the logic of metropolitan domination, the evaluation will shift in favor of Hong Kong television.

Table 8.4 compares the evaluations held by the two groups of Chinese and Hong Kong television programs, respectively. The respondents were asked to specify whether Hong Kong or Chinese television was better on given dimensions. First, let us make the within-group comparison. The group with the best access to Hong Kong television finds that Chinese television is inferior to Hong Kong television in terms of variety (–81.6 percent), production quality (–63.4 percent), entertainment value (–83.5 percent), emotionality (–76.1 percent), social reflectiveness (–15.3 percent), and opinion representation (–9.2 percent). A similar pattern is observed in the group without Hong Kong television in regard to variety (–75.2 percent), production quality (–41.3 percent), entertainment value (–72.7 percent), and emotionality (–67.7 percent). But the observed pattern is reversed on criteria of social reflectiveness (13.9 percent), opinion representation (15.1 percent), and information reliability (19.1 percent).

These statistical patterns indicate that both groups with and without access to Hong Kong television tend to show much higher evaluation of Hong Kong programs in regard to variety, quality, entertainment value, and emotionality, which are dimensions that pertain mainly to entertainment programs such as drama series and variety shows. However, the evaluation patterns in the group without Hong Kong television are reversed on social reflectiveness, opinion representation, and informational reliability, which are dimensions pertaining to informational programs.

It is further noticed that between-group differences for Chinese TV in table 8.4 are all negative and those for Hong Kong TV are all positive. This attests to the influence of accessibility to Hong Kong television in enhancing the perceived general competitive edge of Hong Kong television, especially with respect to quality, social reflectiveness, opinion reflection, and information reliability. Indeed, as we have hypothesized earlier, when capitalist and socialist television cultures meet in a socialist marketplace, the entertaining function of the former will outshine its informational role.

Impact on Satisfaction with TV

As television viewing is voluntary, the audience's satisfaction with television channels should more or less match their exposure patterns. It follows that the two

Table 8.4. Evaluations of Chinese and Hong Kong TV by Hong Kong TV Receivability: Positive Evaluations

| | HK TV Receivability | | | | Within-Group Difference | | Between-Group Difference | |
| | Yes | | No | | | | | |
Comparative Dimensions	Chinese TV (%) (a)	HK TV (%) (b)	Chinese TV (%) (c)	HK TV (%) (d)	Yes (%) (a–b)	No (%) (c–d)	Chinese TV (%) (a–c)	HK TV (%) (b–d)
Variety	4.9	86.5	7.8	83.0	-81.6	-75.2	-2.9	3.5
Production quality	11.3	74.7	21.0	62.3	-63.4	-41.3	-9.7	12.4
Entertainment values	5.3	86.8	10.8	83.5	-83.5	-72.7	-5.5	3.3
Emotionality	7.7	83.8	12.8	80.5	-76.1	-67.7	-5.1	3.3
Reflecting social reality	35.5	50.8	49.6	35.7	-15.3	13.9	-14.1	15.1
Reflecting people's opinion	41.3	50.5	49.2	34.1	-9.2	15.1	-7.9	16.4
Information reliability	42.6	41.1	50.8	31.7	1.5	19.1	-8.2	9.4

Minimum subsample size: "Yes" group = 300; "No" group = 120

Question format: Comparing Chinese television and Hong Kong television, which do you think commands greater variety? The same question is repeated to ask the respondents which television commands "higher production quality," "more reliable information," "higher entertainment value," "more emotional engagement," "higher representativeness of local reality," and "higher reflectiveness of public opinion." The response can be "neutral," "Chinese TV," or "Hong Kong TV."

groups should show different levels of satisfaction with the domestic media. The group accessible to Hong Kong television is expected to exhibit less satisfaction with Chinese television, while the reverse would be true with the other group.

Table 8.5 relates the levels of television satisfaction of the two groups. The respondents were asked to rate their satisfaction with each television channel, using a five-point Likert scale ranging from "very dissatisfied" to "very satisfied." The scale is collapsed into three categories for analysis.

Three observations can be made: One is that the patterns of satisfaction quite match the viewing frequencies as summarized in table 8.1 and table 8.2. In the group without Hong Kong television, the more popular Zhujiang TV and Guangzhou TV receive the greatest satisfaction ratings (74.7 percent and 73.3 percent). The same is true with the group having access to Hong Kong television, where TVB Jade and ATV Home, the two most watched Hong Kong channels, are highly rated (83.7 percent and 75.8 percent).

The second observation is that the domestic media are found to be less satisfying in the group with access to Hong Kong television. For instance, only 55.7 percent of members in this group rated Zhujiang TV as satisfying, whereas the other group registers a corresponding figure of 74.7 percent. In general, the group with access to Hong Kong television is less satisfied with domestic television, especially with Zhujiang TV and Guangzhou TV. This shows that the availability of more attractive cultural products made available by cross-border television transmission may reduce the audience's satisfaction with domestic channels.

Table 8.5. Satisfaction with TV Channels by Hong Kong TV Receivability

| TV Channels | HK TV Receivability | | Difference (%) |
	Yes (%)	No (%)	
Chinese TV			
CCTV	38.7	45.5	-6.8 (ns)
Lingnan TV	34.0	43.5	-9.5 (ns)
Zhujiang TV	55.7	74.7	-19.0*
Guangzhou TV	62.9	73.3	-10.4**
HK TV			
Jade	83.7	—	—
Home	75.8	—	—

Minimum subsample size = 189

Question format: How satisifed are you with (1) CCTV, (2) Lingnan TV, (3) Zhujiang TV, (4) Guangzhou TV, and (5) TVB Jade, ATV Home? The response is a five-point Likert scale, beginning with "very satisfied" and moving through "satisfied," "so-so," and "dissatisfied" to "very dissatisfied."

* p = 0.001

** p = 0.05

Impact on Perceived Functions of TV

Perceived media functions relate to media content and exposure. As the television menu and viewing patterns of the two groups differ, the functions of television as perceived by its members should differ as well. It is expected that the group with access to Hong Kong television, given the entertainment-oriented programming coming from Hong Kong, will stress the entertainment function more than will the other group. On the contrary, the group without access to Hong Kong television, which is served mainly by Chinese television, is expected to emphasize the knowledge and information functions of television.

Table 8.6 shows the most important function that the two groups attach to television. Television is found to be more of an entertainment medium in the group with access to Hong Kong television than in the without group (12.6 percent). On the contrary, it is regarded more as a knowledge medium in the latter than in the former (-9.5 percent). However, the two groups share similar evaluation of television as an information source (-1.4 percent) and time killer (-0.05 percent). This pattern reinforces the previous observation of the outstanding entertainment quality of Hong Kong television. It also attests to the essential function of television as an informer and time killer regardless of its origin.

Impact on the Evaluation of News Sources

We observed earlier that the entertainment qualities of Hong Kong television are recognized more than are its informational credentials. To further investigate the impact of Hong Kong television on the respondents' informational use

Table 8.6. *Most Important Function of TV by Hong Kong TV Receivability*

Most Important Function	HK TV Receivability		
	Yes (%)	No (%)	Difference (%)
Entertainment	47.9	35.3	12.6
Knowledge	12.2	21.7	-9.5
Information	20.3	21.7	-1.4
Killing time	17.4	17.9	-0.5
Others	2.1	2.4	-0.3
	99.9%	101%	
	($N = 409$)	($N = 235$)	
	$X^2 = 15.00$, $df = 4$, p < 0.005		

Question format: Which is the most valuable function you derive from (1) watching TV, (2) listening to radio, (3) reading newspapers, and (4) reading magazines? The response options include (1) for entertainment, (2) for knowledge, (3) for information, (4) killing time, and (5) others.

Table 8.7. *Most Valued Functions of News Sources by Hong Kong TV Receivability*

| Perceived Area of Excellence | HK TV Receivability | | | | | | Between-Group Difference | | |
| | Yes | | | No | | | | | |
	Chinese TV (%) (a)	HK TV (%) (b)	Chinese Press (%) (c)	Chinese TV (%) (d)	HK TV (%) (e)	Chinese Press (%) (f)	Chinese TV (%) (a–d)	HK TV (%) (b–e)	Chinese Press (%) (c–f)
Depth	13.5	< 41.4	> 37.5	31.7	> 8.8	< 51.7	−18.2	32.6	−14.2
Objectivity	22.8	< 46.0	> 12.4	44.9	> 12.4	< 31.2	−22.1	33.6	−18.8
Credibility	26.1	< 34.3	> 25.8	48.1	> 10.7	< 29.2	−22.0	23.6	−3.4
Source of international news	21.2	< 52.4	> 19.7	54.0	> 11.8	< 24.5	−32.8	40.6	−4.8
Source of Chinese news	39.7	> 21.1	< 31.1	55.6	> 5.0	< 30.1	−15.9	16.1	1.0

Minimum subsample size: "Yes" group = 401; "No" group = 233

Question format: Which of the following sources excels in providing you with (1) the most detailed news, (2) the most trustworthy news, (4) international news, and (5) national news? The responses included Chinese newspapers, Chinese TV, Hong Kong TV, Chinese radio, Western radio, Chinese magazines, relatives, and family members.

of media, respondents were asked to evaluate various media as news sources with respect to the following dimensions: depth, objectivity, credibility, provision of international news, and provision of Chinese news.

Table 8.7 cross-tabulates the evaluation of media as news sources on various dimensions with the group types. It only includes the evaluations for the more important media: television and newspapers. The respondents were asked to rate how helpful each medium was as a news source, using a five-point Likert scale ranging from "very useful" to "very useless." For analysis, the scale is collapsed into three categories.

The two groups show markedly different evaluation patterns of news sources. Hong Kong television is perceived to be inferior to Chinese television and newspapers on all comparative dimensions in the group without access to Hong Kong television. Chinese television leads in objectivity (44.9 percent) and credibility (48.1 percent), as well as in the provision of both international (54 percent) and Chinese (55.6 percent) news. Chinese newspapers stand out in terms of depth (51.7 percent).

To contrast, with the exception of the provision of Chinese news (21.1 percent), Hong Kong television in the group with access to it outdid both Chinese television and newspapers in depth (41.4 percent), objectivity (46 percent), credibility (34.3 percent), and provision of international news (52.4 percent). It should be noted that Hong Kong television compares favorably with Chinese newspapers (37.5 percent) even in terms of depth, contradicting the newspapers' universal excellence in this area. It speaks to the severe lack of competitiveness on the part of Chinese media as a news source.

Provision of Chinese news is an exception because Chinese news is only a minor component of Hong Kong television news. The respondents were asked in another question about their interest in various types of information. As many as 81.1 percent of the respondents in the group having access to Hong Kong television expressed interest in Chinese news carried on Hong Kong news programs. In contrast, only 62.4 percent show interest in watching news about Hong Kong. The group without access to Hong Kong television shows similar patterns, but at a subdued level. About 69.3 percent find Chinese news in Hong Kong news programs interesting, and 56 percent regard Hong Kong news as interesting. In other words, if Hong Kong television continues its trend of carrying more Chinese news, it may serve as a formidable alternative source of Chinese news.

The impact of Hong Kong television on Guangzhou residents' evaluation of news sources becomes even more obvious if the between-group differences in table 8.7 are examined. Hong Kong television gains on all comparative dimensions at the expense of Chinese television and, to a lesser extent, Chinese newspapers. Access to Hong Kong television even reinforces the perceived weakness of Chinese television (–15.9 percent) as a source of Chinese news.

Impact on Consumption of Movies and Pop Music

Television is linked to other forms of popular culture, such as popular music and movies, which owe their popularity to their exposure on television. It has been a practice for Hong Kong to feature its popular singers and actors in variety shows, drama series, music programs on television, and in movies. Movies from Hong Kong and elsewhere are shown daily on television as well. This leads to the expectation that exposure to Hong Kong television is positively related to the consumption of other forms of popular culture from Hong Kong.

Table 8.8 summarizes the results of cross-tabulating the respondents' exposure to popular music and movies with the audience groups. Respondents were asked to indicate how often they chose to listen to or view popular songs and movies from various places, using a five-point Likert scale ranging from "very frequent" to "very infrequent." The scale is collapsed into three categories for analysis.

It is first observed from table 8.8 that, for both groups, Hong Kong movies (57.6 percent and 43.5 percent) and popular music (54.2 percent and 48.8 percent) exceed by far the popularity of comparable products from China, Taiwan, and Western nations. The between-group differences show that access to Hong Kong television appears to have a positive impact on the reception of Hong

Table 8.8. Exposure to Movies and Popular Music of Various Origins by Hong Kong TV Receivability (percentages indicating "very frequent" and "frequent" exposure)

| | HK TV Receivability | | | | Between-Group Difference | |
| | Yes | | No | | | |
Origin of Popular Culture	Pop Music (%) (a)	Movies (%) (b)	Pop Music (%) (c)	Movies (%) (d)	Pop Music (%) (a–c)	Movies (%) (b–d)
China	21.3	11.0	29.8	17.1	–8.5	–6.2
Hong Kong	54.2	57.6	48.8	43.5	5.4	14.1
Taiwan	13.6	17.7	13.8	21.8	–0.2	–4.1
Western nations	25.2	10.1	22.4	12.5	2.8	–2.4

Minimum subsample size: "Yes" group = 252; "No" group = 189

Question format: How often do you view or listen to (1) Chinese movies, (2) Hong Kong movies, (3) Taiwan movies, (4) Western movies, (5) Chinese pop songs, (6) Hong Kong pop songs, (7) Taiwan pop songs, and (8) Western pop songs? The response is a five-point Likert scale, starting with "very frequently" and continuing through "frequently," "occasionally," and "rarely" to "extremely rarely."

Table 8.9. Correlating Hong Kong TV Exposure by Exposure to Movies and Pop Songs of Various Origins (r) *in the Group with Access to Hong Kong TV*

Origins of Pop Culture	Jade	Home
Movies		
China	—	—
Hong Kong	.23***	.28***
Taiwan	—	.14**
Western nations	.11*	.15**
Pop Songs		
China	-.11*	—
Hong Kong	.33***	.32***
Taiwan	.12**	.18***
Western nations	—	.13*

*p ≤ 0.05
**p ≤ 0.01
***p ≤ 0.001

Kong movies (14.1 percent). The corresponding impact on movies of other origins is not so obvious. At the same time, the influence of Hong Kong television on the reception of pop songs is in the expected direction, but again not very noticeable (5.4 percent).

To explore the influence of Hong Kong television and the consumption of popular culture in the group with access, we correlate exposure to Hong Kong television with exposure to movies and pop songs of various origins. As table 8.9 indicates, Hong Kong television is significantly correlated in most instances with popular culture from Hong Kong (for example: Jade, movies: r = 0.23, p < 0.001; pop music: r = 0.33, p < 0.001).

To further gauge the impact of Hong Kong popular music on Guangzhou residents, the respondents were asked to name their favorite singer. It is found that about 88 percent of those answering the question named a Hong Kong singer. The top three favorite singers named were three of the so-called Four Kings (*si da tianwang*) promoted by TVB and other Hong Kong media (Jacky Cheung, Li Ming, and Lau Tak Wah). This suggests that Hong Kong popular music has an overwhelming influence on Guangzhou residents as a whole.

Impact on Attitudes

This study does not include what Gerbner (1973) called "message system analysis." To investigate the impact of exposure to Hong Kong television on the attitudes of Guangzhou residents, therefore, I draw on my long-term understanding of Hong Kong and Chinese television to identify some probable systematic differences between their messages.

Like other media, television in China is considered as part of the Chinese Communist Party's ideological apparatus, which toes the party line and promotes puritanism, equality, patriotism, socialism, and collectivism (Chan 1994). Capitalist values associated with individualism, materialism, inequality, and freedom are either suppressed or criticized. On the other hand, television in Hong Kong is a private enterprise that operates in a commercial environment. To attract an audience, Hong Kong television tends to include whatever elements will entertain. Consequently, materialism, sexual permissiveness, individualism, and social stratification are often produced and reproduced on television.

If television can shape the attitudes, values, and worldview of viewers, as some studies (for example: Gerbner and Gross 1976; Gerbner et al. 1994; Bandura 1978, 1994) have suggested, the above characterizations of television in Guangzhou and Hong Kong would lead us to expect that the group with access to Hong Kong television would be more money-minded, receptive to premarital sex, individualistic, and tolerant of the gap between rich and poor than are members of the other group.

Table 8.10 summarizes the mean differences between the two groups in respect to the aforementioned values. It shows that the mean differences for two of the four attitudes, namely, acceptance of premarital sex (md = 0.21, t = 3.46, p = 0.001) and selfish behavior (md = 0.14, t = 2.61, p = 0.01), are statistically significant. The mean differences for the other two values, money as the best indicator of one's achievement (md = 0.08, t = 1.11, ns) and tolerance of the gap between rich and poor (md = 0.03, t = 0.45, ns), are statistically insignificant but fall in the expected direction.

Table 8.10. Comparing the Values of the Groups with
and without Access to Hong Kong TV

| | Accessibility to HK TV | | | | |
| | Yes | No | Mean difference | | |
Attitudinal Statements	(a)	(b)	(a-b)	t (df)	p
"Money is the best indicator of one's achievement."	2.00	1.92	.08	1.11 (614)	—
"Premarital sex is acceptable."	1.56	1.35	.21	3.46 (524)	.001
"One may have to pursue personal interest at the expense of public interest."	1.43	1.29	.14	2.61 (520)	.01
"The gap between rich and poor is acceptable."	2.26	2.23	.03	.45 (595)	—

Table 8.11. Attitudes by Exposure to Hong Kong TV:
"Very Agreeable" and "Agreeable"

| Attitudinal Statements | Exposure to HK TV | | | Gamma | (N) |
	Low	Medium	High		
"Money is the best indicator of one's achievement."	21.9	40.9	47.8	.29***	(382)
"Premarital sex is acceptable."	11.3	15.2	26.5	.18*	(378)
"One may have to pursue personal interest at the expense of public interest."	8.8	10.5	17.2	.24**	(373)
"The gap between rich and poor is acceptable."	48.6	52.4	60.3	.09	(378)

Question format: The respondents were given a five-point Likert scale to indicate how agreeable or disagreeable they found the value statements. The scale began with "very agreeable" and moved through "agreeable," "neutral," and "disagreeable" to "very disagreeable." A higher score indicates higher acceptability.

  *p ≤ 0.05
 **p ≤ 0.01
***p ≤ 0.001

These findings suggest that, at least, exposure to foreign television—perhaps any television which teems with certain attitudes or values—tends to cultivate similar inclinations among the audience. This may happen even if the attitudes and values are contradictory to those propagated by the state media. However, the influence is uneven with respect to different values, perhaps depending on the explicitness and redundancy, as well as trustworthiness and social compatibility, of the value messages.

Summary and Discussion

By this quasi-experiment (the posttest-only design with nonequivalent groups), television is found to have notable and systematic influence over Guangzhou residents at various levels. First, it lures audiences away from Chinese television. Second, it appears to have changed their frame of reference in their evaluation of television, resulting in reduced satisfaction with domestic television and lowered estimation of the role of domestic media as news sources. Third, Hong Kong television is recognized first for its entertainment values, thus enhancing the general perception of television as an entertainment medium. Fourth, Hong Kong's television-linked popular culture, such as movies and pop songs, relates positively to audience access to Hong Kong television. Finally, Hong Kong television is observed to have cultivated in Guangzhou residents some attitudes that it presumably carries. However, the last observation must be qualified, as only two out of the four measured attitudes had a statistically significant result.

Taking all the aforementioned influences as a whole, the cultural impact of Hong Kong television on Guangzhou residents is significant. Indeed, as Gold (1993) has observed, popular culture from Hong Kong and Taiwan has made inroads into China. Hong Kong, as mediated in popular culture, represents a more advanced way of life. As long as Hong Kong's economy and media industry remain vibrant, it will have an edge in setting the trends and tastes for the Chinese urban population in general and for Guangdong residents in particular.

INSTITUTIONAL IMPACT

Radio broadcasting based in Guangzhou was also dominated by its Hong Kong counterparts in the early 1980s. It was this stiff competition posed by Hong Kong radio that motivated radio reforms in Guangzhou (Chan 1994). Guangdong People's Radio thus adopted and reinvented the program formats and professional practices of Hong Kong radio. The reforms succeeded in recapturing the local audience. The triumph of Hong Kong television in Guangzhou poses similar pressures on Guangzhou television to imitate and to reinvent itself, based on what can be learned from the "Hong Kong model." Guangdong television tried to learn from its Hong Kong counterparts about points such as camera techniques, formats, genre, ideas, and management practices.[4] However, the result is far from impressive. Guangdong television continues to be dominated by Hong Kong television. This begs an explanation.

The different nature of television and radio helps account for the relative lack of success on the part of television reforms. Radio is, in the main, a more localized medium, able to resist foreign competitors more readily than can television. That explains why the Zhujiang Economic Radio, the most successful radio to emerge from the reforms, covers mainly Guangzhou and the Pearl River Delta. This geographical focus makes it more appealing to its target audience. On the contrary, television, by its audiovisual character, is a less localized medium. This makes it more difficult for Guangdong television to exploit its local touch, particularly in the Pearl River Delta neighboring Hong Kong. Besides, television operations are more costly than radio, whose reforms, in turn, require much resource input. It is thus more difficult to narrow the resource gap between Guangdong and Hong Kong television.

The degree of open-mindedness among the television regulators and operators involved also makes a difference on the scope and success of reforms. Given Guangzhou TV's municipal status, it enjoys a higher level of autonomy than does the provincial Guangdong television. As a new station that started to operate in 1988, it was much more open to influence from Hong Kong television. It went so far as to coorganize a "beauty pageant" with ATV Home in Hong Kong, in spite of Beijing's general ban on such activities.[5] The more liberal approach has scored formidable ratings during the first few years of its operation. However, its reforms still fall short of achieving the kind of flexibility and autonomy necessitated by a highly competitive environment.

Since Guangzhou TV and Guangdong TV target the city of Guangzhou as a common market, competition between the two stations is quite keen. Before their productions can match those from Hong Kong, they often resort to Hong Kong programming to compete with each other and to prevent any larger share of the audience from drifting toward Hong Kong television. The cable networks operating in Guangzhou also carry Hong Kong television in order to attract subscribers and to fill up the air time. Another important incentive for them to carry Hong Kong television is the opportunity to replace its advertising with local ads. In this way, the cable networks can generate advertising revenue with minimal cost.

The strong presence of Hong Kong television in Guangdong imposes an immense structural pressure on Guangdong and Guangzhou television to re-engineer and even to reconfigure the industrial arrangement. That explains why "the Hong Kong factor" is always mentioned as a rationale for justifying requests from Guangdong TV and Guangzhou TV for approval from the provincial and central authorities of programming reforms.[6] These proposals stand a better chance of being approved if the seemingly liberal reforms are framed as measures to counterattack bourgeois influences from Hong Kong and the West. Such measures, in spite of their political overtones, serve an important economic function. They are also intended to increase the competitiveness of Chinese television, which in turn will bring in a larger audience share and larger advertising revenue.

The domination of local television by Hong Kong television will restrict the development of Guangdong's networks as long as the latter are restricted from making autonomous decisions. The unrestrained use of Hong Kong programs will only help perpetuate the weaker position of Guangdong television. The domination by Hong Kong television will turn functional only if Guangdong television receives full autonomy and is allowed to compete across provincial boundaries and at the national level.

As I revise this article for publication, Hong Kong has celebrated the first anniversary of its return to China. Hong Kong and Guangdong have been cooperating more closely on many fronts since reunification. But the issue of cross-border television remains outside the official agenda. One significant move by Guangdong TV in 1997 has been its launch of a national satellite TV service, which has quickly become an important revenue generator for the television station. Exploitation of the national market, indeed, is a way out for Guangdong TV in the face of continuing competitive pressure from Hong Kong. Meanwhile, TVB is planning to establish a satellite TV service with China as the main target. It will be interesting to see how China will respond to TVB's request for downlinking. Should China eventually let in Hong Kong television, the competition between Guangdong and Hong Kong definitely will intensify.

METROPOLITAN DOMINATION

The proliferation of Hong Kong popular culture in Guangdong can be viewed as a form of metropolitan domination, an effect that occurs when there is a critical gradient between two neighboring places in terms of cultural, economic, and political resources. The weaker is always subordinate to the stronger. Media culture, for instance, tends to flow from the stronger to the weaker economy. The direction of cultural flow may change as a result of the introduction of policy controls or shifts in economic resources. Hong Kong and Guangzhou, and, for that matter, Hong Kong and Shenzhen, are increasingly locked in such a domination structure. Metropolitan domination as such is not unique to Hong Kong and Guangzhou; it applies to the cultural influence that Shanghai, for instance, has over its neighboring cities and counties.

The influence of terrestrial Hong Kong television begins to wane beyond the Pearl River Delta. Its presence is felt in other provinces on occasions when Hong Kong programs are broadcast as a result of barter-trade, piracy, or purchase. Hong Kong television will have a wider coverage of China when its programs are dubbed or subtitled and broadcast via satellite television and redistributed by cable networks. This is no longer a hypothetical scenario, as Guangdong TV has been carrying some Hong Kong programs in its satellite television service, launched in 1997. In fact, many of its own programs bear some imprints of Hong Kong television.

As the sovereignty of Hong Kong changed hands in 1997, the relationship between Hong Kong and China has been fundamentally transformed. Reunited with China, Hong Kong is no longer considered a separate entity. Hong Kong media productions will gradually be regarded as less alienating. The Hong Kong media will likely enhance their effort in lobbying the central authorities to allow them to distribute their products across the border and to coproduce and form joint ventures with Chinese counterparts. Hong Kong media owe their competitive edge to their capital, technical knowledge, and familiarity with both the China market and the world market (Chan 1996). Given the new political status of Hong Kong, the pressure on China to further open its media market to Hong Kong is bound to grow, in spite of China's suspicion of external media. While Hong Kong media are at present inhibited by China's adherence to media protectionism, they will become more active in negotiating with the Beijing authorities for a more open playing field in China.

Notes

The author would like to express his gratitude to the South China Research Program at the Chinese University of Hong Kong for its generous support.

1. The estimates are based on figures provided in *Asiaweek,* June 9, 1993, 15.

2. Based on interviews with a veteran television broadcaster in Guangzhou.

3. Based on an interview with an executive of Guangdong TV.

4. Based on an interview with three different media executives at Guangdong TV.

5. Based on an interview with an ATV Home executive. To avoid irritating the Beijing authorities, the "beauty pageant" was held under the designation of a "Miss Advertising" contest.

6. Based on an interview with an executive and a veteran broadcaster of Guangdong TV.

Bibliography

Bandura, Albert. 1978. "Social Learning Theory of Aggression." *Journal of Communication* 28:12–19.

———. 1994. "Social Cognitive Theory of Mass Communication." In Jennings Bryant and Dolf Zillmann, eds., *Media Effects: Advances in Theory and Research.* Hillsdale, N.J.: Lawrence Erlbaum.

Blumler, Jay. 1979. "The Role of Theory in Uses and Gratifications Studies." *Communication Review* 6:9–36.

Boyd-Barrett, Oliver. 1977. "Media Imperialism: Towards an International Framework for the Analysis of Media Systems." In James Curran, Michael Gurevitch, and Janet Woollacott, eds., *Mass Communication and Society.* London: Edward Arnold.

Chan, Joseph Man. 1993. "Media Commercialization without Independence." In J. Cheng and M. Brosseau, eds. *China Review 1993.* Hong Kong: Chinese University Press.

————. 1994. "Media Internationalization in China: Processes and Tensions." *Journal of Communication* 44(3):70–88.

————. 1996. "Television Development in Greater China: Structure, Exports, and Market Formation." In John Sinclair, Elizabeth Jacka, and Stuart Cunningham, eds., *New Patterns in Global Television: Peripheral Vision*. Oxford: Oxford University Press.

Chu, Godwin, and Yanan Ju. 1993. *The Great Wall in Ruins: Communication and Cultural Change in China*. Albany: State University of New York Press.

Cook, Timothy, and Donald T. Campbell. 1979. *Quasi-Experimentation: Design and Analysis for Field Settings*. Chicago: Rand McNally.

DeFleur, Melvin, and Sandra Ball-Rokeach. 1982. *Theories of Mass Communication*. New York: Longman.

Elasmar, G., and J. Hunter. 1996. "The Impact of Foreign TV on a Domestic Audience: A Meta-Analysis." In *Communication Yearbook 20*, 47–69.

Featherstone, Mike. 1992. "Global Culture: An Introduction." In M. Featherstone, ed., *Global Culture: Nationalism, Globalization and Modernity*. London: Sage.

Gerbner, George. 1973. "Cultural Indicators: The Third Voice." In George Gerbner, Larry Gross, and William H. Melody, eds., *Communications Technology and Social Policy*. New York: Wiley.

Gerbner, George, and Larry Gross. 1976. "Living with Television: The Violence Profile." *Journal of Communication* 26(2):173–99.

Gerbner, George, Larry Gross, M. Morgan, and Nancy Signorielli. 1994. "Growing Up with Television: The Cultivation Perspective." In Jennings Bryant and Dolf Zillmann, eds., *Media Effects: Advances in Theory and Research*. Hillsdale, N.J.: Lawrence Erlbaum.

Gold, Thomas. 1993. "Go With Your Feelings: Hong Kong and Taiwan Popular Culture in Greater China." *China Quarterly* 136:907–1125.

He, Zhou. 2000. "Chinese Communist Party Press in a Tug-of-War: A Political-Economy Analysis of the *Shenzhen Special Zone Daily*." In Chin-Chuan Lee, ed., *Power, Money, and Media: Communication Patterns and Bureaucratic Control in Cultural China*. Evanston: Northwestern University Press.

Katz, Elihu, Jay Blumler, and Michael Gurevitch. 1974. "Utilization of Mass Communication by the Individual." In Jay Blumler and Elihu Katz, eds., *The Uses of Mass Communication*. Beverly Hills, Calif.: Sage.

Lee, Chin-Chuan. 1980. *Media Imperialism Reconsidered*. Beverly Hills, Calif.: Sage.

————. 1994. "Ambiguities and Contradictions: Issues in China's Changing Political Communication." In Chin-Chuan Lee, ed., *China's Media, Media's China*. Boulder, Colo.: Westview.

Liao, Kuang-Sheng. 1990. *Antiforeignism and Modernization in China*. Hong Kong: Chinese University Press.

Liebes, Tamar, and Elihu Katz. 1990. *The Export of Meaning: Cross-Cultural Reading of "Dallas."* New York: Oxford University Press.

Lull, James. 1991. *China Tuned On: Television, Reform and Resistance.* London: Routledge.

McCombs, Maxwell. 1994. "News Influence on Our Pictures of the World." In Jennings Bryant and Dolf Zillmann, eds., *Media Effects: Advances in Theory and Research.* Hillsdale, N.J.: Lawrence Erlbaum.

McCombs, Maxwell, and Donald Shaw. 1972. "The Agenda-Setting Function of Mass Media." *Public Opinion Quarterly* 36:176–87.

McQuail, Dennis. 1994. *Mass Communication Theory.* Newbury Park, Calif.: Sage.

Morley, David. 1992. *Television, Audiences and Cultural Studies.* New York: Routledge.

Noelle-Neumann, Elisabeth. 1984. *The Spiral of Silence: Public Opinion, Our Social Skin.* Chicago: University of Chicago Press.

Pan, Zhongdang. 2000. "Improvising Reform Activities: The Changing Reality of Journalistic Practice in China." In Chin-Chuan Lee, ed., *Power, Money, and Media: Communication Patterns and Bureaucratic Control in Cultural China.* Evanston: Northwestern University Press.

Pan, Zhongdang, Steven Chaffee, Godwin Chu, and Ju Yanan. 1994. *To See Ourselves: Comparing Traditional Chinese and American Values.* Boulder, Colo.: Westview.

Petty, R., and J. Priester. 1994. "Mass Media Attitude Change: Implications of the Elaboration Likelihood Model of Persuasion." In Jennings Bryant and Dolf Zillmann, eds., *Media Effects: Advances in Theory and Research.* Hillsdale, N.J.: Lawrence Erlbaum.

Preston, R. 1991. "Central Place Theory and the Canadian Urban System." In Trudi Bunting and Pierre Filion, eds., *Canadian Cities in Transition.* Toronto: Oxford University Press.

Robertson, R. 1992. *Globalization.* London: Sage.

Rubin, Alan. 1994. "Media Uses and Effects: A Uses-and-Gratifications Perspective." In Jennings Bryant and Dolf Zillmann, eds., *Media Effects: Advances in Theory and Research.* Hillsdale, N.J.: Lawrence Erlbaum.

Schiller, Herbert I. 1991. "Not Yet the Post-Imperialist Era." *Critical Studies in Mass Communication* 8:13–28.

Tichenor, Phillip J., George A. Donohue, and Clarice N. Olien. 1970. "Mass Media Flow and Differential Growth of Knowledge." *Public Opinion Quarterly* 34:159–70.

To, Y. M., and T. Y. Lau. 1995. "Global Export of Hong Kong Television: Television Broadcasts Limited." *Asian Journal of Communication* 5(2):108–21.

Tomlinson, John. 1991. *Cultural Imperialism: A Critical Introduction.* Baltimore: Johns Hopkins University Press.

Turner, Graeme. 1990. *British Cultural Studies.* Boston: Unwin Hyman.

Willnat, Las. 1991. "The East German Press During the Political Transformation of East Germany." *Gazette* 48:193–208.

9

One Event, Three Stories

Media Narratives from Cultural China
of the Handover of Hong Kong

ZHONGDANG PAN, CHIN-CHUAN LEE,
JOSEPH MAN CHAN, AND CLEMENT Y. K. SO

A t midnight, June 30, 1997, a "solemn and meticulously scripted" ceremony of lowering and raising the flag crowned a series of events leading to Britain's handover of Hong Kong to the People's Republic of
China (PRC).[1] The historical and political significance of this ceremony went
beyond a simple rite of diplomacy and symbolized a host of imagined fundamental clashes such as colonialism versus nationalism, capitalism versus Communism, and East versus West. The handover loomed larger than life also
because of the world's lingering memory of the Tiananmen crackdown, which
continued to be a source of uneasiness for Hong Kong. As a global "media
event" (Dayan and Katz 1991), the handover attracted more than eight thousand journalists from around the world, making Hong Kong a site of ideological
contestation over which various national discursive communities would construct the overriding narrative of the event. Lee et al. (2000) provides an overall
comparison of media representations by eight "national" perspectives. This
chapter seeks to analyze how the media from the PRC, Hong Kong, and Taiwan—three contentious discursive communities in what Tu (1991) calls "Cultural China"—tried to make sense of what undoubtedly would constitute a
watershed event in Chinese history.

Discursive Community and the Handover of Hong Kong

A "discursive community" is a group of people who share a framework for interpreting their "lived and living" everyday experiences and who resort to a
common set of conventions to talk about those experiences (Fish 1980; Wuthnow 1989; Lincoln 1989).[2] The discursive binding of such a community shines

at critical moments or around special occurrences which function as reference points and furnish a rich repertoire of cultural symbols. As public stages, mass media rank among the most important institutionally regulated venues for each community to express discursively its shared experiences and to disclose its underlying cultural and ideological premises (Edelman 1988; Esherick and Wasserstrom 1994). Events of historic importance mobilize the resources of each community's public arena (Hilgartner and Bosk 1988) and reinforce its core values. In writing about the U.S. media, Gans (1980:37) said that foreign news was treated as a variation on domestic themes "relevant to Americans or American interests" and "with interpretations that apply American values." This is also true of other media systems. The world media tend to selectively "domesticate" (Cohen et al. 1996) an event such as the handover of Hong Kong in consonance with the "enduring values" (Gans 1980), national interest, and foreign policy agendas (Lee and Yang 1995) of their home countries. They draw metaphors form their own cultural repertoire to make the event seem more relevant and meaningful to their home audiences. Of course, the journalist's personal biography, the organizational constraints of the media, and the larger media environment all come to influence news production with varying strength.

In each society, the political system is a paramount structural apparatus for building its media narrative. The media always favor an unusual event full of drama, suspense, emotion, and vivid images. The prescheduled nature of the handover enabled the media to plan ahead of time the resources needed for knitting their "news net" and for developing their interpretative canons (Tuchman 1978). The process of regime change turned out to be so surprisingly smooth and peaceful, however, as to rob the story of the elements essential to make a good "media event" (Dayan and Katz 1992). Journalists thus had to "hype" news elements of spectacle, festivity, and theatricality in order to attract audience attention. Staged conflict was a frequently used technique to achieve this effect, while producing "color" stories that purported to capture the "mood" was another. These commonalties notwithstanding, the media also created narratives that varied with the "institutional configurations within the media and the social order" (Dahlgren 1991:9), thus painting different "colors" and catching different "moods" in their coverage. In general, the market-based media systems must adhere to the ritual of journalistic objectivity (Tuchman 1972) and orient themselves toward the entertainment logic (Altheide and Snow 1979; McManus 1994). Consequently, as a self-professed guardian of Hong Kong's liberty after the British exit, the U.S. media harped pessimistically on Hong Kong's imminent erosion of democracy, press freedom, and human rights. The British media showed a strong sense of "imperial nostalgia," even going out of their way to stress that Britain had brought civilization to the world and left a good legacy in Hong Kong. The Japanese media were primarily interested in Hong Kong's continued stability, to protect their own business opportunities, while remaining oblivious to its democratic yearnings. In contrast, the Chinese Communist organs sought to uphold the kind of national glory that Taiwan did not aspire to and that Hong Kong felt ambivalent about (Lee et al. 2000).

Thus conceptualized, this chapter will examine how the three Chinese discursive communities authored their media accounts of the handover event. Borrowing from Gamson, we employ a form of framing analysis to deconstruct the media stories and then reconstruct them into what he calls discursive "packages" (Gamson et al. 1992; Gamson and Modigliani 1987, 1989). Each package is a textual conglomerate with a primary frame (Goffman 1974), a conceptual scheme that threads the observable signification devices into a coherent whole. The signification devices include concrete textual elements (such as images, catchphrases, metaphors, depictions, and exemplars) that reflect the underlying structures (thematic scheme and grammar) of the story (Pan and Kosicki 1993; van Dijk 1988). This analysis thus makes a semiotic comparison of media narratives along the paradigmatic axis and the syntagmatic axis (Fiske 1982). Paradigmatically, we examined the choices of textual units as small as words, images, metaphors, and catchphrases and as large as sources and historical exemplars. Syntagmatically, we unpacked the rules or conventions that "structure" such textual units into a coherent narrative.

Our analysis covered the period between June 16 and July 5, 1997, straddling the formal handover on July 1. We analyzed texts—routine news, special reports, documentaries, and live coverage—from twenty-eight media outlets (including eight from the PRC, nine from Taiwan, and eleven from Hong Kong), all chosen for their significance and representativeness.[3] We also interviewed many journalists from these media outlets: eleven from the PRC, eight from Taiwan, and ten from Hong Kong. The interviews probed the journalists' background, interests, and beliefs. More important, we explored the ways their organizations wove the "news net" or utilized available resources to meet challenges in a competitive environment.

Resource Mobilization: Political versus Market Games

Treating the handover of Hong Kong as a political game, the PRC authorities orchestrated a massive media mobilization effort to stage a "national ceremony" for an event that had been touted as a major achievement of the Chinese Communist Party (CCP). In early April, the CCP's Propaganda Department began to organize a workshop, urging more than eighty chief editors from party newspapers to create a "more hospitable opinion atmosphere" for Hong Kong's return to the motherland. A month later, the Propaganda Department and the Ministry of Radio, Film, and Television held a similar workshop with directors from provincial radio and television stations. In its wake, the Propaganda Department and the Office of Hong Kong and Macao Affairs of the State Council issued guidelines stipulating the principles of media coverage and the political terms and language to be used. The policy was to be implemented down to the very basic unit in the propaganda system.

Of the sixteen media outlets chosen to cover the handover, the big three—China Central Television (CCTV), the *People's Daily,* and the Xinhua News Agency—not only accounted for the lion's share of an entourage numbering 610 members but also established command centers at their Beijing headquarters. These skillful journalists were given lengthy training sessions to review Deng's speech on "one country and two systems," the Basic Law, and the general conditions of Hong Kong. The scale of CCTV's operation was particularly grand: It formed a special team in 1996, headed by the director himself, and then set up a Hong Kong office in March 1997, altogether involving 1,600 people (of whom, 289 were in Hong Kong and 100 were sent to cover responses in eight different cities in China and fifteen cities abroad). Xinhua's handover team consisted of eighty-nine reporters in Beijing and twenty-five from the Hong Kong bureau; the *People's Daily* dispatched twenty-seven reporters and editorial writers to join the five members of its Hong Kong bureau.

The CCP wanted to harness the national ceremony as a condensed and crystallized expression of patriotic emotions and at the same time, mindful of historical precedents, was determined to contain the mass euphoria. To that end, the authorities organized tightly controlled, simultaneous extravaganzas visually appealing for live television coverage in eight strategically selected cities, including Shanghai (the CCP's birthplace), Nanjing (where the treaty ceding Hong Kong was signed), Guangzhou (the capital of Guangdong Province, adjacent to Hong Kong), Shenzhen (a special economic zone next to Hong Kong), and Dongguan (a small city along the Hong Kong border where the burning of British opium triggered the war that lost Hong Kong). Moreover, to create the semblance of a unified voice, the party-state accorded special advantages to the big three official organs. The Office of Hong Kong and Macao

Affairs in Beijing and the Hong Kong branch of the Xinhua News Agency acted as liaison between the official organs and the Hong Kong members of the transition team to facilitate the officially scripted coverage.

Contrary to official Chinese media's big-splash coverage, the Hong Kong media had since 1984 chronicled every minute development in the tumultuous process of political transition (Chan and Lee 1991). What needed to be told had been told. Even though the handover itself was only part of an unfolding story, every media outlet still summoned every bit of resources to meet the challenge. Comparing coverage to a war mission, an editor from the mass-circulated *Oriental Daily News* boasted that his boss "did not care about spending money" and granted every budget request made by reporters. Every paper published a special commemorative issue on July 1. Local television stations devoted twenty-four to forty-eight hours to live coverage; TVB (Television Broadcasts Ltd.) alone reserved four hundred people for the project. All told, 106 media outlets registered a total of 2,816 journalists with the handover organizers to, in the words of a leading political editor, "document the history." The broadcast industry (two commercial stations, one cable system, and one public channel) formed a voluntary consortium that supplied signals through satellite feed to the world. Instead of being mobilized from the political center, the media followed a mixture of political and market imperatives; standing sentry over the political environment in flux was, after all, a major source of their economic interest. An editor from the English-language *South China Morning Post* admitted that the media were also fighting to shed off their "timid" and "self-censorship" images (see Lee 1998). Echoing this sentiment, an editor from *Ming Pao Daily News* claimed that the paper was trying seriously to pursue hard facts and capture "public mood" rather than simply do "song and dance stories."

Across the strait, Taiwan, as a nonparticipant, found itself a likely victim of the handover. Since the "one country, two systems" policy was originally conceived to lure Taiwan into ultimate reunification with China, Taiwan could become the next target after Hong Kong of the PRC's pressure. Taiwan's forty-two media outlets dispatched a contingent of 528 journalists to Hong Kong, a representation ranking fifth in size among those of all other countries. They mapped out their own "news nets" (Tuchman 1978) with utmost attention paid to what kind of media strategies their rivals were devising, but political democratization had ruled out the possibility of government meddling. TTV (Taiwan Television Company), the largest network, having formed a "'97 Group" and begun to air a special series titled "The Uncertain Future," now assigned a staff of thirty-nine, armed with a fat budget of U.S. $4 million, to Hong Kong. TVBS (Television Broadcasts Ltd. Satellite) teamed up with TVB, its Hong Kong parent company. Favoring a status quo relationship with mainland China, the two leading newspaper chains—the *United Daily News* and the *China Times*—each posted a twenty-member team, led by the chief editor, in an effort to outwit the other. The cash-rich *Liberty Times,* which preferred Taiwan's secession from China, did not opt to mount a comparable operation but concentrated on domestic reactions instead. The *Central Daily News,* a ruling party organ, found itself ideologically too awkward and financially too strained to face journalistic competition. The fringe, proindependence *Minzhong Daily* had only a stringer on the spot to cover the extravaganza. Overall, the Taiwan media suffered from having discriminatory access to news makers from Britain, the PRC, and Hong Kong, who had granted frequent interviews with major foreign and PRC media but consistently ignored similar requests from Taiwan journalists.

Media Narratives: Celebration, Rejection, and Uncertainty

Although media outlets from the same political system might construct different narratives, this internal variation was dwarfed by comparison to the vast media contrast reflecting the constituencies, concerns, and signification of the three distinctly different Chinese systems. Following Gamson and Lasch (1983), we constructed the "signature matrix" to summarize the distinct discursive packages found in the media coverage. In sum, we observe that China's media played up an ideologically and emotionally charged show of national festivity, the Hong Kong media revealed a sense of uncertainty and confusion about the territory becoming a part of China, and the Taiwan media rejected Beijing's effort to extend the Hong Kong formula to the island nation. There was little overlap in these packages.

THE PRC MEDIA: A "NATION–FAMILY CELEBRATION"

The PRC media articulated the thesis of national celebration through four major discursive packages—national achievement, national festival, national family, and a brighter future—each distinguished by a central organizing scheme and corresponding signification devices. Together they recreated a highly politicized myth of the Chinese as a nation-family (*guojia*). National festivity being a family affair, expression of patriotic feelings was mingled with the rituals of ancestral worship. On the eve of the handover, for example, a CCTV program featured a family memorial of Lin Zexu, the official who had ordered the burning of confiscated British opium and triggered the Opium War in 1840. The caption read, "The family commemorating the ancestor and welcoming Hong Kong's return." After a high-ranking official and the most senior member of the family clan read a eulogy in a hometown gathering, three hundred descendants recited a pledge of patriotism to their distinguished ancestor. Similarly, CCTV and the *People's Daily* repeatedly quoted jubilant citizens as saying that they felt "happier than celebrating the Chinese New Year," a traditional holiday for family reunion. They profusely praised all "children of the Yellow Emperor" who should be united as closely as "flesh and bones" in the "big motherland family."

The "children of the Yellow Emperor" all over the world were to be embraced by Mother China from Beijing. For days, the *People's Daily* carried special sections featuring various overseas Chinese communities honoring Hong Kong's return. Special care was taken to reflect geographical balance and to create a global appearance. For example, on July 2, this special section carried stories originating from London, Washington, Tokyo, Melbourne, and Johannesburg, thus representing each continent. CCTV sent twenty-two crews to cover different cities within China and around the world; activities in various locations were synchronized on the same screen to construct a mythical concept of the "Chinese" that transcended spatial divide.

Visually revealing of this spatial orientation toward the nation-family in Beijing, CCTV centered its coverage on a "countdown clock" at the center of Tiananmen Square. "The countdown clock has forever become a monument in the people's heart," a CCTV anchor announced in Beijing on July 1. It was followed by a camera shot of a sea of people surging toward the clock. Then came a passionate voice-over: "This is a spectacular festival for the Chinese nation, a ceremony of the century." The camera shot shifted to a prerecorded live scene of the June 30 midnight celebration on Tiananmen Square, which started with a CCTV reporter exclaiming to the camera: "Friends, let's count down. 10, 9, 8, . . . Hong Kong has come home!" Thousands of people gathered and roared around him. Then a giant television screen placed on Tiananmen Square showed CCTV's live coverage of the handover ceremony in Hong Kong. The screen was now jammed with scenes of national flags, fireworks, and dances accompanied by the sound of the national anthem and thunderous acclamations from the Square. Then, the CCTV report cut to one city after another, repeating the same jubilant scene and acclamation.

The head of the nation-family is the CCP. News commentaries emphasized that washing away 150 years of national humiliation by reclaiming Hong

Kong was only possible under the CCP's "correct leadership." CCTV quoted a uniformed railway worker as saying with excitement, "Without the CCP, there would be no new China; without the CCP, there would be no reform and openness; without reform and openness, there would not be a strong motherland; without a strong motherland, there would be no return of Hong Kong." The opening paragraph of the *People's Daily* editorial on June 30 read:

> Tomorrow, July 1, is the seventy-sixth anniversary of the Chinese Communist Party, also the happy day of Hong Kong's reunification with the motherland to wash away one hundred years [*sic*] of national humiliation. Having two celebrations in one day is a rare moment in our country's political life. All party comrades and people of different ethnic groups, with unparalleled excitement, warmly celebrate the reunification of Hong Kong and praise our great party!

TAIWAN MEDIA: OUR NATION, NOT YOUR FAMILY

Contrasting with Beijing's euphoria was the subdued mood of the Taiwan media. While showing a "national achievement" package in their coverage, the Taiwan media credited Hong Kong's return to the Chinese *people,* not the CCP. The other discursive packages — "one country, one better system," future of Taiwan, say "no" to Chinese expansion, and celebration hysteria — all drew sharp distinctions between Taiwan and the PRC.

The government held a historical exhibition showing that it was the Kuomintang (KMT) government, not the Communists, who had led China to victory against the Japanese invasion and brought the country to international prominence. Also retrieved from KMT archives for display was an original copy of the Nanjing Treaty which ceded Hong Kong to Britain. Citing this document, Foreign Minister John Chang claimed that only the Republic of China (ROC) had historical continuity with the history of the Chinese *nation* (*minzu*), a deliberate reference to an identity larger than that of the PRC. He was quoted by the *China Times* as saying: "Had Britain negotiated with us over the return of Hong Kong, there would have been much less uncertainty because there would be no need to have 'one country, two systems'; all would [be governed by] the ROC's free democratic system." President Lee Teng-hui (Li Denghui) and Vice President Lian Zhan, in their interviews with domestic and foreign media, repeatedly refuted Beijing's "one country, two systems" and promoted what they called "one country, one system — a better system," meaning Taiwan's flourishing democracy.

Taiwan's mainstream media echoed the official position that there was one China (as a *nation*) with a divided sovereignty enjoyed equally by two separate governments (as sovereign *states*). They reported prominently Vice President Lian's proclamation, to NBC's Tom Brokaw, that "Taiwan is part of China, but not part of the PRC" (*China Times,* June 22). While expressing satisfaction at Hong Kong's returning to "the Chinese *nation,*" the head of Taiwan's Mainland Affairs Committee announced that Taiwan as a sovereign *state* would not accept a local government status under the PRC's "one country, two systems" policy (*China Times,* June 16). The proindependence media such as the *Liberty Times* even treated China and Taiwan as two separate political entities; to them, the distinction between a nation and a state was irrelevant. The paper (on June 24) warned that if *China's* leaders should refuse to listen to the voice of the *Taiwan* people and should seek to impose "Chinese nationalism," there would be bloodshed. On June 29, its report on a "Say No to China" rally was headlined, "Opposing Chinese Annexation, The Whole Taiwan Expresses Her Wish." Taiwan was portrayed as a homogeneous entity separate from China.

While the PRC media tried aggressively to incorporate various spatially scattered Chinese communities into the confine of its nation-family, the Taiwan media focused their attention on Taiwan's future, which meant paradoxically both bringing Taiwan closer to the PRC and distancing itself from the PRC. The *China Times* ran an exclusive interview in three parts with Zhou Nan, then the PRC's chief representative in Hong Kong. A front-page story printed Zhou's assurance that it would be "more convenient for Taiwan people to visit Hong Kong after July 1." In a wide-ranging "question and answer" report, Zhou was quoted as telling Taiwan to "put away its worries." The third report, written by its chief editor, heaped praises on Zhou. Similarly, the media were preoccupied for weeks with whether a senior Taiwan representative, Gu Zhenfu, would be invited to attend the handover ceremony, whether he would accept the invitation, where he would be seated among all the dignitaries, and whether he would visit with PRC or new Hong Kong officials to resume long-stalled negotiations with the mainland. Despite the difficulties in obtaining interviews with key British, PRC, or Hong Kong officials, the Taiwan media seemed alive and wide ranging in reporting about their own government activities, protest rallies, and Taiwan's political status and future business opportunities in Hong Kong. In contrast, the PRC media reports of festivity and jubilation were abstractly framed and devoid of concrete, real-life experiences.

HONG KONG MEDIA: UNCERTAIN OF BEING PART
OF THE NATION–FAMILY

Serving a former colony inhabited by political and economic refugees from the Chinese Communist revolution, Hong Kong's media had always reflected deep-seated suspicion and fear of the PRC as a source of disturbance. The handover was a fait accompli arranged by Britain and China, over which the Hong Kong people did not have any say (Chan and Lee 1991). The main concern now was whether China would indeed honor its promise to prevent "one country" from interfering with the "two systems." The media coverage displayed four discursive packages: the "one country, two systems" model, the quest for democracy, the British legacy, and mixed feelings.

Capturing the essence of these discursive packages was the July 1 special issue of the *South China Morning Post,* which ran the full text in both English and Chinese of President Jiang Zemin's speech at the handover ceremony. The headline read, "Pledge on Rights and Noninterference." At the center of the page, Jiang's huge close-up shot was juxtaposed with photos of other world leaders and their brief greetings, as if to convey that "the whole world is watching." The mass-circulation *Apple Daily* also designed a striking front page, taken up in its entirety with a picture of Chinese and Hong Kong SAR flags being hoisted; it ran a caption in huge boldface that expressed a mixture of hope and fear: "Hong Kong *should* have tomorrow." Even *Ming Pao Daily News,* which had been accused of accommodating Beijing for years (Lee 1998), placed on its July 1 front page a story quoting from the inaugural speech by the newly installed chief executive to say that Hong Kong would enjoy an "unparalleled amount of autonomy."

This mixed feeling of hope and fear has ideological and cultural roots. Ideologically, Hong Kong was slowly establishing a nascent democracy in the 1990s to respond to the growing needs of economic prosperity and to forestall Communist interference, but it was a move China abhorred. Typical of the "quest for democracy" package, a *South China Morning Post* editorial (July 1) urged China to leave what was sometimes called "the Hong Kong virus" alone and to accept the fact that Hong Kong was different. It said that allowing Hong Kong to continue its own way of life was in keeping with the Sino-British Joint Declaration and a key to its economic success. The paper also devoted the entire second page of the July 1 issue to reporting various protests organized by the ousted Democratic legislators and other dissidents. By publishing various polls, the media reflected widespread public fear that China's People's Liberation Army (PLA), which had suppressed Tiananmen protesters in 1989, might upset stability in Hong Kong. The PLA's low pay was a topic of media scorn because failure to resist material seduction might lead it to abuse power. On the other hand, *Ming Pao Daily News* carried a long article by Louis Cha (July 1), its former owner and a renowned political commentator, warning Hong Kong people against challenging Beijing's authorities as a way of preserving their own existing freedoms.

Hong Kong people identified with Chinese culture but rejected the Communist system, as an *Apple Daily* editorial (July 1) asserted. A columnist asked rhetorically (June 24), "Why do so many people feel unsettled and alienated as Hong Kong bids farewell to colonial rule?" Public polls were often reported to show sharply divided feelings about becoming Chinese nationals. In a feature story tracing the history of opinion poll measures of public confidence (July 1), *Ming Pao Daily News* singled out the Tiananmen crackdown as the worst nightmare for Hong Kong people. The *Apple Daily* also reported on the eve of the handover that people were not optimistic about the future of democracy, freedom, human rights, and the economy in Hong Kong. Conversely, many local media praised British legacies, as dramatized by a columnist's ironical admonition:

> Liu Binyan [a Chinese journalist in exile] once told me that we have to thank the Opium War. Without this war, . . . it would have been impossible for Hong Kong's public opinion to monitor China's power all these years. It may not be appropriate to "thank the Opium War," but to say "thank you" to what the colonial rule has brought to Hong Kong is consistent with facts. (*Apple Daily*, June 28)

The British farewell was covered with sentimental and nostalgic fanfare. Television cameras zeroed in on huge crowds lining up to catch a glimpse of the departing Governor Chris Patten. On June 30, the *Apple Daily* captioned a photo of a man holding Chris Patten's photo and seeking his autograph, "Long Live Chris Patten!" The *South China Morning Post* also reported the "hugs, kisses, and tears all around" the farewell to Patten.

Historical Scripts of the Media Narratives

Each media narrative connected the handover story to a much larger historical framework to achieve coherence. Such a framework functioned as a "script" with which the media could structure various seemingly isolated episodes into compelling stories endowed with a distinct causal sequence. It was a template for the media to contextualize a series of activities in terms of their overall historical or political significance. In so doing, the media linked two different "modes of interpretation" (Zelizer 1993) and placed a micro local report about the handover in the macrocontext of Chinese history. The media were at once covering the handover and writing the history—in light of their technological needs (especially for television cameras) and the "media logic" (Altheide and Snow 1979) of their own countries. For the media, a historical script represents an unfolding story of conflict, with a starting point and a directional flow toward a future. As summarized in table 9.1, the three media systems have followed these scripts to define how the Hong Kong conflict unfolds and where the current status is, replete with a roster of heroes and villains.

These media systems did not dispute the authenticity of happenings—which had a clear chronology of various regime changes in Hong Kong—but their historical significance. While the PRC and Taiwan media marked the Opium War as the beginning of national humiliation and imperialist exploitation of China's weakness, the Hong Kong media seldom broached this issue at all. To construct Hong Kong as a *different* part of China, the *Oriental Daily News* staff were explicitly instructed to "look forward" instead of settling scores on historical controversies surrounding the colonial past. On this issue, the media seem largely to endorse a historical script proposed by Governor Patten in his farewell address:

Table 9.1. Features of the Historical Scripts of the Media Narratives

	PRC	**Hong Kong**	**Taiwan**
Starting point	The Opium War in 1840	Historical accidents that occurred 150 years ago	The Opium War in 1840
Hero	The CCP, Mao, and Deng Xiaoping	British legacy, Patten, Hong Kong people, and the Democrats	Chiang Kai-shek, the Taiwanese people
Villain	Western imperialists, typified by Patten	Chinese Communists, the PLA	Western imperialists, Chinese Communists
Historical flow	Linear and continuous	Linear and punctuated	Linear, interrupted, and restarted on a separate cause
Historical present	National pride and celebration; "One country, two systems" works	Hong Kong's future certain; Chinese identity in flux	Hong Kong's future certain; Taiwan's status unclear
Historical future	Greater national achievement, brighter future	Uncertain	Uncertain

[The chapter of the British responsibility in Hong Kong] began with the events that from today's vantage point, at the end of the following century, none of us here would wish or seek to condone. But we might note that most of those who live in Hong Kong now do so because of the events in our own century which today would have few defenders.

Settling a definite starting point for an event has profound implications for assigning roles to the actors in storytelling. The PRC media told of a history that both involved Western imperialists as villains, albeit with an obligatory acknowledgment of Chinese corruption in the Qing Dynasty, and particularly accentuated the CCP's heroic role as a savior of China, both as a *nation* and as a *state*. In this script, the history ran linearly from weak China losing its territorial integrity to strong China washing away past humiliation.

In comparison, the Taiwan media constructed two separate and more complex story lines. One of them, while vilifying Western imperialists, portrayed a history in which Communist insurgence had prevented Chiang Kai-shek's nationalist government from recovering Hong Kong and was continuing to jeopardize Taiwan's democratic existence. The other story line depicted Taiwan either as a democratic sovereign *state,* sharing divided sovereignty with the PRC, or as an independent *nation* in and of itself sharing no necessary political linkage with the PRC. Media construction of this second story line had a murky starting point, given the difficulty in linking the KMT's past authoritarianism to today's democratization.

Unlike the PRC or Taiwan media, Hong Kong's media depicted the territory's history as developing linearly from a barren fishing village to an open and rich international metropolis. This linear progression was only punctuated by the Sino-British Joint Declaration in 1984 and the brutal Tiananmen crackdown in 1989. However, the handover marked the end of this progression and activated the horror images of the CCP, the PLA, and the Tiananmen crackdown as major villains—all against the heroic backdrop of the "Hong Kong people," who wrote a success story with diligence and intelligence; the democrats, who had courage to stand up to Beijing's intimidation; and the British colonialists, who left a good legacy.

Conclusion

With a high degree of belief congruence in the intrasystem media narratives, the three media systems brought very different historical scripts, organizational resources, and ideological lenses to bear on the handover of Hong

Kong and, at this key interpretative moment, revealed very different constructions of China and the Chinese. There were hence three broadly divergent versions of the Hong Kong handover story. To recapitulate, first, the PRC media's nation-family notion was based on mythical blood and ancestral ties; the Taiwan media rejected this expansive framework, while the Hong Kong media were rife with identity uncertainty. Second, the PRC media attempted to integrate all people of Chinese descent across spatial reach in a national celebration. The Taiwan media were intent on drawing different boundaries from the PRC, and the Hong Kong media had, on the one hand, to acquiesce in China's presence and, on the other, to distance itself ideologically and psychologically by emphasizing Hong Kong's "uniqueness." Third, taking different starting points for their "historical scripts," the three media systems defined the Hong Kong handover with very different significance, wrote different story lines, and recognized different heroes and villains. Fourth, the media inscribed their narratives with the prevailing ideology and interests of their respective constituencies. In sum, journalists marshaled their own meaning systems, narrative skills, and visual grammar, and firmly anchored their accounts in their home-based interests. These factors contribute to the coherence of media narratives and reinforce the discourse of their own cultural selves. Domestication in foreign news making is thus a process of articulating discursive binding in a society.

It is often said that journalists write the first draft of history, but they are producers and reproducers of national ideology in the international context. Three necessary ingredients constitute a discursive community: its shared means of interpretations, its shared conventions of signifying practices, and its shared social and political conditions of discourse. With this concept, we can bring either societies or time periods or both together into a common analytical framework (Wuthnow 1989). The concept also has broad theoretical implications today, when media conglomerates, given their reach, have enormous potential to transform regional and local occurrences into global media events (Katz 1992; Dayan and Katz 1992). But stories about these presumably global events are still being—and will continue to be—told through domestic lenses, bearing an imprint of their political system and prevailing ideology. With the concept of discursive community, we can see how, through such storytelling, each society or culture reassesses itself and copes with potential tensions to achieve internal coherence in the face of globalization (Cohen et al. 1996). This is the essential tension between globalization and localization.

Notes

This chapter is part of a larger project entitled "Mass Media and Political Transition," supported by a grant from the Universities Grants Committee, Hong Kong. The able research assistance of Winnie Kwok is gratefully acknowledged.

1. In this project, we examined media accounts of sixty-eight media organizations from eight different countries. For reasons of space limitation, we refrain from making explicit reference to the media sources of the quotations used in this chapter.

2. For an extensive exposition of ideas related to "discursive community," see Zelizer (1993); Radway (1984); Jensen (1990); Snow and Benford (1992); Snow et al. (1986); Dahlgren (1991); Morley (1980); Schroder (1994); and Darnton (1975).

3. Within the context of the PRC's "commandist system" (Lee 1990), we selected media outlets by their official status, including those at the center (for example, the *People's Daily* and CCTV) and those playing a more complementary role. In Hong Kong and Taiwan, we chose media outlets with market shares (the *Apple Daily* and *Oriental Daily News* in Hong Kong, the *China Times* and *United Daily News* in Taiwan) and those with prestige among the elite and journalists (for example, the *South China Morning Post* and *Ming Pao Daily News* in Hong Kong). In these two societies, we also included those with distinctly different ideological positions (for example, the *Liberty Times* and the *Minzhong Daily News* in Taiwan, and the pro-Communist *Wen Wei Po* in Hong Kong). Finally, we included dominant TV networks: CCTV in the PRC, TVB and ATV (Asia Television Ltd.) in Hong Kong, and TTV in Taiwan.

Bibliography

Altheide, David L., and Robert P. Snow. 1979. *Media Logic.* Beverly Hills, Calif.: Sage.

Chan, Joseph M., and Chin-Chuan Lee. 1991. *Mass Media and Political Transition: The Hong Kong Press in China's Orbit.* New York: Guilford.

Cohen, Akiba A., Mark R. Levy, Itzhak Roeh, and Michael Gurevitch, eds. 1996. *Global Newsrooms, Local Audiences: A Study of the Eurovision News Exchange.* London: J. Libbey.

Dahlgren, Peter. 1991. "Introduction." In Peter Dahlgren and Colin Sparks, eds., *Communication and Citizenship: Journalism and the Public Sphere.* London: Routledge.

Darnton, Robert. 1975. "Writing News and Telling Stories." *Daedalus* 103(2):175–94.

Dayan, Daniel, and Elihu Katz. 1992. *Media Events: The Live Broadcasting of History.* Cambridge, Mass.: Harvard University Press.

Edelman, Murray J. 1988. *Constructing the Political Spectacle.* Chicago: University of Chicago Press.

Esherick, Joseph W., and Jeffrey N. Wasserstrom. 1994. "Acting Out Democracy: Political Theater in Modern China." In Jeffrey N. Wasserstrom and Elizabeth J. Perry, eds., *Popular Protest and Political Culture in Modern China.* 2nd ed. Boulder, Colo.: Westview.

Fish, Stanley Eugene. 1980. *Is There a Text in This Class? The Authority of Interpretive Communities.* Cambridge, Mass.: Harvard University Press.

Fiske, John. 1982. *Introduction to Communication Studies.* London: Methuen.

Gamson, William A., David Croteau, William Hoynes, and Theodore Sasson. 1992. "Media Images and the Social Construction of Reality." In Judith Blake and John Hagan, eds., *Annual Review of Sociology* 18:373–93.

Gamson, William A., and Kathryn E. Lasch. 1983. "The Political Culture of Social Welfare Policy." In Shimon E. Spiro and Ephraim Yuchtman-Yaar, eds., *Evaluating the Welfare State: Social and Political Perspectives.* New York: Academic Press.

Gamson, William A., and Andre Modigliani. 1987. "The Changing Culture of Affirmative Action." In Richard G. Braungart and Margaret M. Braungart, eds., *Research in Political Sociology* 3:137–77.

———. 1989. "Media Discourse and Public Opinion on Nuclear Power: A Constructionist Approach." *American Journal of Sociology* 95:1–37.

Gans, Herbert J. 1980. *Deciding What's News: A Study of CBS Evening News, NBC Nightly News, Newsweek and Time.* New York: Vintage.

Goffman, Erving. 1974. *Frame Analysis.* New York: Harper and Row.

Hilgartner, Stephen, and Charles L. Bosk. 1988. "The Rise and Fall of Social Problems: A Public Arena Model." *American Journal of Sociology* 94:53–78.

Jensen, Klaus Bruhn. 1990. "Television Futures: A Social Action Methodology for Studying Interpretive Communities." *Critical Studies in Mass Communication* 7:129–46.

Katz, Elihu. 1992. "The End of Journalism? Notes on Watching the War." *Journal of Communication* 42:5–13.

Lee, Chin-Chuan. 1990. "Mass Media: Of China, about China." In Chin-Chuan Lee, ed., *Voices of China: The Interplay of Politics and Journalism.* New York: Guilford.

———. 1998. "Press Self-Censorship and Political Transition in Hong Kong." *Harvard International Journal of Press/Politics* 3(2):55–73.

Lee, Chin-Chuan, Joseph Man Chan, Zhongdang Pan, and Clement Y. K. So. 2000. "National Prisms of a Global Media Event." In James Curran and Michael Gurevitch, eds., *Mass Media and Society.* 3rd ed. London: Arnold.

Lee, Chin-Chuan, and Junghye Yang. 1995. "National Interest and Foreign News: Comparing U.S. and Japanese Coverage of a Chinese Student Movement." *Gazette* 56:1–18.

Lincoln, Bruce. 1989. *Discourse and the Construction of Society: Comparative Studies of Myth, Ritual, and Classification.* New York: Oxford University Press.

McManus, John H. 1994. *Market-Driven Journalism.* Thousand Oaks, Calif.: Sage.

Morley, David. 1980. *The National Audience.* London: British Film Institute.

Pan, Zhongdang, and Gerald M. Kosicki. 1993. "Framing Analysis: An Approach to News Discourse." *Political Communication* 10:55–75.

Radway, Janice. 1984. *Reading the Romance: Women, Patriarchy, and Popular Literature.* Chapel Hill: University of North Carolina Press.

Schroder, Kim Christian. 1994. "Audience Semiotics, Interpretive Communities and the 'Ethnographic Turn' in Media Research." *Media, Culture and Society* 16:337–47.

Snow, David A., and Robert D. Benford. 1992. "Master Frames and Cycles of Protest." In Aldon D. Morris and Carol McClurg Mueller, eds., *Frontiers in Social Movement Theory*. New Haven, Conn.: Yale University Press.

Snow, David A., E. Burke Rochford Jr., Steven K. Worden, and Robert D. Benford. 1986. "Frame Alignment Process, Micromobilization, and Movement Participation." *American Sociological Review* 51:464–81.

Tu, Wei-ming. 1991. "Cultural China: The Periphery as the Center." *Daedalus* 120 (2):1–32.

Tuchman, Gaye. 1972. "Objectivity as Strategic Ritual." *American Journal of Sociology* 77:660–79.

———. 1978. *Making News: A Study in the Construction of Reality*. New York: Free Press.

van Dijk, Teun Adrianus. 1988. *News as Discourse*. Hillsdale, N.J.: Lawrence Erlbaum.

Wuthnow, Robert. 1989. *Communities of Discourse: Ideology and Social Structure in the Reformation, the Enlightenment, and European Socialism*. Cambridge, Mass.: Harvard University Press.

Zelizer, Barbie. 1993. "Journalists as Interpretive Communities." *Critical Studies in Mass Communication* 10:219–37.

10

The Paradox
of Political Economy

Media Structure, Press Freedom,
and Regime Change in Hong Kong

CHIN-CHUAN LEE

Rights and Freedoms, including those of the person, of speech, of the press, of assembly, . . . will be ensured by law in the Hong Kong Administrative Region.

—Sino-British Joint Declaration, 1984

Is freedom of the press indivisible? Does a newspaper which compromises on a minor issue thereby forfeit its editorial virginity forever or will Hong Kong's pragmatism prove a better way of dodging through the maze ahead than publish and be damned? And what if a newspaper decides to devote less space to reporting critics of Beijing? Is it not the right of a newspaper to determine its own political line?

—Jonathan Fenby, a former editor in chief of the *South China Morning Post,* in a BBC interview in April 1997 (HKJA 1997:48)

Why are the privileged [Hong Kong] people kowtowing to Beijing? They wouldn't be doing it if most of them didn't have foreign passports in their back pockets.

—Chris Patten, the governor of Hong Kong from 1992 to 1997 (Elliot 1996)

A confident wine maker would choose to be minimally interventionist, allowing the wine to make itself. After all, there is no way for the wine to escape the bottle.

—Raymond Chien, an economist and a managing director of a food-and-beverage conglomerate, to the Preparatory Committee (Gargan 1996)

As Hong Kong is being rebonded with the People's Republic of China (PRC), mass media—as a cultural commodity and ideological apparatus in modern capitalism—bear the brunt of the momentous sociopolitical transformation. The media, grounded in the fertile native soil of a language and culture not to be easily uprooted to an alien environment, are particularly sensitive to the realignment of power structures and power relationships in society. Absorbing political and economic pressure from dominant power blocks on the one hand, the media also define issues, focus public attention, and expand or narrow the range of social debate and imagination. However, they must compete fiercely with other information goods in circulation by satisfying consumers' needs. They must ultimately cater to stratified taste cultures of the audience and advertiser, some of which may not be holy or even decent. But no media organizations—whether those of downright vulgarity or those of serious purpose and high instinct—can survive the critical market test if their reportage or commentary should be seen as seriously lacking credibility or consistency. This chapter will analyze this dual role that requires the media, facing momentous regime change, to attend not only to state legitimation but also to their own legitimation in a market economy.[1]

Mass media reflect unevenly the perspectives of the power structure and thus react unevenly to the changing power relations in society. Should there be a collapse of elite consensus or should the power structure face a legitimacy crisis, the media may construct conflicting realities. Reconfiguring the power structure significantly affects the media's political realignment, which results in changes in organizational routines and cultural production. Once the political order is restored, the media may be brought back in line with the resettled consensus, thus returning form a strayed trajectory to their normal (perhaps narrower) range of latitude (Chan and Lee 1991). In a similar vein, Donohue, Tichenor, and Olien (1995:15) propose a "guard dog" hypothesis: "Media perform as a sentry not for the community as a whole, but for groups having sufficient power and influence to create and control their own security systems." Despite their notable differences, many writers (Hall 1977; Dreier 1982; Tuchman 1978; Gitlin 1980; Herman and Chomsky 1988; Chomsky 1989; Hallin 1986b; Said 1981; Entman 1989) have developed important insights on the media's substantial, but not total, dependence on the power structure.

Lance Bennett (1990) argues that the media "index" legitimate voices in the news according to the range of views expressed by prominent officials and members of institutional power blocs likely to influence the outcome of a situation. Voices falling outside the official range of debate can be admitted occasionally, but they are largely marginalized. In so doing, the media regularly put up their antennas to receive cues of environmental change. Under ordinary circumstances, media inertia resists change. If change should become inevitable, they prefer to narrow its scope. They may try to fix part of their news routines and "journalistic paradigms" in order to save the whole paradigmatic structure (Chan and Lee 1984, 1991; Bennett et al. 1985). Systemic change would occur only if partial fixing of such paradigms is seen as incapable of addressing problems arising from major turbulence in the external environment. Now that the Hong Kong media seem to feel encircled by an unfriendly environment, self-censorship may arise. This important insight should not, however, fall into the reductive trap. As Raymond Williams (1977) persuasively argues, the media uphold the dominant reality and weaken alternative or oppositional realities by incorporating, marginalizing, or directly opposing them, but this dominance is continually contested.

What challenges face Hong Kong's media? As the new authoritarian sovereign takes over a mature capitalism that may have a different inner logic, there are and will be a series of ongoing struggles involving the mediation "between civil society and the market economy" as well as the mediation between "civil society and the bureaucratic state" (Dahlgren 1995:128). These struggles, in other words, boil down to the dialectic of political economy. Can Beijing promise Hong Kong's autonomy while constantly threatening its freedom of the press?[2] Can Hong Kong remain economically viable without a free press? Can the market forces withstand or countervail potential political intervention? As the capitalistic logic pursues "profit rationality," how does the economic environment in which the media operate enhance the media's own calculations? Will information as a "public good" give the media needed prestige and legitimacy while putting state controllers on the defensive? But, then, as the capital accumulation may sacrifice noneconomic values, how does it distort cultural production? How would citizen rights and freedoms be defined in ways that may intrude on and restrict media expression in civil society? Finally, how does this economic calculation interact with political pressure, both positively and negatively?

In this chapter, I take a broadly defined political economy approach to historically examine the conditions of Hong Kong's press change and the limits to press freedom.[3] I shall first account for the rise and fall of what Seymour-Ure (1974) calls "press-party parallelism"—a system in which the press is aligned organizationally, financially, or ideologically with political parties—in relation to the stages of political transition. This parallelism can be seen as the way in which the colonial regime tried to position itself—and to walk a fine line—between opposing Chinese forces in the past five decades. The transition from British dominance to Sino-British dual power centers and finally to China's resumption of supremacy has led to a radical redistribution of political power and realignment of social forces. During this process, the impact of the new political economy on media structure and content has been uneven and paradoxical. First, avoiding serious (and dangerous) political journalism and turning that pent-up energy into the pursuit of maximum profit have produced many antidemocratic tendencies, among which media mergers and takeovers by large business interests—many of whom are actively courting Beijing's favor—stand out, with the implication that the diversity of opinions is being severely limited in ways that had not existed before. Second, specifically, both in anticipation of and under Chinese rule, self-censorship has set in among media workers and their organizations (Lee 1998a). Third, during the regime change, the media surely must revamp their "news net" (Tuchman 1978) in order to accommodate new patterns of authority configuration. In the midst of this situation, however, economic concerns of the media create a political space for their workers to operate, to breathe, and even to deflect or resist state stricture; moreover, the creed of journalistic professionalism provides them with a source of legitimacy for autonomy (Lee 1998a). These paradoxical influences speak for the need to analyze the political economy from both liberal-pluralist and radical-critical approaches as outlined in chapter 1.

Press-Party Parallelism and Stages of Political Transition

Hong Kong's media had spanned the entire ideological spectrum, representing an anomalous case of what Seymour-Ure (1974) calls "party-press parallelism." This parallelism is an enduring historical legacy in many European countries and much of the Third World, applying more strongly to press editorials than to broadcast media (Patterson and Donsbach 1993; Donsbach and Klett 1992; Freiberg 1981; Hadenius 1983; Suine 1987; Kocher 1986). In contrast, the U.S. media system prides itself on being "professional" and "nonpartisan" (meaning "centrist"), albeit predicated on an unarticulated commitment to the established order and mainstream values (Tuchman 1978; Gans 1979; Schudson 1978; Fishman 1980; Weaver and Wilhoit 1996; Manoff and Schudson 1986). The Hong Kong press had been ideologically divided on the line of conflict between *exogenous* regimes (the PRC and Taiwan), rather than being linked to *indigenous* political parties. But the ideological landscape of the media was transformed in three stages.

FIRST STAGE (1949 TO 1984)

The founding of the People's Republic on the mainland in 1949 coincided with the beginning of the Cold War. From then to the conclusion of the Sino-British Joint Declaration in 1984, the British colonial regime held the unchallenged power in Hong Kong, subjugating external Chinese forces to subservient positions. Hong Kong served as China's major avenue to the Western world and generated some 40 percent of its much needed foreign exchanges. In the 1950s and early 1960s, Xinhua, China's command post in Hong Kong, and the local Communist press assumed a low profile under the instruction of Premier Zhou Enlai (Man 1996).

The colonial regime disfranchised the local masses but co-opted a tiny circle of Chinese elite from business and professional backgrounds (including some media owners) into the governing bodies in substantive or advisory capacities (Lau 1982; King 1975). Local political parties were banned, and the pattern of electoral representation "hardly progressed beyond the nineteenth century as far as franchise extension was concerned" (Harris 1978). While controlling the rules of the game, the British allowed different Chinese interests to operate their propaganda bases against each other. The much celebrated "press freedom" in Hong Kong should be understood as the latitude that allowed the media to criticize the PRC and Taiwan, but strong criticism of the colonial regime was rare (Mitchell 1969). The media acted as a means to fine-tune administrative bureaucracy and to forestall popular discontent rather than to initiate change (Miners 1977).

Serving Chinese refugees who saw Hong Kong as a temporary shelter, the Chinese-language press was primarily preoccupied with Chinese politics and relatively unconcerned with local political affairs. During the Cultural Revolution (1967 to 1976) most media supported the British against China as the colonial regime broke up local Communist organizations (Xu 1994). Against the backdrop of continuing press-party alignment, a group of popular-centrist newspapers began to emerge around 1970 and quickly established a centrifugal place in the market. They owed much of their success to the rapid economic growth that provided a strong advertising revenue base and to the demographic transformation with the local-born population outnumbering mainland immigrants. Pursuit of the market logic necessitated that they pledge their primary allegiance to local interests while being more detached from the CCP-KMT rivalry.

Social movement was sporadic and narrowly based. The government maintained a huge and sophisticated apparatus—that is, the Government Information Services (GIS), which attached staff officers to all departments—to manage its public relations and, to borrow Gramscian language, manufacture social consent conducive to maintaining colonial hegemony (Lee 1985; Lee and Chan 1990a). The media were overwhelmingly pro-British. This came to light when the British held the press as a "public opinion trump card" to play against China's "sovereignty card" before, during, and after the sovereignty negotiations from 1982 to 1984. The media supported continued British rule in various formulations.

SECOND STAGE (1984 TO 1989)

The Sino-British Joint Declaration of 1984 engendered a dualistic power structure whose legitimacy was questionable. The British could no longer justify colonial rule, much less defend their failure in fulfilling repeated promises to gain China's concession for de jure or de facto British rule over Hong Kong after 1997. They could only try to retain public trust by projecting the image of an active, positive, and "accessible" government. The PRC's resumption of sovereignty over Hong Kong was an act of fait accompli forced upon the local people without their prior consent, so China must overcome a doubting population by improving its public image (Lee and Chan 1990a). While the British prepared for an honorable exit in due course, China shared a guardian responsibility toward Hong Kong. Both regimes competed fiercely to bolster their own legitimacy by co-opting media support while cooperating with each other to foster a climate for smooth transition. The media had a confusing and often contradictory role to play in the midst of this struggle filled with twists and turns.

The media first of all tried to play duplicitously with the twin authority structures as the latter competed to dispense tangible (advertising and news) or intangible (status, attention, and access) rewards to the socioeconomic elite. The colonial regime sharpened its traditional politics of entitlement (bestowal of British honors) and elite absorption (recruitment into advisory boards) that had been practiced with skill and effect for decades (King 1975). It became friendlier to the media. In what Ambrose King (1988) characterized as the "political absorption of economy," the PRC also took pains to emulate the same political style by appointing many pro-British figures (including media owners and "star" journalists) to the power circle as symbolized by the Drafting Committee and the Consultative Committee of the Basic Law. Deng Xiaoping and other leaders listened to various prominent leaders from Hong Kong; cooptation enabled the PRC to form cordial institutional ties with local media (Chan and Lee 1991; Xu 1994).

The media were also energized by their newfound opportunities to cover and galvanize the activities of pressure groups and political activists that had surged since the mid-1980s. This new activism drew impetus from China's rhetoric of "letting Hong Kong people run Hong Kong" and was given life by Britain's decolonization policy aimed to accord local people greater autonomy (King 1988). The indeterminacy of the transition made the media become at once an uncertain "looking-glass mirror" (using a metaphor borrowed from Lang and Lang 1981) through which both power structures tried to gauge each other's intentions and to fathom their own strategies. The ambiguities involved in concretizing the Basic Law as a mini-Constitution to govern future Hong Kong also put the media at the forefront of a public forum in which various interest groups—power holders and challengers—joined battles. The media could only acquiesce to the eventuality of Chinese sovereignty retrocession and, within the parameter of the Basic Law, struggle to obtain the most favorable conditions. Urging them not to engage in self-censorship, the colonial regime was obviously intent on harnessing the local media to counter China's rapid inroads into the political market in Hong Kong. The media were emboldened to criticize the colonial regime for its considerable hesitancy in fulfilling its promise to implement democratic reforms.[4] The British did not want to court China's wrath and would install democratic reform only at a pace they could control, and this halfhearted measure ended up frustrating many of their democratic critics and media allies. Little in the way of democratic development was accomplished in these intervening years. The Tiananmen crackdown in 1989 altered the contour of political dynamics, forcing the media to acknowledge that China's "one country, two systems" policy should be fully carried out to its letter and spirit, which was the very concept they had criticized before 1984 (Chan and Lee 1991; Lee and Chan 1990a).

THIRD STAGE (1990 TO 2000)

The third and final stage, entered in 1990, marked the "fading out" of British power and the "ushering in" of the PRC's dominance. The Sino-British relations took the worst turn, as Beijing fumed at Hong Kong and its media for the outpouring of vital support given to the Beijing student protesters in the prodemocracy movement of 1989. In contrast to China's influence in Hong Kong, which had grown in proportion to proximity to July 1, 1997, surveys registered declining trust in the Hong Kong government from 76 percent in 1986 to 49 percent in 1988 to 43 percent in 1990 (Lau 1992). The approval ratings seemed to hover around 40 percent in the period leading to the handover. Co-optation by the colonial administration was less alluring for political advancement than was seeking China's endorsement and recruitment (Tse 1995). With the sovereignty issue effectively closed, co-optation was less pertinent, and the PRC hardened its position. The renewed belligerence showed that Chinese party-state leaders could not afford to appear weak vis-à-vis foreign power or international pressure. Feeling even less inhibited to lash out at the lame-duck British regime, the press was increasingly apprehensive about offending the new sovereign.

In 1992, Christopher Patten—a professional politician, rather than a conventional bureaucrat from the Colonial Office or a "China hand" from the Foreign Office—became governor and saw his term in office as a last opportunity for the British to broaden electoral participation on the eve of China's takeover. He presided over a series of elections during 1994 and 1995, culminating in the formation of a new Legislative Council in 1996, with two-thirds of its members popularly elected. China's intimidation could not prevent the Democratic Party from triumphing over the pro-Beijing party and a bourgeois-elitist party in such elections. The PRC repudiated these elections as violating the Joint Declaration, the Basic Law, and the agreements exchanged between Beijing and London, while castigating Patten as "sinner of a millennium" (qiangu zuiren). Refusing to negotiate with Patten, Beijing installed its own power organ: the Hong Kong Affairs Advisers and the Special Administrative Region (SAR) Preparatory Committee, neither of which was provided for by the Basic Law (Dimbleby 1997). Only the pro-China elite was recruited, while critics of China, including former media co-optees of the 1980s, were excluded.[5] On July 1, 1997, a Beijing-appointed Provisional Legislature came into office to replace the 1995 fully elected Legislative Council, reintroducing several more restrictive laws.[6] A year later, popular legislative election resumed, but at much a smaller scale.

During this stage, reflecting self-interest and public concerns, the media thoroughly covered various sets of controversies that developed between Britain and China, between Governor Patten and Xinhua, and among different political groups in Hong Kong. In view of the media's structural dependence on the power structure to make news, "legitimate controversies" (Hallin 1986b) over the definition of situation and distribution of interests allow the media to expand their editorial boundary by presenting the various sides of opinion. But this time, the media exhibit no enthusiasm to reestablish a parallelism with the three newly emerged and precarious local parties, thus sending old press-party parallelism into bygone history. As shall be seen, this stage has seen the diminishing of the party press and the toning down of the partisan press, while the popular-centrist press engages in significant self-censorship and experiences major changes in both ownership and content (Lee 1998b).

Since the handover of July 1, 1997, Beijing has striven to honor its promises as laid out in the Basic Law. China's hostility toward the colonial regime has been replaced by its support for the SAR government, without exercising the overt and heavy-handed interference with the civil life of Hong Kong that many had envisioned. Having confidence in its choice of the chief executive and its control of the legislature, China has kept its distance and has handled many of its earlier threats with caution. Reporting on China's dissidents and on Hong Kong's June 4 commemoration remains prominent, the SAR government and Chief Executive Tung Chee-hua continue to come in for vigorous media criticism and scrutiny, while radio talk-show hosts and cartoonists are unrestrained in satirizing political figures and policies (Hong Kong Journalists Association [HKJA] 1998). The Hong Kong media seem to have heaved a sigh of relief, but that does not mean that they have rebuilt full confidence in China. Doubts remain; uncertainties abound. These doubts and uncertainties have pushed the popular-centrist press not only to tone down its criticism of Chinese authorities but also to become so apolitical and vulgar as to blur the traditional boundaries of cultural taste (Lee 1998b). There are "no grounds for complacency," warns the Hong Kong Journalists Association (HKJA 1998), because self-censorship continues unabated as a serious structural problem; the SAR government's attitudes to the disclosure of government-held information have been markedly less open; access of Hong Kong journalists to the mainland remain restricted;[7] and the SAR government is likely to reintroduce more restrictive laws. As the press duopoly in the mass market deepens, the standard of professional ethics declines. Media organizations with financial difficulties are either edged out of the market or provide opportunities for mainland Chinese interests to gain a stronger voice in Hong Kong, thereby "casting a longer shadow in an already uncertain environment" (HKJA 1998). Public discontent with transgressions of media ethics led to an unsuccessful government attempt to install a media council with regulatory power in 1999.

The Party Press

An immediate impact of the political transition was the demise of the pro-Kuomintang (Guomindang, or, hereafter, KMT) newspapers in rapid succession. The pro-KMT press had a substantial anti-Communist following in the 1950s, only to become gradually weakened in the subsequent decades. When it appeared certain that Chiang Kai-shek was not to recover the mainland, the KMT's influence in Hong Kong began to wane and finally be consigned to marginality. The colonial regime also came under Beijing's pressure to suppress pro-KMT activities, including denial of entry visas to Taiwan officials and the banning of sensitive Taiwan-made films. This decline of the KMT's influence was coterminous with the attrition of its supporters due to aging, death, or departure, whereas the rising tide of the postwar generation grew increasingly impatient with the traditional CCP-versus-KMT polemics.[8] In the early 1980s, Deng Xiaoping implored the KMT elements to remain in Hong Kong after 1997, though on condition that they abide by the "one China" policy and not create unrest. The line between legitimate activities and the "one China" policy is highly unclear. Once the Joint Declaration was concluded in 1984, however, the KMT institutions became even less relevant to the political life of Hong Kong.

The first newspaper on which these forces took their toll was *Kung Sheung Yat Pao* (*Industrial-Commercial Daily*), owned by the pro-KMT Ho family.[9] Stridently anti-Communist despite the sea change in demographic and political environments, this once influential paper saw its readership base continually stolen away in the 1970s by upstart centrist competitors. By the decade's end, it had reached a low point from which it would never regain its vitality. With its prospect further dimmed, the paper bid farewell to its readers in November 1984, two months after the Joint Declaration was initialed. The KMT's official mouthpiece, *Hong Kong Times* (*Xianggang Shibao*), continued to operate for another decade, but a serious internal rift briefly erupted over whether to adopt a more flexible editorial policy to suit the new political ecology (Shi 1985).[10] As Taiwan lifted its martial law in 1987, the KMT could not draw as freely on the national treasury as in the past to subsidize unprofitable and self-serving operations. The paper's closure became inevitable in February 1993, causing bitter resentment among the local KMT old guards.

In 1992, the two largest newspaper chains in Taiwan tried to test the waters in the Hong Kong market by publishing a local edition of the *United Daily News* and *China Times Weekly*. Both aspired to reach into mainland China, falsely inspired by the sudden collapse of the Soviet Union and the growing rapprochement between Beijing and Taipei. The Taipei parent company of the *United Daily News* was the target of a boycott campaign in 1992 for its alleged pro-Beijing and pro-unification stance.[11] Its Hong Kong edition was serious on China reporting and highly critical of Taiwan's president Lee Teng-hui (Li Denghui). *China Times Weekly* started out playing up the tune of "Chinese unification" and promoting closer ties between mainland China and Taiwan. The political approach did not seem to pay off, so the magazine, briefly re-named *China Times Economic Weekly*, championed a globally integrated Chi-nese economic system. But the economic emphasis did not catch on, however, so it reverted to its original name, dropping "economic" from the title. Both outlets failed to survive in the already crowded Hong Kong market.[12] Their ef-fort to establish joint ventures with mainland media also fell through, because Beijing insisted on having complete editorial control. Even the softened eco-nomic approach taken by *China Times Weekly* could not ease Beijing's restric-tions. Cultivating the mainland market not only proved illusory but began to stir ethnic controversy in Taiwan. In 1992, China began to verbally vilify Gov-ernor Patten's political reform in Hong Kong, and, further, it launched missile threats against Taiwan in 1995 and 1996. Taiwan's deteriorated economic con-ditions over China's military provocation prompted both outlets to retreat from Hong Kong, in the midst of a price war, at the end of 1995. Media voices representing Taiwan have been virtually extirpated.

On the opposite side, the PRC has, since 1989, tightened its control of such press organs as *Ta Kung Pao* and *Wen Wei Po*. In the 1980s, both papers undertook localization programs; Xinhua imposed less rigid control of their work as part of a pattern of gestures meant to show Beijing's commitment to the "one country, two systems" policy. However, when the Tiananmen pro-tests broke out in 1989, these papers sided with the reformist faction of Premier Zhao Ziyang against the ultimately triumphant hard-liners (Lee and Chan 1990b). Bitter purges in the wake of the protests resulted in the ouster of pub-lisher Lee Tze-chung of *Wen Wei Po* and his top assistants, who together founded the short-lived *Contemporary*, a news magazine. From 1989 to 1997, hard-liners took control of the Hong Kong and Macao Affairs Office under State Council and Xinhua's Hong Kong branch. Xinhua staffed many top edi-torial positions at both papers with ideologically loyal mainland appointees on a rotation basis rather than employing local recruits who might have cognitive and emotional ties to Hong Kong (Song 1995).

Despite its low credibility and dismal circulation, the leftist press secured handsome advertising revenues from mainland Chinese companies and their local governments, courtesy of Deng Xiaoping's rejuvenated economic policy changes in 1992. The once rebellious main ideological stalwart, *Wen Wei Po*, received more funds from the PRC to "repair the image of June 4," whereas the second-fiddle *Ta Kung Pao* developed its mainland market through a net-work of ties with provincial party secretaries (Song 1995). Both papers were highly profitable from 1992 to 1994; *Wen Wei Po*'s 1995 circulation ranked twelfth, but its advertising revenues stood in fifth place. The paper blasted former Governor Patten daily and printed commentaries written by Xinhua under pseudonym to intimidate China's critics. The efforts to strengthen China reporting—*Wen Wei Po* had twelve reporting stations staffed primarily by mainland reporters of Hong Kong origin—were futile under rigid party control (Ho 1996). Competing for the same small pool of readers and revenues, the two ideological siblings have subtly sniped at each other. The *Hong Kong Commercial Daily,* a pro-China publication of lesser importance, fell to the control of the leftist Joint Publishing Group. *Ching Pao* (*Crystal Daily*) and the *New Evening Post* folded.

After the handover, Beijing's institutions—including Xinhua and the leftist press—have lowered their public profile for fear of undermining the SAR government's authority. The ideological function of the leftist press has eroded now that the colonial masters have gone home, and local media have been more accommodating to Beijing. China has altered the nature of its United Front strategy from "contradictions with the enemy" to "contradictions within the people," with Hong Kongers being pushed into the ambit of "the people." Furthermore, both leftist papers invested their advertising profits heavily into real estate in the mid-1990s, only to see their values virtually evaporated in the Asian financial crisis in 1998. The tough-minded Premier Zhu Rongji would sever their subsidies, giving rise to merger discussions.[13] The future of the leftist press looks dim.

The Partisan Press

The other major impact on the press structure was a progressive blurring of boundaries between the centrist (popular) and rightist (partisan) newspapers. Both the partisan-rightist press and the popular-centrist press catered to the market and allied with the colonial regime. But the partisan-rightist newspapers had been founded long before the Communists took power in China, and were thus historically supportive of the KMT, whereas the popular-centrist press did not arise until 1970 and owes no binding loyalty to the KMT. The two most significant partisan-rightist daily papers were *Wah Kiu Yat Pao* (*Overseas Chinese Daily*) and *Sing Tao Jih Pao* (*Star Island Daily*), founded in 1925 and 1939, respectively.[14] With the advance of regime change, the partisan-rightist press has lessened its partisanship by accommodating the market forces, leading to a clear convergence between the partisan press and the popular-centrist press.

Xinhua began to co-opt these two papers in the mid-1980s. *Wah Kiu Yat Pao*'s family owners responded positively, but *Sing Tao Jih Pao*'s reaction was much more circumspect. In any case, both papers tried hard to play a balancing game with the Chinese and Hong Kong authorities, while managing not to alienate their KMT friends (Chan and Lee 1991). But their loosening of traditionally pro-Taiwan ties was facilitated by continued erosion of the KMT's base in Hong Kong and the gradual warming of the relationship across the Taiwan Strait. Meanwhile, local-born Taiwanese have wrested the KMT's leadership from the traditional mainlander core on the island.

Keen market competition—along with political uncertainty—has not been particularly kind to the weaker of the two: *Wah Kiu Yat Pao.* Having lost HK $40 million per year during the 1980s, the family owners were eager to dissolve it. Eyeing the tantalizing China market, Rupert Murdoch, having taken control of the prestigious English-language *South China Morning Post* (*SCMP*), acquired *Wah Kiu Yat Pao* in 1992 for HK $46 million, presumably as a first step toward setting foot in the Chinese press market (Fung and Lee 1994). The paper severed its traditional tilt toward the KMT. Before long, however, Murdoch left the local press business and moved over to run the Hong Kong–based Star satellite television, the signal of which reaches the whole of Asia, including the Chinese mainland, where official bans on satellite reception have been sporadic and ineffective. Robert Kuok, a Malaysian-Chinese business tycoon with strong ties to the PRC, took a controlling interest of the *SCMP,* which owned *Wah Kiu Yat Pao. Wah Kiu Yat Pao* continued to struggle unsuccessfully under different hands until its closure in January 1995.

Beijing had long extended an olive branch to *Sing Tao Jih Pao,* offering to return confiscated properties to its publisher, Sally Aw, and to treat her with high honor if she would visit the mainland. Distrusting the Communists, however, she relocated the paper's headquarters to Australia in 1985. With *Sing Tao* publicly incorporated the following year, Aw sought to diversify her investments in the nonmedia areas (Chan and Lee 1991). But her losses, after initial gains, in real-estate investments became so vast as to invite the creditors' intervention, forcing her to refocus on core newspaper business.[15] Thus in 1992, Aw accepted an invitation to visit Beijing in hopes of pursuing market opportunities and was warmly received by President Jiang Zemin and Premier Li Peng. (Soon afterward, other publishers, including Ho Man Fat of *Sing Pao* and Ma Ching-kuan of the *Oriental Daily News,* followed suit and visited mainland China.) To distance herself from a somewhat critical stance toward the PRC and to tone down the politics, Aw hired a new Singaporean chief editor

(Zhang 1995b:107). By 1995, she had invested in a variety of publishing projects in mainland China for a total of HK $250 million, resulting in what could only be described as financial debacles.[16]

Sing Tao now resembles *Ming Pao* in editorial orientation, effectively obfuscating traditional distinctions between the rightist and centrist newspapers. Meanwhile, at the end of 1996, Aw decided to close down the once popular but now highly unprofitable *Sing Tao Evening News,* while *Qingsiu (Delicate and Pretty) Weekly* was also closed to protect the profit base. However, the decline of *Sing Tao Jih Pao* continued unabated. Stolen away by the *Oriental Daily News* and the *Apple Daily,* its readership (a different measure from actual circulation) had almost been halved in one year—from 218,000 at the end of 1996 to 120,000 in February 1998 (HKJA 1998). Aw was named as a coconspirator in an alleged fraud to falsify circulation data for the *Hong Kong Standard.* An attempted acquisition of the *Sing Tao Jih Pao* by a pro-China businessman fell through due to the severity of its financial woes. The paper was finally sold at a bargain price in 1999 to Lazard Asia, whose parent company owns the *Economist* and *Financial Times.*

The Popular-Centrist Press

The popular-centrist press group of newspapers has ascended since the late 1960s to bring about a weakening of the partisan press and to mark a progressive delinking of the traditional press-party ties. This group is composed of two "taste cultures" (Gans 1974): intellectual (notably, *Ming Pao* and the *Hong Kong Economic Journal*) and mass (notably, the *Oriental Daily News,* the *Apple Daily, Sing Pao,* and the *Tin Tin Daily News*). Stratification of taste cultures among the *audience* is assumed to parallel stratification of media *content* in an intertwined way. Wilensky (1964) argues that television has the power to cut across diverse taste and class strata. But given the more demanding cognitive skills it involves, newspaper reading must be more rigidly stratified. Schudson (1978:119) distinguishes "a newspaper of information" from "a newspaper of story," whereas Hallin (1986b:130) characterizes the differences as between "a journalism of policy" and "a journalism of experience." In trade terms, it is the quality press versus the quantity press. Together the popular-centrist newspapers account for two-thirds of newspaper circulation and advertising.[17] As is typical of the "professional" press in the United States (Gans 1979; Tuchman 1978; Schudson 1978; Manoff and Schudson 1986), they are deeply oriented toward market economy, middle-class liberalism, and the centrally legitimated institutions to the exclusion of views that fall outside the boundary of social consensus. They support the current system that benefits them and interpret the PRC-Taiwan conflict from Hong Kong's vantage point.

THE INTELLECTUAL PRESS

International capital has flowed into Hong Kong as a springboard to get into mainland China. The prime example is the *South China Morning Post (SCMP)*. Akin to the power stratification in the colony, the press has perpetuated a two-tier structure in which an overwhelming majority of the local populace read the Chinese-language press, while the English-language *SCMP* serves a small but powerful constituency consisting of the expatriate community and elite Chinese. The *SCMP* came closest to what Ithiel de Sola Pool (1952:120) calls a "prestige paper," in that it "functions to express the views of the [British and Chinese] elite and to disseminate to the elite information and judgments needed by them to function as an elite in society."[18] Xu Jiatun (1994), former director of Xinhua's Hong Kong branch, disclosed in his memoirs that China made a failed attempt to acquire the *SCMP* in the mid-1980s. Now the paper's ownership was transferred through Murdoch to Kuok in 1993. Kuok holds a controlling interest of the paper (34.9 percent of the stock, worth HK $349 million) and also owns 33 percent of TVB, the largest television station. Appointed by Xinhua as a Hong Kong Affairs advisor, he also sat on the SAR Preparatory Committee and Selection Committee (Fung and Lee 1994). Besides, as a sign of increasing mainland capital in Hong Kong's media, Liu Changle, said to have close connections to the Chinese military, acquired the financially losing Asia Television in 1998.

Kuok's close business ties with China prompted the *Eastern Express,* newly published by the *Oriental Daily News* group, to advertise itself as "the *only* independent English-language newspaper in Hong Kong." It has been noted that the *SCMP* constitutes only a small fraction of Kuok's total assets and that the paper has diluted its political reporting about China since his takeover (HKJA 1996). Even after 1997, the *SCMP* can be expected to enjoy a freer rein than its Chinese-language peers. Most authoritarian regimes in the world are more tolerant of the English-language press within their countries because it appeals to a more sophisticated audience and has a direct bearing on their external image. The *Eastern Express,* which never seriously threatened the *SCMP,* was terminated in 1996, after only two years of operation. Neither can the *Hong Kong Standard* (owned by the *Sing Tao* group) menace the *SCMP*'s leading role. But the *SCMP* is not—and will never be—as dominant as it was. On the eve of the handover, the *SCMP* hired a senior Beijing journalist as its editorial adviser, causing public concern.

Murdoch's bold foray into satellite television — despite his original boast of wanting to use satellite communication to topple Communist regimes — is motivated not so much by journalistic merits as by the elusive aim of breaking into China's market.[19] Murdoch has, in fact, mobilized his global media empire to ingratiate himself with China's leaders. His New York–based publishing firm, HarperCollins, sponsored a much publicized trip to the United States in 1995 for Deng Rong to promote her inauspiciously received biography of her powerful father, Deng Xiaoping. Murdoch dropped the BBC World Service, at which Beijing takes offense, from the northern part of Star satellite TV's footprint covering East Asia. Symbolizing a strange marriage of money and politics, his Phoenix TV satellite channel provides entertainment fare to China's state-owned cable system, while leaving its news to strict official control. Many of the staff at the Star satellite were hired from China's state-run TV fully aware of the boundaries of Beijing's tolerance. In 1998, to avoid provoking Beijing, Murdoch ordered his British publishing company to cancel a book contract with Chris Patten; Patten (1998) ended up being published by Random House, which advertised the memoirs as the "book Rupert Murdoch refused to publish." Murdoch made a private showing of the movie *Titanic* for President Jiang, who praised it. The film, produced by Twentieth Century Fox, was imported with Jiang's blessing (China imports ten foreign films per year) and reaped huge profits. Jiang has also lauded Murdoch for his "objective coverage" of China and his effort to "further enhance friendly cooperation to present the world with a better understanding of China."[20]

The most significant change of ownership on the Chinese-language press side has been that of the intellectual-oriented *Ming Pao* (*Enlightenment Daily*). Under the mantle of its founder, Louis Cha, a renowned editorialist and novelist, the paper was widely acclaimed for its expertise on China watching and for its insightful political analysis during the Cold War era. Having been scathingly critical of China's radical-left leadership faction during the Cultural Revolution, Cha entered the 1980s as a firm supporter of Deng's economic reform policy, even forbidding his paper to criticize Deng by name. As a leader in drafting the Basic Law, he authored a conservative proposal in 1988 opposing any effort to hasten democratic elections, for fear of putting the well-organized Communist Party at an advantage (Chan and Clark 1991). He even used his paper to promote his proposal, provoking angry protesters to burn copies of *Ming Pao* in front of its premises. Cha ignored the Hong Kong Journalists

Association's admonition not to take part in the Basic Law Drafting and Consultative Committees to avoid a serious conflict of interest. He finally resigned from these bodies to protest against Beijing's brutal crackdown in 1989 (Chan and Lee 1991). But he quickly mended his relationship with Beijing and expressed "understanding" about why force had to be used in 1989.

Cha sold his paper to Yu Pun-hoi in December 1991. Fancying himself to be a Chinese media empire builder, Yu ventured to set up a global Chinese Television Network (CTN) with capital of HK $312 million. Yu proceeded in his venture against Cha's counsel that under no circumstances would Communist China yield the control of the media, the military, and the party to outsiders. Not allowed to operate in China, CTN became a financial drain. In 1993, Yu also initiated the ill-fated tabloid *Hong Kong Today* and Guangzhou's *Modern Mankind Daily,* both at heavy losses. Press revelations of Yu's criminal record while studying in Canada did further damage to his credibility, status, and financial standing and forced him to resign as chairman of the Hong Kong Newspapers Association. Yu's real-estate investment in mainland China was a debacle, and new printing facilities added to *Ming Pao*'s financial problems. Debt commitments compelled Yu in 1994 to sell 10 percent of the paper's share to Oei Hong Leong, the Indonesian-Chinese publisher of the pro–China *Wide Angle* magazine, who had close business ties with China.[21] But the move could not save Yu from the need to relinquish his short reign over *Ming Pao* in 1995 to the Malaysian-Chinese publisher, Tiong Hiew King, also known to have significant business investment in China. Yu retained the control of the unprofitable CTN until 1996, when it was finally sold to Taiwanese interests.

Ming Pao boasts of most comprehensive China coverage; in the mid-1990s, eleven of its fourteen China Page editors were former mainland journalists. Characteristic of its rigidly nationalistic tone,[22] *Ming Pao* published several long editorials (for example, February 17 to 18, 1995) advocating the notion of "running a Chinese paper" that would view the questions of Tibet and other world affairs "through a Chinese prism." To be a paper for Hong Kong was not good enough, it said; it must be a paper for all Chinese—a point that invited heated rebuttals from some readers as "hegemonic." Even so, the paper had a strained relationship with Beijing and was repeatedly singled out by Xinhua for blame. The tension culminated in the arrest of the reporter Xi Yang in September 1993 under provisions of the Chinese state security law. Having migrated from his native Beijing just two months earlier, Xi returned there on a reporting assignment and wrote about an expected policy change in interest rates and an international gold sale. He was charged with the alleged crime of "probing and stealing state secrets," even though many other papers, including the PRC-controlled *Wen Wei Po,* had reported the same information. Publisher Yu yielded to his staff's pressure and openly applied pressure on Beijing. The paper argued that Xi had broken no laws and that China did not try him openly and fairly. The staff, led by the chief editor, took part in protest rallies. The paper printed highly critical interviews with experts and postcard letters from readers, further suggesting that this case would chill the Hong Kong people and damage China's international image (Qi 1993).

No offense was thought to be more serious than an open defiance that in effect accused Beijing's paternal-authoritarian leaders of wrongdoing. Through personal connections, Yu pleaded with Beijing for clemency and apologized, in person and in the paper, to the agitated authorities, but all in vain. Xi Yang was given a stiff twelve-year imprisonment sentence in March 1994, sending a chilling message to Hong Kong journalists (Qi 1993). Earlier, a female reporter from the *Express Daily* was similarly detained in Beijing for conspiring to "steal" an advance copy of President Jiang's speech. Her low-key boss rushed up to Beijing to make an apology, and the reporter was released within days. But Yu could not remain silent, under the pressure of his staff to protect the reputation of Hong Kong's premier paper. As China showed little signs of conciliation, *Ming Pao,* having lost HK $22.7 million in China, terminated almost all the investment projects there between 1995 and 1996. The paper's avoidance of strident criticisms of the PRC in the editorials has been notable in recent years (HKJA 1996:42).[23] China has treated *Ming Pao* better under its new owner; Tiong managed to secure the release of Xi Yang shortly before the handover.

THE MASS PRESS

The mass-circulated press field was led by the *Oriental Daily News* and *Sing Pao* (*Success Daily*) — until the *Apple Daily* entered the fray — pampering the audience with vivid, vulgar, and sensational accounts of crime stories, mixed with a large dose of entertainment gossip and daily tidbits of soft pornography. These papers copy and outwit each other to offer new variations on the same theme. The *Oriental Daily News* boasts of a contingent of eighty spot-news reporters and thirty others covering "societal news," with reporting vehicles and devices to eavesdrop on police radio communication, priding itself on the ability to beat the police in speeding to the scene of crimes or accidents. By contrast, the paper only has ten political reporters and twenty economic reporters. Deliberately apolitical, these papers cultivate a pro-underdog image befitting their working-class readers. Their relationship with the Chinese authorities is more ambiguous: not wanting to offend Beijing on the one hand, while feeling less pressured to ingratiate themselves with China on the other.[24] As long as they are not too critical of China, these "yellow" newspapers may offend the sensibilities of the morally puritan Beijing regime without threatening its hegemonic power. Beijing's officials have repeatedly chided that Hong Kong people will be allowed to keep the trappings of their decadent way of life, such as horse racing, pornography, and other capitalistic trifles.

The market equilibrium was upset when Jimmy Lai, who had made a fortune in the garment business, began publishing *Next* magazine. *Next*'s surprising market success provoked the *Oriental Daily News* to publish a similar magazine, *Eastweek,* and both magazines thrive on the "sex and violence" themes. Both publications either shun political affairs or sensationalize them for commercial exploitation. Inspired by his own success, Lai set out to launch the highly publicized HK $700-million *Apple Daily* in mid-1995, prepared to lose a lot of money before it turned profitable. The paper modeled itself after *USA Today* in its colorful, eye-catching graphic design and its brisk, brief writing. Sold for HK $3 per copy (at a 60 percent discount) for the first month, it was bolstered by an HK $100 million promotional campaign. Offering higher salaries, Lai lured ten managers and 235 reporters from other papers to embellish his crime-gossip-sex formulas. Every day the paper exploits pictures of nude females and advises its readers where and how to obtain sex services, along with articles written in lively and highly personable Cantonese vernacular. In the name of "muckraking," moreover, the paper relentlessly exposes personal secrets and the dark underside of the lives of entertainment celebrities to satisfy the reader's peeping curiosity. Reporters were sent out as "doggy teams" (paparazzi) to tail and record every move of some targeted personalities (So 1996). Within months, the paper climbed to near the top of the pack, amassing a circulation of 300,000 copies, cutting into the commanding lead of the *Oriental Daily News*.[25] Accused of not playing fair, Lai retorted that it was not his responsibility to look after his competitors' weak spots (HKEJ 1995).

Lai defied popular wisdom by entering the newspaper competition against the backdrop of enormous political uncertainties and capital flight. The PRC had suspended Lai's Giordano garment store in Beijing (resulting in his resignation from the company's board of directors and, later, liquidation of all his shares) to retaliate against his personalized editorial in *Next* magazine in which he called Premier Li Peng a "bastard idiot." His well-publicized anti-Communist attitude notwithstanding, Lai appeared to display calculated oscillation in shaping his edi-

torial policy, while gauging pressure points of the regime change. His first im-
pulse was to steer this expensively invested and commercially successful paper
away from political trouble, and he proclaimed on the eve of the handover that
it "would no longer be anti-Communist."[26] But the *Apple Daily* was cleverly
cashing in on the weaknesses of its competitors, which had been recoiling from
confronting Beijing, to stir a reservoir of deep-seated public doubts by playing up
anti-Communist sentiments and by lending a strong voice to the Democratic
Party. With a small political desk, the *Apple Daily* is far from being a thoughtful
political paper, but it has developed a smart *business* strategy to *commodify the politics*. The paper borrows proven methods from crime stories and treats political
agendas and anti-Communist feelings as salable items — often in such a populist
and demagogic format, language, and style that the articles not only grab the attention of the readers but also earn their admiration for its supposed political
courage. Also taking on the incompetence of local politicians and the greed of
business tycoons (such as the leading real-estate developer, Li Ka Shing), Lai also
makes himself a friend of the "little guys." Despite Beijing's continued effort to
bar the entry of his reporters to the mainland, the paper has excelled in "domesticating" (Gans 1979) China news into the familiar themes of "eroticism, gam-
bling, drugs, darkness, and deviousness" and molding it according to traditional
crime-news formulas. China news is a taken-for-granted extension of Hong
Kong news, thus whetting readers' voracious appetite for more "familiar yet ex-
otic" crime stories "scripted" by mainland rather than local characters (Ho 1996).
Lai has justified everything his paper does as meeting the public's wants — as if this
claim would insulate him from Beijing's ire or free him from the charges of ethical degradation — but he has "revolutionized" the yellow press by breaking away
from traditional decency and responsibility.

THE PRICE WAR

Most papers had at this time been suffering from a slack economy and depressed
advertising revenues, made worse by the doubling in one year of newsprint
prices due to a global shortage.[27] They complied with the cartel-set price instead of matching Lai's price reduction. The *Oriental Daily News* saw its peers'
vulnerability as perfect timing for revenge and sharply cut the cartel-imposed
price from HK $5 to HK $2 per copy in early 1996.[28] This time, most papers
could not sit idly. In a manner akin to what a Chinese proverb describes as
"drinking poison to quench thirst" (*yin zhen zhi ke*), they competed to cut
prices and offer raffle tickets for such grand prizes as an automobile or an apart-
ment. But it took only two weeks to claim the lives of those less fit to survive:

the *Express* (which reappeared from 1996 to 1998), the *United Daily News,* the *Television Daily,* and the *South China Economic Daily.* A total of six hundred news workers lost their jobs.

The price war lasted for six months and ended only when Lai negotiated in person with Ma. During the price war, newspapers attacked each other, kept changing the prices for no good reason, and constantly broke their promises to readers. Most outlets suffered huge losses, and overall press stocks were significantly devalued. Thanks to market segmentation, only the two English-language newspapers (the *SCMP* and the *Hong Kong Standard*) and the two financial newspapers (the *Hong Kong Economic Journal* and the *Hong Kong Economic Times*) were relatively unharmed. Even though the newspaper price was restored to HK $5 per copy in July 1996, an advertising war intensified. Because of the bad economic conditions, the Hong Kong press industry has been hard hit by a sharp decline in advertising revenues (which, for example, totaled only HK $4.37 billion in 1995, a 12 percent drop from the previous year). To fill up the advertising space, many newspapers offered deep discounts—in the depressed real-estate areas, advertisers paid as low as 30 percent of the regular prices—and some even were willing to provide free service. The combined factors of high inflation, low advertising revenues, rising newsprint cost, and the growth in salaries (10 percent annually)—on top of the price war and a strong competition posed by the *Apple Daily*—reduced the profit of the Oriental Press group and the Sing Tao group each by two-thirds, while turning *Ming Pao*'s profit into a net loss.[29] Most other papers did not fare any better. The unfavorable profit structure was directly or indirectly responsible for the closure of the *Eastern Express, Sing Tao Evening News,* and *Qingxin (Delicate and Pretty) Magazine.* With the press market having become saturated, the fact that the *Apple Daily* posted a total circulation of 360,000 copies at the end of 1996 means an average loss of 10 percent in circulation for its peers. Despite its profitability, *Next,* the parent company of the *Apple Daily,* has failed twice, in 1995 and 1997, to become a public company, because it could not find a guarantor willing to risk a bad relationship with Beijing. The *Oriental Daily* has since launched three rounds of price cuts to reclaim its lead in circulation, causing more newspapers and magazines to fold (four hundred more journalists unemployed), but the *Apple Daily* is too strong to be devastated. Besides, *Next* has branched out to publish *Sudden Weekly* and *Eat and Drink* and spawned other imitators (including *Oriental Touch* by the *Oriental Daily News*). The *Oriental Daily* launched a highly vulgar *Sun Daily* in 1999 in an effort to lure young readers away from the *Apple Daily.* Press ownership will be further consolidated.

Market-Driven Journalism

Market forces have intensified merger and takeover activities by international and pro-PRC capitalists (Fung and Lee 1994) and have also produced certain blatantly antidemocratic and antijournalistic tendencies. The road to conglomeration was paved in the mid-1980s, when many papers became public corporations in order to attract public funds and minimize the owners' capital risks posed by political uncertainties. But the huge sum of capital they collected had to be invested, resulting partly in acquisition of other media outlets and real-estate properties. *Ming Pao, Sing Tao Jih Pao,* the *Oriental Daily News,* and the *Apple Daily* have branched out into publishing a variety of newspapers and magazines or into ownership of other nonmedia businesses. Robert Kuok is a further example of cross-media ownership, controlling the *South China Morning Post* and 33 percent of TVB.

Corporate ownership not only makes it difficult for family-owned papers to survive but it also prevents potential competitors from entering the market, thus diluting the diversity of views and opinion in circulation (Garnham 1990; Golding and Murdock 1991; Jansen 1991; Keane 1991; McManus 1994; Mosco 1996). Theoretically, when the media are owned by diverse families, parties, and constituencies, no single owner is able to exert disproportionate amount of influence because "economic exchange and power repel each other" (Caporaso and Levine 1992:165–68). In an oligopolistic market, however, large firms have far greater potential power as "price makers," capable of affecting such economic parameters as output levels, technology, and tastes (Caporaso and Levine 1992:167). Media barons, as Jimmy Lai's example shows, enjoy immense direct and indirect power. Directly, they give free publicity to their own media; indirectly, they set the rules of the game (Golding and Murdock 1991). They can use their financial power to ward off potential challengers and elbow weaker competitors out of the market by raiding creative talents, fixing prices (through, for example, price wars), and launching expensive promotional campaigns. They can also siphon off advertising revenues from their rivals because of their market reach and their ability to offer big discounts to advertisers. Moreover, they can harass their critics with legal action.

Capital concentration sets broad boundaries for exercising "allocative control" (Murdock 1982) in the larger media environment, which may in turn influence how specific media organizations implement "operational control" within that environment. Structurally, since the onset of political transition, Hong Kong has seen a rapid and vast dwindling in the number of diverse media outlets. Moreover, both the survivors and (very few) newcomers have competed to offer more of the same themes and images, as the center of gravity increasingly moves from journalistic achievement to the pocketbook. Once the *Apple Daily* launched itself with fanfare and an initial capital of HK $700 million, and once the *Oriental Daily News* matched it with equally hefty investment, the door of the market was essentially shut to individuals or companies long on journalistic ideals but short on money. The Big Two own the best equipment and many of the premium talents in town, all for the sake of what commentators call "shit digging." With their huge vested interest at stake, big capitalists tend to be politically conservative (with the dubious exception of Jimmy Lai, as explained above) and commercially clever. Many papers have followed the lead of the Big Two to pursue more escapist infotainment—cheap entertainment fares, investigative gossip, sex, violence, and scandals disguised as news—which is not only politically safe but commercially rewarding. Despite China's intense disdain of yellow journalism, such fare poses no real threat to its power and hence will be tolerated in Hong Kong. Unless politics can be turned into money, the big-money media are likely to use slick production to dodge serious journalism rather than to strengthen journalistic vigor. Even quality newspapers, which have been losing readers to the Big Two, are no longer immune from trends in the mass market; to meet the corrosive competition, they— notably, *Ming Pao*—have gradually borrowed from mass dailies such editorial style as attention-grabbing pictures and headlines (HKJA 1998).

These newspapers make claims and counterclaims about their circulation figures and resort to outrageous marketing strategies to stimulate their sales. Claiming well above 70 percent of the total newspaper readership (different from circulation figures), the Big Two marginalize other competitors who can only share the leftovers. In an environment ruled by crude sensationalism, good cultural taste and serious journalism must fight an uphill battle. Even the once strong *Sing Tao Jih Pao* is having difficulties surviving, let alone a host of many other publications that have been forced to fold. The surviving mass-market dailies, for survival's sake, will have to develop their own niches in the market. This deepening duopolization of the newspaper market will likely exacerbate more publications to close down (HKJA 1998). The *Nineties Monthly,* generally regarded as one of the best political magazines around, one that had been put on Beijing's "enemy list," closed down in 1998 not because of direct political pressure but because of a declining interest in serious political discussion, especially among the younger generations. Before this, several well-respected political magazines, such as *Pai Shing* and *Contemporary,* had been bought out and then closed down by pro-China businessmen. Once providing a vital forum for journalists and critical intellectuals from global Chinese communities, Hong Kong's political journals may have a dim future. As a small antidote, in 1996, a noted talk-show host published a short-lived *Mad Dog Daily* to "bite" Beijing. The PRC and its allies also publish a gamut of magazines (including *Mirror*, *Wide Angle*, *Economic Journal*, *Bauhinia*, and *Window*), but their collective influence is marginal.

The unethical journalistic practices of the Big Two have led to a steep deterioration of professional standards, but as long as the market responds favorably to sensationalism, papers using these practices will not be deterred by moral or professional criticism. Despite their wide circulation, as will be seen in table 10.1, both papers were held in low esteem by media professionals. They invade privacy, fabricate stories, and throw out the window the dos and don'ts of journalistic ethics. The *Oriental Daily*, given its resources, has hired full-time attorneys to bring scores of libel lawsuits against a wide array of individual critics and other media outlets on the most trifling counts. Few if any of such cases can be established in court, but the time and effort taken to answer these charges are threatening enough to silence potential dissenters. This harassment tactic seems to have achieved its aims, for media critics have largely stayed away from reproving the *Oriental Daily*, even though other publications remain fair game for criticism. The paper was cited for contempt of court after a full month of vicious editorial attacks on the judiciary, which it preceded by sending a paparazzo to tail a High Court judge (called "swinish white-skinned") for several days to avenge what it perceived to be a ruling partial to the *Apple Daily* in a copyright case.

The weakened market position of many mainstream media outlets opens a door to their acquisition by those who have close personal, business, or political connections with Beijing leaders. *Sing Tao Jih Pao* was to be taken over by Cha Chi-min, a conservative pro-China tycoon who abhorred implementing "British-style socialism" in Hong Kong, because it "corrodes social morality," before he withdrew upon discovering the paper's horrid financial condition. The financially embattled Asia Television (ATV) sold its controlling 51 percent stake to a consortium of two companies led by businessmen with strong mainland backgrounds and connections. The largest new shareholder, Dragon Viceroy, is partly owned by Liu Changle, a former Chinese army officer. In addition to ATV, Liu had purchased from Rupert Murdoch part of the Phoenix Chinese Channel on Star TV and persuaded Beijing to tolerate the reception of its signal by mainland viewers (HKJA 1998). It may not be totally justified to impute a direct cause-effect relationship between media ownership and media content (Murdock 1982), but, in this case, concerns about possible erosion of editorial independence run deep.

Table 10.1. Journalists' Perceived Credibility of Major Hong Kong News Media

Media Organization	1990 (mean)	1996 (mean)	Difference
RTHK	7.6	7.07	-0.53*
TVB	7.6	7.07	-0.70*
ATV	7.2	6.72	-0.72*
HK Economic Journal	7.4	7.38	-0.02
SCMP	7.7	7.20	-0.50*
Ming Pao	7.0	7.16	0.16
HK Economic Times	6.7	6.75	0.05
Sing Tao Daily News	6.9	6.73	-0.18
HK Standard	6.6	6.55	-0.05
Oriental Daily News	6.9	5.85	-1.05*
Sing Pao	6.5	5.74	-0.76*
Tin Tin Daily News	5.5	5.12	-0.39*
Apple Daily	—	5.03	—
HK Commercial Daily	5.0	4.90	-0.10
Wen Wei Po	5.1	4.69	-0.42*
Ta Kung Pao	5.1	4.66	-0.44*
Hong Kong Times	5.1	—	—

*Statistically significant differences. The range of perceived credibility was from 1 to 10. The 1990 survey had a sample of 522 journalists, and the 1996 survey had a sample of 551 journalists, selected according to systematic random sampling method. Sources: So, Lee, and Fung (1996).

If the mass press uses the market forces to defuse political pressure (since China seems indifferent to media sensationalism in Hong Kong), the journalistically serious press seems to be seeking a balance between political demands and economic interests in an intertwined and paradoxical way. The serious press is politically submissive enough to exercise self-censorship but practical enough to want to protect its fragile professional reputation, which is a legitimizing source of their economic interests. To protect their economic interests, they have to make peace with the authorities that dispense vital rewards and punishments, but to be seen as fair, bold, and trustworthy, they must risk irking the powers that be (Lee 1998b). Insofar as this tug-of-war may make the media highly vulnerable, we must watch how media owners with heavy business ties with China behave differently—according to specific issues, conditions, and situations—from those whose media interests are solely in Hong Kong.

Self-Censorship and Professionalism[30]

Despite its antipathy to press freedom, China is conscious that a measure of editorial independence in Hong Kong is acceptable, even necessary, as long as that freedom does not offend China's central concerns or objectives. China cannot impose naked coercion or install a tight censorship system in Hong Kong; as part of its United Front work, it has actively co-opted some media people while harshly ostracizing others. The media have been trying to be conciliatory toward China but to uphold their own fragile legitimation as well. These paradoxes have shaped inconsistent and uneven patterns of journalistic self-censorship.

Self-censorship is defined as a set of editorial actions ranging from omission, dilution, distortion, and change of emphasis to choice of rhetorical devices by journalists, their organizations, and even the entire media community in anticipation of currying reward and avoiding punishments from the power structure. It thus deviates from relatively clear and widely agreed-upon norms of journalistic professionalism. Inasmuch as news making is anchored in centrally legitimated institutions, where facts can be gathered more efficiently (Tuchman 1978), Hong Kong's handover may redefine what Hallin (1986a) calls the "sphere of consensus" and the "sphere of deviance." That the media turn the limelight to the SAR government may not alone constitute a case of self-censorship. It enters into the realm of contention, however, if they knowingly or unknowingly play up or down information and perspectives consequential to regime change.

In evidence are the press's tendency to dodge political controversy, the hiring of pro-China staff to assume responsible posts, the shift of editorial tone in line with Beijing's policy, the redesign of space to reduce its political overtone, the firing of high-risk contributors, the dissemination of writing guidelines on "sensitive" stories, and the placing of sensitive stories in obscure positions.[31] In 1996, the media busied themselves with the excitement of guessing who was ahead or behind in the highly orchestrated and undemocratic races for the SAR chief executive post and for the Provisional Legislature seats, seemingly unperturbed by China's tampering with the rules of the game in violation of both the Basic Law and the Sino-British Joint Declaration of 1984 (P. Lee and Chu 1998).[32] Many media organizations appear to be voluntarily accepting certain boundaries of expression; for example, TVB, CTN, and even the Chinese edition of Marie Claire have reportedly exercised self-censorship on issues regarding secession of Tibet, Taiwan, and Xinjiang from China (HKJA 1998). All these signs point in an unmistakable direction: that of trying not to agitate Beijing.

It is found (Lee 1998b; So, Lee, and Fung 1996) that many Hong Kong journalists were fearful of criticizing the Chinese government, while few dreaded offending the outgoing colonial regime; the amount of deference shown to big business, probably out of the desire to be on good terms with those who foot the press bills, was somewhat surprising. Most Hong Kong journalists claim to subscribe to Western norms of professionalism — such as objectivity, balance, and impartiality — even if their performance may fall short of the goal; and to maintain professional integrity has been a real struggle (Lee et al. 1996). They despise state control, but nonetheless must do something to neutralize Beijing's pressure. Table 10.1 also shows that there was a significant erosion of media credibility from 1990 to 1996 as perceived by Hong Kong journalists due to a combination of cutthroat competition, vulgarization, and self-censorship. None of the outlets made any gains in the amount of perceived credibility during this period. There is nonetheless a stable hierarchy of credibility, with the elite press (such as TVB and *SCMP*) leading the mass-market press (such as the *Oriental Daily News* and the *Apple Daily*) but with the leftist press (*Wen Wei Po* and *Ta Kung Pao*) at the bottom.

According to Lukes (1974), Galbraith (1983), and Boulding (1990), power can be wielded through reward and punishment and, more fundamentally, through a process of hegemony which conditions one's belief in such a way that submission to authority is assumed and unrecognized. Kelman (1961) also outlines three processes of opinion change: compliance, identification, and internalization. Given China's vast power over reward and punishment (Chan and Lee 1991:52–62; Allen 1997), self-censorship among the Hong Kong media seems to typify a process of compliance with external demands based on the perception of limited or no better choices rather than from volition. Compliance implies verbal or overt changes to attain certain instrumental goals without accompanying changes in belief. It is motivated by a concern with "social effect of behavior" (that is, rewards and punishments) rather than by a concern with "social anchorage of behavior" or a concern with "value congruence of behavior" (Kelman 1961). Compliance may eventually combine with — or develop into — identification and internalization, thus moving from instrumental considerations of reward and punishment to hegemonic conditioning of beliefs. But at present, self-censorship is primarily an act of compliance. Hong Kong's media seem inherently suspicious of China. They had stridently supported the British vis-à-vis the PRC — over issues ranging from sovereignty negotiations and democratic reform to party formation — until such a position became untenable. While avoiding confrontation with Beijing, they abhor pro-China labels for fear of damaging their own credibility. Their posture is highly defensive.

Self-censorship could occur individually and organizationally. There are three broad categories of self-censorship: direct and indirect external pressure on a media organization, pressure within a media organization, and assimilation of values by journalists (HKJA 1997:50–57). Organizational culture of the media regulates—in the sense of filtering pressure through to influence—professional norms of individual journalists, thus ensuring a high degree of belief consistency and value homogeneity (Sigelman 1973; Chan and Lee 1988). Exercising belief control through self-selective or deliberate mechanisms at the point of recruitment is augmented by what Breed (1955) calls "socialization in the newsroom." Journalists continually absorb, internalize, and reinforce the organizational culture by learning the dos and don'ts from various patterns of signs, symbols, and practice that surround them. Editors may occasionally issue explicit orders on what story to avoid or tilt, but journalists habitually stay within bounds without having to be told. In Hong Kong, those journalists who do not feel subjected to strong control by company guidelines far outnumber those who do (Chan and Lee 1988). They have, in short, "naturalized" the organizational perspectives as a standard of taste, conduct, and judgment.

Self-censorship, given its huge social cost, is used as a preventive defense. The external pressure can be real, imagined, or both. Real pressure is exerted behind the scenes, if possible, to avoid public criticism. Imagined pressure can sometimes be more intimidating because the consequences of failing to succumb to it are ambiguous. Self-censorship is directly related to the "*imagined boundaries*" of how tolerant China will be and what it will do in the way of reward and punishment. Allport (1937) argues that public opinion involves an "imagined crowd" and the power of public opinion lies in the way others perceive it. Noelle-Neumann (1984) further predicts that the perceived "climate of opinion" may induce people to support the seemingly more popular views while stifling dissenters from public debate. The "crowd psychology" in a gauging game can be tortuously contagious.

Hong Kong's handover, under the "one country, two systems" policy, is unprecedented. It has many uncertain and contradictory possibilities but fewer fixed battlelines. The media-state relationship in a capitalistic market remains fluid, and its modes of operation are unsettled. All contending parties must constantly ask themselves: "How far can I go?" Neither side knows the "correct" answers, and calculation of the other side's behaviors may provoke or constrain one's own imagination. How can China control Hong Kong's media without discrediting its announced policy? How can the media court political and economic rapport with Beijing without casting doubt on their professional credibility, which is the direct source of their business interest? Often, these boundaries can be *subjectively imagined* under the influence of the presumed "climate of opinion" with or without objective basis in reality. They are constantly being contested and adjusted to accommodate the dynamics of social movements that articulate the changing visions, risks, and possibilities. Public struggles "out there" may interact with the struggles within the newsroom. Public criticisms of a media outlet's sudden switch of allegiance may strengthen the internal "democratic" faction in moderating if not warding off China's real and imagined interventive pressure.[33]

On the other hand, in "indexing" legitimate voices (Bennett 1990), the popular-centrist press may appeal to a professionalism rooted in middle-class consensus. The marketplace of opinions is assumed to be normally distributed, with the center covering the widest segment of the population. It can thus be argued that the official view in an open system overlaps with a substantial area of social consensus that forms the media's point of departure (and, often, a point of return) to anchor their news perspectives. Media sociologists (Tuchman 1978; Gans 1979; Fishman 1980; Schlesinger 1978; Cohen and Young 1981) have argued that the media focus their "news net" on the centrally legitimated institutions, hence the rhythm of news work is in tandem with the cycle of such institutions. Hallin (1986a) maintains that the media will follow the institutionalized agendas rather than propose new or innovative approaches to the problem. No doubt the media have been shifting their focus from the Hong Kong colonial government to the SAR government, and from Britain to the PRC, as primary news sources and reality definers. What about those social groups, notably the Democrats, which have been severely denounced by the PRC but have enjoyed the most popular support in Hong Kong's electorate (with 64 percent of the vote in the 1995 direct election)? By refusing to take part in the China-picked Provisional Legislature, Democrats complained about receiving insufficient media attention. The pro-PRC forces became more visible and more vocal both in the political arena and in media coverage. After the Democratic Party won a victory in the 1998 legislative election, however, its leaders seemed to have shared the media limelight with leaders of other parties. Insofar as the Democrats remain as a significant political force, the media would give them their share of voice, which, however, won't be as dominant as it was in the early 1990s.

Strategic Rituals

While scholars of the New Left display insight in explaining the impact of in-creasing media concentration on journalistic integrity, their excessively nega-tive interpretations of media professionalism—as an ideological construction to support the status quo (for example, Hall 1977; Tuchman 1978; Fishman 1980; Gitlin 1980)—seem to have more dubious relevance to Hong Kong. The plu-ralists, who uphold media professionalism as an ideological buffer against arbi-trary state control, seem to throw light on Hong Kong's media under political pressure. In chapter 1 of this volume, I contrast these two perspectives on the political economy of communication. Pertinent to the present context is the fact that norms of professionalism have necessitated media organizations to es-tablish and follow what Gaye Tuchman (1978) calls "strategic rituals." Such rit-uals refer to key routines and conventions—ranging from determination and interpretation of facts, attribution of sources, and credit and blame to choice of narrative forms—developed by media organizations to guide their news-gathering activities and render reality intelligible in ways that would shield them from public criticism. Tuchman (1978) contends that "strategic rituals" tie the media's "news net" too closely to the perspectives of the centrally legit-imated institutions in society. Media professionalism thus serves to reproduce the dominant ideology and marginalize dissent.

While acknowledging the contribution of her brilliant thesis, I am redefining Tuchman's concept—in a more positive tone than she had in-tended—to refer to the peculiar and twisted ways that media organizations routinize their news work in order to credibly meet extraordinary political pressure and to uphold their own limited legitimacy. Since "peculiar" and "twisted" connote something that deviates from "normal" practice, this pro-cess signifies the "normalizing" of the abnormal. Once these "abnormal" practices are gradually absorbed into the stable organizational framework, they are taken for granted as part of the "normal" routine. That said, without any intention to romanticize or overestimate its power, I would contend that media professionalism, by way of developing "strategic rituals," may serve as a "weapon of the weak" (Scott 1988), especially when the weak are devoid of stronger means of resistance. Media professionalism enables journalists and the media to appeal to socially accepted principles of fairness, objectivity, and im-partiality—often in the names of "consumer interests," the public's "right to know," or whatever. By following the established conventions, they are enti-tled to claim superior expertise on their craft and privileged access to facts, the soul of journalism. Possessing media professionalism as an imperfect ideal, they may wedge a greater space to fend their daily practice against external infringement and to justify the society's bestowal of enormous power on the media. This can be as defensive a measure as media self-censorship, even though the results diverge.

In the case of Hong Kong, I have identified three kinds of illustrative "strategic rituals"—juxtaposition, editorial division of labor, and more neutralized forms of narrative—with which the media seek to cope credibly with the uncertain tides of change. More empirical and historical studies are needed to discover or uncover a catalogue—and the structure—of other "strategic rituals."[34] Market competition on the one hand depoliticizes the media, as previously described, and, on the other, obliges them to protect their own fundamental legitimation. The media's effort to establish "strategic rituals" seems quite paradoxical: These rituals sometimes hide the acts of self-censorship but at other times morally justify media workers' resistance to (or subversion of) perceived censorship, and this is a point worthy of further analysis. On the ideological level, however, most Hong Kong journalists subscribe to norms of media professionalism, and perceived media credibility is positively associated with its level of professionalism (Lee et al. 1996; Lee 1998b); any outlet seen as recklessly caving in to China's pressure would not survive in the market. But balancing the need to maintain the appearance of autonomy and the need to minimize political risks is a treacherous task.

JUXTAPOSITION

If given a choice, China would undoubtedly prefer to wield influence on the media informally and subtly rather than to level an assault on them openly. Xinhua has done both. It assembles a sizable coterie of writers in its propaganda department, each given an area of responsibility to watch over several newspapers and rebut unfavorable opinions by firing off their own articles or letters to the editor. Xinhua is known to have applied this tactic for some time. Its ideological straitjacket has not only found its way to the Communist-controlled press in the form of "public commentary" or "citizen's voices," its ghostwritten articles have appeared in the non-Communist press with increasing frequency. How does an editor treat such unsolicited propaganda articles from Xinhua? To ignore or reject them is not a viable policy. The solution may lie in what I would call *juxtaposition*, which means that the editor may, in the same issue, display opposing points of view, sometimes side by side, a practice legitimized by professional canons of balance and objectivity, thus treating

Xinhua's view as one of several views in an ideological spectrum. For the media organization, adopting this "strategic ritual" serves to neutralize cross-pressure, present the least offense to all sides, and, consequently, offer a defense for its own professional reputation.

EDITORIAL DIVISION OF LABOR

Inasmuch as editorial positions are viewed as the responsibility of the media organization, they tend to be more sensitively predisposed to the perspectives of the power structure. Expressions in the popular daily columns, which are a diverse lot and usually buried in the inside pages, are commonly assumed to be at the discretion of individual writers, relatively free from organizational meddling.[35] Many of the popular columns remain lively and excruciatingly critical of Chinese authorities, in contrast to their timid editorial counterparts. With historical precedents, the ideological incongruence between editorial positions and those of individual columnists is preserved as a way to effectively resolve the friction between a desire to dodge political pressure and a need to yield to market demand.[36] The media can defend this inconsistency, strangely, in the name of professionalism. The *Hong Kong Economic Journal,* which offers the most trenchant political commentaries, has continued to rely heavily (as high as about 70 percent) on contributions by freelance writers from various Chinese communities around the world. This has the advantages of saving on overhead costs, ensuring the expression of a diversity of ideological perspectives, and, not insignificantly, shielding the paper itself from the potential ire of the powers that be. Of course, no single pattern of media practice exists. The process of counterhegemony is open-ended, uneven, and contradictory, while there are also severe limits to the sphere of counterhegemony (Williams 1977). Several papers have canceled anti-Communist columns, but critical columnist Lee Yee continues to write a serious daily column for the vulgarly populist *Apple Daily. Ming Pao* has added many soft and nonpolitical columns to make political subjects look less weighty; yet so far as the political subjects are concerned, the paper has deliberately created a semblance of balance by inviting people from divergent ideological ranks to write columns.[37] By so doing, the editor uses the "marketplace" metaphor to underscore the supposed pluralism of voices and, in a way, to absolve himself from moral and political responsibility. Under extraordinary circumstances the Chinese authorities may cajole and pressure individual columnists or publishers, but this undue pressure can only be exercised discreetly. Moreover, publishers can only accommodate this pressure sparingly and selectively. Both sides would seek to avoid embarrassing publicity.

NARRATIVE FORMS

The narrative forms also are part of the emerging "strategic rituals." First, the media would be more likely to criticize the PRC government than to attack its leaders personally. The PRC government or the Communist Party is more ambiguous, abstract, and diffuse than individual leaders as targets of criticism. Chinese leaders have tended to use external media to strengthen their factional position in the internal power struggles (Hood 1994), and media attacks on specific leaders may invite immediate retaliation. In the 1980s, Louis Cha astutely forbade *Ming Pao* to criticize Deng Xiaoping. In the mid-1990s, however, Jimmy Lai paid a heavy price for his personal attack on Premier Li Peng in *Next* magazine. Criticisms of the Chinese authorities would be couched in collective terms, so that it becomes more difficult to fix the blame on specific leaders. Criticisms of particular events or leaders, if any, would also be framed with reference to the selectively interpreted Basic Law.[38]

Second, the elite media are expected to report more straightforward factual accounts while quoting sources in a "neutral" and nonjudgmental way without explicit commentary. Even though the "neutral" news is ultimately embedded in certain enduring values and ideological underpinnings (Tuchman 1978), it is far less thorny than overt opinions in the eyes of power holders. Third, the media may resort more frequently to the "on the one hand, on the other hand" rhetorical format and couch their otherwise critical views behind a cacophony of conditional statements, especially on critical issues. After former governor Patten sniped at the once pro-British privileged class for kowtowing to China (Elliot 1996), the local press scolded him for undermining public confidence but then quickly turned around to urge that China keep a good record to prove Patten's prognosis wrong. This tactic of using circular, ambiguous, and conditional language in the Orwellian Newspeak fashion is a device to smooth the rough edge of criticisms and make them less grating to the ear. The press may also selectively quote paramount leaders of China (such as the officially canonized Deng Xiaoping) as a framework within which to chastise the current policy.

The Question of Press Freedom

Hegemony is not singular, total, or exclusive. It is a process that "has continually to be renewed, recreated, defended, and modified," and is also "continually resisted, limited, altered, challenged" by alternative and oppositional ideologies (Williams 1977:112–13). Political pressure can be ignored, negotiated, compromised, subverted, or fought back against. Control breeds anticontrol. Hong Kong's press freedom will hinge importantly on the contradictory influences of the political economy of the media that involve antijournalistic forces of depoliticization, self-censorship, and media conglomeration against those of professionalism.

History has a different side than the one written from the top. To assume that external forces, imposed from above, are so overwhelming as to render the agency and voices of the Hong Kong people totally impotent would be self-defeating. At many key moments, the Hong Kong people and media have actively deflected China's pressure on issues ranging from Patten's reforms, party formation, and elections to implementation of the Basic Law (Chan and Lee 1991). To cope with the new situation, media organizations have developed a range of professional strategies to absorb or defuse political pressure. Professional ideology has provided a certain political breathing space in which rank-and-file journalists, daily columnists, and professional editors can struggle over various meanings of reality. It is doubtful that China can manipulate all media owners or dismiss all critical writers, especially if they touch on Hong Kong's nerve and command strong popularity.

From the cultural point of view—one that is born in a unique political-economic context—the 1997 issue has bred a new Hong Kong identity differentiated from the Pan-Chinese identity, for it means a test of will to defend one's way of life.[39] This stands in stark contrast to the "refugee mentality" of the 1950s and 1960s, in which grandiose Chineseness subsumed everything that was about Hong Kong. Nowadays, the press is filled with discussions about how to nurture this emerging ethnic identity, and politicians of all colors boast of their "pro-Hong Kong" positions—so much so that even the pro-China party calls itself Democratic Alliance for Betterment of Hong Kong (DABHK), and pro-China candidates, too, present themselves as "pro-Hong Kong" and "prodemocracy." Its leader, Tsang Yok-shing, proclaimed his party as "pro-China, but even more pro-Hong Kong," complaining that the public did not appreciate this point and the media often distorted it. The party also packages itself as a party for grassroots services, not as a "yes-party" to China.[40] After the handover, political parties have converged toward the center on certain public issues to get votes while the SAR government, not Beijing, has had to absorb harsh media criticisms.

Holding the Hong Kong identity to heart is a constituent part of media credibility. It was no small wonder that *Ming Pao* backfired by editorially presenting itself as a paper for all Chinese rather than for the Hong Kong people.

Some pro-China columnists have taken pains to urge Beijing to display greater sensitivity toward the local interests, values, and viewpoints of Hong Kong. This ethnic identity, fueled by the "one country, two systems" rhetoric, may accomplish what political and economic factors have failed to do: put the ball in Beijing's court. Even with its power and resources, China cannot impose full ideological hegemony on the Hong Kong people, who have a deep-seated distrust of the Beijing regime—a sentiment to which the media contribute mightily. Seen in this light, Chris Patten was perhaps not entirely unjustified in saying: "You can dismantle institutions, but I don't think you can destroy the values that have helped make Hong Kong such a special place" (Elliot 1996). In 1998, no sooner had a pro-China figure, Xu Simin, blasted the publicly funded Radio Television Hong Kong (RTHK) at a high-level political conference in Beijing than most Hong Kong media outlets chided him for inviting the central government to intervene in local affairs.[41]

Press freedom is always precarious. It is plainly written in the Sino-British Joint Declaration and the Basic Law. Laws not being self-protective, even the PRC's constitution formally guarantees freedom of speech and the press. Writing and enforcing the law is inherently a political process. Even the interpretations and enforcement of the First Amendment in the United States have fluctuated significantly, with periods in which popular movements demanded broader speech rights (Kairys 1982). Struggle for press freedom is a struggle between the state and the civil society, and a struggle between the political and the economic; in Hong Kong, it will depend substantially on the integrity of the "free market" system, social pluralism, and citizen vigilance.

On the legal front, the Democrats criticized the British throughout the 1990s for being too late and too slow in abolishing draconian colonial laws and in revising other illiberal instruments.[42] China, however, denounced British late conversion to the cause of democracy in the colony as hypocritical, seeking to dismantle Patten's political reforms and to reverse the ordinances he had liberalized. Of the more than forty revised ordinances, six specifically restricted the arbitrary executive power over freedom of assembly, emergency situations, public order, and the management of broadcasting and telecommunications (including the government's authority to revoke licenses on security grounds and to censor films or prebroadcasting television content). To preempt the new sovereign, the colonial government introduced an amendment to the Public Order Ordinance in 1996 that ruled out speech as part of antistate crimes. On the very day of the handover, however, the China-picked Provisional Legislature amended the Public Order and Societies Ordinance to make its coverage more restrictive concerning approval for demonstrations and the formation of societies and organizations. On the question of theft of state secrets, the colonial government contradicted itself by transplanting—with the PRC's tacit consent—the highly inhibiting Official Secrets Act from Britain to Hong Kong without modification, a law that may affect press freedom negatively. The futures of the Bill of Rights and the Freedom of Information Act are dubious. But most ominous is Article 23 of the Basic Law, which authorizes the SAR government to enact laws to prohibit acts of "treason, secession, sedition and subversion against the Central People's Government or theft of state secrets." There is much concern about the importation of China's legal concept—widely framed and severely restrictive—into the Hong Kong common law system (HKJA 1998).

Viewing the process of struggles dynamically, I believe that the multiplicity of political and economic pressures may trigger media reactions in highly situational, erratic, partial, and even contradictory patterns. The media will be cyclically bold and tame, public-spirited and self-serving. Lacking a grand conception about the world, the practically minded editors may deal with the external pressure on an ad hoc and piecemeal basis. As long as a journalist, an editor, or a media organization happens to break a sensitive story at a particular moment, however, other competitors are bound to pick it up and expand it, irrespective of political pressure. As "public goods," information is not exclusively enjoyed by its producers or purchasers; once a story is broken, it enters into the public domain for widespread dissemination, which may then give rise to public attention. Once a story has broken, market competition demands and legitimizes its pursuit by media outlets. In the end, journalists and their organizations have to juggle constantly various sets of pressure against their professional standards and their peers' collective behavior. Hong Kong's vaunted press freedom may have corroded under Chinese rule, but the degree of its societal transparency remains relatively high.

The Sino-British conflict has been replaced by the conflict between the PRC's central government and Hong Kong's local governance. Beijing's emphasis on "one country" is a counterpoint to Hong Kong's preference to highlight "two systems" that grants its autonomy (Chan and Clark 1991), thus foretelling some of the potential rifts in the years ahead. The PRC had hoped to set Hong Kong as an example for wooing Taiwan into reunification, but its military threats against Taiwan in 1995 and 1996 strayed away from this stated course. Whether the aim of courting Taiwan will moderate Beijing's attitude toward Hong Kong is being tested. In sum, the media are expected to defend

Hong Kong's local interests against Beijing's encroachments by offering alternative and sometimes opposing interpretations of reality. Technical issues may be negotiable, but the basic "one country, two systems" policy that constitutes the outer limits of press freedom is not.

One can argue that social and political freedoms are the indispensable "software" to the "hardware" of Hong Kong's economic miracle, and that if the PRC truly values Hong Kong's economic and functional contributions to its modernization, then freedom of the press and free flow of economic information should be a cherished pillar of the Hong Kong success story. Flow of economic and cultural information would not be severely hampered; in many respects the Hong Kong media may improve their interaction with the mainland economic and cultural institutions. The right of the press to report freely about the political authorities and even criticize them is, however, more precarious, but not impossible to achieve and defend. On the political front, Hong Kong has sometimes been wrongly compared to Singapore to underscore the point that economic prosperity can be maintained at the sacrifice of press freedom. This argument seems reminiscent of the theme that economic development serves to consolidate what Guillermo O'Donnell (1973) calls "bureaucratic authoritarianism" rather than to advance democracy. This comparison is, however, misleading. If Hong Kong's press freedom is curtailed from "more" to "less," Singapore could move from having "little" to "some" freedom. Hong Kong is too complex and contradictory to be sanitized, the bud of political activism inspired by the political transition cannot be nipped, and those who have tasted the first fruits of elementary democracy may need more, not less, to satisfy their appetite. As an increasingly pluralistic society with diverse interests, competing ideologies, and different power bases, Hong Kong cannot be pushed back to what it was thirty years ago. It is also doubtful if Singapore's current authoritarian paternalism will survive beyond the strong father figure of Lee Kuan Yew. Furthermore, unless martial law (armed with huge and complex coercive apparatuses) is imposed, neither will Hong Kong's press be as restrictive as its counterparts in Taiwan or South Korea in their days of authoritarian control (Lee 1993). Unless the "one country, two systems" policy totally collapses, Hong Kong's press freedom is unlikely to degenerate to the level existing in mainland China.

The ultimate guarantee of press freedom in Hong Kong lies in China—in China's continued liberalization and its determination to carry out faithfully the "one country, two systems" policy. Economic reform has transformed China from a totalitarian regime into an authoritarian regime, marked by greater tolerance for what Isaiah Berlin (1969) calls "negative freedom" and media diversity in nonpolitical areas, a phenomenon resembling Taiwan under martial law in many ways.[43] But "positive freedom," in Berlin's sense, for democratization is nowhere yet to be seen in China. It should not be overlooked that Hong Kong has begun to set agendas for south China and other coastal provinces in terms of popular culture and media tastes, along with Hong Kong-sponsored trade, financial, and economic undertakings (Gold 1993). In relation to China, a geographically and politically peripheral Hong Kong may act as a center of cultural, economic, and technological innovations (Tu 1991). Beijing's influence on Hong Kong is not necessarily unidirectional, and the "one country, two systems" policy is fraught with tensions and contradictions liable to sway with a host of conditions and issues. A crisis implies an opportunity. These tensions and contradictions will be fertile ground for the struggle against state control, while the glaring incongruity between Beijing's public commitment to Hong Kong and its vacillating policy whims will provide leakage in ideological control. China cannot, in the final analysis, fully close off the public space from liberal struggle in Hong Kong.

Notes

1. As part of the larger project entitled "Mass Media and Political Transition in Hong Kong," on which I am the principal investigator, a project supported with funds from Universities Grants Committee in Hong Kong, this chapter updates Lee (1997) and incorporates perspectives from Lee (1998a, 1998b). The research assistance of Dr. Anthony Fung is gratefully acknowledged.

2. In the mid-1980s, Deng Xiaoping, the paramount leader, boasted that the Communist Party would not be afraid of being "cursed down," but warned the opposing forces in Hong Kong (which presumably included some media outlets) not to incite disturbance or to advocate "two Chinas." After the Tiananmen crackdown, President Jiang Zemin and other leaders lost no time in denouncing Hong Kong and its media for meddling in mainland affairs. The Basic Law has subsequently outlawed "subversive" activities against socialist China, but the line between legitimate criticism and subversion is never clearly drawn. In the 1990s, Beijing has sent the same message using different language, proclaiming that Hong Kong is, historically, an "economic city" rather than a "political center." In their midst, Beijing sarcastically assured the Hong Kong media that they would not lose their discretion to carry pornography, horse racing, and other decadent capitalistic trappings—that is, anything but politically critical materials. Lu Ping, a senior Chinese official, warned that after 1997 "advocating" (rather than "reporting" about) two Chinas would be banned. In 1996, Vice Premier Chen Qichen served notice that the Hong Kong media should not "create falsehood" or "personally attack national leaders" after 1997, but he did not define those terms.

3. This chapter should be read in conjunction with chapter 1, where two approaches to the study of political economy are compared.

4. In 1984, the colonial government issued a white paper intended to develop a more representative polity, with measured steps to increase the number of elected members and to decrease the number of appointed members in the District Boards and the Legislative Council (Ching 1992; Walden 1993). Democratic representation had eluded the British colony for nearly a century and a half, and the sudden change of mind by the British was clearly an attempt to introduce a system that would curtail Beijing's arbitrary power after 1997. The proposal was, however, met with objections from China, particularly vehemently in 1987 and 1988 over the direct election issue.

5. Of the ninety-six Hong Kong members of the Preparatory Committee (an additional sixty-four members are from the mainland), half own major companies and grew rich under the British; they now need mainland friends to stay rich. It has been commented that "business and Communist leaders share a hunger for Hong Kong's wealth, and they need each other to keep it flowing" (see Elliot 1996). In early 1996, the Preparatory Committee obligingly voted, 149 to 1, to scrap Hong Kong's elected Legislative Council after the handover. The lone dissenter was officially reprimanded.

6. The Preparatory Committee selected the Selection Committee. All four hundred Selection Committee members were Hong Kong residents; half of them represented commercial and industrial circles. Sixty-three percent of the members were affiliated with the PRC, including (a) deputies to the National People's Congress or the National People's Political Consultative Committee (15 percent); (b) representatives of the existing leftist elite organizations (23 percent); (c) representatives of the existing leftist grassroots organizations (16 percent); (d) representatives of the newly emerging leftist elite organizations (8 percent); and (e) representatives of the newly emerging leftist grassroots organizations (1 percent). Adding other pro-China politicians to this list, the PRC could effectively control 70 percent of the members. See *Ming Pao,* November 5, 1996.

Four candidates, all acceptable to Beijing, raced for the SAR chief executive post, and the Selection Committee finally chose Tung Chee-hwa by an overwhelming majority. Subsequently, in what the PRC lauded as a "fair" election, the committee further picked sixty members to sit on the Provisional Legislature. Of the sixty members chosen, 85 percent were members of the Selection Committee themselves; another 10 percent bore PRC-appointed posts (including deputies to the provincial-level People's Congresses); only two had no ties with the PRC. See *Ming Pao,* December 24, 1996, C6. In addition, the sixty-member chamber included twenty-three current members and eight former members of the Legislative Council. The largest bloc in the Legislative Council, the Democratic Party, and its allies refused to participate in the process. The chief benefactors were pro-PRC political organizations. Several prominent pro-Beijing members of the Provisional Legislature, including Tsang Yok-shing (the DSBHK party leader), were defeated in the 1995 direct election.

7. Since 1989, Beijing has issued a set of seven regulations to screen and control those media organizations and journalists wishing to report on the mainland. Notably,

the *Apple Daily* has been denied entry into China. Journalists who are permitted to work in China face surveillance from the authorities — at times harassment and detention (HKJA 1998).

8. Mainland refugees increased Hong Kong's population from 1.6 million at the end of 1946 to an estimated 2.36 million by the spring of 1950. The Hong Kong–born population has increased from 32.5 percent in 1931 to 47.7 percent in 1961, to 56.4 percent in 1971, and to 60 percent in 1991. See *Hong Kong 1991 Population Census: Summary Results.*

9. Founded in 1925, at the time of the anticolonial Canton–Hong Kong General Strike–Boycott, the paper warned in its inaugural editorial that the burgeoning tide of Communism would spell a "disaster" for China (Lin 1977). Robert Hotung was part of the local pro-British establishment elite, while his heir, General Ho Shili, had served as Chiang Kai-shek's deputy defense minister.

10. Despite its small circulation and marginal public influence, the *Hong Kong Times* symbolized the presence of Taiwan's KMT, a presence significant enough to warrant a close watch by the colonial regime. Former Governor Edward Youde, a China expert, admitted reading five Chinese-language newspapers daily, including the *Hong Kong Times* and *Wen Wei Po.*

11. When Taiwan was under martial law, the *United Daily News* sided with the KMT's conservative faction, whereas the *China Times* endorsed its liberal wing (Lee 1993). Since martial law was lifted in 1987, the *United Daily News* has supported the conservative splinter group and holdovers of the old KMT regime who are hostile to President Lee, the first Taiwanese president, and to the opposition Democratic Progressive Party (DPP) for advocating secession of Taiwan from China. The DPP's followers had been seeking revenge, and President Lee handed them a perfect opportunity by telling a group of DPP leaders that he was so disgusted with the *United Daily News* as to refuse to read it. This set off a large-scale boycott campaign in 1992 on the unfair charge against the paper as "a Taiwan edition of the *People's Daily.*" The paper lost 90,000 copies in circulation. Its chief rival, *China Times,* also an advocate of Taiwan's ultimate unification with China, has, however, managed to support President Lee without alienating his foes and has even enjoyed some trust from the DPP.

12. Circulation of the *United Daily News* in Hong Kong briefly soared to twenty thousand copies when it serialized an exclusive memoir of Xu Jiatun (Xu 1994), the former director of Xinhua's Hong Kong branch who has taken refuge in the United States since 1990, but it then settled down to a meager three thousand copies. The paper invested a total of HK $2 billion in Hong Kong but lost HK $5 to $6 million in 1994 alone.

13. *China Times,* September 11, 1998, 14.

14. Until the late 1980s, both had borne on their mastheads the official "Republic of China" chronological designation and had celebrated October 10 as the national day of the Nationalist government. Registered in both Hong Kong and Taiwan, they mirrored Hong Kong's prevailing popular sentiment in being mildly critical of the mainland Communist regime (Lee 1985).

15. Having made HK $300 million from Hong Kong's real estate during 1985 and

1989, Aw plunged more deeply into short-term speculations. In one year alone (1988 to 1989), she purchased properties worth HK $500 to $600 million in Canada, Britain, and New Zealand. In early 1989, she acquired a commercial building in Hong Kong for HK $750 million, 90 percent of which was from bank loans, in addition to taking over Culture Communications, which owned the *Tin Tin [Everyday] Daily News*. In late 1989, Aw had incurred a mountain of debt totaling HK $1.96 billion as overseas property markets started to tumble and Hong Kong's market was devastated by the Tiananmen crackdown. She was pressured by major bank creditors to reorganize her board of directors and to refocus on the core publishing business (Zhang 1995a).

16. Aw published a nonpolitical monthly, *Xingguang Monthly (Starlight)*, a joint venture with the *People's Daily*, which was folded on account of "reorganization of the editorial department." Aw published *Shenggang Economic Times* in Shenzhen from 1993 to 1998. *Huanan Jingji Ribao (South China Economic Daily)*, briefly available to mainland subscribers, ceased operation in 1995 (Zhang 1995b, 1995c). In October 1994, her English-language *Hong Kong Standard* was to be printed by the *China Daily* for distribution to Beijing's major tourist hotels, but the three-year contract was abruptly terminated on short notice after only four months (Ji 1995:94). Since April 1995, *Sing Tao Jih Pao* has printed a weekly economic news section produced by Shanghai's *Liberation Daily*, but *Sing Tao*'s news cannot appear in the latter.

17. According to a report by Survey Research Hong Kong (January 1996), the *Oriental Daily News* claimed 26 percent of the total newspaper readership (1.4 million), followed by the *Apple Daily* (23 percent), *Sing Pao* (11 percent), and the *Tin Tin Daily News* (9 percent). The four popular newspapers accounted for 69 percent of the readership. *Ming Pao*, by comparison, captured 7 percent. Note that readership is based on the circulation figure multiplied by a mathematical factor.

18. Its circulation (115,000 copies) accounts for 87 percent of the English-language press market; it is highly profitable and highly respected among journalists.

19. Since Murdoch acquired Star TV in 1994 from the real-estate tycoon Li Ka-shing for U.S. $1 billion, it has not been profitable. The loss in 1996 stood at U.S. $100 million. Advertising dollars, though meager, generated 82 percent of Star TV's revenues, whereas the subscription base was so weak as to account for only 18 percent. This contrasts with a typical cable or satellite television network, which garners 80 percent of its revenues from subscription fees. *Hong Kong Economic Journal*, December 13, 1996.

20. *South China Morning Post*, December 12, 1998.

21. Oei, born in Indonesia and educated in China during the Cultural Revolution, controls China Strategic Investment, which invested U.S. $400 million in China's beer, rubber, and paper-making businesses. He bought China's failing state-owned enterprises and owned up to thirty joint ventures in places like Shaanxi, Hangzhou, Ningbo, and Dalian. Received by top Chinese leaders Jiang Zemin and Li Peng, Oei has been awarded several honorary professorships and advisorships by Chinese universities. But his wheeling and dealing courted a sharp criticism by Beijing's *Financial Times;* Oei denied any wrongdoing and blamed the problem on China's underdeveloped legal system. See *The Nineties*, June 1996, 7–8.

22. In fact, according to Ju (1995a, 1995b), they were far more critical of Taiwan than were several inside-page columns written by Luo Fu (a former deputy chief editor of the Communist-controlled *Ta Kung Pao*, who was once detained in Beijing for several years) and Huang Wenfang (former deputy secretary-general of the local Xinhua branch in charge of the Taiwan affairs).

23. Besides, the day after Wang Dan, a prominent Beijing democratic dissident, was sentenced in 1996 to a eleven-year prison term, most Hong Kong papers published editorials expressing concern. *Ming Pao* was silent on that day. It waited for one more day (and after many phone calls from the readers) to offer an ambiguously worded editorial.

24. The *Oriental Daily News* was once considered pro-Taiwan not because of its content (which was primarily apolitical) but because its owner jumped a jail bond on charges of drug trafficking and had been taking refuge in Taiwan, with which Hong Kong does not have a repatriation treaty.

25. In one year, the *Apple Daily* firmly captured one quarter of the circulation but only accounted for 10 percent of the total newspaper advertising revenues. See *Hong Kong Economic Journal*, August 9, 1996, 4.

26. *China Times*, November 22, 1996. Two former top assistants to Lai told me that Lai would or would not be an anti-Communist publisher depending on whether anti-Communism is a profitable commodity.

27. The price of newsprint rose from between U.S. $300 and $400 to between U.S. $700 and $800 per ton. According to Dharmala Securities, newsprint accounts for 43 percent of the total cost for the *Oriental Daily News;* the corresponding figures are 20 percent for *SCMP,* 30 percent for *Ming Pao,* and 16 percent for *Sing Tao Jih Pao.*

28. Hong Kong dollars have been pegged to U.S. dollars at the rate of 7.74 to 1.

29. During the six months from March to September in 1996, the Oriental Press group and the Sing Tao group posted a gain of HK $30.07 million and $4.92 million (or 78.3 percent and 76.2 percent drops from March to September 1995), while *Ming Pao* reported a loss of $18.53 million. See *Hong Kong Economic Journal*, December 28, 1996, 9.

30. This section is adapted from Lee (1998a).

31. For example, Edward Gargan, "New Hong Kong Editor: He Edits What, Exactly?" *International Herald Tribune,* April 18, 1997; Joseph Kahn, "A Hong Kong Newspaper Softens its Voice," *Asian Wall Street Journal,* April 22, 1997.

32. It should be noted that Lee and Chu (1988) offer a model which is too formalistic and too static to account for the dynamic interplay between political and economic factors. Their overemphasis on political determinants neglects the economic logic as a potential countervailing check on state power.

33. When the Democratic Party leaders toured North America in early 1997 to raise funds, many of the rallies they attended turned into embarrassing forums against *Ming Pao*'s alleged pro-Beijing attitude — especially in Vancouver and Toronto, cities which in the last decade have seen an influx of more than 600,000 Hong Kong emigrants of middle-class and professional backgrounds (people relocating there precisely

out of fear of China's takeover of the colony) and in which *Ming Pao* publishes its local editions. The paper did not escape the public eye when it, along with the Communist press, blackened its usually red masthead to mourn the death of China's paramount leader, Deng Xiaoping. Public attacks on its credibility, fueled by a notable decline in circulation and the resignation of disgruntled senior reporters, seemed to have curbed the pace of *Ming Pao*'s caving in to Beijing's pressure. Its tendency toward vulgarization, however, remains unabated.

34. It is a painstaking task to identify the dynamics of discursive formation in the media. My colleagues and I will do several case studies involving press coverage of the June 4 candlelight vigils (since 1990), the death of Deng Xiaoping, the PRC's national day on October 1 (since 1990), the selection of the SAR chief executive and the Provisional Legislature, and China's missile threats off Taiwan's waters in 1995 and 1996.

35. A typical paper prints about fifteen small daily columns covering a wide range of topics (many on politics, but others on historical events, cultural criticism, food and wine, and moneymaking), all commissioned to freelance writers rather than penned by its own staff. Though varying in nature and quality—some serious and well researched; some witty and lighthearted; some sarcastic; others esoteric—these columns overall approximate a vital intellectual "public sphere" (in a Habermasian sense) where diverse, even opposing, views are expressed and often debated.

36. In the 1980s, most of *Ming Pao*'s editorials, which were composed by Louis Cha, endorsed China's major policies, while many of the columns it carried, especially one by the satirist Ha Gong, were devastatingly critical of Beijing. Cha confided to Xu Jiatun, Xinhua's head, that he retained Ha Gong because the column was popular, not because Cha agreed with Ha. Xu expressed his understanding, saying that, had Cha not invited Ha Gong to write, other papers would have lost no time in doing so (Xu 1994). Xu had actively befriended many other anti-Communist writers, but their carefully cultivated cordiality was later undermined by his hard-line successor.

37. Among them are Szeto Hwa, a noted China critic and Democratic Party leader; a writer from Xinhua; and another younger critical writer. Having for years inveighed against *Ming Pao* for its softened position on China, Szeto decided to accept its invitation to write a column twice weekly only because he felt that his party should maintain a media forum. In his inaugural column, he warned the paper not to use him as a propaganda ploy. He has continued to rebuke *Ming Pao* in his column from time to time—something that the editors cannot help but swallow.

38. For example, when Beijing sentenced a leading student dissident, Wang Dan, to a second prison term of eleven years in 1996, almost all Hong Kong media—from *Ming Pao* to *Ta Kung Pao*—argued that, after 1997, Hong Kong should be ruled by the Basic Law rather than the PRC's laws. From that premise, each paper proceeded to offer different views. Wang was released to the United States in 1998 before President Clinton's visit to China.

39. A poll by the Chinese University of Hong Kong found that 36 percent of Hong Kong's people see themselves as Chinese, while 49 percent identify themselves as "Hongkongese." See *New York Times,* June 8, 1996, 4.

40. *Eastweek,* August 11, 1993.

41. China had never been fond of RTHK. In the mid-1980s, the British aborted an attempt, under China's pressure, to turn RTHK from a government unit to an autonomous public corporation like the BBC (Davies 1993). China insisted on having a right to use RTHK as a propaganda arm after 1997. Instead of being a propaganda arm, according to Xu's complaint, RTHK took an adversarial posture toward Beijing and Tung Chee-hua. Beijing leaders quickly dissociated themselves from Xu and announced that it would be a matter for the SAR government to decide.

42. Hong Kong's ordinances run into the hundreds, of which more than thirty bear direct relevance to the media. Had these all been faithfully executed, Hong Kong would have written a very dark page in the history of press freedom. Many of the ordinances were enacted to cope with the leftist forces, but the British have generally refrained from invoking them. It was feared that such ordinances would assist the Chinese regime that was only too eager to control.

43. For media changes in China, see White (1990), Yu (1990), Dittmer (1994), Zhao (1998), and many chapters (especially those by Pan, He, Lynch, and Rosen) in this volume. To draw a comparison between the PRC and Taiwan, see Lee (1994).

Bibliography

Allen, Jamie. 1997. *Seeing Read China's Uncompromising Takeover of Hong Kong.* Singapore: Butterworth-Heinemann Asia.

Allport, Floyd. 1937. "Toward a Science of Public Opinion." *Public Opinion Quarterly* 1:7–23.

Bennett, Lance. 1990. "Toward a Theory of Press-State Relations in the United States." *Journal of Communication* 40(2):103–25.

Bennett, Lance, Lynn Gressett, and William Haltom. 1985. "Repairing the News: A Case Study of the News Paradigm." *Journal of Communication* 35(2):50–68.

Berlin, Isaiah. 1969. *Four Essays on Liberty.* Oxford: Oxford University Press.

Boulding, Kenneth. 1990. *Three Faces of Power.* Newbury Park, Calif.: Sage.

Breed, Warren. 1955. "Socialization in the Newsroom." *Social Forces* 33:326–36.

Caporaso, James A., and David P. Levine. 1992. *Theories of Political Economy.* New York: Cambridge University Press.

Chan, Joseph Man, and Chin-Chuan Lee. 1984. "Journalistic Paradigms on Civil Protests: A Case Study in Hong Kong." In Andrew Arno and Wimal Dissanayake, eds., *The News Media in National and International Conflict.* Boulder, Colo.: Westview.

———. 1988. "Press Ideology and Organization Control in Hong Kong." *Communication Research* 15(2):185–97.

———. 1991. *Mass Media and Political Transition: The Hong Kong Press in China's Orbit.* New York: Guilford.

Chan, Joseph Man, Paul Siu-nam Lee, and Chin-Chuan Lee. 1996. *Hong Kong Journalists in Transition*. Hong Kong: Chinese University of Hong Kong, Hong Kong Center of Asia-Pacific Studies.

Chan, Ming K., and David Clark, eds. 1991. *The Hong Kong Basic Law: Blueprint for "Stability and Prosperity" under Chinese Sovereignty?* Hong Kong: Hong Kong University Press.

Chan, Ming K., and Tuen-yu Lau. 1990. "Dilemma of the Communist Press in a Pluralistic Society." *Asian Survey* 30(8):731–47.

Ching, Frank. 1991. "Implementation of the Sino-British Joint Declaration." In Joseph Y. S. Cheng and Paul C. K. Kwong, eds., *The Other Hong Kong Report, 1992*. Hong Kong: Chinese University Press.

Chomsky, Noam. 1989. *Necessary Illusions*. Boston: South End Press.

Cohen, Stanley, and Jock Young, eds. 1981. *The Manufacture of News*. Beverly Hills, Calif.: Sage.

Dahlgren, Peter. 1995. *Television and the Public Sphere*. London: Sage.

Davies, Simon T. 1993. "Hong Kong Broadcasting." In Po-King Choi and Lok-sang Ho, eds., *The Other Hong Kong Report, 1993*. Hong Kong: Chinese University Press.

Dimbleby, Jonathan. 1997. *The Last Governor*. London: Warner Books.

Dittmer, Lowell. 1994. "The Politics of Publicity in Reform China." In Chin-Chuan Lee, ed., *China's Media, Media's China*. Boulder, Colo.: Westview.

Donohue, George A., Phillip Tichenor, and Clarice Olien. 1995. "A Guard Dog Perspective on the Role of Media." *Journal of Communication* 45(2):115–32.

Donsbach, Wolfgang, and Bettina Klett. 1993. "Subjective Objectivity. How Journalists in Four Countries Define a Key Term of their Profession." *Gazette* 51:53–83.

Dreier, Peter. 1982. "The Position of the Press in the U.S. Power Structure." *Social Forces* 29:298–310.

Elliot, Dorinda. 1996. "Betrayed?" *Newsweek*, May 13, 37–38.

Entman, Robert M. 1989. *Democracy without Citizens: Media and the Decay of American Politics*. New York: Oxford University Press.

Fishman, Mark. 1980. *Manufacturing the News*. Austin: University of Texas Press.

Freiberg, J. W. 1981. *The French Press: Class, State and Ideology*. New York: Praeger.

Fung, Anthony, and Chin-Chuan Lee. 1994. "Hong Kong's Changing Media Ownership: Uncertainty and Dilemma." *Gazette* 53:127–33.

Galbraith, Kenneth. 1983. *The Anatomy of Power*. Boston: Houghton Mifflin.

Gans, Herbert. 1974. *Popular Culture and High Culture*. New York: Basic Books.

———. 1979. *Deciding What's News*. New York: Pantheon.

Gargan, Edward. 1996. "New Jitters from Hong Kong: In Economics, as in Politics, China Exerts Control." *New York Times*, May 18.

Garnham, Nicholas. 1990. *Capitalism and Communication*. London: Sage.

Gitlin, Todd. 1980. *The Whole World Is Watching*. Berkeley: University of California Press.

Gold, Thomas. 1993. "Go With Your Feelings: Hong Kong and Taiwan Popular Culture in Greater China." *China Quarterly* 136:907–25.

Golding, Peter, and Graham Murdock. 1991. "Culture, Communications, and Political

Economy." In James Curran and Michael Gurevitch, eds., *Mass Media and Society.* New York: Arnold.

Hadenius, Stig. 1983. "The Rise and Possible Fall of the Swedish Party Press." *Communication Research* 10:287–310.

Hall, Stuart. 1977. "Culture, the Media and the 'Ideological Effect.'" In James Curran, Michael Gurevitch, and Janet Woollacott, eds., *Mass Communication and Society.* London: Arnold.

Hallin, Daniel. 1986a. "Cartography, Community, and the Cold War." In Robert Manoff and Michael Schudson, eds., *Reading the News.* New York: Pantheon.

———. 1986b. *The "Uncensored" War.* New York: Oxford University Press.

Harding, Harry. 1993. "The Concept of Greater China: Themes, Variations and Reservations." *China Quarterly* 136:660–86.

Harris, Peter. 1978. *Hong Kong: A Study in Bureaucratic Politics.* Hong Kong: Heinemann Asia.

Herman, Edward, and Noam Chomsky. 1988. *Manufacturing Consent.* New York: Pantheon.

HKEJ. 1995. "Jimmy Lai: 'I Have No Obligation to Take Care of My Opponents.'" *Hong Kong Economic Journal,* June 20 (in Chinese).

Ho, Leung-mou. 1996. "China News in the Hong Kong Press." Unpublished M.Phil. thesis, Chinese University of Hong Kong (in Chinese).

Hong Kong Journalists Association (HKJA). 1996. "China's Challenge: Freedom of Expression in Hong Kong." Annual report.

———. 1997. "The Die Is Cast: Freedom of Expression in Hong Kong on the Eve of the Handover of China." Annual report.

———. 1998. "Questionable Beginnings: A Report on Freedom of Expression in the Hong Kong SAR One Year after the Change of Sovereignty." Annual report.

Hood, Marlowe. 1994. "The Use and Abuse of Mass Media by Chinese Leaders During the 1980s." In Chin-Chuan Lee, ed., *China's Media, Media's China.* Boulder, Colo.: Westview.

Jansen, Sue Curry. 1991. *Censorship.* New York: Oxford University Press.

Ji, Wen. 1995. "Hong Kong Media." *Nineties Monthly,* February, 94–95 (in Chinese).

Ju, Zhong. 1995a. "Assumptions Behind Commentaries on Taiwan." *Hong Kong Economic Journal,* July 13–14 (in Chinese).

———. 1995b. "Listen to the Voices of People on Taiwan." *Hong Kong Economic Journal,* June 20, 22 (in Chinese).

Kairys, David. 1982. "Freedom of Speech." In David Kairys, ed., *The Politics of Law: A Progressive View.* New York: Pantheon.

Keane, John. 1991. *The Media and Democracy.* Cambridge: Polity Press.

Kelman, Herbert C. 1961. "Processes of Opinion Change." *Public Opinion Quarterly* 25:57–78.

King, Ambrose Y. C. 1975. "Administrative Absorption of Politics: Emphasis on the Grass Roots Level." *Asian Survey* 15:422–39.

King, Ambrose. 1988. "The Hong Kong Talks and Hong Kong Politics." In Jürgen Domes and Yu-ming Shaw, eds., *Hong Kong: A Chinese and International Concern.* Boulder, Colo.: Westview.

Kocher, R. 1986. "Bloodhounds or Missionaries: Role Definitions of German and British Journalists." *European Journal of Communication* 1:46–65.

Lang, Gladys, and Kurt Lang. 1981. *Battling for Public Opinion.* New York: Columbia University Press.

Lau, Siu-kai. 1982. *Society and Politics in Hong Kong.* Hong Kong: Chinese University Press.

———. 1992. "Hong Kong People's View of the Government." *Wide Angle Monthly,* No. 238.

Lee, Chin-Chuan. 1985. "Partisan Press Coverage of Government News in Hong Kong." *Journalism Quarterly* 62:770–76.

———. 1993. "Sparking a Fire: The Press and the Ferment of Democratic Change in Taiwan." *Journalism Monographs,* No. 138. Also included in Chin-Chuan Lee, ed. *China's Media, Media's China.* Boulder, Colo.: Westview.

———. 1994. "Ambiguities and Contradictions: Issues in China's Changing Political Communication." In Chin-Chuan Lee, ed., *China's Media, Media's China.* Boulder, Colo.: Westview.

———. 1997. "Media Structure and Regime Change in Hong Kong." In Ming K. Chan, ed., *The Challenge of Hong Kong's Reintegration with China.* Hong Kong: Hong Kong University Press.

———. 1998a. "Conglomeration, Professionalism, and Strategic Rituals: The Hong Kong Press and Political Transition." Paper presented at the annual convention of the International Communication Association, Jerusalem, July 20–25.

———. 1998b. "Press Self-Censorship and Political Transition in Hong Kong." *Harvard International Journal of Press/Politics* 3(2):55–73.

Lee, Chin-Chuan, and Joseph Man Chan. 1990a. "Government Management of the Press in Hong Kong." *Gazette* 46:125–39.

———. 1990b. "The Hong Kong Press in China's Orbit: Thunder of Tiananmen." In Chin-Chuan Lee, ed., *Voices of China: The Interplay of Politics and Journalism.* New York: Guilford.

Lee, Chin-Chuan, Chi-hsien Chen, Joseph Man Chan, and Paul Siu-nam Lee. 1996. "Partisanship and Professionalism: Hong Kong Journalists in Transition." *Gazette* 57:1–15.

Lee, Paul Siu-nam, and Leonard Chu. 1998. "Inherent Dependence on Power: The Hong Kong Press in Political Transition." *Media, Culture and Society* 20:59–77.

Lin, You-lan. 1977. *History of the Hong Kong Press.* Taipei: World (in Chinese).

Lukes, Steven. 1974. *Power: A Radical View.* London: Macmillan.

Man, Cheuk-fei. 1996. "How Did Xinhua Launch its Propaganda Work through the Leftist Newspapers (1949–1982)?" *Hong Kong Economic Journal Monthly* 226 (January):10–17.

Manoff, Robert K., and Michael Schudson, eds. 1986. *Reading the News.* New York: Pantheon.

McManus, John H. 1994. *Market-Driven Journalism.* Thousand Oaks, Calif.: Sage.

Miners, N. J. 1977. *The Government and Politics in Hong Kong.* Hong Kong: Oxford University Press.

Mitchell, Robert E. 1969. "How Hong Kong Newspapers Have Responded to 15 Years of Rapid Social Change." *Asian Survey* 9:673–78.

Mosco, Vincent. 1996. *The Political Economy of Communication.* London: Sage.

Murdock, Graham. 1982. "Large Corporations and the Control of the Communication Industries." In Michael Gurevitch, Tony Bennett, James Curran, and Janet Woollacott, eds., *Culture, Society, and the Media.* New York: Methuen.

Noelle-Neumann, Elisabeth. 1984. *The Spiral of Silence.* Chicago: University of Chicago Press.

O'Donnell, Guillermo A. 1973. *Modernization and Bureaucratic-Authoritarianism.* Berkeley: Institute of International Studies, University of California.

Patten, Christopher. 1998. *East and West: China, Power, and the Future of Asia.* New York: Random House.

Patterson, Thomas E., and Wolfgang Donsbach. 1993. "Press-Party Parallelism: A Cross-National Comparison." Paper presented at the International Communication Association conference, Washington, D.C., May 28.

Pool, Ithiel de Sola. 1952. *Prestige Papers.* Stanford, Calif.: Stanford University Press.

Qi, Xin [Lee Yee]. 1993. "To the Granddaddy Up There, Your Little Servant Confesses a Mistake." *Hong Kong Economic Journal,* October 18 (in Chinese).

Said, Edward. 1981. *Covering Islam.* New York: Pantheon.

Schlesinger, Peter. 1978. *Putting "Reality" Together.* Beverly Hills, Calif.: Sage.

Schudson, Michael. 1978. *Discovering the News.* New York: Basic.

Scott, James. 1988. *Weapons of the Weak.* New Haven, Conn.: Yale University Press.

Seymour-Ure, Colin. 1974. *The Political Impact of Mass Media.* Beverly Hills, Calif.: Sage.

Shu, Yufei. 1985. "The *Hong Kong Times*'s Quarrel in Taipei," *Nineties Monthly,* March (in Chinese).

Sigelman, Lee. 1973. "Reporting the News: An Organizational Analysis." *American Journal of Sociology,* 72:132–51.

So, Clement Y. K. 1996. "Pre-1997 Hong Kong Press: Cut-throat Competition and the Changing Journalistic Paradigm." In Mee Kau Nyaw and Si Ming Li, eds., *The Other Hong Kong Report, 1996.* Hong Kong: Chinese University Press.

So, Clement Y. K., Chin-Chuan Lee, and Anthony Fung. 1996. "How Do Media Workers View Press Credibility?" *Ming Pao,* December 5, C5.

Song, Lingqi. 1995. "The Infighting Between the Two Leftist Papers." *Open Monthly,* May, 74–75 (in Chinese).

Staniland, Martin. 1985. *What Is Political Economy?* New Haven, Conn.: Yale University Press.

Suine, Karen. 1987. "The Political Role of Mass Media in Scandinavia." *Legislative Studies Quarterly* 12:395–415.

Tse, Patricia Wen-sei. 1995. "The Impact of 1997 on Political Apathy in Hong Kong." *Political Quarterly,* 210–20.

Tu, Weiming. 1991. "Cultural China: The Periphery as the Center." *Daedalus* 120 (2)1–32.

Tuchman, Gaye. 1978. *Making News.* New York: Free Press

Walden, John. 1993. "Implementation of the Sino-British Joint Declaration." In Po-king Choi and Lok-sang Ho, eds., *The Other Hong Kong Report, 1993.* Hong Kong: Chinese University Press.

Weaver, David, and G. Cleveland Wilhoit. 1996. *The American Journalist in the 1990s.* Mahwah, N.J.: Lawrence Erlbaum.

White, Lynn T., III. 1990. "All the News: Structure and Politics in Shanghai's Reform Media." In Chin-Chuan Lee, ed., *Voices of China: The Interplay of Politics and Journalism.* New York: Guilford.

Wilensky, Harold. 1964. "Mass Society and Mass Culture: Interdependence or Dependence?" *American Sociological Review* 29:173–97.

Williams, Raymond. 1977. *Marxism and Literature.* New York: Oxford University Press.

Xu, Jiatun. 1994. *Hong Kong Memoirs.* 2 vols. Hong Kong: United Daily News (in Chinese).

Yoon, Youngchul. 1989. "Political Transition and Press Ideology in South Korea, 1980–1989." Ph.D. diss., University of Minnesota.

Yu, Jinglu. 1990. "The Structure and Function of Chinese Television, 1979–1989." In Chin-Chuan Lee, ed., *Voices of China: The Interplay of Politics and Journalism.* New York: Guilford.

Zhang, Shengru. 1995a. "Hu Xian [Sally Aw]: The Tigress Who Inherits Her Father's Fortune." *Next,* No. 257, February 10, 86–90 (in Chinese).

———. 1995b. "The Rise and Fall of Hu Xian." *Next,* No. 259, February 24, 102–8 (in Chinese).

———. 1995c. "The Tigress Who Turned the Paper Profitable." *Next,* No. 258, February 17, 98–104 (in Chinese).

Zhao, Yuezhi. 1998. *Media, Market and Democracy in China: Between the Party Line and the Bottom Line.* Urbana: University of Illinois Press.

11

Mainland Chinese News in Taiwan's Press

The Interplay of Press Ideology, Organizational Strategies, and News Structure

RAN WEI

Contradictory and multifaceted changes have characterized Taiwan's press coverage of mainland China. The decades-old anti-Communist propaganda has given way to press fever for mainland reporting in the late 1980s followed by a coexistence of paradoxes in the 1990s. These developments reveal patterns of interaction between sociopolitical changes and the behaviors of news organizations. This chapter intends to analyze the changes in mainland Chinese news within the contexts of Taiwan's democratic transition and the intensified competition in its media market.[1] Specifically, it examines the interplay of external political, market, and social forces with internal factors of organizational ownership, ideology, and structure. The central concerns include the following: (1) What are the influences that impinged on the press coverage of mainland China ideologically, strategically, and structurally? (2) How did different types of press respond organizationally to the pressure of and constraints on mainland China reporting? (3) And to what extent do the environmental uncertainties and tensions set the boundaries for mainland China coverage? I shall start by viewing historically the three stages of mainland China reporting and will then offer a conceptual explication of key influences and an organizational analysis of Taiwan's leading newspaper organizations.

Press Structure in Taiwan and Stages of Mainland China Coverage

Shortly after the Republic of China (ROC) government took refuge in Taiwan in 1949, the ruling Kuomintang (the Nationalist Party, hereafter the KMT)

imposed martial law on the island. Under martial law, a political system characteristic of one-party authoritarian rule took shape (Tien 1989; Winckler 1984),
in which the press was explicitly subjected to the domination of the KMT ideology and pervasive government control (Lee 1992; 1994). The government relied particularly on the "press ban" imposed in 1951 to shape and restrict press
coverage (Chen and Chu 1987). The ban froze the total number of newspapers
at thirty-one, limited the number of pages per issue to eight, and restricted publication to a single location, be it in northern, central or southern Taiwan.

Furthermore, half of the thirty-one papers permitted to publish were owned
by what Chin-Chuan Lee (1994) calls the "triple alliance" of the KMT, the government, and the military; chief among them were the *Central Daily News* (the
KMT's major organ), the *Taiwan New Life Daily* (owned by the government), the
Youth Daily News and the *Taiwan Daily News* (both controlled by the military).
They formed the core of the "official press," competing with the privately
owned "Big Two" (the mass-circulated *United Daily News* and *China Times*) and
the so-called Ben Tu Pao (the indigenous press), those papers owned and run by
local-born Taiwanese.[2] Because the "press ban" policy allowed for the existing
newspapers to be traded while maintaining the total number of newspapers at
thirty-one, the *United Daily News* and the *China Times* were able to purchase additional newspaper licenses to form giant press groups.

Ideologically, the official press took the orthodox anti-Communist stance.
Financially, the party and government papers received preferential treatment in
subscription sales and advertising booking. The KMT-owned *Central Daily
News* was the leading mouthpiece. The military *Youth Daily News* and the *Taiwan Daily News,* controlled by the Department of National Defense, were explicitly designated as vehicles for "political warfare" against the Communist
regime across the Taiwan Strait. Staffed by military personnel, these two papers
were both conservative and intolerant of liberal intellectual critics (Lee 1994).
Government offices and public schools were required to subscribe to the *Central Daily News* or other government-run dailies. Besides, government agencies
and offices gave primary consideration to the official papers in buying advertisement space. Not surprisingly, the official press claimed more than 80 percent of newspaper circulation in the 1950s and 1960s, but that percentage
gradually declined in the 1970s due to strong competition from the emerging
"Big Two." The chronic decline made the official press hover near bankruptcy
in the 1980s.

The KMT-led government's control of the commercial "Big Two" and
other private newspapers, in comparison, was "less than total" and "indirect"

(Chen and Chaudhary 1990:255). In discussing different types of press control, Chan and Lee (1991:28) referred to them as an example of state incorporation, in which the press "garners huge profits from crass commercialism or state favoritism, while politically subservient to the state." Rather insignificant in the 1950s and 1960s, the *United Daily News* and the *China Times* came to challenge the dominance of the official press when they surpassed a million each in circulation in the early 1980s. Accounting for two-thirds of Taiwan's total circulation of 3.5 million, they left the official papers far behind in market shares and clout (Goldstein 1985). Shortly afterward, the owners of these two giants replaced the publisher of the KMT-owned *Central Daily News* in holding a seat on the elite KMT standing committee, which is the most powerful decision-making body within the ruling party.

The dominance of the "Big Two" dwarfed other privately owned newspapers, particularly those owned and run by native Taiwanese, such as the *Independence Evening Post* and the *Minchung Daily News* (Lee 1998). These papers continuously struggled for survival in the limited market niches left by the "Big Two" and the official press, numbering no more than a half dozen papers at any one time. Even the once influential *Independence Evening Post* had a circulation of less than 100,000 (Chen and Chu 1987).

Under martial law, for a long time, no newspapers except the official ones were allowed to handle mainland China reporting to fulfill their mission as state propaganda apparatuses. Mainland Chinese news had been off-limits to privately owned papers in the name of "maintaining national security." The monopoly of the official press over mainland China reporting was broken in the mid-1980s when the KMT-led government, in an effort to strengthen its anti-Communist publicity campaign, granted the "Big Two" the privilege of starting their own in-house libraries to process mainland news. They relied heavily on secondary sources, mostly foreign news agencies, such as Reuters, Associate Press, United Press International, Agence France-Presse, and Kyodo; mainland Chinese news agencies, namely Xinhua and China News Service; publications from Hong Kong; and Taiwan's official Central News Agency. The coverage was characterized by one critic as "little in amount and devoid of substance" (Rong 1994). Readers were largely indifferent to news about the mainland during this period because it contained nothing but anti-Communist slogans and official pronouncements of little interest or relevance to them.

After martial law was lifted in 1987, however, mainland Chinese news became a hot topic almost overnight, reaching a peak during the Tiananmen protests in 1989. As opportunities emerged for Taiwan residents to visit the

Chinese mainland, the general public showed a strong interest in mainland reporting that focused on home visits, family reunions, and sightseeing spots to satisfy their deeply ingrained curiosity about the mainland. Official clichés in mainland Chinese news became obscure. It was during this period that the giant *United Daily News* and *China Times* started their own mainland news pages, paralleling those in the official *Central Daily News* and *Youth Daily News.* The "Big Two" also built up an unprecedentedly large mainland news division, employing a staff of some twenty journalists. Even small-scale indigenous papers added a "Mainland China" page for the first time in their history. Altogether, a total of twelve newspapers, about one-third of Taiwan's press, set up a page devoted to mainland news (Press Council 1996:17).

These unprecedented developments in mainland China coverage took place in the context of rapid sociopolitical changes in Taiwan. First, the monopoly of political power by the ruling KMT came to an end in 1987. The first real opposition party, the Democratic Progressive Party (hereafter the DPP), was formed. The DPP has pursued a dual goal of democratizing Taiwan on the one hand, and indigenizing the mainlander-dominated power structure on the other (Tien 1989). Local-born politicians who had been deprived of political participation now had more opportunities than ever before to share power with the dominant yet minority mainlander politicians. Significant inroads made by the DPP in gaining legislative seats through popular votes ushered in competitive party politics.[3] The growth of the opposition party was coupled with a surge of social movements. The dominant majority of native Taiwanese (85 percent of the total population), whose full political rights had been suppressed, began to voice social dissent on a wide range of issues. Some seventeen social movements were observed in 1988, ranging from consumer and environmental protection to feminist and student rights (Hsiao 1989:7). The number of interest groups at the grassroots level also surged to a record high of one thousand (Zich 1993:20). A pluralistic society was taking shape as the decades-old KMT authoritarian rule phased out.

The government attempted to balance considerations of political democratization (thus indigenization) with those of accommodation with mainland China. The sweeping political reforms also led to a shift in the government's policy toward the Chinese mainland. In 1987, many of the mainlanders who had followed the KMT to Taiwan in 1949 were allowed for the first time to visit their relatives left behind on the mainland. Four years later, the government further declared an end to the state of war with the People's Republic of China (PRC). Increasing relaxation of cross-strait tensions brought about increasing people-to-people contacts through exchange of goods and tourist travel. Taiwanese businessmen played a leading role in establishing close ties with the mainland by investing a total of U.S. $3 billion during the later 1980s and early 1990s (*Republic of China Yearbook* 1993:145). Mainland China has become a "critical variable" affecting Taiwan's politics and economy (Lasater 1990:65).

Coterminous with these developments, the press market was thrown open in January 1988, a change marked by the lifting of the thirty-seven-year "press ban." Soon enough, within two and a half years, the number of newspapers mushroomed from 31 to 216 (*Republic of China Yearbook* 1992:315). Although very few of the new papers have gained significant market strongholds, competition among the established outlets intensified. Meanwhile, the government retreated from press control; mainland China reporting was no longer taboo. (For a detailed political-economy analysis of the media structure in post-martial-law Taiwan, see Lee [2000].) The sweeping political reforms have created a liberal and tolerant climate that enabled Taiwan journalists to cover the mainland firsthand and to conduct one-on-one interviews with top mainland officials. As thousands of Taiwan's mainlander parents brought their children to the "mysterious" homeland, after being cut off from it for forty years, the press jumped on the mainland bandwagon. Mainland news now became a key basis for competition among the Taiwanese newspapers.

The intensified competition added fuel to the aggressive, sometimes reckless pursuit of breakthroughs in mainland reporting. Newspapers had to figure out ways to outsmart each other, as scooping was the name of the game in the postban years, and mainland news of substance provided the right ingredients for exclusive reporting. Covering the post-Mao market reforms in China, as Wang Chen-bang (1994), mainland news editor of the *United Daily News,* put it, opened up "a whole new world." Mainland coverage presented different opportunities and challenges to the official press, the "Big Two," and the indigenous press.

Shortly after the "mainland craze" between 1987 and 1989 subsided, mainland China coverage entered a new stage in the 1990s, one marked by contradictory developments. The three types of press have shown differential performance in their reporting on mainland China. The "Big Two" continued to be enthusiastic about giving mainland Chinese news a high priority, with a news hole consistently large and always increasing. The staff involved in producing mainland news, including the mainland beat, has increased steadily, and now numbers twenty.

In contrast to the actions of the "Big Two," at this point the indigenous papers cooled off the enthusiasm for reporting mainland news that they had displayed in 1989. Mainland news no longer commanded a priority. The editorial space devoted to mainland reporting had ups and downs but has in general decreased. Staff in charge of mainland news fluctuated between assigning and not assigning the mainland beat. Even when a mainland staff existed, however, its size never exceeded two people. The official papers fell in between the "Big Two" and the indigenous papers. Characteristically, they covered news from mainland China with an attitude neither enthusiastic nor unenthusiastic, but lukewarm. Mainland news was not neglected, but neither was it a priority. The news hole assigned to mainland news stayed at about a half page. The size of staff responsible for mainland coverage, too, was constant, hovering at around five. Table 11.1 summarizes the differential performance on mainland China coverage among the three types of press.

The handover of Hong Kong to Chinese rule in July 1997 revived press interest in covering mainland China. A total of 528 reporters representing forty-two Taiwan-based news organizations reported firsthand the departure of the last British governor, Chris Patten, and the founding of the Special Administrative Region (*Asia News* 1997:24). However, the revival proved to be short-lived, by no means comparable to the 1989 peak.

Table 11.1. Differential Performance on Mainland Coverage
in Taiwan's Three Types of Press

	Official Press	**"Big Two"**	**Indigenous Press**
Representative newspapers	*Central Daily News* *Youth Daily News* *China Daily News* *Taiwan Daily News*	*United Daily News* *China Times*	*Independence Evening Post* *Liberty Times* *Taiwan Times* *Minchung Daily News*
Attitude toward mainland coverage	Lukewarm	Enthusiastic	Apathetic
Editorial priority given to mainland news	Low	High	None
Editorial space devoted to mainland news	News hole stable	Sustained increase in news hole	Decrease in news hole
Staff size charged with mainland reporting	Medium (about 5)	Large (about 20)	Small (fewer than 2)

Press Ideology, Business Strategies, and News Structure

As James Mann (1999:106) argues, mainland China is "too big, too complex and too diverse to be captured in a single or simplistic frame." Moreover, amidst the emergence of ideological diversity and the development of different business strategies in the Taiwan press, mainland China coverage became a site of ideological contestation between the mainlander-owned papers that stress Taiwan's shared origin with the mainland and those indigenous papers that emphasize Taiwan's native origin and its yearning for secession from China.

IDEOLOGICAL REALIGNMENT

The influence of press ideology is one of the "most important aspects of a news media organization's control" (Chan and Lee 1988:194). John Plamenatz (1970:15) defines it conceptually as "a set of closely related beliefs or ideas, or even attitudes, characteristic of a group or community." Critical theorists (Gitlin 1980; Hall 1982) maintain that press relations with dominant powers are the most important factor in the formation of political ideology of a given news organization and that press ideology is often aligned with the dominant ideology of the society at the expense of alternatives, resulting in a narrow ideological spectrum. Nevertheless, when the political power of a society is redistributed, the press will reflect the changing power structure and shifting power relations. Though the press may still be aligned ideologically with the ruling elite in a society, it may no longer be unconditionally faithful to a single power center. At the same time, alternative voices can be clear and loud in a diversified press, thus broadening the range of ideological boundaries (Lee 1994; Yoon 1989).

Taiwan's press has expanded its ideological spectrum. Under martial law, the official "anti-Communism" and "recovery of the mainland" ideology dominated the monolithic press. The democratic transformation that broke the KMT's monopoly of power after 1987 has given rise to ideological diversity among political parties. Given the close relationship between parties and the press since the 1950s, the newly emerged political pluralism was duplicated in press ideology. The previously monolithic press began to side with different ideological groups. The range of press ideology now includes pro-unification and proindependence tendencies, with a middle position for the maintenance of the "status quo," or peaceful coexistence between Taiwan and mainland China. In a larger sense, all the newspapers favored the perpetuation of the status quo. But on a relative scale, the "Big Two" represent the pro-unification stance with a Pan-Chinese orientation; the indigenous press is ideologically proindependence, with an explicit "Taiwan-first" perspective, while the official press follows the KMT "status quo" line. As subsequent analysis reveals, the increasingly demarcated ideological differences among the newspapers hold explanatory power for the differential coverage of mainland China.

CONTROL OF MEDIA OWNERS

Closely related to the influence of press ideology is the control of media owners, another crucial determinant on a news organization's ideological realignment. Media ownership has been found to exert a key ideological control over news organizations in such societies as Hong Kong and South Korea (Lee 1985; Chan and Lee 1991; Yoon 1989). As John Lent (1978, 1982) noted, media owners tended to be deeply involved with politics and politicians, especially in Asian countries, including Taiwan.

As outlined earlier, two types of press ownership in Taiwan—official and private—have produced differential journalistic performance. Official news organizations, as part of the state and ruling KMT apparatus, had predictably and rigidly reflected the anti-Communist ideology and advanced the official policy. As the first local-born president, Lee Teng-hui (Li Denghui), gradually gained full control of the KMT after 1988, he insisted that Taiwan and mainland China hold equal status in the international community before eventual reunification. The party and government papers soon shifted their editorial stance to accommodate this change in the official line. The ideological realignment of the private commercial newspapers was influenced by their owners as well. In the adjusting process, ethnic origin of the owners in terms of birthplace and allegiance (local Taiwanese who had migrated to Taiwan for centuries versus mainlanders who followed the KMT to Taiwan in 1949) played a deciding role. The ruling KMT was fractured by leadership struggles between rising native Taiwanese politicians and declining mainlander politicians. Papers owned by mainlanders were co-opted into the KMT system during martial law, but they now began to take different sides in the KMT's factional fights. Some remained close to the KMT old guard. Many Taiwanese-owned papers at this time began to cultivate close ties with the opposition movement as well as to side with the KMT under President Lee Teng-hui's leadership. The ideologies and political beliefs of mainlander owners differed fundamentally from those of Taiwanese owners. Mainlander-owned papers were consistent with their pro-unification stance in the post-martial-law era. Taiwanese-owned papers tended to be proindependence. The ideological repositioning of the press was, in sum, also largely driven by political and business considerations in light of larger power realignment and intensified press competition (Lee 2000).

ADJUSTMENTS IN BUSINESS STRATEGIES

The influence to consider next is the news organization's formation of post-press-ban business strategies, their road maps for coping with market uncertainties. Under the circumstances of intensified competition and audience fragmentation after 1988, three coping business strategies surfaced in Taiwan's press: The first was the niche-seeking strategy, which aimed narrowly at claiming market niches consisting of small audience segments defined using such demographic characteristics as age, occupation, or area of residence. The second was the mass audience strategy, which required the deemphasis of partisan news treatment so as to attract cross-party, cross-ethnic-group, and cross-region readers. The third strategy pursued segmentation through an explicit ideological slant on news coverage that targeted a single but large segment of the audience, instead of a mass audience.

The official press pursued the niche strategy, which allowed it to avoid competing head-to-head with the commercial press. The "Big Two" positioned themselves as mass-appeal papers. They were no longer blindly loyal to the ruling KMT at the expense of other social and political forces. Such a balancing strategy intended to attract readers regardless of which political party they supported, which ethnic group they belonged to, or where they lived. The indigenous press built its strategy by playing up oppositional politics and taking sides in the KMT's internal fights in hearty favor of President Lee. Coupled with aggressive marketing initiatives, it appealed to segments made up of the dominant native Taiwanese. Newspapers with such a market-driven strategy included the *Minchung Daily News* (in Kaoshiung), the *Taiwan Times* (in Chiayi), the *Independence Evening Post,* and the *Liberty Times* (both in Taipei). Similar to the influence of press ideology, diverse business strategies would also have a far-reaching impact on mainland China coverage in the post-press-ban era.

BEARINGS OF SOCIAL AND ETHNIC GROUPS

Audience fragmentation contributed to the formation of the above described business strategies among the newspapers. Amidst the sharp increase of new titles as well as the flourishing of cable TV and satellite broadcasting services in the late 1980s and early 1990s, new audience segments were carved out from among supporters of political parties or party factions, partisan interest groups, ethnic groups, and regions of residence. The segments that comprised the commanding majority of Taiwanese became critically important for the survival or growth of a paper.

In general, native Taiwanese, many of whom were die-hard supporters of the opposition and President Lee Teng-hui vis-à-vis his mainlander opponents, preferred to read the indigenous papers published by local-born Taiwanese. Not surprisingly, the mainlander-owned "Big Two," emphasizing the shared origin between Taiwan and the mainland, had difficulties penetrating those segments. The indigenous press, which promoted Taiwan's strategic interests from a native perspective rather than in the Pan-Chinese context, had made painstaking efforts to target them by stressing its local roots and ethnic kinship. As the initial interest in mainland Chinese news died down on the island after 1989, the sentiment of wanting politically little to do with the mainland grew strong. Given such a swing of local sentiments, it would be almost suicidal for the indigenous press to give priority to mainland news.

ORGANIZATIONAL INTEREST

Defined as the articulation of organizational goals and the pursuit of desired outcomes, the interest of news organizations was found to influence the way news events were covered and presented (Gans 1979; He and Zhu 1994). Under the former martial law regime, no Taiwan news organizations could possibly develop any interest in publishing and distributing their papers on the Chinese mainland. The total separation between the two societies under the Cold War ruled out this possibility. Between 1987 and 1989, covering the mainland presented an opportunity to scoop competitors for the private commercial papers, particularly the dominant *United Daily News* and *China Times*. The 1989 student-led protests, concentrated at Tiananmen Square, and the historical visit of Gorbachev to China attracted more than one thousand overseas journalists to Beijing. Among them were 150 reporters from Taiwan. News about student protesters and dissidents occupied up to twelve pages an issue, an unprecedented number. The "Big Two" came to realize the value of mainland news as a unique selling point for attracting readers at home. After 1992, when mainland China sped up marketizing its centrally planned economy, they were more eager than were any other papers to explore growth opportunities on the other side of the Taiwan Strait.

Accordingly, emerging organizational interest has shown marked variations from the high demonstrated by the "Big Two" to the low seen in the official and indigenous press. Mainland coverage presented different business opportunities to the Taiwan newspaper organizations. Varied organizational interests, in return, affected the coverage itself.

RESOURCE REALLOCATION

The choice of a particular business strategy by a news organization affects pro-foundly its resource allocation in staffing and news hole. As Michael DuBick (1978) points out, resource deployments rest upon the strategic goals of the news organization. Taiwan's newspapers have added capital, built new printing facilities, and hired new recruits after 1988. The amount of new investments, operational expansion, increases in staff, and addition of new titles by the major papers between 1988 and 1989 made records (Chang 1997). The *United Daily News* and the *China Times* injected N.T. $3 billion (U.S. $115 million) and N.T. $2.7 billion (U.S. $107 million), respectively, into their news operations. The *Liberty Times* added N.T. $1 billion (U.S. $4 million) to expand its news-gathering and production capacity, while the *Independence Evening Post* invested more than N.T. $25 million (U.S. $1 million) in upgrading its printing machines. The *China Times* hired 150 new recruits, while the *United Daily News* and the *Liberty Times* recruited 200 new staff respectively. Even the military's *Youth Daily News* had 20 new staff members.[4] In addition, all of the papers expanded their editorial pages per issue, doubling first from twelve to twenty-four and later to any desirable number.

However, the reallocation of the added resources in these newspapers was dictated by their organizational strategies. The self-directing efforts of the de-clining official press focused on survival. To have another lease of life was of paramount importance. Accordingly, resources in these papers were consoli-dated to build their niches at home. Expansion in mainland coverage was ruled out. The allocation of budget, manpower, and news hole was balanced in the "Big Two." They expanded all kinds of news reporting, including news about mainland China, to attract every major segment of the mass market. In contrast, the sole coverage of local politics and affairs at the expense of other news was the top priority for the indigenous papers. Resources poured into the reporting of Taiwan affairs. Resource reallocation would have a more direct influence on mainland reporting than any other organizational factors.

NEWS STRUCTURE

Uneven resource reallocation among the Taiwan newspapers led to internal structural changes. Structure here concerns the level of differentiation of a paper in organizing its mainland China operation. (The level of differentiation was determined by the following structural attributes: [1] whether an indepen-dent mainland department or desk was in place; [2] the size of mainland staff; and [3] the number of full-time mainland beats.) Specifically, how did the paper organize mainland coverage in terms of division of labor, distribution of staff, and role specialization (creating specialists whose job involves solely the coverage of mainland China)?

The "Big Two" have developed a highly differentiated mainland division featuring a stand-alone "Mainland News Center" with about twenty full-time staff and at least five mainland beats. The official papers, such as the *Central Daily News* and the *Youth Daily News,* maintained a moderately differentiated mainland desk employing five staff members. All of the indigenous papers had a less differentiated mainland operation without either an independent desk or a beat. According to the renowned historian of management Alfred Chandler (1962), structure follows strategy; the structural differences among Taiwan's papers would enhance the influences of press ideology, business strategies, and organizational interest on the coverage of mainland China.

Table 11.2 summarizes a variety of organizational factors that influence the gathering and processing of mainland news in Taiwan's press. The first five factors are influences that legitimize or delegitimize mainland coverage; the remaining two are concerned with organizational mechanisms and journalistic practices that deal with such coverage.

Table 11.2. Organizational Factors Influencing Mainland Coverage

	Official Press	**"Big Two"**	**Indigenous Press**
Ideological tendencies and cultural orientations	Status quo	Ultimate unification with China	Proindependence
Ownership	KMT/government/military	Mainlanders	Local Taiwanese
Post-martial-law business strategies	Niche	Mass audience	Segmentation
Relations with social groups controlled by native Taiwanese	None or few	Exclusion or incorporation	Close and mutually supportive
Organizational interest in publishing on the Chinese mainland	Low	High	Low
Resource allocation of budget, manpower, and news hole	Consolidated	Balanced	Disproportionate ("Taiwan first")
News structure of mainland reporting	Moderately differentiated	Highly differentiated	Less differentiated
Representative newspapers	*Central Daily News Youth Daily News China Daily News Taiwan Daily News*	*United Daily News China Times*	*Independence Evening Post Liberty Times Taiwan Times Minchung Daily News*

Organizational Strategies

To achieve a coherent understanding of the differential performance among the three types of press, we next analyze the heightened factors that act as influences and determinants on mainland China coverage. The analysis starts with the official press, followed by the "Big Two" and the indigenous press.

THE OFFICIAL PRESS

The breakdown of the KMT's monopoly of political power and the opening of the press market dealt a fatal blow to the flagging official press. Its influence further declined; several of the official papers, such as the *China Daily News* (northern edition) and the *Modern Daily News* (formerly *Shangkung Daily News*), closed down. Problems persisted for the survivors, including the KMT's *Central Daily News,* the government-run *Taiwan New Life Daily,* and the military-controlled *Youth Daily News* and *Taiwan Daily News.*

Before the internal split within the KMT hierarchy between the mainlander elite and the Taiwanese faction led by President Lee Teng-hui, the official press was presumed by mainlander loyalists to toe party lines. After the split in the years following 1987, the power struggle within the KMT caused the official press to shift its ideological stance. The shift occurred because its finance and staff were controlled by the one who led the KMT. As party appointees under the supervision of the KMT's Department of Cultural Affairs, publishers of the party and government papers were in no position to challenge the new KMT leadership. Even though the origins and historical ties of the official press were akin to the old KMT group, it had to switch allegiance to the KMT under Lee Teng-hui. It now anchored its ideological position to the KMT line, which stresses the existence of the Republic of China on Taiwan as a political entity equal to the People's Republic of China on the mainland.

Nevertheless, the official papers differed in their pace of adjusting to the new KMT leadership under Lee Teng-hui. The *Central Daily News* switched allegiance faster than did its siblings. Changes in its editorial positions attested to this. In 1992, it deliberately missed out on a big Mother's Day story about Lee's opponent, Premier Hau Pei-tsun. Hau talked in public, with tearful eyes, about his fond memories of his mother, an unusual and news-making move for the tough-minded retired general. Because of their closer ties with mainlander politicians and military generals, the military-controlled papers were initially resistant to Lee Teng-hui's leadership. For instance, the *Youth Daily News* voiced objection to direct presidential elections, which Lee favored. Such an election would allow—for the first time in Taiwan's history—the commanding majority of local Taiwanese to choose a president through voting. It took the change of several publishers and editors before the paper was tamed.

Moreover, the continued decline in circulation has hastened the departure of the official press from its traditional Pan-Chinese orientation, which viewed Taiwan as part of China. The strategic interests of Taiwan for its own sake were now stressed as critically important. Losses in advertising revenues (in 1990, as compared to 1989, the *Youth Daily News* lost 65 percent and the *Central Daily News* lost 13 percent) made them further dependent on the KMT's or the state's financial subsidy and compulsory subscription sales to government offices and public schools. However, the decades-old practice of compulsory subscription and preferential treatment in receiving government advertisement bookings became difficult to support in postauthoritarian Taiwan. In July 1996, the opposition DPP mayor of Taipei, Chen Hsui-pien, banned the subscription of the *Central Daily News* by the city government and metropolitan schools. The city government offices were also prohibited from placing advertisements in the paper. In response to their declining influence, the official papers sought market niches as a viable business strategy for survival. The *Youth Daily News* no longer targeted the general public, but reverted to being a military publication; whether this niche-seeking strategy will work for the official press remains to be seen. Most recently, to date, the military-owned *Taiwan Daily News* printed its last issue in July 1996. Its historical legacy of being a military mouthpiece against the opposition movement and liberal intellectuals under martial law was one of the causes for closure (it was later bought out by private investors). The complete marginalization of the official press seems to be only a matter of time.

The niche strategy adopted by the official papers affected deeply their editorial priorities, particularly with regard to the coverage of mainland China. Mainland Chinese news had not been a top editorial priority for these papers, despite the fact that, due to their privileges as state and KMT organs, they were the earliest papers on the island to publish such mainland news routinely. The *Youth Daily News,* for example, has maintained a mainland news page (originally known as "News About the Enemy") since the 1960s. Their monopolistic advantages over mainland reporting disappeared in the postban era, but these papers cannot afford to ignore their historical legacy as the first to process mainland news. Accordingly, they had neither an enthusiastic nor an apathetic but a lukewarm attitude toward the reporting of mainland China. As party and military papers, they also encountered additional difficulties in covering the mainland firsthand, with the exception of reporting its annual conferences of the National People's Congress (China's nominal parliament) and the People's Political Consultative Conference open to all Taiwan journalists. The mainland authorities have turned down almost all of their requests, at the papers' initiative, for reporting trips to mainland China. Among the official newspaper organizations, the interest in publishing across the Taiwan Strait was low. The idea of publishing on the mainland was tempting, but they felt it to be not worth pursuing for the moment.

The lukewarm attitude toward mainland reporting, together with limited budgets and manpower, prohibited the official press from expanding its mainland operation. For instance, the *Central Daily News* has maintained its five-member desk. The *Youth Daily News* depended on a small desk, supplemented by two or three foreign correspondents reporting about mainland China to home papers in Japan and the United States. These two papers had expanded the original news hole devoted to news about the mainland from a half page to a full page in 1988, but recently both have reverted to a half page of regular mainland China coverage.

The official press was once dependent solely on wire service reports and Hong Kong press accounts for news about the mainland. After 1989, when it became difficult to have firsthand and timely stories on mainland China due to new restrictions imposed on Taiwan journalists by the mainland authorities, the mainland page in the *Central Daily News* printed many contributions from mainland students studying overseas. At the same time, it solicited Taiwanese citizens and veterans to write about their experiences on the mainland. A great proportion of stories also covered medical, health, and cultural topics and events. The *Youth Daily News,* on the other hand, still relied on the Central News Agency (which was reorganized from party ownership to state ownership) and leading foreign services to fill its mainland news hole. Story selection has maintained its traditional focus on exposing the dark side of the mainland to score propaganda points. The anti-Communist thrust lingered on.

THE "BIG TWO"

Democratic transition and the lifting of the long-standing press ban destabilized Taiwan's oligopolistic press structure dominated by the *United Daily News* and the *China Times.* These two papers historically had cordial ties with the KMT during martial law; the *United Daily News* even had three members sitting on the powerful KMT central committee. The *United Daily News* used to side with the conservative wing of the KMT, while the *China Times* leaned toward its liberal faction (Lee 1992, 1994). But ideologically, Yu Chi-chung, owner and publisher of the *China Times,* and Wang Tih-wu, who had owned the *United Daily News,* shared a Pan-China perspective and a vague sense that, eventually, Taiwan and China would be reunified. The *United Daily News* had been well known on the island as a staunch anti-Communism and anti-independence paper. Because of the close ties between the owners of the two giants and the ruling KMT under Chiang Ching-kuo (whom Lee Teng-hui succeeded in February 1988), the *United Daily News* and *China Times* became the first two nonofficial papers to have their own in-house coverage of mainland China in the mid-1980s. The mission was to counter the mainland's heightened "united front plot" against Taiwan.

The new balance of power after 1987, and particularly the rise of President Lee Teng-hui, forced the two giant papers to reconsider party affiliation and to realign ideologically with different political forces. In the realigning process, Wang Tih-wu and Yu Chi-chung differed markedly in their approaches. Wang made no secret of his dislike for Lee and his followers; and the *United Daily News* has regularly criticized Lee by name, sometimes very harshly. Wang continued to side with the "nonmainstream" faction led by Lee's political foes, who were primarily the KMT's old guards. When Hau Pei-tsun, leader of this faction, was appointed premier as a political compromise in 1992, the *United Daily News* threw full support behind him. Because of the long-standing ties between Wang and the conservative wing, the paper has published the largest number of exclusive stories on mainlander politicians of the KMT. On the other hand, the Presidential Office, under Lee's control, has publicly corrected the errors in that paper's news reports on a number of occasions, apparently to discredit it.

Publisher Yu, on the other hand, has been more pragmatic. The *China Times* initiated an "indigenization" drive in response to the transforming political environment. The drive was intended to ease tensions and clashes between the Taiwan-on-its-own-merits and the Taiwan-as-part-of-China positions. Politically, Yu was trying to maintain a good tie with Lee, but not at the expense of the established relations with mainlander politicians. At the height of factional strife within the KMT leadership between the rival "mainstream" and the "nonmainstream" factions, Yu personally ordered the paper to stop criticizing Lee and his protégés by name. Nevertheless, the Pan-China cultural attachment and the emphasis of a shared origin and common bond between Taiwan and China made the "Big Two" symbolic of the pro-unification papers in Taiwan, even though reunification was seen as nothing more than a remote goal.

What was more, the *United Daily News* had not only distanced itself from President Lee, but also alienated the opposition movement at the grass roots.

Under these circumstances, it fell victim to a boycott campaign in 1992. President Lee had singled the paper out for criticism on a number of occasions; in 1992, he accused it of trying to scare the Taiwanese public when it quoted Li Rui-huan, chairman of the People's Political Consultative Conference on the mainland, as saying that Beijing might use force against Taiwan if Taiwan should seek independence. Lee's criticism triggered fifteen groups, led by the proindependence Taiwan Presbyterian Association and the Association of Taiwan Professors, to launch a boycott campaign, calling on the public not to read the *United Daily News* because of its alleged sellout of Taiwan and its role as a "mouthpiece" of the mainland. The campaign cost the paper a loss of circulation in the neighborhood of 100,000 copies (Ting 1993). The boycott indicated that mainland coverage was significantly affected by the changing relations between the *United Daily News* and the political forces on the island. The coverage has also become part of the battlefield of ideological contestation between the local interests and the Pan-Chinese forces of which the paper was a symbol.

The *China Times* escaped being a target of the boycott, though its report had used the same quote from Li Rui-huan. Unlike the *United Daily News,* the *Times* had attempted to incorporate rather than exclude the opposition and social movement in its news coverage, even back to the 1980s. Views and activities of social groups controlled by native Taiwanese received no priority, but they were not neglected altogether. It further articulated its balancing approach in a mass appeal business strategy in the 1990s. Huang Chao-hsung (1994), its editor in chief, put the strategic goals of the *China Times* as based on "Lichu Bentu" (grounded in the grassroots on the island). The paper has set up regional editorial offices and printing outlets in central (Taichung) and southern (Tainan) Taiwan to make further inroads into the home market. Over the past few years, the number of its local editions increased to eighteen, one in each county.

The "Big Two" remained big, still accounting for two-thirds of Taiwan's newspaper circulation and advertising revenues in the 1990s. Given the saturated press market at home, they began to explore growth opportunities in the mainland, where the Beijing authorities shifted their Taiwan policy from emphasizing the use of force to a soft "united front" approach intended to win the minds and hearts of Taiwan people. Under such circumstances, the *China Times* was able to conduct a full-page exclusive interview with Yang Shang-kun, president of the People's Republic of China, in September 1990. The interview was the first ever granted to a Taiwan-based news organization.

New impetus in mainland coverage came after the 1992 southern tour by China's paramount leader, Deng Xiaoping, which accelerated the momentum in reforming China's economy into a market-driven one. As Taiwanese annual investments in the mainland increased from U.S. $3 billion in 1992 to U.S. $3.5 billion in 1996 (second only to Hong Kong), the outward-looking *United Daily News* and *China Times* envisioned publishing mainland editions. Wang Tih-wu told the *Global View* magazine in 1994 that, if allowed, he would publish a paper in each of the thirty mainland provinces. The mainland was now not only a topic for news, but also a huge potential market for the two aggressive giants. The largest investments of the "Big Two" in exploring the mainland market were in establishing the N.T. $7 billion (U.S. $270 million) *Hong Kong United Daily News* in 1992. As the first step in building a gateway to the mainland, the mission of these two new outlets was "to cover the mainland's interaction with Taiwan and Hong Kong."

Therefore, at a time when other Taiwan newspapers cooled off their mainland fever in the 1990s, the "Big Two" rekindled enthusiasm in reporting the mainland. They kept increasing resources allocated to the mainland operation. The *United Daily News* expanded its mainland operation, set up in 1989, into a full-scale division known as the "Mainland News Center," now one of the fastest growing departments in the organization. The division employed twenty-one journalists, including twelve mainland beats, in 1994. The setup of the *China Times* mainland operation was similar; the number of staff members at its own mainland news center has increased to some twenty in total. They claimed between a quarter and a third of the entire paper's annual budget between 1992 and 1993 in the amount of N.T. $25 million (U.S. $1 million). Moreover, the staff of the mainland news center at both papers was dominated by people with special knowledge about the mainland: Yu Yu-lin, who was in charge of the mainland division at the *China Times,* holds a graduate degree in China studies, as does Wang Chen-bang of the *United Daily News*. Actually, nine members of the *China Times* staff majored in China studies, and only two majored in journalism.

The news hole devoted to mainland news, which was expanded at the *United Daily News* and the *China Times* into a full page in January and April of 1988, respectively, has remained large. Mainland news also showed continued expansion in scope and topics. Soft news of human interest increased in proportion to the traditional hard news about mainland politics and military affairs. Such news included stories on veterans' home visits and scenic spots on the mainland that Taiwan residents had read about from childhood. The coverage of the cross-strait relationship also emerged as a popular topic. In addition, to produce more news useful to readers at home, the *China Times* initiated a series of in-depth reports on eleven mainland provinces (eight were actually printed) and distributed them as supplements (at a cost to produce of N.T. $500,000 or U.S. $20,000 each) between 1992 and 1994. This series was unprecedented in the history of mainland coverage. The *United Daily News* has used the most contributions by such mainland activists in exile as Yan Jiaqi.

In the meantime, firsthand coverage of the mainland has become increasingly difficult during this period. The mainland authorities imposed the so-called four restrictions on Taiwan journalists to restrict their topics, interviewees, geographic movement, and duration of stay (to less than a month) while reporting from the mainland. Most frustrating of all, no news bureau was allowed to set up on the mainland for fear of Taiwan's role in promoting "peaceful evolution," aimed at toppling the Communist regime. To overcome this institutionalized barrier, the *United Daily News* and the *China Times* have had to rotate their reporters on a monthly basis since 1990. This practice has given rise to a costly "relay system" that only the "Big Two" can afford. Even so, a mainland beat reporter can visit the mainland no more than three or four times a year, with a fear of being denied entry each time.

Without a news bureau on the mainland, the *United Daily News* and the *China Times* experienced great difficulties in developing an extensive news net and cultivating long-term relations with sources. The mainland beat reporter had to rely on personal friends, mostly journalists and scholars, to get a story; both papers set aside a fixed budget for gifts and banquet expenses. The competition in covering mainland China between the *United Daily News* and the *China Times* thus boiled down to a competition for sources. The competition between these two oligopolies required that each get the same story as the other did and to get scoops whenever possible. This was the reason why articles of Fang Lizhi, China's leading dissident, once appeared in both papers on the same day! The exclusive interview with China's President Yang Shang-kun in 1990 was a major competitive triumph for the *China Times*. It gradually became a common practice for the mainland beat reporters to "report first and check later" in the highly competitive atmosphere of mainland coverage.

Another approach taken by the "Big Two" to alleviate the problems of access to the mainland and of the shortage of firsthand reporting was to produce more "enterprise stories," such as the *China Times*'s unprecedented series on eleven mainland provinces. Enterprise stories were possible because most of the mainland beats of the two giant papers had trained as China specialists. The

"Big Two" also tried different methods to solicit contributions from mainland writers to fill up the mainland page. Some were more successful than others. The *China Times* started a weekly column—"Forum for Mainland Scholars"— in 1995, for instance, publishing articles on issues regarding China's continued economic reforms by such economists and political scientists as Hu Angang and Wang Shaoguang. The column, however, was later discontinued when contributions, seemingly filled with recycled ideas, were coldly received by Taiwan readers.

The competition between the "Big Two" took place on other fronts as well. Between 1992 and 1996, they competed for potential business partners in seeking a foot in the enormous mainland market. The *China Times* established news swaps with the state Xinhua News Agency in Beijing and almost closed a deal with the *Liberation Daily* in Shanghai on a joint publication featuring business news. The *United Daily News* maintained good ties with the Shanghai-based *Wenhui Daily*. However, none of the deals materialized, because political considerations prevailed in spite of the attempts made by the "Big Two" to defuse political concerns in the interest of business gains. Publisher Yu Chi-chung was said to have asked the *China Times* not to use too many contributions from mainland dissidents. But China's restrictive policy regarding overseas investments in the media kept the door closed; the mainland authorities were particularly angered by the *United Daily News*'s sustained attention to Chinese dissidents abroad and its continued criticism of human rights violations in the mainland.

Finally, the ups and downs in the precarious Taiwan-China relations conditioned mainland reporting in the Taiwan press. During the years 1995 and 1996, Beijing fired missiles off Taiwan to protest President Lee Teng-hui's private trip to the United States. Cross-strait relations took a sharp downturn and sealed any prospects the "Big Two" might have had for publishing on the mainland. As a result, both the Hong Kong-based *China Times Weekly* and the *Hong Kong United Daily News* folded, with the former reportedly losing more than U.S. $13 million. Even the on-line version of *China Times,* which committed no investment in the mainland but depends on the global Internet medium, was blocked by the mainland (Tu 1999).

THE INDIGENOUS PRESS

The indigenous papers, owned and run by the locally born Taiwanese, were small players that survived under the shadow of the official press and the mainlander-owned dominant "Big Two." These papers were scattered around geographically, the better to find market niches and avoid head-on competition with the official papers and the two giants. The oldest, *Independence Evening Post,* established in 1947, had a circulation hovering around 100,000 in the late 1980s, even though it had been influential before 1987 as a quasi-outlet for the outlawed "Dang Wai" (opposition) voices, which were then denied in the official press and slighted by the "Big Two." The *Independence Evening Post* built its reputation as the most liberal of Taiwan's newspapers — breaking silence on sensitive topics and reporting what the official press ignored and the "Big Two" envied. Moreover, as the island's long-standing pro-opposition paper, the *Post* had a closer tie with grassroots groups made up of the dominant Taiwanese majority than did any of the other papers.

The *Independence Evening Post* was the first news organization in Taiwan to send two reporters to the mainland in late 1986 in contravention of the government policy. The trip itself was a news-making event designed to gain a competitive edge at home. The lifting of martial law made it possible for the opposition to gain fair coverage, so now the *Post* made an attempt to use mainland news as a competitive advantage. At the height of the 1989 student-led demonstrations in Beijing, one of the *Post*'s two reporters, Huang Teh-pei, was even arrested for trying to help student leaders flee the country. The *Post* also initiated a deal in 1989 with the Shanghai-based reformist *World Economic Herald* to exchange news, but the deal collapsed when the mainland authorities closed down the outspoken *Herald.* However, as the *Post* experienced increasing financial hardship in the 1990s because of losses incurred in launching the sister paper, the *Independence Morning Post,* such enthusiasm evaporated. The peak of the *Post*'s mainland coverage ended with the 1989 student-led prodemocracy movement in Beijing.

Structurally, the operation of mainland reporting was informal and unstable in the *Independence Evening Post.* It set up a makeshift mainland desk with two political reporters in 1989 to cope with the sudden need to cover the student demonstrations. Hsu Lu, one of the two journalists who broke the law to make the first reporting trip to the mainland, was never a member of the mainland beat, because the *Post* had no formal beat structure. In the 1990s, when mainland reporting turned out not to be commercially profitable, the *Post* focused on pursuing indigenous loyalty. It consolidated its resources to focus on domestic coverage of local interests, concentrating on what Lee Yong-teh (1994), its editor in chief, calls the "revitalization of the flagging native Taiwanese culture," which was pushed to the periphery by classic Chinese culture over the past four decades. The *Post* group cut ninety-seven staff reporters in 1990 and more than two hundred in 1991, respectively. Its small and makeshift mainland desk was also closed, and the added mainland news page was dropped. News about the mainland appearing in the paper was now mostly re-written wire reports and stories carried in the Hong Kong press. Financial difficulties finally forced the *Post* to change hands in December 1994; in 1998, it was under a new owner and on the verge of bankruptcy.

The redistribution of political power from mainlanders to local Taiwanese politicians and the end of the press ban, in particular, brought opportunities for growth to the indigenous press. As political repression was phased out, the most important change these indigenous papers made was to further localize their Taiwan-oriented ideology. The interests of Taiwan on its own merit rather than in the context of a symbolic China commanded their attention first and foremost. At the same time, they were more outspoken about their anti-unification stance than were the "Big Two." In 1990, the opposition DPP in-cluded the pursuit of Taiwan independence in its platform. The *Independence Evening Post* was its sole defender, claiming views of political parties should be freely expressed as long as they were not translated into action. In return, ideo-logical indigenization helped these Taiwanese-owned papers deal with com-petitive pressures by differentiating them from the Pan-Chinese "Big Two." The *Minchung Daily News* and the *Taiwan Times,* for instance, were able to es-tablish themselves in the cities of southern Taiwan as the most popular papers. They ignored the coverage of mainland affairs, for the interest of their readers did not go beyond the waters surrounding the island.

The "Taiwan first" ideological tendency together with the marketing ap-peal to large segments of indigenous readers has made the *Liberty Times* a partic-ular success. Before 1988, it was a small and insignificant paper published in central Taiwan; the *Liberty Times* has subsequently ridden atop the tide of shift-ing power relations. Viewed as politically correct in the eyes of lower-class read-ers, the die-hard opposition, and Lee Teng-hui supporters, this paper was, according to its slogan, "A Paper Defending the Interests of the 21 Million Tai-wanese." Seeking domestic business opportunities took precedence over those on the mainland. The *Liberty Times* launched a number of costly promotions, including, in 1992, an N.T. $2 billion (U.S. $77 million) campaign offering gold bars and luxurious cars like Mercedes-Benzes (Chang 1997). But nothing like this kind of investment was put into mainland coverage. In addition, the *Liberty Times* attacked the "Big Two" for not "putting Taiwan's interest first" but, rather, "promoting the Pan-China chauvinism" on the island (Chiang 1994).

More important, given President Lee's popularity with the dominant majority of local-borns, the *Liberty Times* thrived on fully supporting Lee and ruthlessly blasting his mainlander opponents. When the KMT infighting continued to seethe at the top, it went so far as to make a public announcement, in May 1994, openly endorsing Lee's fight against the mainlander politicians. It thus earned itself a solid reputation as a "pro-Lee paper." Finally, the claim to "speak for the grass roots" made the *Liberty Times* an outlet for releasing the grievances and expressing the sentiments of its native readers; many of them defected from the "Big Two." In 1992, the *Liberty Times* claimed a circulation of half a million, becoming the third-largest paper in Taiwan. When the "Big Two" raised their prices in late 1995 from N.T. $10 to N.T. $15, under the pressure of a steep rise in the cost of newsprint, the *Liberty Times* did not follow suit; it kept its price at N.T. $10 per copy. The decision helped its circulation. The *Liberty Times* further claimed in 1996 to be the largest paper in Taiwan, though the claim was highly questionable.

The "Taiwan first" ideology and segment strategy of the indigenous press has had profound consequences for mainland coverage. The indigenous papers categorically had a low interest in mainland news, in contrast to the enthusiasm of the *United Daily News* and the *China Times*. The *Liberty Times* has never had a mainland desk nor assigned any mainland beat. It did not do so even after its staff increased from 400 in 1990 to more than 1,000 in 1993. Consequently, it has depended on an ad hoc contingency structure. A political beat reporter covered the mainland as part of his portfolio. He stayed in Taipei most of the time, making far more telephone calls than reporting trips to the mainland.

Without a full-time mainland beat, reporting on mainland China was surely constrained among the indigenous papers. They were unable to keep up with the amount of coverage offered by the "Big Two" or by the official press. Their coverage was narrow in scope. From the perspective of Taiwan's interest and concern for security, the *Liberty Times* emphasized cross-strait news rather than news about the mainland alone. Stories on mainland dissidents, which were routinely covered by the official press and the "Big Two," were close to none. With no intention to befriend the mainland authorities, the tone of reporting in the indigenous press was often critical of the mainland for threatening an invasion of Taiwan and for pressuring Taiwan's allies to break diplomatic ties. The *Liberty Times,* the *Taiwan Times,* and the *Minchung Daily News* even addressed China without the modifier "mainland," implying that China was a country foreign to Taiwan.

Conclusion

Using the year 1988 as a watershed, a systematic content analysis of six leading newspapers representing the three types of press over 10 years (five years before and five years after the lifting of the "press ban") provided more supportive evidence. Measured by the amount of coverage, of the three newspaper types, the official papers published the most mainland news under the five-year press ban (64.7 percent), thanks to their privileged position. In the five postban years, however, more mainland news stories appeared in the "Big Two" (53.6 percent) than in the official papers (33.3 percent), which in turn did better than the indigenous papers (13.2 percent). Changes in story size and in the number of staff-filed stories showed similar patterns. The "Big Two" published the longest stories about the mainland (8.8 percent), while the official papers had fewer long stories (6.3 percent), and the indigenous papers had the fewest stories longer than one-eighth of a page (1.6 percent). The two giants also outperformed both the official (19.8 percent) and the indigenous papers (13.7 percent) in putting out the largest number of stories filed by their staff reporters (32.4 percent), thanks to their large beat systems (see table 11.3).

In qualitative measures, the "Big Two" showed the largest percentage of highly prominently placed stories (3.8 percent), while the indigenous papers had the smallest (2.2 percent). Before 1988, more negative stories appeared in the official and indigenous papers, in contrast to the overall neutral tone of the "Big Two." After 1988, the negative tone in the official papers persisted. The overall tone of the indigenous papers changed to neutral, taking a stance similar to that of the "Big Two." However, a close examination of the story topics across the six papers reveals a pattern focusing narrowly on Beijing as the core of mainland coverage and on politics as essential in news reported about the Taiwan-China relationship. Stories on power struggles within the Communist regime, including the heated speculation about Deng Xiaoping's death, appeared routinely. Taiwan journalists wrote more stories on the possibility of "liberating Taiwan in a bloodbath," the resurgence of the independence movement, and the prospect of a cross-strait summit meeting than on any other topic, in the hope of scoring a scoop, although there has been, in fact, little change in the mainland's official pronouncements toward Taiwan (Press Council 1996).

This chapter concludes that the recent multifaceted and contradictory changes in Chinese mainland news reported in Taiwan's press were the result of a wide range of interacting external and internal influences, particularly the interplay of press ideology, business strategy, organizational interest, and news

Table 11.3. Characteristics of Mainland News by Press Types and Stages (1983–1993)

	Official Press (%)	"Big Two" (%)	Indigenous Press (%)
Amount of Coverage			
During press ban			
(N)=419	64.7	25.8	9.5
After press ban			
(N)=1,383	33.3	53.6	13.2
Story Prominence			
During press ban			
Low	92.6	88.0	92.5
Moderate	6.6	12.0	2.5
High	0.7	0.0	5.0
(N)	(271)	(108)	(40)
After press ban			
Low	87.4	87.2	95.1
Moderate	9.3	9.0	2.7
High	3.3	3.8	2.2
(N)	(460)	(741)	(182)
Story Size			
During press ban			
Small	73.1	77.8	70.0
Medium	25.8	17.6	30.3
Large	1.1	4.6	0.0
(N)	(271)	(108)	(40)
After press ban			
Small	67.6	64.2	81.3
Medium	26.1	27.0	17.0
Large	6.3	8.8	1.6
(N)	(460)	(741)	(182)
News Source			
During press ban			
Staff	17.3	21.3	20.0
Wires	58.3	57.4	60.0
Other	24.4	21.3	20.0
(N)	(271)	(108)	(40)
After press ban			
Staff	19.8	32.4	13.7
Wires	56.1	36.3	34.6
Other	24.1	31.3	51.6
(N)	(460)	(741)	(182)
News Tone			
During press ban			
Positive	0.0	0.9	0.0
Neutral	11.8	49.1	22.5
Negative	88.2	48.1	77.5
Mixed	0.0	1.9	0.0
(N)	(271)	(108)	(40)
After press ban			
Positive	5.7	7.7	11.0
Neutral	41.4	60.3	55.8
Negative	50.3	26.4	28.2
Mixed	2.6	5.6	5.0
(N)	(449)	(736)	(181)

The *Central Daily News* and the *Youth Daily News* were included for the official press, while the *Independence Evening Post* and the *Liberty Times* were used to represent the indigenous press. Story size was measured by estimated page size, while the measure of story prominence was based on story size and placement. The coding of news tone was inferred from choice of words, editorial emphasis, and nature of coverage. For more details, see Wei (1995).

structure. The production and presentation of news about the mainland were blended with Taiwan's rapid sociopolitical transformation from an authoritarian society into a democracy. The demarcated differences in ideology among the newspapers had a primary influence on mainland coverage. The lack of enthusiasm in such coverage in the indigenous press was a protestation against the hegemonic Pan-Chinese perspective. Moreover, newspapers jockeyed for position in light of intensified competition; mainland coverage became an integral part of their organizational strategies. The resultant differential performance was a testimony to the consequences of pursuing diverse business strategies and of varied emerging organizational interests. Marked differences in resource reallocation and news structure reinforced the influences of press ideology, business strategy, and organizational interest.

As the division between those favoring renunciation and those favoring independence deepens in Taiwan, the coverage of mainland China will reflect more dramatically the ideological rift between the native Taiwanese emphasis and the Pan-China orientation. The enthusiasm of the outward-looking "Big Two" in dealing with mainland news has had an adverse effect, as demonstrated in the 1992 boycott campaign. Their pursuit of business opportunities in the mainland turned out to be a double-edged sword. Following the rising sentiments at the grass roots favoring Taiwan's secession, the downplay of mainland news in the inward-looking indigenous press is expected to continue. Furthermore, the constraints on mainland coverage set by Taiwan's internal power reconfiguration, its changing policy toward the mainland, as well as mainland China's shifting policy toward Taiwan will likely persist in the near future (Hong 1997; Lee 1998). So will the heightened tensions between marketization and continued political control in China. These external pressures have set the boundaries for the Taiwan press in mainland reporting over the past ten years. Meanwhile, the opposition DPP candidate, Chen Shui-pien, has been elected president, ending fifty years of the KMT's power monopoly. It is still too early to determine the implications of his victory for press reporting about the PRC.

Notes

1. This study was based on my dissertation, completed at Indiana University. I wish to thank the China Times Cultural Foundation in New York for the generous dissertation grant that helped support this study and Dr. Chin-Chuan Lee for his helpful comments on previous versions of this chapter.

2. A large number of Chinese emigrated to Taiwan in the mid-seventeenth century. The descendants of these Chinese immigrants, who are known as "Taiwanese," account for more than 85 percent of Taiwan's population. They are distinguished from those who migrated to Taiwan with the Chiang Kai-shek regime in 1949, who are known as "mainlanders."

3. The KMT dominated the popular vote, holding 72 percent in the 1980 legislative election. In the 1986 legislative election, it had 68 percent of the popular vote, while the newly formed DPP received 22 percent. The balance of the vote was further tipped in favor of the DPP in the 1989 election of lawmakers. The popular vote for the DPP increased to 25 percent, while the popular vote for the KMT further declined to 60 percent. Independent candidates took the remaining 12 percent. In the general legislative election in 1995, the KMT took 85 seats out of 164, with a record low of 46 percent of the popular vote; the DPP won 54 seats and 33 percent of the vote; and the New Party came third with 21 seats and nearly 13 percent of the popular vote.

4. Data provided to the author by these news organizations.

Bibliography

Asia News. 1997. "The News Media Eye on the 1997 Handover." May 19–25:24–30.

Chan, Joseph Man, and Chin-Chuan Lee. 1988. "Press Ideology and Organizational Control in Hong Kong." *Communication Research* 15(2):185–97.

———. 1991. *Mass Media and Political Transition: The Hong Kong Press in China's Orbit.* New York: Guilford.

Chandler, Alfred D. 1962. *Strategy and Structure.* Cambridge, Mass.: MIT Press.

Chang, Jonathan Y. H. 1997. "A Study on Newspaper Management in Post-Press-Ban Taiwan." Taipei: World Journalism University Press (in Chinese).

Chen, Anne, and Anju Chaudhary. 1990. "Asia and Pacific." In John Merrill, ed., *Global Journalism.* 2nd ed. New York: Longman.

Chen, Kuo-hsiang, and Chu Ping. 1987. *Forty Years of Newspaper Evolution in Taiwan.* Taipei: Independence Evening Post (in Chinese).

Chiang, Antonio. 1994. Publisher of the *Journalist,* interview, Taipei, June 29.

DuBick, Michael. 1978. "The Organizational Structure of Newspapers in Relation to Their Metropolitan Environment." *Administrative Science Quarterly* 23:418–33.

Gans, Herbert. 1979. *Deciding What's News.* New York: Pantheon.

Gitlin, Todd. 1980. *The Whole World Is Watching.* Berkeley: University of California Press.

Goldstein, Carl. 1985. "Dominance of Taipei's Big Two." *Far Eastern Economic Review,* December 25, 27–29.

Hall, Stuart. 1982. "The Rediscovery of 'Ideology': Return of the Repressed in Media Studies." In Michael Gurevitch, Tony Bennett, James Curran, and Jane Woollacott, eds., *Culture, Society, and the Media.* London: Methuen.

He, Zhou, and Jian-hua Zhu. 1994. "The 'Voice of America' and China: Zeroing in on Tiananmen Square." *Journalism Monographs,* No. 143.

Hong, Junhao. 1997. "Media/Cultural Product Exchanges between China and Taiwan: Cultural Interaction and Political Integration." *Gazette* 59(1):61–75.

Hsiao, Michael H. H. 1989. "Emerging Social Movements and the Rise of a Demanding Civil Society in Taiwan." Paper presented at Conference on Democratization in the R.O.C., Taipei.

Huang, Chao-hsung. 1994. Editor in chief of the *China Times,* interview, Taipei, July 1.

Lasater, Martin. 1990. *A Step toward Democracy: The December 1989 Election in Taiwan, ROC.* Washington, D.C.: AEI Press.

Lee, Chin-Chuan. 1985. "Partisan Press Coverage of Government News in Hong Kong." *Journalism Quarterly* 62:770–76.

———. 1992. "Post-Authoritarian Press in Taiwan: A Political Economy Analysis." In Leonard Chu and Joseph Man Chan, eds., *Communication and Societal Development.* Hong Kong: Chinese University of Hong Kong (in Chinese).

———. 1994. "Sparking a Fire: The Press and the Ferment of Democratic Change in Taiwan." In Chin-Chuan Lee, ed., *China's Media and Media's China.* Boulder, Colo.: Westview.

———. 1998. "Media Market and Political Conflict: A Decade of Media Interaction between Mainland China and Taiwan." *East Asia Quarterly* 29(2):43–57 (in Chinese).

———. 2000. "State, Market, and Media: The Case of Taiwan." In James Curran and Myung-Jin Park, eds., *De-Westernizing Media Studies.* London: Routledge.

Lee, Yong-teh. 1994. Editor in chief of the *Independence Evening Post,* interview, Taipei, July 25.

Lent, John A. 1978. "Press Freedom in Asia: The Quiet, but Completed, Revolution." *Gazette* 24:41–60.

———. 1982. *Newspapers in Asia: Contemporary Trends and Problems.* Hong Kong: Heinemann Asia.

Mann, James. 1999. "Framing China." *Media Studies Journal* 13 (Winter):102–7.

Plamenatz, John. 1970. *Ideology.* London: Pall Mall Press.

Press Council. 1996. *How the Taiwan Media Covered Mainland China.* Taipei: National Press Council of the R.O.C. (in Chinese).

Republic of China Yearbook. 1992; 1993. Taipei: Kwanghua.

Rong, Fu-tian. 1994. "Ethical Issues in Mainland China Coverage." *Journalism Forum* 1(1):38–47. Taipei: Graduate School of Journalism, National Taiwan University.

Tien, Hung-mao. 1989. *The Grand Transition: The Political and Social Evolution in Taiwan.* Taipei: China Times Press (in Chinese).

Ting, Hsuan-yang. 1993. "Why Wang Tih-wu Has Offended Lee Teng-hui: The *United Daily News* under Fire." *Wealth* (January):251–54 (in Chinese).

Tu, James N. C. 1999. "New Media and Cross-Strait Exchanges: The Case of *China Times* On-Line." Paper (in Chinese) presented at the Conference on the Impact of New Communication Technologies upon Cross-Strait Media Exchanges. Organized by Institute of Communication Studies, National Chiaotung University, Taipei, May 20–21.

Wang, Chen-bang. 1994. Director of the Mainland News Center of the *United Daily News,* interview, Taipei, June 16.

Wei, Ran. 1995. "China in Taiwan's Press: A Study of the Selection of Mainland Chinese News, 1983–1993." Ph.D. diss., Indiana University, Bloomington.

Winckler, Edwin. 1984. "Institutionalization and Participation on Taiwan: From Hard to Soft Authoritarianism?" *China Quarterly* 99:481–99.

Yoon, Youngchul. 1989. "Political Transition and Press Ideology in South Korea, 1980–1988." Ph.D. diss., University of Minnesota.

Zich, Arthur. 1993. "The Other China Changes Courses: Taiwan," *National Geographic* (November):2–33.

Notes on Contributors

Joseph Man Chan is a professor in the School of Journalism and Communication at the Chinese University of Hong Kong. His research interests include international communication, political communication, social impact of information technology, and media development in greater China. A prolific writer, he is also the coauthor of *Mass Media and Political Transition: The Hong Kong Press in China's Orbit* (1991) and *Hong Kong Journalists in Transition* (1996). He was a Harvard-Yenching Fellow.

Zhou He is an associate professor of journalism at San Jose State University and the City University of Hong Kong. A former journalist, he has written on the media profession, media technologies (old and new), media effect, and consumerism. His publications include *Mass Media and Tiananmen Square* (1996) and *China's Mass Media: A New Perspective* (coauthor, 1998, in Chinese).

Chin-Chuan Lee is a professor of journalism and mass communication at the University of Minnesota, where he directs the China Times Center for Media and Social Studies. He has previously been a professor of journalism and communication at the Chinese University of Hong Kong and a visiting professor at the Academia Sinica in Taiwan. Among his English publications are *Media Imperialism Reconsidered* (1980), *Voices of China: The Interplay of Politics and Journalism* (editor, 1990), *Mass Media and Political Transition: The Hong Kong Press in China's Orbit* (coauthor, 1991), *China's Media, Media's China* (editor, 1994), and *Hong Kong Journalists in Transition* (coauthor, 1996). He has also been widely published in Chinese as an author and editor. He was the founding president of the Chinese Communication Association.

Tahirih V. Lee is an associate professor at Florida State University Law School. She teaches Chinese law, international business transactions, and civil procedure. She is the editor of *Chinese Law: Sociological, Political, Historical, and Economic Perspectives* (1997).

Daniel C. Lynch is an assistant professor of political science at the University of Southern California. His publications include *After the Propaganda State: Media, Politics, and "Thought Work" in Reformed China* (1999).

ZHONGDANG PAN is an associate professor of journalism and communication at the Chinese University of Hong Kong, having previously taught at Cornell University and the University of Pennsylvania. His research interests include political communication and China's media reforms. He is coauthor of *To See Ourselves: Comparing Traditional Chinese and American Cultural Values* (1994).

STANLEY ROSEN is a professor of political science at the University of Southern California specializing in Chinese politics and society. He is the author and editor of books and articles, writing on topics such as the Cultural Revolution, the Chinese legal system, public opinion, the media, youth, gender, and human rights. His current project, funded by the Smith Richardson Foundation, seeks to identify the major debates preoccupying the policy-making elites and those trying to influence them, to clarify the major fault lines between different schools of thought, and to ascertain how these debates enter the political realm.

CLEMENT Y. K. SO, a former newspaper editor in Vancouver, is an associate professor of journalism and communication at the Chinese University of Hong Kong.

RAN WEI is an assistant professor of journalism and communication at the Chinese University of Hong Kong. His research interests focus on comparative media systems, media effects, advertising and lifestyles in cultural China, and the impact of new media technologies. His work has been published in the *Gazette, Journal of Broadcast and Electronic Media, International Journal of Public Opinion Research, International Journal of Advertising, New Media and Society,* and *Telematics and Informatics.*

GUOGUANG WU is an assistant professor of government and public administration at the Chinese University of Hong Kong. His research focuses on China's political change in the reform era and its impacts on domestic institutions and foreign policy. He is a contributor to many journals and volumes and the author of *Political Reform under Zhao Ziyang* (1997, in Chinese).

Index

advertising 15, 308
  content, 127–28
  enterprise sponsorship, 85–86, 88
  influence on newspaper operation, 14
  revenues in PRC newspapers, 58, 73
  role in market dominance, 125–27
  space and news hole, 114–15
Althusser, Louis, 31, 74
Apple Daily (Hong Kong), 280, 281,
  305–8, 309, 310, 311, 314, 319
Asian Television (ATV), 252, 254, 257,
  266, 311
Aw, Sally, 300

Basic Law (Hong Kong), 221, 223, 226,
  229, 233, 235, 274, 293, 294,
  295, 296, 303, 304, 314, 321,
  322, 323
BBC World Service, 303
Beijing Youth Daily, 16–18, 54, 73, 218
  approval rating, 156
  debates in
    recent, 158–73
    significance of, 174–75
  pioneer in news packaging, 155
  removal of chief editor, 158
  testing limits of investigative report-
    ing, 156–57, 158
Bennett, Lance, 74, 289, 316
Berger, Peter, 8, 10, 96
Berlin, Isaiah, 325
bourgeois liberalization, 198, 249
Breed, Warren, 315
Brzezinski, Zbigniew, 3, 45
British colonial regime (Hong Kong),
  292–96

bureaucratic-authoritarian regimes, 34,
  324

capital concentration and media merg-
  ers, 308, 309–11
Carey, James, 30, 33
Central Daily News (Taiwan), 276, 338,
  339, 340, 348, 349, 350, 351
"central place theory," 247
Cha, Louis, 281, 303–4, 320
Chan, Joseph Man, 10, 57, 62, 71, 73,
  80, 104, 247, 248, 249, 263, 265,
  268, 275, 280, 289, 290, 293,
  294, 300, 314, 315, 321
Chang Tsan-kuo, 7, 25, 113, 115
Cheek, Timothy, 72, 101
Chen Hsui-pien, 350
Chiang Ching-kuo, 352
Chiang Kai-shek, 297
China. *See* People's Republic of China
China Daily, 100, 219, 220, 221, 224, 235
China Times (Taiwan), 338, 339, 340,
  346, 347, 359
  investment in Hong Kong, 279, 297–
    98, 356
  mainland coverage, 354–56
  relationship with the KMT, 351–53
Chinese Central Television (CCTV),
  11, 17
  covering Hong Kong handover, 274,
    276, 277, 278
  impact vis-à-vis Hong Kong TV,
    252–54
  versus cable programming, 20
Chinese Television Network (CTN),
  304, 313

Chomsky, Noam, 31, 32, 33, 117, 289
command communication, commandist
        media, 45, 69, 70, 74, 89, 97, 104
Communist Youth League, 11, 54, 165,
        166
Cultural China, 4, 9, 24, 26, 28, 31, 271
    center-periphery axis, 5-6, 325
    and the Cold War, 6, 7
    "Economic China," 6
    epistemology of, 8-10
    esoteric communication in, 24-26
    insiders versus outsiders, 7-8
    marginality in the United States, 6
    media narratives about Hong Kong
        handover, 6, 276-81
    "Political China," 6
    political economy of the media, 28,
        31-32
    "social knowledge" model versus
        propaganda model, 113, 115
    as a system of knowledge, 5-10
    three symbolic universes of, 5
cultural globalization, 247
Cultural Revolution, 22, 34, 144, 163,
        167, 186, 249, 292, 303
Curran, James, 28, 30, 116

Dahlgren, Peter, 272, 290
Democratic Progressive Party (DPP),
        340, 362
Deng Xiaoping, 11, 54, 58, 78, 99, 144,
        238, 297, 298, 303, 320, 359
Department of Propaganda, 11, 51,156,
        158, 171, 186, 211, 212, 215, 274
discourse analysis, 208, 273
    code words, 228-29
    double messages, 234
    historical scripts, 281-83
    media narratives, 271-72, 276
discursive community, 271-73, 284
Dittmer, Lowell, 10, 144
domestication, 74, 272, 307
Downing, John, 28

Economic Daily, 12, 153
economism versus politicism, 26-27
enduring values, 35, 272
esoteric communication, 24-26
    "bystander public," 25
    face-to-face versus mass media, 25
    "looking-glass mirror," 25, 294
    use of symbols in power struggle, 24-25
ethnographic or field study, 69-70, 75-78

First Amendment (U.S. Constitution),
        322
Fishman, Mark, 25, 83, 291, 316, 317
frame analysis, 129-30, 132, 273
Friedman, Edward, 19

Gamson, William, 273
Gans, Herbert, 25, 35, 272, 291, 301,
        307, 316
Garnham, Nicholas, 28, 31, 309
Gerbner, George, 246, 262, 263
Giddens, Anthony, 30, 68, 69, 75, 96,
        103, 105
Gitlin, Todd, 23, 33, 74, 78, 129, 317
Golding, Peter, 29, 32, 89, 309
Goldman, Merle, 16, 46
Gorbachev, Mikhail, 11
Gouldner, Alvin, 32
Guangming Daily, 12, 55, 153, 216
Guangzhou Daily, 113
Guangzhou TV, 250, 252, 253, 254,
        257, 265, 266
"guard dog" hypothesis, 289
Guomindang. See Kuomintang

Habermas, Jürgen, 30, 33
Hall, Stuart, 23, 29-30, 31, 33, 289, 317
Hallin, Daniel, 35, 289, 295, 301, 311,
        313, 316
Harding, Harry, 6
hegemony, 22-23, 31, 33, 293, 304,
        314, 319, 320-21
    Communist, 70, 73-74

Hong Kong
    absorption of Chinese elite, 292, 293,
        295
    British colonial regime, 292–96, 316
    CCP-KMT rivalry, 292
    contribution to PRC's economy, 292
    Democratic Party, 295, 316
    identity, 321
    influences on the PRC, 292, 325
    Legislative Council, 226, 231, 295
    "one country" versus "two systems,"
        294, 323
    "political absorption of economy,"
        293
    post-handover press freedom, 296
    Provisional Legislature, 316, 322
    refugee mentality, 321
    relationship with Guangzhou, 248
Hong Kong Special Administrative
        Region (SAR), 220, 222, 224,
        226, 230, 233, 234, 235, 289,
        302, 314, 316, 321
Hong Kong Times, 297
Hu Angang, 135, 356
Hu Qili, 190, 191, 192
hype, 272

ideology. See hegemony; Party Publicity
        Inc.
    defined, 343
    ideological state apparatuses, 74
    "practical" versus "pure," 15
improvisation, improvising reform
        activities, 68–105
    ad hoc and opportunistic nature, 71,
        79, 80, 83, 104
    following instinct, 78, 81, 82
    knowledgeable actors, 96–103
    "minding the degree," 82
    organizational strategies, 80–81
    political limits, 102
    reciprocity, 90–96

routine versus nonroutine measures
        78–83
    routines and ideological hegemony,
        73–75
    symbolic markers, 96
    symbolic resources, 74, 96, 97–98,
        99, 103
    under Communist hegemony, 70–73
    web of subsidies, 83–90
Independence Evening Post (Taiwan), 339,
        345, 347, 357, 358

Jeffersonian democracy, 33, 34
Jiang Zemin, 144, 174, 219, 227, 280,
        300, 303, 305
journalistic paradigm, 74, 289–90
journalistic reform, 68, 69, 70–71, 74–
        75
"junk-food journalism," 114

Katz, Elihu, 26, 245, 271, 272, 284
Keane, John, 30, 34
Kelman, Herbert, 314
King, Ambrose, 292, 293, 294
Kung Sheung Yat Pao, 297
Kuok, Robert, 300, 302
Kuomintang (KMT), 145, 278, 283,
        296, 297, 299, 300, 337, 338,
        339, 340, 341, 344, 349, 350,
        351, 352, 362
    internal power struggle, 349–50, 359

Lai, Jimmy, 306–8, 309, 320
Lasswell, Harold, 180
Lee, Chin-Chuan, 4, 10, 31, 68, 116,
        118, 121, 129, 145, 247, 249, 273,
        275, 280, 289, 290, 291, 293, 294,
        300, 309, 313, 314, 315, 318, 321,
        324, 338, 341, 343, 344, 351, 362
Lee Kuan Yew, 324
Lee Teng-hui (Li Denghui), 26, 278,
        297, 344, 345, 349, 352, 353,
        356, 359

Legal bureaucracy and media (PRC).
See media and legal bureaucracy
(PRC)
Legal System Daily, 210, 212, 219, 221,
223
Li Peng, 224, 225, 231, 300, 306, 320
Li Rui-huan, 353
Li, Victor, 214
Lian Zhan, 278, 279
liberal democracies versus Third World
countries, 33–34
liberal pluralism
endorsement of "responsible capitalism," 34
influence on student movements in
China, 34
role of the state according to, 34, 35
theories of political economy of the
media, 33–36
theory of democracy, 34
views on media professionalism, 35–
36
Liberation Daily, 113, 356
Liberty Times (Taiwan), 276, 279, 345,
347, 358, 359
"looking-glass mirror," 25, 294

Mainland Affairs Committee (Taiwan),
279
Mao Zedong, 181, 210
market competition, 115, 123–24
market-driven journalism, 309–12
press freedom resulting from, 35
price war resulting from, 307–8
Marx, Karl, 117
mass media
effects on worldview, 245–46
as "guard dog," 289
in Hong Kong, 5
co-optation by the power structure, 294
coverage of the handover, 275,
280–81, 283

declining credibility, 311–12
demise of political journals, 310
market-driven journalism, 309–12
media owners with investments in
the PRC, 301, 302, 304
partisan press, 299–301
party press, 296–99
political economy of, 28, 288–325
popular-centrist press, 301–7
PRC capital in, 302, 311
press criticism after the handover,
296
press freedom, 320–25
press investments in the PRC, 301,
304
price war, 307–8, 310
pro-PRC press, 298–99
pro-Taiwan press, 296–98
self-censorship, 312–16
sensationalism, 306, 307
stages of political transition and,
291–96
strategic rituals used by, 317–20
TV influence on China, 5, 8, 252–
68
in modern capitalism, 289
power structure of, 289–90
in the PRC. See also telecommunications (PRC); newspapers
(PRC)
compared with Taiwan, 20, 145
content and ideology in, 16–18,
129–37
"continuist" versus "reformist"
perspective on, 46
decentralization of, 47–53
depiction of problems in Hong
Kong under British rule,
231–33
Hong Kong handover as a national
celebration, 273–75, 276–
78, 283
interaction with Taiwan, 24–26

and the law, 22–23, 208–38
marketization of, 57–63
marketization of political manage-
    ment in, 10
objective reporting in, 36
press conglomeration in, 12–13
reform in, 10–23
serving two masters, 16, 102
socialization in, 53–57
sociology of news in, 14–16, 68–
    105
structure of, 10–13, 45–63
uneven development of, 11
in Taiwan, 5, 24, 28, 35. *See also* press
    (Taiwan)
coverage of Hong Kong handover,
    275–76, 278–79, 283, 342
interaction with China, 5, 24–26,
    354, 356, 357
press ban, 338
press investments in Hong Kong,
    297–98, 356
reporting on mainland China, 337–
    62
structure under martial law, 24,
    337–39
media
"big" versus "little," 21, 203
commercialization (PRC)
influence on salary structure, 12,
    121–22
and legal bureaucracy, 216–19,
    236–38
marketization and liberalization,
    46, 61–63
press conglomeration, 12–13, 113
reduction of state subsidies, 71–72
rise of mass-appeal newspapers, 12
and uneven development, 11
depiction of events, 271, 272, 282
"color" stories, 272
hype, 272
staged conflict, 272

finance, 122
incentive system, 121–22
self-sufficiency, 113
imperialism, 247
law, 22–23, 101. *See also* media, and
    legal bureaucracy (PRC)
in colonial Hong Kong, 322–23
hegemony and, 22–23
media as sources of, 22, 23
"public" role of media, 23
rule of law versus rule by law, 23
and legal bureaucracy (PRC), 208–38
adjudication supervision/trial
    supervision, 214, 215
bureaucracy's use of media to pro-
    pound law, 209–16
channels and target audience, 212–
    13
commercialization, 216–19, 234–
    38
compared with the Soviet Union,
    Taiwan, and the U.S., 236,
    238
control by party central, 211–12,
    215
court system's reliance on media
    communication, 213–15
domestic versus foreign message,
    221
Hong Kong as a case study, 219–35
media providing authoritative
    interpretations of law, 208,
    210, 211, 214–15
on-line computer databases, 237
professionalism, 291, 313, 314, 316
checks and balances, 35, 317
erosion of ethics, 114, 139–40
journalists' redefined roles, 114
news net, 317
radical critique of, 33, 317
strategic rituals, 317–19
as weapon of the weak, 317
reform (PRC), 10–23

influence on journalists' practical
   ideology, 15
news improvisation, 15–16
structure
   "Big Two"
      Hong Kong, 310
      Taiwan, 338, 339, 342, 348,
         351–56
   duopoly, 296
metropolitan domination, 246–47, 248,
      267–68
Merton, Robert K., 8
Mills, C. Wright, 10
Ministry of Information Industries (for-
      merly Ministry of Posts and Tele-
      communications), 21, 186, 187,
      188, 189, 190, 191, 192, 193,
      194, 196, 197, 198, 200
Ministry of Radio, Film, and Televi-
      sion, 274
Ming Pao (Hong Kong), 275, 281, 303–
      5, 310, 319, 320
Mosco, Vincent, 29, 32, 309
Murdoch, Rupert, 300, 311
   befriending China, 303
Murdock, Graham, 29, 32, 89, 309

Nanfang Daily, 12, 113
National People's Congress, 52, 132,
      214, 215, 223, 229, 237, 351
National People's Political Consultative
      Committee, 52, 351, 353
nationalism, 230, 276–79
   definition of China and Chinese, 284
   distinguishing nation and state, 279,
      344
   Hong Kong handover as national cel-
      ebration, 273–75, 276–78, 283
   linking nation and state, 276–78, 283
   patriotism, 162
   versus colonialism, 233
New York Times, 98, 197

news net, 84, 96, 272, 275, 291, 316,
      355
newspapers (PRC). See also mass media,
      in the PRC
   central versus local, 48
   circulation, party organ, 59, 152–53
   comprehensive versus professional, 52
   mass-appeal, 11, 152–53
   party organ versus nonparty organ, 56
news subsidies, 84
Noelle-Neumann, Elisabeth, 23, 246,
      315

O'Donnell, Guillermo, 34, 36, 63, 324
Office of Hong Kong and Macao
      Affairs, 274, 298
"one country, two systems," 222, 224,
      274, 278, 294, 315, 323, 324, 325
Opium War, 282
Oriental Daily News (Hong Kong), 275,
      282, 300, 305, 306, 308, 309,
      310, 311, 314
Orientalism, 6–7

paid journalism, 16, 85–87, 90, 137–39
Pan, Zhongdang, 250, 273
Patten, Chris, 226, 281, 288, 295, 298,
      303, 320, 322, 342
patron–client relationship, 31, 35
Party Publicity Inc., 13–14, 143–48
   compared with KMT propaganda sys-
      tem, 145
   deemphasizing ideology, 113, 144–45
   in post-Deng era, 146
   problems of, 145–48
   versus party mouthpiece, 115
   versus propaganda model, 117
People's Daily, 17, 20, 51, 55, 57, 60, 71,
      79, 85, 100, 113, 114, 174
   coverage of Hong Kong handover,
      274, 277, 278
   declining influence of, 11, 12, 59, 153
   as transmitter of law, 210, 214, 216

People's Liberation Army (PLA), 163,
230, 280–81, 283
use of telecommunications, 186, 189,
190
People's Republic of China (PRC), 3,
4, 5
central government budget deficits,
187
compared with Soviet Union and
Eastern Europe, 11, 45, 236,
238
compared with Taiwan, 236, 238
control-relaxation cycle in politics
and party press, 115–16
esoteric communication, 24–26
Press and Publication Administration,
12, 51, 71, 72
relationship with Taiwan, 24–26
reports about in Taiwan's press, 337–62
U.S. media coverage of, 7
political economy of media and communication, 4, 10, 13, 15, 26–36,
116. See also market competition;
capital concentration and media
mergers
allocative versus operational control,
309
authoritarian states, 5, 118
corporate control, 305, 309–12
in Cultural China, 28, 31–32
culturalist view of, 31–32
economism versus politicism, 26–27
five operating modes, 119
in Hong Kong, 288–325
instrumentalist view of, 31–32
liberal-pluralist approach toward, 33–
36
limitations of Anglo-American literature on, 4, 27–28, 116–18
military-industrial complex, 31
politics-centered versus state-centered
approach toward, 13, 46, 117
price war, 307–8, 310, 358–59

radical-Marxist approach toward, 28–
33, 117
socialist alternatives to, 32–33
socialist market economy, 118
structuralist view of, 31–32
tug-of-war model, 116–19
Polumbaum, Judy, 8, 10, 72, 102, 133,
216, 218, 219
Pool, Ithiel de Sola, 18, 302
Poulantzas, Nicos, 31
press
control, 209–10, 338–39
methods of, 71, 133, 218–19
freedom, 101, 322
in Hong Kong, 292, 320–25
in post-handover Hong Kong,
296
threats to, 322–23
versus Singapore, 324
versus Taiwan, 324
and market competition, 35
and marketization, 61–63
and media professionalism, 35
negative versus positive, 325
1980s versus 1990s (PRC), 16–18,
153–54
as political process, 322
in political versus nonpolitical matters, 11, 16, 18, 46
ideology, 343
in Taiwan. See also Taiwan; mass
media, in Taiwan
anti-Communist, 338, 339, 343,
344
of the "Big Two," 351–56
of the indigenous press, 356–59
influencing mainland news coverage, 347–49
influencing press structure, 337–42
official press, 349–51
and organizational strategies, 349–59
and power realignment, 349–50,
352–53, 358–59

and price war, 358–59
relation to control of media owners, 344–45
Press and Publication Administration
(PRC), 2, 51, 71, 72
press-party parallelism, 290, 291, 295
prestige paper, 302
price war, 307–8, 310, 358–59
Progressive Movement, 35
public sphere, 30, 35, 202
as the third way, 30

Qian Qichen, 132, 227
Qiu Shi, 153
quasi-experimental design, 246, 252,
264

radical-Marxist approach
grand narratives, 33
socialist alternatives, 32
totalizing discourse, 33
Radio-Television Hong Kong
(RTHK), 322
reciprocity
defined, 90
favors, 95
good faith, 93
improvisation, 90–96
source-journalist relationship, 94
Reference News, 59
Republic of China. See Taiwan
River Elegy, 153
Rogers, Everett M., 181, 236
routine versus nonroutine practices
in the macroenvironment, 78–79
in news operation, 74, 78–79, 85, 89,
96, 104
in shaping media's role, 25–26

Said, Edward W., 6, 7, 33, 289
Schiller, Herbert I., 18, 31, 32,
247
Schlesinger, Peter, 33, 316

Schmitter, Phillip, 32, 63
Schramm, Wilbur, 21
Schudson, Michael, 27, 30, 69, 116,
291, 301
Schurmann, Franz, 15, 50
self-censorship, 133, 208, 236
categories of, 315
compliance, 314
defined, 313
during Hong Kong regime change,
312–16
imagined boundaries, 315
and media organizations, 315
in Ming Pao, 319, 321
Orwellian Newspeak, 320
in South China Morning Post, 275
Shanghai Legal System News, 212, 219
Shenzhen Special Zone Daily, 14, 16, 18,
112–48
career choices at, 138–39
compared with Shanghai media, 143
competition with other papers, 122–
25
content, 129–37
controversy over special economic
zone, 135
ethics, 139–40
financing, 122
incentive system, 121–22
institutional structure, 120–21
Party Publicity Inc., 143–48
proximity to Hong Kong, 129
staffing, 121
Sing Tao Jih Pao (Hong Kong), 124, 299,
300, 301, 310, 311
Singapore, 21, 324
Sino-British Joint Declaration, 220,
221, 222–23, 226, 229, 280, 293,
297, 314, 322, 331
Smythe, Dallas, 32
South China Morning Post (SCMP)
(Hong Kong), 275, 280, 281,
300, 302–3, 308, 314

Southern Weekend, 11, 18, 59, 154
"sphere of consensus" versus "sphere of deviance," 313
"spiral of silence" hypothesis, 23, 246
spiritual pollution, 249
Staniland, Martin, 26, 28, 34, 36
Star TV, 300, 303, 311
state, role of, 13
    radical-Marxist approach to, 30–31, 32
    liberal-pluralist approach to, 34–35, 117–18
strategic rituals
    defined, 317
    editorial division of labor, 319
    juxtaposition, 318–19
    media professionalism, 317–18
    narrative forms, 320
    as weapon of the weak, 317

Ta Kung Pao (Hong Kong), 225, 298, 314
Taiwan, 31. *See also* press, in Taiwan; mass media, in Taiwan
    ethnic politics, 345–46
    lifting of martial law, 297, 339–40, 343
    Pan-Chinese versus "Taiwan-first" orientation, 343–44, 346, 350, 352, 358, 362
    power struggle within the KMT, 349–50, 359
    rejecting "one country, two systems," 278–79, 323
    relationship with China, 340–41, 344, 353, 356
technological determinism, 18
    in authoritarian regimes, 19
    in "little" versus "big" media, 21
telecommunications (PRC), 3, 8, 18–22, 179–204
    fax, 181, 195–96
    foreign ownership of, 22, 198

ideological implications, 21–22, 179, 185, 198, 199
as indicators of development, 183
Internet, 20, 180, 181, 196–98
Intranet, 21
investment in, 21
Liantong and Jitong, 190–92
mobile phones, 184
on-line computer databases, 237
paging services, 184, 193
and the People's Liberation Army, 186, 189, 190
social effects of, 198, 202–3
state control of, 19, 21, 181, 185, 186, 201–4
technological determinism, 18
versus mass media, 179, 185, 186, 198, 199
television (Hong Kong). *See also* Television Broadcasts (TVB)
    impact on attitudes, 262–64
    impact on consumption of movies and pop music, 261–62
    impact on evaluations of Hong Kong and Chinese TV, 254–55
    impact on perceived functions of TV, 258–61
    impact on satisfaction with TV, 255–57
    impact on viewing patterns among Guangzhou residents, 252–55
    institutional impact, 265–67
    spillover to China, 249
    uneven access to, by Guangzhou residents, 249–51
Television Broadcasts (TVB) (Hong Kong), 252, 254, 257, 267, 275, 276, 313, 314
thought work (PRC), 182, 188
    telecommunications versus mass media, 179, 185, 198, 199
Tiananmen crackdown, 12, 13, 142, 146, 152, 153, 154, 195, 230, 271, 281, 294, 298, 339, 346

Tomlinson, John, 33, 247
Tu Weiming, 4, 5, 271, 325
Tuchman, Gaye, 14, 25, 33, 78, 83,
    272, 289, 291, 301, 313, 316,
    317, 320
Tung Chee-hua, 296

United Daily News (Taiwan), 338, 340,
    341, 346, 347, 359
  boycott campaign, 297, 353
  investment in Hong Kong, 297–98,
    356
  mainland coverage, 353, 354–56
  relationship with the KMT, 351–53
United Front, 313, 353
United States
  relationship with China, 3
  as source of knowledge about Cul-
    tural China, 6–7
USA Today, 98

Vogel, Ezra, 7, 209

Wah Kiu Yat Pao (Hong Kong), 299,
    300, 301
web of facilitation, 95, 96
web of facticity, 83, 95
web of subsidies, 83, 96
Wenhui Daily (Shanghai), 12, 113, 163,
    356

Wen Wei Po (Hong Kong), 298, 299, 314
White, Lynn T., 10, 57, 143
Williams, Raymond, 23, 29–30, 33, 73,
    290, 319, 320
World Economic Herald, 16, 55, 153, 216,
    357
  and Zhao Ziyang, 16
World Trade Organization, 21–22, 222,
    226

Xinhua News Agency, 51, 71, 100, 113,
    339, 356
  China's command post in Hong
    Kong, 292, 298, 299
  co-optation by, 300
  coverage of Hong Kong handover,
    219–20, 233, 274
Xinmin Evening Daily, 12, 113
Xu Jiatun, 293, 302

Yang Shangkun, 353, 355
Yangcheng Evening Daily, 12, 59, 73

Zhang Yimou, 216
Zhao Yuezhi, 16, 114
Zhao Ziyang, 16, 144, 153, 298
Zhou Enlai, 292
Zhou Nan, 279
Zhu Rongji, 299
Zhujiang TV, 252, 253, 254, 257